The Interpretation of the Flesh

The 'riddle of femininity', like Freud's reference to women's sexuality as a 'dark continent', has been treated as a romantic aside or a sexist evasion rather than as a problem to be solved. In this first comprehensive study, Teresa Brennan suggests that by placing these ideas in the context of Freud's work as a whole, we will begin to understand why femininity was such a riddle for Freud. Brennan argues that by turning to Freud's work and his concrete questions about femininity, a psychical state which occurs in men and women alike, the problem is clearly a soluble one, provided that Freud's concern with energy is taken into account. The real riddle of femininity is as much a problem for thinking about physicality as a problem for the subject who suffers from what Freud described as 'femininity's negative effects on curiosity, intelligence and activity.

The Interpretation of the Flesh

Freud and Femininity

Teresa Brennan

London and New York

First published 1992
by Routledge
11 New Fetter Lane, London EC4P 4EE

Simultaneously published in the USA and Canada
by Routledge
a division of Routledge, Chapman and Hall, Inc.
29 West 35th Street, New York, NY 10001

© 1992 Teresa Brennan

Typeset in 10 on 12 point Garamond by Intype, London
Printed in Great Britain by Clays Ltd, St Ives plc.

British Library Cataloguing in Publication Data
Brennan, Teresa
   The interpretation of the flesh: Freud and femininity
   I. Title
   155.333092

Library of Congress Cataloging-in-Publication Data
Brennan, Teresa
   The interpretation of the flesh : Freud and femininity /
   Teresa Brennan.
       p.   cm.
   Includes bibliographical references and index.
   1. Femininity (Psychology) 2. Freud, Sigmund, 1856–1939—
   Contributions in psychology of femininity. 3. Femininity
   (Psychology)—History—20th century. 4. Psychoanalysis and
   feminism. 5. Mind and body. I. Title.
   BF175.5.F45B74   1992
   155.3'33—dc20   91–39866

ISBN 0-415-07448-7 ISBN 0-415-07449-5 (pbk)

For Columb Brennan,
Flora Brennan,
and Joan, my mother.

Where is my Metapsychology? In the first place, it remains unwritten. Working-over material systematically is not possible for me; the fragmentary nature of my observations and the sporadic character of my ideas will not permit it. If, however, I should live another ten years, remain capable of work during that time . . . then I promise to make further contributions to it.

(Freud, correspondence with Lou Andreas-Salomé)

But at least, if strength were granted me for long enough to accomplish my work, I should not fail, even if the results were to make them resemble monsters, to describe men first and foremost as occupying a place, a very considerable place compared with the restricted one which is allotted to them in space, a place on the contrary prolonged past measure – for simultaneously, like giants plunged into the years, they touch epochs that are immensely far apart, separated by the slow accretion of many, many days – in the dimension of Time.

(Proust, *A la Recherche du temps perdu*)

Contents

Preface

This study of Freud's theory of femininity was shaped by two casual observations. The first was that women in analysis commented more on feeling exhausted or wrung out at certain key points of the analytic process. For men, the process seemed more verbal. This was not true of all the men I knew in analysis, or all the women, but there was a definite weighting towards women and energy, men and words.

This was not a clinical observation, and it was highly context-specific. The context was a mainly white, largely academic feminist community in which psychoanalysis, following Juliet Mitchell's initiative, was more and more an issue. As the theoretical interest escalated, so did the number entering analysis and discussing it. The odd thing was that none of the numerous theoretical turns in the debate between psychoanalysis and feminism addressed the energetic dimension of psychical life. Neither the linguistic turn of Lacanian-influenced feminism, nor the familiar constellation of object-relations theory, took it into account.

This is odder still, given that a close investigation of Freud's own riddle of femininity reveals that energy is its cornerstone. Having said that, and while I trace the theoretical developments and feminist debates at issue, this book is more embedded in the contemporary theoretical context than its mode of presentation reveals. The way that the 'return to Freud' helps undo the links between maleness and masculinity, and femaleness and femininity, respectively (any being could take up either position), and the Lacanian insistence that the subject was constructed, not self-generating, provide pointers to rethinking the energetic issues. They do so if the idea that the self-contained, self-generating subject is an illusion is pushed as far as it will go, which brings me to the second observation.

At one level, the second observation is self-evident. In the relations between beings, emotions as well as positions are interchangeable. A man or woman can be the beloved one year, the lover the next. Even in the briefer time-frame of an argument, for instance, positions and their attendant emotions or affects can be reversed. At a certain moment one party is hysterical, in the colloquial sense of the term, while the other is rational.

But if the hysteric assumes the rational mantle, the dramatic and irrational emotions sometimes pass over to the previously rational interlocutor. It is as if, in the first case, the more independent beloved is in fact dependent on the other's dependence. In the second, rationality seems to require that the other carry the emotions that otherwise interfere with the dispassionate position. What is of interest here is not the distinction between the lover and the loved as such, or the binary opposition between reason and emotion, which have received ample attention. The interest lies in how these positions and their attendant emotions are exchangeable in a dynamic process, which makes it seem as if an emotion is an entity in its own right. If one party drops it, the other picks it up. To put it more emphatically, it seems that emotions can cross the boundaries between individual persons; they do not necessarily originate or stay within them. My point here is that if it is allowed that the subject is decentred in other ways, we should investigate the assumption that individuals are the sole and self-contained points of origin for their emotions.

The stronger point, and it is here that the two observations that founded this book come together, is this: if the idea that emotions are contained is relinquished, one can account for Freud's riddle of femininity. For Freud, emotions and affects are tied to drives, and drives to psychical energy. Femininity was a riddle because Freud could not explain why certain drives and affects were turned against the subject in a disabling way. Indeed femininity, for Freud, means a specific psychical state that is always disabling. Womanhood, or the feminine (whatever that is), is not identical with femininity in Freud's sense. Freud could almost explain his disabling femininity in women, but not in men.

Unlike many feminists, I have no quarrel with Freud's belief that a disabling femininity exists. Where I depart from Freud is this: he worked with a model of a human being who was energetically self-contained. It was a thermodynamic model, relying, Freud thought, on the physical laws of inertia. In this assumption he was wrong. In reality, Freud's is a theory of a *constructed* inertia. It is different from and at odds with the concept of 'inertia' in Newtonian physics. For Newton (and physicists after and before him) 'inertia' did not entail the absence of motion. It meant that degrees of motion would stay unchanged without interference. For Freud, inertia meant the lack of motion or tendency towards fixity. At the same time, Freud's mistaken theory can be read, as I read it here, as a theory of how the illusion that beings are energetically self-contained is born. It is born together with the unconscious that represses knowledge of the energetic connections between beings. Without this repression, a human being could not establish the barriers that maintain its sense of a distinct identity.

Whether all human beings depend on a distinct identity is actually a cross-cultural and historical question, although I do not investigate that here. But understanding how identities can be or are constructed differently should be abetted by this enquiry. Despite the recent concern with deconstructing identities, the barriers that construct a self-contained western identity have not been fully investigated. By my argument, these barriers depend on a constructed sense of time and space. Of course, the idea that time is a construction takes Freud closer to Einstein than to Newton, but this is not something Freud anticipated or explored. One might wish that his correspondence with Einstein had gone beyond mutual compliments and mutual concern for troubled times, but it did not.

Now the idea that the sense of space is also psychically constructed reconnects this theory with another poststructuralist concern: the relation between space, deferral, and language. In turn, this means the theory proffered here bears on the critique of metaphysics. But it does so in an unorthodox way. Freud dreamt that metaphysics could be transformed into metapsychology, and he might have been right. Except that metaphysics, in this transformation, would have to take on another meaning, a meaning it once had. 'Metaphysics' would refer to a theory supplementary to the theory of physics, rather than a series of transcendental claims about a self-contained, self-originating subject. Metapsychology, for Freud, was an attempt to unify his often conflicting insights; my argument is that his attachment to the idea of a self-generating ego meant he missed the metaphysical, or metapsychological, standpoint that might have enabled him to do so.

I realize as I write this preface that it may give some inaccurate impressions about the contents of this book. The book is part of a longer-ranging project in which constructed inertia will feature more; I intend to write a follow-up study. This book itself is more about the riddle of femininity; the energetic physical issues come to the fore because of my conviction that femininity can be understood only in terms of how the drives and emotions of the one cross over to the other. At this point, my hypothesis about how the illusion of a psychically self-contained subject is constructed is raw, not refined.

Another possible impression I should correct concerns the fact that I prefaced this book with observations. I did this because in the end it is the everyday experience of femininity I wish to explain. However this attention to observations and the personal experience they invoke may mislead the reader into thinking that this book is written in a constant dialogue with personal reflection. It is not. This is a book which tries to locate Freud's riddle of femininity in the context of his theory overall, and this means that there are several threads in the weave of its argument, threads based on a detailed reading of Freud's corpus. The reader who is familiar with Freud's theory of femininity and the psychoanalytic and feminist debates surrounding it can bypass the second chapter. The reader who is not might find this chapter useful as a summary. But in general, those reading because of their interest in femininity, rather than Freud, might be best advised to read the book's conclusion, before going through the preceding arguments on Freud's texts. On the other hand, to be remotely convinced by the solution to the riddle of femininity the conclusion outlines, the Freud or psychoanalytic scholar would first have to read the chapters that lead to it.

That disclaimer aside: personal experience returned again and again in conversations with the many women and men who provided facilitating environments for writing this book. I suppose it began in Sydney over a decade ago, so some of it has survived the test of Horace. I am indebted to Linda Burnett and Pauline Garde for their assistance in drafting an initial outline, and to R. A. Brooks for his understanding. The project was then deferred. I resumed it because of the encouragement of a remarkable Freud scholar, the late Professor A. F. Davies. Desley Deacon, Suzanne Dixon, and Deborah Mitchell also gave things a push at that time. Practically, I benefited from grants from Melbourne University (special thanks to Arthur Huck), from the Archbishop Mannix Foundation of Newman College, and the Cambridge Commonwealth Trust.

I completed writing with the help of two interlocking groups. One is a geographically scattered group of feminist scholars: my deep thanks to Parveen Adams, Drucilla Cornell, Jane Gallop, Alice Jardine, Juliet Flower MacCannell, Philipa Rothfield, and Gayatri Chakravorty Spivak, for many conversations. The second group, unexpectedly, I found in Cambridge, where most of this was written. I thank the following women for the general intellectual stimulation and companionship they provide, as much as any conversation about this theory as such: Gillian Beer, Marilyn Butler, Ann Caeser, Anne Marie Goetz, Elizabeth Guild, Marion Hobson, Sheena Jain, Susan James, Jennifer Jarman, Sarah Kay, Naomi Segal, and Michelle Stanworth. I was initially convinced that an over-reliance on social approval and social identification was one reason why femininity, as a disabling state, persisted. I am now convinced that it is only possible to tell the truth about it with the aid of a sustaining social community.

Other debts. Peter Lambley and Sourayya Azam Shinwari lent me their houses at key points in writing. Sourayya's friendship, and that of Anthony Giddens gave this project its continuity over time. Colleagues at Queen Mary and Westfield College, including Lisa Jardine and Morag Shiach, provided many helpful pointers. So did my colleagues at the University of Amsterdam; I owe special thanks here to Elisabeth Lissenberg, who introduced me to a missing piece in the puzzle of femininity. Margaret Whitford's detailed observations on an earlier draft were much appreciated. As the book has changed radically since then, the traditional absolution of responsibility for errors is more necessary than ever. I am grateful too for Malcolm Bowie's and John Forrester's careful comments on a complete manuscript, to Liana Giorgi, Ingrid Scheibler, and Simon

Goldhill for intellectual counsel, to Elizabeth Wright, for correcting my German, to my cousin Kay Hollingshead and the unswerving Sarah Green, who helped deliver me of this book, and to the women at Routledge over three years' association. For this book, thanks go to my desk editor, Jill Rawnsley, and especially to my publisher Janice Price, who is responsible for the completion of more feminist and other critical projects than she knows. My final debt is to Daphne Lambert, who lightened the weight of the other within. This book is dedicated to Flora Brennan, as she knew, my father, who did his best to pass on the craft of writing, and my courageous mother, whose faith in the logic of this book persisted at unlikely moments.

Abbreviations

GW Sigmund Freud, *Gesammelte Werke, chronologisch geordnet,* edited by Anna Freud, Edward Bibring, Willi Hoffer, Ernst Kris, and Otto Isakower, in collaboration with Marie Bonaparte, vols 1–17, London, Imago, 1940–52, vol. 18, Frankfurt am Main, S. Fischer Verlag, 1968.

Letters *The Complete Letters of Sigmund Freud to Wilhelm Fliess, 1887–1904,* edited and translated by Jeffrey Moussaieff Masson, Cambridge, Mass., Harvard University Press, 1985.

Origins Sigmund Freud, *The Origins of Psycho-Analysis: Letters to Wilhelm Fliess, Drafts and Notes, 1887–1902,* edited by Marie Bonaparte, Anna Freud, and Ernst Kris, translated by Eric Mosbacher and James Strachey, introduction by Ernst Kris, London, Imago, 1954.

SE *The Standard Edition of the Complete Psychological Works of Sigmund Freud,* edited and translated by James Strachey, in collaboration with Anna Freud, assisted by Alix Strachey and Alan Tyson, London, Hogarth Press and the Institute of Psychoanalysis, 1953–74, 24 vols.

Studien Sigmund Freud, *Studienausgabe,* Frankfurt am Main, S. Fischer Verlag, 1969–75, 10 vols.

IJPA *International Journal of Psycho-Analysis*

IZP *Internationale Zeitschrift für Psychoanalyse*

Life Ernest Jones, *Sigmund Freud Life and Work* (1st edn) 3 vols, vol. 1, 1953, vol. 2, 1955, vol. 3, 1957, London, Hogarth Press.

Minutes *Minutes of the Vienna Psychoanalytic Society,* H. Nunberg and E. Federn, translated by M. Nunberg with N. Collins, New York, International Universities Press, 1962–75.

PQ *Psychoanalytic Quarterly*

Note on translations and texts

In addition to Sigmund Freud's *Gesammelte Werke* (*GW*), I have referred to the *Studienausgabe* (*Studien*), which has the advantage that it refers to James Strachey's extensive emendations to Freud's works. The English text of Freud employed throughout is *The Standard Edition of the Complete Psychological Works of Sigmund Freud* (*SE*), under the general editorship of James Strachey. References to Freud are to the date of publication, followed by the page number in the *SE*. Where a reference to the *GW* or the *Studien* is made, its page number is given first, and the second page number refers to the *SE*. Strachey's translation, although notably not his editorship – which is 'standard' in German as well as English – of Freud's works has been criticized, especially in the last few years. Where appropriate, I have indicated the nature of these criticisms. I have made one major modification to Strachey's translation. This is the substitution of 'drive' for 'instinct' in the translation of *Trieb*. References to Freud's *Project for a Scientific Psychology* (1950b) are only to Strachey's translation; the German edition of this work is so inaccurate, and Strachey's corrections to it so extensive, as to make a reference to the German transcription of Freud's manuscript superfluous.

To avoid quoting lengthy passages from the original German, where the point concerns only one or two words, all nouns have been put in the nominative case.

References throughout the text are cited by the year of the edition used as given in the bibliography. Where this date differs from the original or an earlier edition, and this has also been consulted, this reference is given in square brackets.

Chapter 1

The riddle of femininity

INTRODUCTION

At the beginning of *The Interpretation of Dreams* there is an epigraph: *flectere si nequeo superos, Acheronta movebo*. These are Virgil's words. Freud does not comment on their context in the *Aeneid*, but it deserves a note. It was Juno who said, 'If I cannot move the heavens, I will rouse hell.' She did so after Jupiter allowed Aeneas the Trojan to become king of Latium. Unable to move the king in heaven, she summoned hell's Furia Allecto, who spurred an attack on the Trojans through the agency of enraged women. The Trojans had come to the women's homeland, Latium, to found the imperialist power of Rome. Rome, born of Latium, will colonize the world through the descendants of Aeneas. This is what Juno would prevent.

But Juno knows, in fact, that her power is limited: she cannot prevent the victory of Aeneas. She is able only to 'put off the hour and bring delay'.[1] 'Saturn's royal daughter', as Virgil calls her, knows in her rage that she has only Saturn's weapons, the weapons of 'detours and delays'.[2]

The Interpretation of Dreams, Freud's greatest work by his own account, begins with an epigraph that obliquely identifies the repressed unconscious he is about to arouse with women who are furious, and the temporal power of delay. This putative identification ends there; it is no concern of the *Interpretation*. But this is not the last time that either delay or negative emotions charged with strong affect will concern us in this book. The strength of any affect – rage, envy, love, and hate – is for Freud the concern of the economic level of psychical organization. Economics are involved because quantities of energy are involved; the quantities of different affects determine their force and the force of the resistance to them. Freud, in one of the least popular aspects of his theory, tried to theorize this economic level in designing his metapsychology. In theorizing it he

---

1 References to Virgil are to Virgil (1934: 25ff, trans. mod.).
2 'Detours and delays' are described as the marks of Saturn by Walter Benjamin. See Sontag's essay on Benjamin, 'Under the Sign of Saturn', in Sontag (1980).

referred to a hypothetical physics, to physical energetic processes, and the machinations of the flesh.

Initially, I am defining metapsychology as Freud's attempt to construct a consistent theoretical framework for the diverse hypotheses that arose in relation to his psychoanalytic work and thought. By metapsychology, Freud himself meant a theory that addresses the economic level, and the topographical (spatial) and dynamic (interactive) levels of psychical organization. Of these three levels, it was the economic or quantitative level that, for Freud, was the most important and puzzling aspect of metapsychology. It was the inadequacy of psychoanalytic formulations concerning quantities, or the economy, of psychical energy and physical excitation that made 'metapsychology', as such, inadequate.[3]

Freud's metapsychology has not been explored in any depth in conjunction with his writings on femininity.[4] Although the quantitative question is basic to his writing on the riddle of femininity, the implications for femininity of Freud's metapsychological (and physical, rather than biological) theories of the mind overall have been neglected, and this is critical in what follows. I shall try to show that Freud's discussion of femininity has to be placed in the context of his metapsychology before his widely misunderstood 'riddle of femininity' can come closer to its solution, and that it is only when Freud's riddle of femininity is placed in a metapsychological context that the real nature of the riddle can be clarified. Moreover it can be clarified only when the economic, physical dimension in Freud's

3 'The indefiniteness of all our discussions of metapsychology is of course due to the fact that we know nothing of the nature of the excitatory process [*Erregungsvorganges*] that takes place in the elements of the psychical systems, and that we do not feel justified in framing any hypothesis on the subject. We are consequently operating all the time with a large unknown factor, which we are obliged to carry over into every new formula. It may reasonably be supposed that this excitatory process can be carried out with energies that vary *quantitatively* . . .' (1920a, *GW*: 30–1, *SE*: 30–1). Note that *Erregung* connotes emotion (fear, rage etc.) as well as excitation in the more technical sense. Note too that Freud's use of the terms 'economic' and 'economy' is very specific. It always implicates energy. This specificity does not hold for other contemporary writers who use the term 'economy'. See below, page 75.

4 Since the early 1970s, the literature on Freud, psychoanalysis, and femininity has expanded dramatically. Yet it has produced few book-length systematic treatments of Freud's theory of femininity. The first is Juliet Mitchell (1974); the second is Sarah Kofman [1980]. Mitchell treats femininity within the context of Freud's theory as a whole, but her project is expository rather than critical in this respect. Kofman is certainly critical, but neglects the overall theory at the expense of concentrating on the texts directly concerned with femininity. Also important is Assoun (1983) and Granoff (1976). Freud's theory of femininity is dealt with at less length in Kristeva (1986), [1987], [1974c], (1980), whose arguments intersect with mine at so many points that this book could have become an exchange with her thinking, in Irigaray [1974 and 1977] and to some extent in Chodorow (1978 and 1989), Gallop [1982], Sprengnether (1990), to name some of the most interesting books, and in numerous feminist articles and in the expanding field of psychoanalysis and literary criticism. But with few exceptions, these books and articles concentrate on Freud's masculinist bias at the expense of his theoretical project overall and, without exception, neglect the real riddle of femininity.

metapsychology is taken into account, at the same time as the reasons for the neglect of the riddle emerge.

Mutatis mutandis, it is only by taking account of femininity that the physical dimension of Freud's metapsychology comes into focus as a near miss, rather than a creaking hydraulic failure. This is not to defend Freud's assumptions about physics, which on the face of it did not go far beyond the water pump model in which the pressure of quantities of drives and affects produce pleasure or unpleasure. It is rather to say that Freud's attention to physics pointed in the right direction, and that his assumptions lead to another physics altogether (one he could not and did not anticipate). This other physics allows one to think of physical processes in other than reductionist terms. For of course it is often assumed that Freud's belief in the physical and economic aspects of the psychical processes he described involves or implies a biological reductionism: material factors are meant to determine psychical processes. The fact that physics and biology have very different deterministic implications is not considered in these criticisms.[5] The things that led Freud to puzzle over the physical issues, such as energetic inertia or rigidity, or the physical alterations wrought by hysteria, are given as little weight as the real riddle of femininity, and we will see that these lacunae are related.

But first a major caveat. As I have indicated, the problem with talking about physicality is that such talk is generally confused with an appeal to a reductionist materialism. As the explanatory power of reductionist materialism is limited, and its ideational fruits sterile, dualism was and frequently is proffered as the reasonable being's alternative, although dualism in its own way is just as inadequate as reductionist materialism. Indeed the fact that dualism is preferred to attempts at thinking about physicality in a non-reductionist way suggests an overwhelming prejudice in thought. Its persistence in the face of arguments to the contrary leads one to suspect that it is almost a psychical necessity. For of course there are arguments to the contrary. Spinoza throughout his work, and Aristotle at points, to name but two of the older and most striking examples, have argued for a non-reductionist materialism, and for the idea that 'mind' is not only a

---

5 The major exception in this stream of neglect is Deleuze, especially Deleuze and Guattari (1972), who makes the economic level, the energetic unconscious, central. A sensitive evaluation of Freud's quantitative and economic dimension is Ricoeur (1970). For a different style of critique of Freud's quantitative account, especially in Freud (1950a), see Derrida (1981 and 1980, especially 281–3). In support of Derrida's otherwise wilful reading of Freud in the latter, which suggests that Freud attempted somewhat disingenuously to distance himself from philosophy in order to buttress his originality, rather than, as seems more probable, to legitimate his enquiries for science, we can note Freud's remark to Fliess: 'I see how, via the detour of medical practice, you are reaching your first ideal of understanding human beings as a physiologist, just as I most secretly nourish the hope of arriving, via the same paths, at my original goal of philosophy. For that is what I wanted originally, when it was not yet at all clear to me to what end I was in the world' (January 1896, *Letters*: 159).

physical thing, but one which can socially and psychically affect the nature of 'matter'.[6] More recently, Merleau-Ponty's (1968) notion of the 'flesh', as that which bridges mind and subject, body and object, has constituted one outstanding critique of dualism, while in Anglo-American thinking, philosophers evoke a 'dual-aspect monism'. (Cf. Hodgson 1991.)

In the long run, to emphasize the non-reductionist nature of certain physical effects, without raising old spectres, the term 'physicality of ideas' may be preferable to 'materialism'. The physicality of ideas means no more than it says. Ideas are physical. We may now feel warmly towards an idea which once made us go cold. In fact, the best illustration of the physicality of ideas lies in our changing feelings towards them. Ideas take time 'to sink in', a process which is accurately recognized in the language used to describe it. We may hear something, agree with it, then not think much about it until and if the full implications sink home. Again, we may accept a notion which is in flat contradiction with all we have previously thought and felt, but it is only possible to live with the contradiction while our agreement with the contradictory idea is formal. Once an idea enters into our physical content, once its form becomes more substantial, we physically change. We change our outlook so that our emotional responses are consistent with the idea. The sinking-in time is the lag between the initial hearing and the gut feeling, between the polite interest and the emotional involvement, the intriguing idea and the lifelong commitment. It is the difference between that which is on the surface and that which is deep, between the external recognition and that which goes to the heart of the matter. Aristotle's belief that anger was tied to the seething of blood around the heart may have been problematic, but all arguments against the heart of the matter cannot be discounted on the grounds that they are 'reductionist', when they are clearly not. One may be angry only momentarily, but when one is, one's blood may race. One's psychical state alters one's physical state; this is the very opposite of the unfortunate thinking that adheres to reductionism.

As I have indicated, uncovering the psychical origins of the prejudice in thought which obscures the physicality of ideas, and developing an alternative which is neither dualistic nor reductionist, depends on elucidating the riddle of femininity.[7] Partly because developing an alternative

6 There is an insistence in feminist critiques that mind/body dualism begins with Plato (see n. 7), but a major controversy over whether Aristotle was dualist or non-reductionist. See Nusbaum and Rorty (1992). Spinoza (1989) is far better known for his propositional proof of the logical mental and physical inseparability of the One Substance, and his argument that they are separated only by the 'power of the imagination' (cf. James 1990) prefigures this interpretation of Freud. Hampshire (1988) has also sensed and written beautifully of the energetic affiliation between Freud and Spinoza.

7 There are outstanding critiques of mind/body dualism and the thinking that underlies it in Keller (1985), Gallop (1988) and Bordo (1987). For other insights, see the collections edited by Harding and Hintikka (1983), Bleier (1986), Harding (1986), and Tuana (1989). Butler's (1990) questions about the inside and outside also open out new perspectives.

means for thinking about the physicality of ideas depends on a prior unravelling of the riddle, the physical concepts in this book are not refined. In general I use the term 'psychophysical' to evoke the conceptual unity of mental and physical processes, but this usage, together with my employment of other, too general, concepts such as 'energy' and 'psychical energy', is pro tem. It should be possible to develop a better vocabulary for the physicality of ideas in subsequent work. But given that unravelling the riddle of femininity is the key to unravelling physicality, we will concentrate in this book on the riddle.[8] The questions Freud scholars have asked about femininity have been remarkably few. And while psychoanalysts and feminists have asked a great many, their questions are never Freud's.

Of course, Freud's observation that woman's sexuality is 'a dark continent'[9] (1926b, GW: 241, SE: 212) and femininity an enigma has been noted, incessantly quoted in fact, and most often by writers who romanticize that dark enigma, in a literature that forms part of the celebration of 'the feminine' as that which is outside discourse, the unrepresentable, and so on.[10] These writers give us a Freud who ruminates on the eternal feminine,

Keller's argument refers to object-relations theory. For a critique of it, which also introduces Cixous's (1981) and Le Doeuff's (1980) perspectives on the limitations of dualism, see Moi (1989). Another (Lacanian) psychoanalytic approach to the body and the senses is found in Grooten (1991). There are outstanding critiques of mind-body dualism and the splitting of language and body in Irigaray's (1985) critique of the economy of metaphor and her (1984) evocations of a 'sensible transcendental' echo Spinoza's argument. At least, I think these evocations echo Spinoza. Whitford (1991) reads Irigaray's diverse deployments of this term as an indication that the 'transcendental', if it is embodied, is also mortal (1991: 140ff). Whatever the case, any effort at rethinking the artificial relation between mental and physical process that points at new directions is significant in the current psychoanalytic, as well as feminist, context, and Irigaray certainly does this through her reiteration of the deadly power of metaphor (cf. Irigaray 1985: 346), a thing which preoccupied Hegel (see Colletti 1973: 163) and which will be an issue later in this book (see pages 131–4).

8 This is why, despite evident overlaps, I have postponed engaging with Merleau-Ponty to some other time, after I have staked out the physical questions in terms of sexual identity. On Merleau-Ponty's neglect of 'gender', see Young (1990). For an excellent discussion of Merleau-Ponty and the flesh, which I read when this book was in press, see Grosz (1992).

9 The full context for that famous expression, which occurs in *The Question of Lay Analysis*, is: 'We know less about the sexual life of little girls than of boys. But we need not feel ashamed of this distinction; after all, the sexual life of adult women is a "dark continent" for psychology' (1926b, GW: 241, SE: 212). It should be said here, in case it does not enter the argument again, that there is of course far more information available now on the sexual life of adult women than there was at Freud's time of writing. Kinsey's, and Master's and Johnson's reports confirmed not only that the phallic, i.e. clitoridal, nature of female sexuality survived, but that it was the condition of orgasm in women, something that Freud did not know. See Sherfey (1972). The sexual life of women is not the enigma confronted in this book; the enigma here is psychical femininity, as Freud defined it.

10 This is especially so with French women writers on psychoanalysis: Kofman [1980] reads Freud's questions on femininity as an insincere appeal to mystery. Cixous in Cixous and Clément [1975] suggests that the feminine is unrepresentable and that Freud's problem originates in attempting to impose a representation on it, and there is a similar, but more developed, suggestion in Irigaray [1977]. The best-known argument on the unrepresentability of the feminine is probably Kristeva [1974a].

with unsatisfactory results. It is an image that Freud, who was capable of heavy-handed romanticism, helped create. In some of his last words on the subject, he quotes Heine's *Nordsee*, noting that, for generations, 'sweating human heads' have been 'knocking against . . . the riddle of femininity' (1933a, *GW*: 120, *SE*: 113). Yet, in the context of his appeal to Heine, Freud also makes it plain that he regards femininity as a problem to be solved, something that he knew too little about.

The real riddle of femininity is neglected partly because Freud's work on femininity is not known for the precise problems he encountered in its investigation. It is known for a characterology of woman. In this characterology, Freud refers to woman as envious, narcissistic, and insincere. She has a convenient sense of justice. She is less capable of loving than of desiring to be loved. In Freud's own terms, what he has to say about women does not always sound 'friendly' [*freundlich*] (1933a, *GW*: 145, *SE*: 135). It is understandable that Freud's most recent feminist critics should respond to Freud's unkindness not by tackling Freud's riddle of femininity as a soluble one, but by valorizing its enigmatic nature, making of mystery an asset. However this response is precisely a contemporary one, coinciding with the rise of postmodernism. A longer-standing response to Freud's writings on femininity has been to condemn their phallocentric bias, and either to dismiss their characterology out of hand, or to seek explanations for it in the phallocentric culture whose social effects on gender went underremarked by Freud.[11] Yet these well-merited responses have served to focus attention on Freud's characterology of woman, at the expense of his specific questions about femininity. For despite his denigratory digressions, Freud's riddle of femininity did consist of specific questions about a psychical state that restricts and inhibits both women and men. Freud of course insisted that femininity, like masculinity, occurs in both sexes. In addition, 'femininity' for Freud is itself a specific term, which we shall shortly define, rather than a generic term for one of the two genders; when the word 'femininity' is used in this book, it means Freud's understanding of femininity.

In terms of Freud's own criteria for health, femininity is not only a characterology. It is also a pathology, although Freud never quite styles it as such. Freud's woman not only has an unfortunate character. She is also less likely to be curious, to have an intellectual capacity for research (indeed her mental life is generally restricted), or to be able to withstand adversity. She is more subject to repression. She is masochistic. In the context of

11 Freud's phallocentrism generated two debates. The first was conducted amongst analysts in the 1920s and 1930s; the second amongst feminists sympathetic to psychoanalysis, and feminist psychoanalysts in the 1970s and 1980s. These debates are discussed in chapter 2. The discussion is limited to those writers who have some allegiance to psychoanalytic ideas, even if they disagree with Freud, or Freud's theory of femininity; the feminist repudiation of Freud and psychoanalysis *tout court* was, of course, one of the topics addressed in Mitchell's (1974) classic *Psychoanalysis and Feminism*.

Freud's metapsychology, these are all marks of pathology. The female sex for Freud has the greater tendency to neuroses.

It is these pathological aspects of femininity that are especially interesting, for these reasons. First, because they have been neglected as such. This is an appropriate point to signal that the pathological aspects of femininity might resonate with the experience of a reader once they are translated into everyday experience: not being able to work well or concentrate, shooting oneself in the foot, feeling anxiously inhibited from time to time. If these things do not resonate with experience, then much of the point of this enquiry, and any relevance Freud's theory of femininity might have to women and men, is lost. The second reason the pathological aspects of Freud's theory are interesting (and this is the main reason for the neglect) is that they emerge as pathological only in the context of Freud's metapsychology, his theory overall. Third, the fact that Freud almost, but *not quite*, styles femininity itself a pathology, raises the question as to why he was hesitant. To begin answering it, we can begin by noting that 'femininity' for Freud performs two tasks. On the one hand, it is an account of a psychical state that occurs in all human beings, men and women alike. On the other, Freud's account of femininity is an account of how the biological female being becomes a woman. Now, if femininity, as an account of the making of the woman, is simultaneously a pathology, this means that Freud's theory implies that the normal state of womanhood is a pathological one. But I do not want to suggest that this unpalatable conclusion consti- tutes of itself an explanation for Freud's hesitancy. The situation is compli- cated because: (i) Freud's views on metapsychology changed. He had, at the minimum, two theories of psychophysical energy, two 'topographies', meaning spatial descriptions of the psyche, and there were other major metapsychological shifts besides; (ii) his theory of femininity changed as well. It is only as his metapsychology develops that the problem 'femininity' poses for it becomes apparent. It is only as his theory of femininity changes that the pathological implications of femininity as a psychical state gradually emerge.[12]

And to complicate matters further, the changes in the theory of femininity mean that femininity becomes less an account of a psychical state in both sexes, and more of a theory of female sexuality specifically. Yet, if we turn to Freud's relatively late formulation of the 'riddle of femininity' as a concrete problem, it is the idea that femininity occurs in men, as well as women, that makes it into a problem to be solved.

---

12 Of course, before the implications of femininity as pathology can be discussed in any depth, the notion that we are dealing with an account that describes both the 'normal' process of becoming a woman and a pathological condition has to be established. This means discussing what pathology means for Freud, and this in turn returns us to his metapsychology. This discussion is pursued in this chapter (pp. 21–2, 30ff), and in the next chapter.

Shortly after quoting Heine, Freud notes that masochism, for instance, is regarded as a truly feminine trait.

> The suppression of women's aggressiveness, which is prescribed for them constitutionally and imposed on them socially, favours the development [*Ausbildung*] of powerful masochistic impulses, which succeed, as we know, in binding erotically the destructive trends which have been diverted inwards. Thus masochism, as people say, is truly feminine. But if, as happens so often, you meet with masochism in men, what is left to you but to say that these men exhibit very plain feminine traits?
>
> (1933a, *GW*: 123, *SE*: 16)

Immediately after this passage, something very interesting occurs. Immediately after saying that masochism, as a passive feminine trait, is also found in men, Freud again refers to femininity as a 'riddle', one that 'psychology [like biology] is unable to solve' (ibid.). As I read this passage, this is the quintessence of the 'riddle' of femininity. It seems to be: why is it found in men? It is not about understanding the mysterious enigma, woman. It is about men.

To understand why femininity is a riddle because it occurs in men as well as in women, we have to take account of Freud's assumption that health is a matter of less rather than more repression (1937: 226), and that 'health' can only 'be defined in metapsychological terms'. In understanding why femininity is a riddle in men, we next have to understand that activity and aggressiveness directed outwards are less likely to result in pathology because they entail less repression (1905b, *Studien*: 139, *SE*: 236). Freud tries to account for why activity and aggressiveness are turned inwards in women, and for the idea (which he will maintain consistently) that women are more repressed than men, on the basis that this inward-turning is meant to contribute to the propagation of the species; impregnation and reproduction are guaranteed by it, and the constitutionally greater activity, aggressiveness, and, indeed, sadism, of the male. But this recourse to biology, aside from the fact that Freud was not content with it, and apart from the biological arguments against it, cannot explain the inward-turning of aggressiveness and masochism in men. Thus the first problem with femininity, the first reason femininity becomes a riddle. It is an energetic or economic problem, in Freud's language, because the inward-turning is counter-productive in terms of the pleasure principle, of which more soon.

There is a further difficulty here, which is that the biological explanation tends to tie masculinity to activity, and femininity to passivity. Freud initially accepted this equation, but progressively distanced himself from it (1905b, *Studien*: 69, n. 4, *SE*: 160, n. 2; 1933a, *GW*: 123, *SE*: 115–16). He is clear that there is a difference between masculinity and activity, but the nature of the difference constitutes a second difficulty in the theory of femininity (and masculinity, for that matter). Anticipating more discussion,

Freud's final position is that masculinity is equivalent to activity plus 'n', and femininity to passivity plus 'n', where 'n' is established, although its nature is not known, by the Oedipus complex. So the first and second problems with femininity concern its relation to passivity and how it is that men, too, turn their aggressiveness inwards, against themselves.

These problems can be borne in mind as we approach a third and a fourth problem via a path which will allow us to consider Freud's theory of femininity in more detail, and note why it has achieved some currency in contemporary feminist writing. Freud has not only been the object of extensive feminist criticism. He has also found feminist advocates on the grounds (i) that the masculinity and femininity he described were not biologically specific states, but found in either sex, and (ii) that his account of femininity makes it into something constructed.[13] Both grounds are right. It is also true that Freud's account of the girl's Oedipus complex refers to 'the female sex', and that the femininity he bestows on her develops in relation to this complex. This reintroduces the matter of the difference between female sexuality and femininity. Are we talking about two types of femininity, one contingent on female sexuality, the other on something else? Or is only one 'femininity' involved? In which case, given that femininity is also found in men, it cannot be contingent on female sexuality.

FREUD'S TWO THEORIES OF FEMININITY

As I indicated, Freud had two theories of femininity, just as he had at least two metapsychologies. In his first theory of femininity, he claimed that the psychosexual development of girls was 'precisely analogous' (1923b, GW: 260, SE: 32) to the Oedipal impulses of boys. Where boys first desired their mothers and wished to do away with their fathers, girls desired their fathers and wished to dispose of their mothers.[14] After 1923, Freud slowly relinquished his first theory of femininity, which we will

13 Brennan (1989). Most of Freud's critics share the assumption (which Freud himself held for a time) that girls are naturally drawn towards their fathers, in a manner analogous to the way boys are drawn to their mothers. They reject Freud's assumptions about femininity (penis-envy is the most notorious); but in constructing alternative theories of gender, they hold to an *a priori* love for the parent of the opposite sex. Freud discounts this when he makes the girl's love for her father a problematic and difficult achievement, based on a turning-away from her first love, the mother. It is the difficulty of this achievement, combined with the implications of her repressed maternal attachment, that leads to the problems and questions about femininity. But it is also, according to Freud's feminist supporters, the theory that has more potential for explaining femininity as a construction that inhibits human potential. See especially Rose (1986).
14 The Oedipus complex was first introduced as a concept by Freud in a letter to Fliess (15 October 1897, *Letters*: 272). It was also referred to in Freud (1900, GW: 267-73, SE: 261-6). However there is a difference between concept and terminology. Freud did not employ the term 'Oedipus complex' until 1910 (1910e, GW: 73, SE: 171). See the discussion in Forrester 1980: 84-95.

call the analogy theory, and subsequently favoured the view that girls, too, first desired the mother.[15]

Freud was forced to change his mind about the course of feminine development because of the implications of the new account of the tripartite structure – id, ego, superego – of the mind developed in *The Ego and the Id* (1923b). This theory still maintained that the development of boys and girls was analogous, but the analogy idea had to be relinquished because of the new theory. It had to be relinquished because of the significance accorded the penis in the dissolution of the Oedipus complex and the establishment of the superego. The penis has a crucial role here, in that it is the threat of castration that leads the boy to abandon his desire for his mother and identify with his father. The boy takes the threat seriously because he has the opportunity to observe beings like himself in other respects who have been 'castrated'.

Writing of the Oedipus complex later in 1923, Freud does not claim an analogy, but instead acknowledges that 'the corresponding processes in the little girl are not known to us' (1923d, *GW*: 295, *SE*: 142).

Officially, while Freud first comments on the lack of correspondence between the girl's and boy's Oedipus complex in 1923, he had observed that the development of boys and girls was not analogous in an earlier study of masochism (1919b). Although Freud basically ceased ignoring the implications of his metapsychology for the analogy theory after introducing the superego in *The Ego and the Id*, his acceptance of the revised thesis was relatively slow, and interrupted by tenacious restatements of the old analogy. Femininity is an area where Freud, the theorist of forgetfulness, failed either to think through the implications of his own discoveries, or even to recall them, with disconcerting regularity. In the early months of 1924, he remembered, in fact developed the view, that there was no Oedipal analogy (in 'The Dissolution of the Oedipus Complex') but he forgot again when writing *An Autobiographical Study* (1925d) later that year, in August and September.

How does one explain Freud's attachment to a view that was thoroughly undermined by the development of his theory of the superego, or, for

15 As I argue below, I doubt that Freud's inconsistency was without a basis: a clinical basis for his belief in the attraction of girls towards their fathers was provided by his studies in hysteria. In addition, Freud says that the factor of parental preference figures in the Oedipus complex. 'We must not omit to add that the parents themselves often exercise a determining influence on the awakening of the child's Oedipus attitude by themselves obeying the pull of sexual attraction [*sie selbst der geschlechtlichen Anziehung folgen*], and that where there are several children the father will give the plainest evidence of his greater affection for his little daughter and the mother for her son' (1916–17, *GW*: 345, *SE*: 333). In fact this is how Freud explains the fact that the mother devotes the same attention to her daughter as she does to her son, 'without producing the same [Oedipal] result' (ibid.). Freud however continues to give priority to the sexual drive constructed in relation to the aim of repeating a pleasure first experienced orally, but the fact that a parental preference factor, however downplayed, coexists with the infant's aim is an indication of a conflict between the imposed 'desire of the other' (to borrow a Lacanian term) and the constructed libido.

that matter, why the obvious escaped Freud for as long as it did? Two reasons for overlooking the obvious are offered by Freud himself. He suggested the vicissitudes of transference as a possible culprit for his inadequate knowledge. He may have overlooked the girl's phase of attachment to her mother 'because the women who were in analysis with me were able to cling to the very attachment to the father in which they had taken refuge from the earlier phase'. He registers that women analysts have had an easier, clearer view of the facts in question because their patients treated the analysts as mother-substitutes (1931b, *GW*: 519–20, *SE*: 226–7).[16] Freud also – and this may be related to the transference difficulty – attributed his inability to come to terms with women to blocks in analytic information. When he asks specifically, and for the first time, about the dissolution of the Oedipus complex in girls, he begins by noting that 'At this point our material – for some incomprehensible reason – becomes far more obscure and full of gaps [*dunkler und lückenhafter*]' (1924c, *GW*: 400, *SE*: 177).

Yet in the same article, some implications of the tripartite theory for femininity were developed, and the full revision of Freud's position followed in 1925. The essential tenet of Freud's revised thesis on femininity, and the shift away from his earlier view, is summed up thus:

> The information about infantile sexuality was obtained from the study of men and the theory deduced from it was concerned with male children. It was natural enough to expect to find a complete parallel between the two sexes; but this turned out not to hold. Further investigations and reflections revealed profound differences between the sexual development of men and women. The first sexual object of a baby girl (just as of a baby boy) is her mother; and before a woman can reach the end of her normal development she has to change not only her sexual object but also her leading genital zone. From this circumstance difficulties arise and possibilities of inhibition which are not present in the case of men.
>
> (1925d, *GW*: 64, *SE*: 36, n. 1, added to the 1935 edn)

While initially the little girl treats her clitoris like a penis, when she compares her organ to that of a 'playfellow of the other sex, she perceives that she has "come off badly" ['*zu kurz gekommen*'] and she feels this as a wrong done to her and a ground for inferiority' (1924c, *GW*: 400, *SE*: 178). Moreover she perceives herself as castrated. And as she cannot fear

---

16 In the case of Dora, Freud is explicit about how his heterosexually biased counter-transference marred the young woman's analysis (1905b). After that case study, Freud wrote nothing on women for fifteen years. There is an extensive literature surmising about and analysing Freud's transference in Dora's case. See especially Gallop [1982] and Bernheimer and Kahane (1985).

what has already occurred, she cannot fear being castrated. With the fear of castration thus removed

> a powerful motive ... drops out for the setting-up of a superego and the breaking-off of the infantile genital organization. *In her, far more than in the boy, these changes seem to be the result of upbringing and of intimidation from outside which threatens her with a loss of love.*
>
> (1924c, *GW*: 401, *SE*: 178; emphasis added)

What this means for the girl's psychical organization is unclear at this point. Freud announces only that she does not tolerate the loss of a penis without seeking recompense. This she finds in the desire for a child from her father: she desires 'to receive a baby from [him] as a gift' (1924c, *GW*: 401, *SE*: 179). The only reason she has for giving up the Oedipus complex is that the wish is unsatisfied. Unconsciously both the wish for a penis and the wish for a child from her father remain strongly cathected. In short, the essence of the revised thesis is an explicit statement of what, as I shall demonstrate at more length in a discussion of how the sexual drive is constructed, has been implicit all along: the girl's primal attachment is to her mother.

The boy resolves his Oedipus complex by anticipating the future: he will have a woman like his mother one day; and this prospect enables him to defer the present unrealizable attachment in favour of a possible future goal. He defers at the same time as he 'smashes' his Oedipus complex by diverting the hostility originally directed towards his mother towards his father. Some of this hostility also finds its way into his sexual drive, which he splits from his affectionate feelings for his mother and represses. Ideally, his Oedipal attachment will not only be repressed; the libidinal drives will be redirected in the process known as sublimation. The lynch-pin in the repression of the masculine Oedipus complex is the threat of castration. This threat, which can be a matter of reality but is usually phantasy, is what prompts the boy to repress his desire for his mother, identify with his father, establish a superego, and ideally redirect his drive in sublimation.

Because this threat has less power in the feminine case, as the girl is already castrated, she has less motive for establishing a superego, and none for giving up her attachment to her mother. Indeed, the problem becomes why she should repress her phallic sexuality, as Freud of course maintains she does, and why she turns from her mother 'in hate', and forms an Oedipal attachment to her father. Rather than terminating her attachment to the parent of the other sex, the castration complex inaugurates it. Freud's main explanation for the girl's repression of her phallic sexuality and for her turning from mother to father is penis-envy. The girl represses her phallic sexuality because of the 'wound to her narcissism' consequent on her lack, and the extent to which she represses her sexuality means that she is unable to redirect it in sublimation. She blames her mother for refusing to supply her with a penis, and turns instead to her father. I have mentioned that the girl's phantasy is that the father will supply her with the missing penis, or a substitute for it in the form of a child. But she has no particular reason for giving up this attachment to her father, and Freud maintains that it persists, and is only worn away by social and slow repression. He also signals that the girl's Oedipus complex is 'a haven of refuge': from the crisis of narcissism, from hostility to her mother. This introduces Freud's third concrete question about the riddle of femininity: despite his emphasis on penis-envy, Freud was still unsatisfied with this as an explanation for why the girl turns from her mother. It also introduces a fourth question: Freud was evidently troubled by the tortuous route the girl had to take to achieve a position where her desire was oriented towards the father, and thence to men. He described this task as psychically exhausting, and added that it resulted in a rigidity in women, an inability to change.

A woman [of 30] often frightens us by her psychical rigidity [*psychische Starrheit*] and unchangeability . . . as though, indeed, the difficult development to femininity had exhausted the possibilities of the person concerned. As therapists we lament this state of things, even if we succeed in putting an end to our patient's ailment by doing away with her neurotic conflict.

(1933a, *GW*: 144–5, *SE*: 135)

Freud signalled that this rigidity also required more explanation, but it was not one he could supply. In more general terms, the explanation of femininity in his second theory of femininity, in so far as it is contingent on a real anatomical difference, will not do in his own terms. It will not do because it will not do for men. The masochism that results from aggressiveness turned back against the self, the repression of active, phallic sexuality, the preference for a passive situation: the numerous feminine traits found in men require another account. Faced with this requirement, Freud offered an explanation founded in phylogeny and innate bisexuality.

Mitigating the severity of his judgement on the effects of the castration complex on women's superego, Freud reiterated that masculinity and femininity existed in 'all human individuals'. They did so 'as a result of their bisexual disposition and of cross-cultural inheritance' (1925c, *GW*: 30, *SE*: 258). The second half of this explanation relies on the Lamarckian suppositions Freud had recourse to in explaining why the Oedipus complex occurred even where the conditions of its occurrence were absent:

Although the majority of human beings go through the Oedipus complex as an individual experience, it is nevertheless a phenomenon which is determined and laid down by heredity.

(1924c, *GW*: 396, *SE*: 174)[17]

Freud's Lamarckian response was also directed to empirical objections to his theory: what if one or all of the conditions of the Oedipus complex were lacking (no father, no mother, no opportunity to see a penis or a woman without one)? These objections, which are the ones most frequently made to the Freudian theory of the Oedipus complex, generated a non-Lamarckian response from Lacan, who insists that what Freud attributed to phylogeny can better be explained by the action of language and the culture's symbolic order.[18] For the time being I am taking up neither option here.

Although there are some ideas associated with Lacan in what follows (they figure in terms in chapter 2 especially; also in chapter 3), not all of these were derived from Lacan; they emerged rather from an enquiry into the internal consistency of Freud's theory of femininity and his metapsychology, especially, but not only, his economic, physical metapsychology. My enquiry began with Freud's questions about femininity, but it concentrates on the consistency and inconsistency of his work overall. As it does so, it outlines a theory which offers another explanation for why femininity is present in both sexes, and also why it is more likely to be found in women. In addition, it is an enquiry which refers more to the physical economic mystery of femininity than to the Lacanian notion that femininity is constructed in relation to language, and the symbolic father who is identified with language. This is not to say language is discounted here; it figures significantly in the latter part of this book, where I will introduce a hypothesis concerning its origins. It is rather that language and the father's role are more end points than beginnings, and these end points are mainly speculative. Overall, the limits on this book are set by its enquiry into Freud's internal consistency: it is not a book on femininity or metapsychology, or even psychoanalytic theories of femininity and metapsychology, let alone psychophysics in general. It is an attempt to think through the consistent implications of, and to examine the inconsistent assumptions in, Freud's theory; it has led to a thesis on how many of Freud's diverse claims might be rationalized, which I shall set out shortly. The fact that I have followed this internal path to the conclusions I reach means that not only Lacan, but Irigaray and Deleuze also figure less than they would if this was a tabulation of relevant cross-references to ideas and concepts. For Irigaray, too, is concerned with physics and spare-time, and Deleuze with the economic level of energy.

17 See also 1919b, *GW*: 208, *SE*: 188: 'Children ... are compelled to recapitulate from the history of mankind the repression of an incestuous object choice.'
18 Lacan (1953b); also [1953–4].

But keeping for now to one of the questions that prompted this enquiry: namely, Freud's problem of how femininity comes to figure in men. Thus far, Freud has given us the alternatives of (i) an intelligible psychical consequence of the anatomical distinction between the sexes (1925c, *GW*: 19, *SE*: 257), and (ii) 'bisexual disposition and cross-cultural inheritance'. Yet there is a sense in which the castration complex and the identifications imbricated in its resolution could offer an alternative explanation of femininity in men. Some of the reasons for the girl's turning away from her mother in hostility apply to boys as well, including the idea that the boundless love of infancy cannot be satisfied. Under these circumstances, the boy's as well as the girl's libido will give up its old position for a new one (1931b, *GW*: 523–4, *SE*: 231). Freud thought that a boy could also identify with his mother, and wish to take her position, that is to say, a passive position in relation to his father. This is the boy's negative Oedipus complex. By the same logic, the girl could and frequently did identify with her phallic mother or father, leading to a masculine position in which she wished to take her father's place in relation to her mother; this is her negative Oedipus complex, and accounts for the masculinity and sublimated masculinity which in turn account for active pursuits in women. In the boy's case however the feminine situation he desired would once again have 'castration' as its phantasmatic consequence, a phantasy which would lead him to repress the feminine attitude.

Yet an insufficient repression of the boy's feminine attitude towards his father could none the less be made to account for femininity in men. But to stress this, as Freud did not, excepting in the remarkable case of the Wolfman (1918a), would have a theoretical price. The theoretical price is that it shifts the emphasis from anatomical sexual difference to identification. Accordingly, it opens out the question as to why identification could not provide a sufficient explanation for the formation of femininity in women, as well as men?

The theoretical price to be paid in pursuing this notion is that Freud's theory of the ego and superego is at stake. So for that matter is his theory of repression, and thus of the repressed unconscious itself. These are at stake because in order to account for the threat of castration taking effect, Freud needs an anatomical difference; it is critical to the castration threat's taking effect that the boy discovers that 'castrated beings otherwise like himself' exist, and believes that he might become one of them. Without this threat, there is no occasion for repressing the incestuous Oedipal attachment to the mother – the core of the repressed unconscious – nor for establishing a superego, nor for redirecting the drives into sublimation. Nor is there a way for mapping masculinity on to men, and femininity on to women; whatever the insistence on bisexuality, Freud continues to suppose that men are more likely to be masculine, women feminine. In short, we are still seeking a consistent explanation for how masculinity is

more likely to be found in men, femininity in women. And this explanation will only be satisfactory if it does not dispense with an account of
how the repressed unconscious is formed.

In fact there is in Freud another, earlier metapsychology of the structure
of the psychical apparatus, and of how repression and the unconscious
are formed; and it is this earlier theory that I intend to pursue at length.

It is a striking fact, and I have tried to indicate it in describing the
masculine and feminine Oedipus complexes, that most of the key terms
Freud uses in describing their course are terms of time and space. The boy
defers his goal, diverts his hostility from mother to father, and redirects his
libidinal drives. The girl does not redirect her drive, divert her hostility,
or defer her goal; she stays in the same place; she 'lingers' in the Oedipus
complex, out of time, and it remains to be seen why she does so.

In Freud's earlier theory of the psychical apparatus, the first topography,
spatial considerations or metaphors are paramount. In it, Freud discusses
how 'excitations' (which owe their economic force to their quantity) are
diverted from hallucinations to actions, and how motor activity directed
towards a goal takes over from wishful phantasies that merely imagine the
goal, instead of altering reality to achieve it. Subsequently, Freud also
credits the ego with this temporal task of deferral, arguing that the ego,
acting in accord with the reality principle, postpones the demands of the
pleasure principle; it defers the immediate satisfaction of a wish, which
the pleasure principle conjures up through hallucination or phantasy, in
favour of longer-term action; in deferring, it represses the wish.

If the reality principle does not hold sway, or if real circumstances make
action difficult, the result is neurosis or psychosis. Psychosis is a denial
of reality as such. Neurosis signifies both an attachment to the past, in
the form of an unconscious attachment to a wish that has been repressed,
and a retreat from action, in which both the repressed wish and conscious
phantasies play a part: the former because it involves the diversion of
psychical energy in maintaining the repression; the latter because they can
substitute for action.

Parallels between masculinity and the healthy ego on the one hand,
femininity and pathology on the other, should now be evident, once this
similarity in the spatial and temporal terms used to describe them are taken
into account. The question now becomes: Are these spatial and temporal
terms merely coincidental, or is there, in this earlier metapsychology, the
beginnings of an alternative explanation of the pathological marks of femininity, an explanation which would account for the occurrence of femininity
in men and women?[19] And if there is, can it be brought to bear on the
mapping of masculinity and femininity on to men and women that is

19 For a related argument, with an intelligent discussion of Freud, see Flax's discussion (1990).
   Another psychoanalytic feminist whose work bears directly on space and sexual identity

consequent on the castration complex? I should stress again that my main concern is not with the actualities of female sexuality, but with whether the exploration of Freud's metapsychology and theory of the ego can account for the pathological marks of femininity in women and men. Recognizing Freud's description of the problems of femininity does not automatically entail accepting the castration complex as an adequate solution; nor, alternatively, need it prevent the realization that the 'solution' of the castration complex overlays a far more complex situation.

The remainder of this Introduction will explore metapsychology and the first topography in more detail, establishing some of the spatial factors to be taken into account. They will be taken into account in understanding the riddle of femininity and the spatio-temporal terms used in the Oedipus complex, and ultimately in reformulating Freud's physics, and the dualism that distorts his theory's explanatory potential. I shall then introduce the concept of psychical reality and elaborate on the first theory of femininity. Psychical reality has received much recent critical attention on the grounds that it was Freud's discovery of it that founded psychoanalysis proper. Later in this book, the question of psychical reality as such will figure. What is of most interest here is that a discussion of psychical reality allows us to elaborate on another critical temporal factor: the timelessness of the unconscious. After this discussion, there is a preliminary outline of my main hypothesis.

METAPSYCHOLOGY AND THE TWO 'SPATIAL' TOPOGRAPHIES

Much of the above discussion of Freud's theory of femininity will be familiar to readers with a broad acquaintance with Freud's theory. So will the discussion in this section. But it is necessary to traverse familiar territory to draw out what will be at stake, particularly in the argument I will introduce on the spatial significance of the concept of 'direction' in the psyche. This will also provide us with an opportunity to define metapsychology in more detail, and it is to this extended definition that I now turn.

In writing on psychoanalysis, metapsychology refers to a notion of an overarching or general theory. Freud's 'metapsychological writings' are the works concerned with theories that try to weld different psychoanalytic hypotheses and theories into a consistent whole. Writing of the only book

is J. Benjamin (1988). Questions of space and time have preoccupied Lacan throughout his work. The significance of space in the formation of the self has also been discussed by Winnicott (for example Winnicott 1965), and by Erikson (1953), whose 'essentialist' concepts of inner and outer space in men and women are based on the idea that women have 'inner' wombs and men have 'outer' penises. But the obvious fact that the terms used to describe the masculine and feminine Oedipus complexes are spatio-temporal ones has escaped attention. Nor has the similarity between these terms and those used by Freud in referring to the ego been remarked.

which he planned but did not complete with the express title of 'Metapsych-ology', he said that metapsychology would 'clarify and carry deeper the theoretical assumptions on which a psychoanalytic system could be founded' (1917a, *GW*: 412, n. 1, *SE*: 222, n. 1).[20] This book has followed suit, in that metapsychology has been defined initially as Freud's attempts to construct consistent theoretical frameworks for the diverse hypotheses that arose in relation to his psychoanalytic work and thought. Yet if we press Freud's own definitions of metapsychology, it seems this general definition should be treated as problematic.

It is problematic because Freud changed and expanded his views, and the result is that the metapsychological writings, the attempts at making psychoanalysis consistent, are themselves inconsistent. According to Wollheim, Freud's work is rife with apparent contradictions, such that 'nonsense' is produced if hypotheses resulting from the problems Freud confronted at different points are juxtaposed.[21] Freud, for Wollheim, has to be read in his chronological context, if these apparent contradictions are to be understood. On the other hand, Freud himself was perennially attempting to 'insert [his] new findings into the picture . . . with which we are familiar' (1931b, *GW*: 520, *SE*: 227). Freud persistently revised previous works, in an attempt to make their hypotheses consistent with his sub-sequent ones. But Wollheim is right; the attempts are not always successful. Yet it is the surviving inconsistencies in particular that will interest us here. For while on the one hand, the inconsistencies can indeed be explained chronologically, in relation to Freud's concerns of the moment, some of these inconsistencies can be resolved in terms of the book's main argument (see pp. 30–6). The inconsistencies become consistent, once they are given a different foundation.

The definition of metapsychology as a consistent theoretical framework is problematic for other reasons. Behind the term lurks a great ambition. 'Metaphysics', Freud writes, should be transformed into 'metapsychology': metapsychology, which Freud here appears to be defining as 'the psy-chology of the unconscious' will provide the key to the great metaphysical questions ('the myths of paradise and the fall of Man, of God, of good and evil, of immortality, and so on') (1901b, *GW*: 288, *SE*: 259). More to the immediate point, by the time Freud said what he meant by metapsy-chology, he had, as I also indicated above, given it a precise technical meaning.[22] This definition is sufficiently technical such that all the terms

20 The book Freud planned to publish would have been titled '*Zur Vorbereitung einer Metapsychologie*' [Preliminaries to a Metapsychology].
21 Wollheim (1973: 9). Wollheim argues that the inconsistencies can be explained by taking account of the situations or problems Freud was addressing at the time.
22 Freud first used the term 'metapsychology' in a letter to Fliess (to whom he addressed much of the correspondence (from 1887 to 1901–2) that reflected his self-analysis, and the origins of psychoanalysis). 'I am continually occupied with psychology – really *metapsych-ology*; Taine's book *L'Intelligence* suits me extraordinarily well' (13 February 1896, *Letters*:

Freud uses to define it need explication: 'when we have succeeded in describing a process in its dynamic, topographical and economic aspects, we should speak of it as a metapsychological presentation [*Darstellung*]' (1915e, *GW*: 281, *SE*: 181). Actually once 'dynamic', 'topographical', and 'economic' are defined, there is one sense in which the two definitions of metapsychology converge. Freud had no general overarching theory of psychoanalysis which was not at one and the same time dynamic, topographic, and economic. However he does not always use these terms in elaborating the different theoretical frameworks which, by common consent, constitute his metapsychological writings.

For that extraordinary editor Strachey, Freud's 'general pictures' of the mind were presented in the seventh chapter of *The Interpretation of Dreams*, which elaborated on an earlier picture outlined in the unpublished *Project* (1950b [1895]); the Metapsychological papers of 1914 to 1917,[23] and the tripartite structure, *The Ego and the Id* (1923b).[24] The tripartite structure is commonly referred to as the second topography; it was presented in 1923, prefiguring the decline of the analogy theory later that year. But while it is referred to as a topography, the 1923 model does not have the spatial connotations the term 'topography' implies. The spatial connotations of the first topography, presented in the *Project* and *The*

172). In other letters, Freud writes, 'Far beyond these considerations [on psychology] lurks my ideal and problem child, metapsychology' (12 December 1896) and metapsychology as 'my psychology that takes one beyond consciousness' (10 March 1898) and see Jones (*Life*, vol. 1: 381–2). Freud's first published use of the term comes in Freud (1901b, *GW*: 288, *SE*: 259). This is the only published allusion to the philosophical ambitions Freud expressed in his correspondence with Fliess, and which he subsequently went to some lengths to disown. Freud does not use the term 'metapsychology' again until his Metapsychological papers of 1914–17, where he gives the technical definition of it discussed in the text.

23 The Metapsychological papers are significant not only because Freud expressly terms them 'metapsychological' (he does not use the term for the other theoretical writings that subsequent psychoanalytic generations have regarded as his metapsychological corpus); they are also significant because only five of the original twelve papers were ever published. The other seven papers Freud either planned to write, or actually wrote, have been lost. Strachey, following Jones, believed that Freud destroyed them. From Freud's correspondence with Lou Andreas-Salomé, it is not clear to me that he actually completed them (2 May 1916, Freud 1972), but see Gay (1988: 373). And in Freud's other correspondence from this period, he refers to five of the topics dealt with in the missing seven papers: Consciousness, Anxiety, Conversion Hysteria, Obsessional Neurosis, and the Transference Neuroses in General. Strachey guesses that the two unspecified papers may have dealt with Sublimation and Projection or Paranoia (Editor's Introduction to the Papers on Metapsychology [*SE*, vol. 14: 106]).

24 To this list, Laplanche and Pontalis (1983), in their summary of Freud's metapsychological writings, add Freud 1911a, 1920b and 1940a [1938]. However as the following discussion will show, we also need to consider the *Studies on Hysteria, Group Psychology and the Analysis of the Ego*, and others of Freud's writings to understand his metapsychology. We will be particularly concerned with 'The Economic Problem of Masochism' (1924b), some critical theoretical formulations in the Schreber case (1911b), and two articles dealing with neuroses and psychoses (1924a and 1924e). For a list of Freud's writings dealing with theory, see *SE*, vol. 14: 259.

Interpretation are plain; it consisted of distinctions between the primary and secondary processes, the conscious, preconscious, and unconscious, and Freud literally drew them out. But the second topography is a model of intrasubjective relations within the psychical apparatus. The superego, ego, and id all enter into relations with one another. The superego becomes the locus of repression, conscience, and reproach; the id the locus of the repressed drives; the ego attempts to balance the demands of both its 'taskmasters' and of its third responsibility: external reality. I have used the term 'locus' in describing these agencies, but they have no spatial relation with each other comparable with the spatial relations of the first topography. But while the second topography has no consistent spatial connotation, it none the less has one 'spatial' implication which, as indicated, will become progressively important in my argument. In using expressions such as 'the superego hammers at the ego', Freud suggests that the superego has a stance in relation to the ego, and that the ego is the object or aim of a certain force. In both its stance and its aim, the superego is *directed* towards the ego. Similarly, libido can be directed away from the ego, or 'turned back on the ego' (in psychosis). It is this notion of direction that has spatial, and indeed temporal, connotations. In addition, both topographies have something else in common: this is the notion of censorship.

In the first topography, Freud imposes a censorship between the unconscious, the preconscious, and the conscious. The censorship tries, not always successfully, to prevent the ideas from one system (and possibly both systems) erupting into the others. The superego, and the ego in one respect, have a similar task in the second topography. The notion that a censor could either prevent, or fail to prevent, the passage of ideas and impulses from one part of the psyche to another introduces the dynamic and economic aspects of Freud's metapsychology.

The topographies are dynamic because the systems or agencies they posit are by definition in conflict. Almost from the beginning, Freud believed that the basis of psychical conflict and the origin of neuroses lay in the censorship, or repression, of ideas, impulses, wishes, and phantasies. These are made unconscious, but continue to strive for self-expression. In doing so they encounter the ongoing opposition of the ego, an opposition based on considerations of reality (which means practicality, morality, and social appropriateness). In brief, topographical issues and dynamic ones are intertwined in that the theories imply each other: the first and the second topographies were theories that explained repression: the division between consciousness and what it was permitted to know, and the repressed unconscious.

It is mainly sexual ideas that are repressed. It is the conflict presupposed in the first topography and theory of sexuality that leads to the quantitative *Unlust* or unpleasure principle, and later to the first theory of the drives

(*Triebe*), in which ego drives are opposed to sexual ones. It leads to it because when confronted with the question, Why, given similar backgrounds and similar circumstances, do some people fall ill when others do not?, Freud answered that a quantitative or economic force was involved, which brings us to the economic factor in metapsychology: sexual impulses and repression alike are variable in their energetic physical force, as indeed must be the strength of the resistance to them. Initially, Freud did not use the term 'drives'. In the *Project* (and *The Interpretation*) he referred to the quantitative factor in terms of 'excitations'. Wollheim (1973), Laplanche and Pontalis (1983), and Strachey (*SE*, vol. 1: 291, edit. n.) believe drives and excitations are the same thing. However I do not agree with this, and besides, the *Triebe* are elaborated by Freud in a manner that excitations are not. He referred to the theory of them as the indispensable 'mythology' of psychoanalysis. Yet it is the earlier quantitative theory of excitations that will have more ultimate bearing on the riddle of femininity, partly because it owes less to biology and more to physics. And while Freud first described the conflict in the drives in terms of the struggle between ego or self-preservative drives and sexual drives, where it was the ego drives that did the repressing, he subsequently refined the conflict in the drives in terms of life and death drives, and this redefinition echoes the 'excitations' model of the *Project*.

But however he expressed it, the quantitative or economic factor remains fundamental to Freud's definition of health and pathology throughout his work. In a late work, he refers to 'the irresistible power of the quantitative factor [*der quantitative Moment*] in the causation of illness' (1937, *GW*: 70, *SE*: 226). In this context, he also refers to how the forces against which repression is directed have various reinforcements.

The strength of the ego is the strength of the repressive force, and this strength can diminish for a variety of reasons. Not all of them are based in psychical reality. The drives are considerably reinforced at puberty and the menopause. The strength of the ego can be diminished 'through illness or exhaustion'. The notion that exhaustion can weaken the ego is discussed by Freud together with other non-psychical factors.

> Here we have a justification of the claim to aetiological importance of such non-specific factors as overwork, shock, etc. These factors have always been assured of general recognition, but have had to be pushed into the background precisely by psycho-analysis. It is impossible to define health except in metapsychological terms: i.e., by reference to the dynamic relations between the agencies of the mental apparatus which have been recognized – or (if that is preferred) inferred or conjectured – by us.
>
> (1937, *GW*: 70, n. 1, *SE*: 226, n. 2)

This quotation is significant because it reveals two things. One is the notion that in order to become psychoanalysis, psychoanalysis had to minimize the external factors which Freud none the less recognizes as possible causes of pathology. He is emphasizing the psychical factor, and, by implication, stressing the significance of psychical reality as the foundational discovery of psychoanalysis. In addition, 'overwork' and 'shock' were current explanations of neurosis in the second half of the nineteenth century especially.[25] But, and this introduces the second point, for Freud these external factors explain nothing unless they are situated in relation to a theory of dynamic and economic psychical relations. Some people fall ill and others do not when confronted with various external contingencies because external contingencies are not the only factors involved. Analysis as a therapy contributes to health by correcting the original processes of repression, 'a correction which puts an end to the dominance of the quantitative factor' (1937, *GW*: 71, *SE*: 227). In doing so, it alters the basis of the original repressions made in early childhood: Freud is insistent that these are the pivot of illness. The ego deals with subsequent conflicts by following the pathways established by the first repressions in a process Freud terms 'after-repression'('*Nachverdrängung*') or 'after-pressure' ('*Nachdrängung*'). In other words, new repressions might be innovative in terms of the content of what is repressed, but the nature of the repression is set by the initial 'primitive defensive measures' of the early ego. Evidently, although Freud does not say this in these terms, the content of new repressions could thus be handled inefficiently, in that they could be subjected to forms of repression which were inappropriate. But enough at this point to say that repression is a complex affair.[26]

Before closing this section, the spatial metaphor of the first topography needs more attention, for it is in this topography that we will find the basis for a redefinition of the unconscious and repression which will make 'femininity' into less of an inconsistency. The term 'spatial metaphor' has been used to describe the first topography because Freud insists that he is not attempting to localize the psychical agencies he describes in cerebral anatomy.[27] Yet the metaphor is extremely elaborate; and in the *Project* at least, the spatial descriptions may well be hypothetical, but they do not appear metaphorical. In addition, even in *The Interpretation*, it seems that Freud is not so much insisting on a metaphor as 'carefully avoid[ing] the temptation to determine psychical locality in any anatomical fashion'

25 Ellenberger (1970: especially chapter 4; also p. 243).
26 This complexity has already been indicated by the complication of after-pressure. Freud's distinction between primal repression and repression proper will be discussed in chapter 3, where the idea of primitive defence measures will be investigated.
27 Freud initially uses the term 'topographical' critically in describing the deficiencies in then current theories of cerebral localization of psychical processes. See the discussion in Forrester [1980]: 14ff. Forrester's discussion however implies that Freud distinguished hypothetical physiological space from anatomical space.

(1900, *GW*: 541, *SE*: 536). That is to say, there is a difference between refusing to speculate about where these systems are, and hypothesizing their spatial existence as such. At one point, Freud suggests that he is introducing a hypothesis 'of the crudest and most concrete description' (1900, *GW*: 541, *SE*: 536). Freud's commentators, Strachey included, favour a completely metaphorical reading. But the text repays a closer investigation.

In fact, Freud's 'crude hypothesis' about the mental apparatus suggests that it might have either a spatial or a temporal arrangement. He pictures it as a 'compound instrument' like a microscope or a photographic apparatus: 'psychical locality . . . correspond[s] to [an ideal] point inside the apparatus at which one of the preliminary stages of an image comes into being' [*Die psychische Lokalität entspricht einem Orte innerhalb eines Apparats, an dem eine der Vorstufen des Bildes zustande kommt*] (1900, *GW*: 541, *SE*: 536). The components of this compound instrument are given the name of 'systems'. Excitational energy can pass through these systems in either a spatial or perhaps a temporal sequence.

> The first thing that strikes us is that this apparatus, compounded of [*psi*]-systems, has a sense [*sic*] or direction. All our psychical activity starts from stimuli (whether internal or external) and ends in innervations. Accordingly, we shall ascribe a sensory and a motor end to the apparatus. At the sensory end there lies a system which receives perceptions; at the motor end there lies another, which opens the gateway to motor activity.
>
> (1900, *GW*: 542, *SE*: 537)

The first thing that strikes us about this quotation is the apparent misprint in the first sentence. The German reads, '*Das erste, das uns auffällt, ist nun, dass dieser aus [psi]-Systemen zusammengesetzte Apparat eine Richtung hat*' (1900, *GW*: 542). There is no 'sense' in this sentence; there is 'direction' (*Richtung*). It seems probable that Strachey had intended to translate *Richtung* as 'sense *of* direction'. Whatever the case, the English loses the emphasis in the German on direction. The expression 'sense *or* direction' brings questions of meaningfulness to mind; 'sense *of* direction', or simply 'direction', suggests an aim in view, intentionality, and perhaps movement towards an aim, which in turn evokes movement through space and time. (Cf. Lacan 1990: 132.) The critical idea here is that of direction. As noted, 'direction' enables us to draw a parallel between the first and second topographies, a parallel which is additional to the more obvious parallel: namely, that both topographies make repression central.

Whether or not movement through space or time is implied in the direction of the psychical apparatus, and whatever Freud's reservations about the actual spatial bearings of his model, space, together with time, is built into the model of the psychical apparatus in more than one respect.

While Freud refuses to think of the spatial dimensions of the psychical apparatus as concrete in the rest of the passage quoted above, where he situates motor activity at one end of the psychical apparatus, perceptual activity at another, and while he says that this relationship could also be described as a temporal one, Freud adheres consistently to the principle which he attributed to Kant, but which is also and more usually attributed to Leibniz, that the one space cannot have two simultaneous occupants. For instance, memory occupies a different space from perception; this is critical to Freud's insistence that memory had to be the province of a system which was distinct from the system of perception: 'there are obvious difficulties involved in supposing that one and the same system can accurately retain modifications of its elements [memory] and yet remain perceptually open to the reception of fresh occasions for modification [perception]' (1900, *GW*: 543, *SE*: 538).[28] So he supposes that the perceptual system is in 'the very front of the apparatus [*ein vorderstes System des Apparats*]' (ibid.). Memories are incorporated in the second system, which lies 'behind it'. Freud is still stressing the hypothetical nature of his thinking here, and we may presume that he retains it when he none the less writes, 'The only way in which we can describe what happens in hallucinatory dreams is by saying that the excitation moves in a *backward* direction [*rückläufigen Weg*]' (1900, *GW*: 547, *SE*: 542). This backward thinking is regression; it is distinct from the '*progressive* [*progrediente*] ... direction taken by psychical processes arising from the unconscious during waking life' (ibid., Freud's emphases, trans. mod.). In fact the discussion of progression is somewhat confusing. Freud also writes that 'in the case of dreams regression may perhaps be further facilitated by the cessation of the progressive current which streams in during the day-time from the sense organs' (1900, *GW*: 553, *SE*: 547). On the face of it, a progressive direction taken by the psychical apparatus cannot be the same thing as a progressive current which 'streams in'. But whichever way they 'stream', ideas and energy follow *directions*. Similarly, only one memory at a time is able to pass through consciousness into 'the breadth [*Weite*] of the ego' (1895b, *GW*: 296, *SE*: 291). Ideas and impulses go from one point to another in the process of coming to consciousness. Alternatively, they can regress.

Freud here uses the term 'regression' in a different, although related, sense from that in which it is usually understood in psychoanalysis. He does not mean regression to an infantile behaviour or disposition. He means that thoughts can go back to their original form. In this form, they are governed entirely by the unpleasure principle and consist of hallucinations. An hallucination is the thought form that is closest in character to perception as such, and the first hallucinations, incidentally,

28 Cf. Freud with Breuer (1895b: 188–9, n. 17).

are visual rather than auditory. So regression involves travelling the direction that leads back to the first thought forms, forms which visit us nightly in dreams. Hallucination is governed by the pleasure principle in that, for instance, if an infant desires the mother's breast, it hallucinates it, and imagines it to be present regardless of the real facts of the matter. This form of satisfaction is of course short-lived, as the hallucination is not sufficient to dispose of the excitations that prompted it.

Hallucination is an immediate process: immediate in the sense that it dispenses with temporal and spatial considerations. This brings us to another spatio-temporal feature of the psychical apparatus. Hallucination in dreams, and for that matter in waking life, is tied to the immediate present tense. In fact, in unconscious processes, the conditional, and necessarily future- or past-oriented 'perhaps's and 'if's are removed. This temporal realization is one Freud came to through the discovery of psychical reality, to which I now turn.

PSYCHICAL REALITY: TIME LOST

However this section will not only touch on time. It will also show how the analogy theory and psychical reality were two sides of the same discovery. Eventually, this two-sided discovery will return us to the spatio-temporal bearings of masculinity and femininity, via the physical phenomena of hysteria. When Freud first claimed ('with a certainty beyond all doubt') that the child's death wish against its parent of the same sex dates back to earliest childhood and 'that a girl's first affection is for her father' (1900, *GW*: 264, *SE*: 257), he illustrated the claim with a vignette from a case of hysteria (1900, *GW*: 265–6, *SE*: 259–60). Throughout his work, hysteria was to remain the neurosis typical of femininity for Freud, just as obsessional neurosis was to be typical of masculinity. The specific example of hysteria Freud uses in announcing the analogy theory concerns a young woman's death wish towards her mother. Let us note at the outset that it is a death wish that points the way to the discovery of the girl's Oedipus complex, rather than the discovery of love for her father. Yet this is also an example, drawn from Freud's clinical practice, of a heterosexual Oedipal dynamic on the woman's part. As such, it raises the question of how far Freud was relying on his clinical practice for his conclusions regarding the analogy theory. Prior to 1900, and the disastrous Dora analysis (1905a), after which Freud was not to write about women for another fifteen years, hysterics were a large part of his private practice. Freud of course began psychoanalysis, as theory and practice, with hysterics. And hysterics were mainly but not exclusively women.

But the study of hysteria was treacherous territory for Freud. In it, he made the 'mistake' of supposing that the accounts of paternal rape or seduction given by his patients were always descriptions of real events.

He revised and qualified that view comparatively rapidly; it was twenty-five years before he revised his views on a girl's first emotional, erotic attachment.

In revising his view of the real event, Freud arrived at his most momentous discovery: the existence of psychical reality.[29] To understand the relation between the real events of seduction, and Freud's discovery of psychical reality in his patients, the meaning of psychical reality, and what Freud thought he had discovered, has to be defined. Psychical reality means that the phantasies a person had entertained but repressed (for instance, desire for a parent) and the reactions to those phantasies (for instance, guilt over the wish to dispose of the other parent) had the same effects on behaviour as if they had been real events. 'As if' becomes 'it is'. Accordingly, as I have indicated, a temporal shift is effected when the phantasy is taken for reality.

Psychical reality has been defined as any of the ideational contents of the unconscious (Laplanche and Pontalis 1983). More precisely, it is the belief that wishes or fears are real. For example, when the infant hallucinates the breast because of the unpleasure contingent on its absence, it founds psychical reality. But it also founds the situation where it believes that whatever it does to the breast or mother in phantasy is real. If it devours the breast, for instance, in phantasy, it unconsciously believes that this event has occurred. The belief that a phantasy is not merely a wish, but something that took place, involves the expenditure of psychical energy precisely when it involves repression. The phantasy is repressed as securely or as relentlessly as a memory of an event that did take place. Psychical energy is not available for outward pursuits. It is flowing backwards, pressing down something that the subject does not want to come up. It is this expenditure of energy that means the subject is tied to the past, and that the phantasy lives on with the full force of a present event.

Now this tie to the past, while it involves a temporal shift ('as if' is 'it is'), is not the same thing as the timelessness of the unconscious, in which the events of today coincide with those of yesterday. It is important to note this as these two temporal or atemporal phenomena are often confused. For on the one hand the unconscious, using the term in what Freud described as a 'descriptive' sense, simply does not recognize the passage of time: it has access to all experiences, and may produce those of two

29 The discovery of psychical reality was based not only on the study of hysteria, but on the psychoneuroses more generally. These included hysteria, 'many phobias and obsessions and certain hallucinatory psychoses' (1894, GW: 59, SE: 45). Freud introduces the term 'psychoneuroses' to contrast one category of clinical entities with another, that of the 'actual neuroses'. The genesis of the latter lies in quantitative factors, degrees of excitation, and in this is more somatic. See Freud (1896a and 1898a). As the label implies, the psychoneuroses have a psychogenesis. The fact that the grouping included some psychoses, which were allied with hysteria through the symptom of hallucination, is also evoked by the term. Concerning the first appearance of a distinction between 'thought reality' (psychical reality?) and external reality, see Freud (1950a: 373, n. 1).

years ago as readily as, and without differentiating them from, the events
of twenty-five years past. But this ready access need not be related to the
repression that gives psychical reality its distinctive character and temporal
effect. I repeat, it is the fact that an imagined phantasy or hallucination
is repressed that ties the subject to the past by the expenditure of energy
involved in this repression, and thereby brings the past into the present.
Moreover the wish that brings psychical reality into being is prompted by
the delay between a need and its fulfilment. It is prompted, for instance,
by the absence of the breast when it is needed. The significance of this is
that in contrast to the descriptive unconscious which knows no time,
psychical reality needs a delay. And there can be no experience of delay
without some experience or concept of time.[30]

Doubtless this side of psychical reality will seem far removed from its
better-known dimension, in which psychical reality makes one feel as
guilty as if the crime had occurred. Yet these two aspects of psychical
reality are ultimately tied together, as we shall see after more investigation
of its better-known aspect.

The implications of psychical reality for real behaviour do not end with
guilt. In the feminine case, it seems the desire and the guilt can be projected
on to the parent; the parent, not the child, is made the point of origin for
blame. Hamlet, for example, is a true male hysteric, marked by exaggerated
scruples of conscience which were actually 'reaction-formations' to his
own desires (1900, GW: 270, SE: 265).

In modifying his view that the paternal seductions his patient reported
were real events, Freud was influenced by the self-analysis that was contemporaneous with, and conducted in the context of, his relationship with
Wilhelm Fliess. This self-analysis revealed his own Oedipal impulse; we
might say that the analogy theory was already presupposed in his re-
evaluation of his hysterical patients' accounts; just as he had found the
Oedipus complex in his psychical depths, so too (he assumed) the analogous impulse lay behind the women he analysed. Freud announced the
Oedipus complex, meaning sexual love for the opposite sex parent, and
jealous hostility towards the other, on 15 October 1897, one month after
the collapse of the seduction theory.[31] He had gone as far as he could
with himself; he assumed there was no hinterland in women. In the
published record, he writes that in recognizing that the accounts of
seduction were not all true, 'I had in fact stumbled for the first time upon
the Oedipus complex, which was later to assume such an overwhelming
importance' (1925d, GW: 60, SE: 34).

But the Oedipus complex Freud discovered in his patients either

30 The complex issue of time and the unconscious and the concept of timelessness is central
   to Hampshire (1974), Derrida (1981), who suggests that Freud is arguing against mechanical,
   Laplacean time, and Forrester (1991).
31 Jones, *Life*, vol. 1: 390.

assumed or led to another great mistake: the analogy theory. Let us reiterate this fact too at the outset. The context for the momentous discovery of psychical reality and the simultaneous discovery of sexual impulses in children is also the clinical occasion for perpetuating the idea that a girl's father, not her mother, is her first love. Thus the discovery and the oversight are two sides of the same picture. This leads to an obvious question. Is psychical reality, is the process whereby 'as if' becomes 'it is', the same in the masculine and the feminine case?[32]

But the main point here is to suggest that because the evidence for the girl's desire for her father is uncovered together with the discovery of psychical reality, Freud had another reason for remaining attached to the analogy theory, despite the fact that it is, as we shall see, logically contradicted by the implications of his other most significant discovery: his theory of infantile sexuality. That is to say, Freud regarded the *Three Essays on the Theory of Sexuality* (1905b) as his second great work; he ranked it alongside *The Interpretation of Dreams*; and both books are regarded by his followers as 'his most momentous and original contributions to human knowledge'.[33] The *andere Schauplatz* of psychical reality is elaborated in *The Interpretation*; the theory of sexuality in the *Three Essays*. They complement each other exactly in that psychical reality is the result of the repression of infantile sexuality. But the complementarity is exact on the masculine side only. Chapter 4 will show this in detail, in a discussion of how the implications of Freud's theory of infantile sexuality contradict the assumptions he made about the analogy theory. But briefly put, and as noted above, the contradiction is that the theory of sexuality shows that the mother's breast is the first sexual object for both sexes, and this is presupposed in Freud's account of how the construction of sexuality is also the construction of a characteristic choice of a 'love-object', in later life, who is prefigured by the child's mother.

There is another point about psychical reality that should be noted. It is commonly supposed that when Freud abandoned the seduction theory, he simultaneously assumed that all the accounts given him of seduction

---

32 Apart from the analogy mistake being built into the discovery of psychical reality, there are other grounds for enquiring about its relation to sexed identity. In terms of its assumptions about activity and passivity, the theory of psychical reality is similar to the seduction theory that preceded it: Freud maintained that while the archetypically feminine neurosis, hysteria, could be traced to passive sexual experience (being seduced), the quintessentially masculine obsessional neuroses originated with active sexual experiences, although this distinction breaks down in that later Freud insists that active sexual experiences are always preceded by passive ones. This in turn raises the problem of how the passive experiences are converted into active ones. Thus the analogy theory was not precisely analogous even at the time of its inception: the active and passive positions that are present in the unresolved masculine Oedipus complex and in the unresolved feminine one indicate why. In addition, in the theory of psychical reality the correlations between activity and obsessional neurosis, passivity and hysteria, were still demanded by 'some facts' (1906a, *GW*: 154, *SE*: 275).

33 Strachey, Editor's Note to Freud (1905b).

were false. This is not correct.[34] Like so much else in Freud's theory, the received view rests on a generalization that Freud not only never made, but counselled against making. Of course, one has to read Freud, and his constant doubts about the universal validity of his conclusions, to find that this is so. In this case, what Freud abandoned was the idea that the sole cause of a psychoneurosis was an actual seduction. In his first published revision of the seduction theory, he wrote that his case material at the time he formulated the seduction theory

> was still scanty, and it happened by chance to include a disproportionately large number of cases in which sexual seduction by an adult or by older children played the chief part in the patient's childhood. I thus over-estimated the frequency of such events (though in other respects they were not open to doubt). Moreover, I was at that point unable to distinguish with certainty between falsifications made by hysterics in their memories of childhood and traces of real events.
>
> (1906a, GW: 153, SE: 274)

The significance of the discovery of psychical reality was less that it discounted the accounts as 'real events', more that it emphasized that phantasies of seduction had similar effects to real events.[35] Not only

34 J. M. Masson's argument that Freud suppressed the seduction theory as the result of a 'failure of courage' proceeds by selective quotation from Freud (1914b and 1925d) and leaves aside Freud's references to real seduction (Masson [1984: 10–11]). When Masson first mentions Freud's public retraction of the seduction theory in 1905, he abstains from quotation. It would have been difficult to sustain an argument that Freud suppressed the seduction theory in the light of the relevant quotations from the initial retraction. In the *Three Essays* of 1905 (and this is the only occasion in that year where Freud refers to seduction theory), Freud lists seduction as the most important of the accidental '*external* contingencies determining sexual activity and neurotic illness' (1905b, GW: 96, SE: 190). There is a postscript to Masson's book, in which he says that (unnamed) critics of his book have pointed out that Freud 'never ceased to believe that seduction played an important role in the origins of neurosis' [1984: 195] from which I conclude that others have made points similar to those that occupy this note. (And apart from this one, there is an excellent critique of Masson in Rose 1986.) Of course had Masson made a case against the manner in which Freud's own views have been discounted in favour of the idea that all accounts of father/daughter incest were phantasies, he would have been on unimpeachable ground.
35 On the other hand, Freud exculpates the father to some degree in a report to the Vienna Psychoanalytic Society (24 January 1912, *Minutes*). And in his first history of the psychoanalytic movement, Freud wrote that the seduction 'aetiology broke down under the weight of its own improbability and contradiction in definitely ascertainable circumstances. Analysis had led back to these infantile sexual traumas by the right path, and yet they were not true' (1914b, GW: 44, SE: 7). Yet the earlier qualification on the renunciation of the seduction theory is echoed again (1925d, GW: 60, SE: 34). Freud records that his confidence in the seduction theory had been increased by cases where the sexual relations with the father or older brother persisted to a point 'at which memory was to be trusted' (ibid.), and also that seduction still played a part, albeit a lesser one, in the aetiology of the neuroses (ibid., GW: 60, SE: 35). These qualifications also reflect Freud's doubts, expressed after the letter in which he first retracted his seduction theory, in other letters to Fliess. Freud's belief in the father aetiology was at one point

because they had a similar effect, but also because other people who had actually been seduced did not fall ill (1906a, *GW*: 155, *SE*: 276), the aetiological concern became the relative force of repression. The failure of repression, the splitting-off of an idea or memory from consciousness, led to the formation of a symptom. The shift in emphasis from the real event to repression meant that

> it was no longer a question of what sexual experiences a particular individual had had in his childhood, but rather of his reactions to those experiences – of whether he had reacted to them by 'repression' [*Verdrängung*] or not.
>
> (1906a, *GW*: 156, *SE*: 277)

This shift in emphasis did not mean that Freud discounted or downplayed the possibility, actually probability, that a real event could have the same impact as or far greater impact than a phantasy. What is critical in his new aetiology is precisely the notion that it is the force of repression that causes illness, whether a phantasy or a real event is at stake. And what is of interest to us now is that that aetiology presents us with a persistent interplay between phantasy and material reality in Freud's model of health and pathology. That aetiology also shifts the focus of Freud's concerns to another foundation stone of psychoanalysis, the relative force of repression. It is in relation to repression that Freud formulated his hydraulic metapsychology, dominated by a physics of quantities of pressure, whose build-up led to unpleasure, and whose release resulted in satisfaction. This hydraulic physics may seem a long way from the spatio-temporal factors which I have argued underpin the Oedipus complex, and the riddle of femininity, but this book's argument should show that the distance between the two is not as great as it first appears. I turn now to a selective summary of that argument, which is intended more as a preliminary outline of its main hypothesis, a memory guide to some of my argument's principal paths, than a comprehensive overview.

MEMORY GUIDE

Freud did note that masculinity is 'ego-syntonic', meaning in harmony with the ego, in a way that femininity is not. But he did not say why. While femininity, like pathology, appears to be tied to the past, the similarities between femininity and pathology, and the account of masculinity and the healthy ego, are obscured. They are obscured because the

---

strengthened (12 December 1897, *Letters*; also 22 December 1897) and his reluctance to reach a final view is entirely consistent with the measure of the emphasis throughout his work as a whole: namely, that sometimes the repression of real trauma was involved in the formation of symptoms; sometimes the symptoms originated in the repression of phantasy.

extent to which the ego is constructed is not fully explored. More accurately, in Freud's theory, the ego appears as something that both is and is not constructed. On the one hand, it is presented as the *given* agent of conscious perception, action, and attention; it arises out of the id as a kind of biologically necessary agent for perceiving reality. On the other, the ego is constructed out of identifications.

Yet if the history of the ego and its identifications is pushed back far enough, it can and will be argued here that the ego's perception is structured, and its capacities for testing and acting on reality are acquired. Perception is structured in that the attentive energy deployed by the five senses is structured along certain pathways, just like the libido. In turn, perception and attention are part of the ego's equipment for testing and acting on reality. These capacities are acquired through a complex process, loosely termed 'identification'. This process has two aspects. One of these is recognized. One is not.

Freud's theory of narcissism presupposes an 'identification' with oneself. (I will continue to use this term until I have established bases for differentiating the processes involved in it).[36] Narcissism presupposes that one sees oneself as if one's image were reflected in a mirror. The idea of seeing oneself is active, but seeing oneself in a mirror is passive because it presupposes being seen. This means that the people concerned are in some sense visualizing themselves, and in this actively *directing their capacity for visualization, or imagination, inwards*, towards a passive end. Moreover this capacity is one form of attention.

With this unexplained confusion between activity and passivity in mind, we can turn to the unrecognized aspect of 'identification'. I will argue that it lies in this: initially, the mother's (or primary other's) capacities for attending, testing, and acting are literally experienced as one's own through an unconscious tie with the mother. Because these capacities come from the mother they are actually not an identification at all, as we shall see. But for the time being, I will say that the mother's capacities are 'identified' with in a way that means that they are also turned inwards; they are not *directed* towards an 'external reality' but constitute a passive ego which then has to be reversed into an active one. It is in this reversal that these capacities, called subjective capacities, for attending, testing, and acting are 'acquired' and the active ego formed. In addition, by postulating that the mother's capacities are first experienced as one's own, and yet experienced passively, two old psychoanalytic disputes can be clarified. The first is whether the ego drives and sexual drives can be separated. The second is about the origin of the superego. I will hypothesize that initially the superego *is* the mother's executive capacities. This supposition makes the superego anterior to the Oedipus complex. The idea that the

36 The imprecision in Freud's use of the term is discussed, from very different perspectives, by Wollheim (1982), Adams (1988), and Borch-Jacobsen (1989).

ego-ideal is formed before the Oedipus complex is not contested in the psychoanalytic corpus; however the idea that the superego predates the Oedipus complex, and is not only its successor, was the heresy of Melanie Klein.[37]

My use of the term 'superego', rather than, or as well as, the term 'ego-ideal' is a considered one. The idea of the superego turned inwards, 'hammering' or observing the ego, occurs in Freud's formulations on masochism, melancholia, and paranoia. This inward-turning superego is in possession of some part of the sexual drive, and of the death drive. It is in possession of the physical, economic, quantitative force of the drives in a way that the inward-turning ego-ideal is not, apparently at least. Now this appearance of a driveless 'ego-ideal' is deceptive, for there is also, according to Freud, a 'seeing' or scopophilic drive; this ephemeral drive is more forceful than it appears at first, but enough to stress here that the concept of the inward-turning superego carries indubitable drives in its train.

Two points need to be made now. The first is that the inward-turning superego can, as Freud says it does, account for certain pathologies. It can account for them independently of the Oedipus complex, in so far, and only in so far, as they can be attributed to an unintegrated 'identification' with the ego's capacities in their passive form. It can account for the appearance of certain feminine traits in men. Masochism is the main illustration of this situation: discussion of it will show that the ego's capacities for judging and acting on reality are 'passed back' to the inward-turning superego. This notion of a superego, which is experienced in the first instance as the ego's capacities opposed to, turned in towards, the self, can help account for the similarity between certain pathologies and the marks of femininity.

The second point to be made is that if it is accepted that the superego predates the Oedipus complex, the ideal resolution of the masculine Oedipus complex can be read as a forging, a union of capacities that were hitherto identified with the mother and original superego, but come to belong to the masculine ego. In this process, the early superego changes its character. Before the Oedipus complex, the active and passive experience of these executive or subjective capacities was a fluid one; the subject was still finding its sexual bearings. The Oedipus complex cements the active deployment of these capacities to the masculine position. But in the feminine case, the capacities for attending to and acting on reality are reversed back to their original passive state. Femininity constitutes a passive overlay on an originally passive experience, and this passive overlay is not restricted to the female sex.

37 The heresy is first apparent in Klein (1928) but not elaborated until Klein (1935). It is a heresy with which Lacan concurred, endorsing Klein's view of 'the first formation of the superego' as 'perfectly original' (Lacan 1948).

We shall see that this cementing of activity to the masculine position, and passivity to the feminine one, is necessary because the ego is unable to carry out its two tasks without reference to an external other. By 'its two tasks', I mean repressing and actively diverting attention and drives towards its goal in external reality, and constructing and maintaining a self-image. This self-image is a condition of its identity. The term 'identity' has come to recent prominence, but it, like 'identification', has not been well defined. However it is enough to say now that for the subject, maintaining its self-image and identity is a task which requires some energetic attention and drive, diverted towards a passive end.

In fact, most people do split the ego's capacities, maintaining their self-image in the manner laid down by the structure of narcissism and the ego-ideal, at the same time as they direct the ego's capacities for testing and acting on reality externally. None the less, the external other is a means for consolidating the spatio-temporal bearings a subject needs to establish in order to function in reality. I say 'consolidate' because the suggestion here is that it is establishing bearings in time and space that bring repression, and, with it, the unconscious and subject-to-be, into existence. As I have indicated, when the subject-to-be represses an hallucination, it establishes a fixed reference point for itself (the beginning of a sense of time) at the same time as it makes the repressed wish or hallucination as real for it now as it was then (that is to say, 'timeless').

In the first instance, the infant's orientation to external reality is as fluid and uncertain as its sense of whether it or the mother embodies the active executive capacities the ego will seek to claim as its own. While the fixed point of an hallucination provides it with its initial temporal orientation, its fully spatial orientation is not cemented until masculine and feminine positions are adopted. In this cementing, the Lacanian idea that the masculine and feminine positions are founded in language comes into its own, as does Derrida's argument on the spatio-temporal structure of language.

As to the question of what comes 'before' this consolidation, and the question of what 'fluidity' consists of: these are questions that can be answered only if one takes the notion that the infant experiences the mother's capacities as its own literally. That is to say, they can be dealt with provided that one pushes this idea back as far as it will go, into our uterine genesis, and hypothesizes, as I shall, that *in utero*, there is no or less delay between the sense of a need and its fulfilment. It is only after birth that the sense of time is born of the sense of delay. Of course this hypothesis, especially where it concerns the origins of delay, relies on the idea of a non-reductionist materialism. It supposes some fleshly memory of a state in which the delay between need and fulfilment did not exist or was less, and where subject and other were not differentiated. But it is precisely this fleshly memory that the unconscious construction of spatio-temporal bearings will conceal. And precisely how it conceals them can be uncovered only after the vested interests of both the masculine and feminine parties are taken into account.

I can hint at these vested interests. The feminine party helps the masculine one with one of the ego's two tasks. By her living attention, she helps maintain his identity, a self-image that accords with acting on the world. He also protects her identity, especially in his function as father. But the extent to which paternal protection has positive or ego-syntonic effects can be undermined by the nature of her relation to the external other, and the nature of the psychophysical impact the external other has on her. To give a broader hint, this impact may mean that she carries an overload of affects that overlay her own narcissistic inward-turning.

In unravelling the riddle, I will explain the nature of this impact in detail, and its tie to the concept of 'identification'. But to begin thinking that the external other has an impact means thinking about intersubjective relations in energetic terms. Thinking about the external other this way means breaking down the illusion that subjects' mental or psychical processes are individually self-contained, an illusion that can only be maintained when these processes are regarded as unphysical. In fact much contemporary psychoanalytic theory recognizes the psychophysical effects of the external other. Although the implications remain untheorized, exactly this assumption underlies much post-Kleinian thought. It employs concepts such as 'counter-transference', in an idiosyncratic sense of that term, where the analyst is meant to *feel* the analysand's feelings. Pick up a recent issue of the *International Journal of Psycho-Analysis*, and you will probably find a statement like: 'the patient entered the room and I felt his depression enter into me'.[38] While it could (and should in lieu of an argument) be objected that the phenomenon of migrating emotions can be explained by other means, the point is that 'counter-transference' presupposes that psychophysical connections operate between beings. We will show that these connections operate at a 'slower' pace than the connections I am supposing exist *in utero*, but they are none the less physical for all that. Indeed their slower pace, together with the initial delays of hallucination, will help explain the peculiar inertia or rigidity of femininity.

But it will take the remainder of this volume to show why. The second chapter, 'The riddle's repression', elaborates on the problems posed by Freud's second theory of femininity, especially the idea that women are more repressed than men. This idea is critical to the economic riddle of femininity, which has been bypassed entirely in both the debates (one in

---

38 See Bion [1962], (1967), and (1970) for theoretical elaborations of this notion of counter-transference. It originates with Paula Heimann's (1950) paper, but was never accepted by Klein herself. Grosskurth tells the story of the young trainee analyst who told Klein that he *felt* the patient's confusion enter into him. Klein replied: 'No, my dear, you are confused' (see the discussion in Grosskurth 1986: 378–9).

the 1920s and 1930s, one in the 1970s and 1980s) generated by Freud's second theory of femininity. This chapter is obliged to discuss those two debates, to show that this is so, benefit from their insights, and sum up the story so far. It is a story that brings the interplay between psychical and material reality to the fore, and a story whose examination enables us to begin giving a more precise definition of 'identity'. Yet it is also a story that bypasses the riddle in an otherwise interesting linguistic turn.

Elaborating on the riddle of femininity and its relation to repression establishes preliminary grounds for a main thesis for this book: the connections between masculinity, femininity, and the vicissitudes of the ego's capacities for testing, acting, and attending. In developing this thesis, chapter 3 turns first to Freud's early work with Breuer on hysteria, which reveals more about the interplay between phantasy and material reality, and begins to illustrate how the ego's capacities are turned inwards in the feminine case, a turning exemplified in the art of the daydream. In a related discussion of attention and psychical reality, Freud's assumptions about physics come into their own. What Freud was in fact describing was how 'inertia' is a psychical construction (an entirely new idea), but he, like some of his nineteenth-century forebears, confused his description with an interpretation of Newton's first and second laws. This emerges through an analysis of the early metapsychology of the *Project*, which also tells us something about energy and excitation, as Freud conceived them.

How this analysis bears back on the riddle of femininity will be clarified after the matter of the drives is discussed in chapter 4. Much of the argument of this chapter, and of chapter 5, has already been outlined. These chapters show how Freud's account of the formation of the sexual drive is an account 'in other words' of the acquisition of the ego's capacities for attention, testing, and acting on reality, capacities which are originally 'identified' with the mother. The fifth chapter, 'The original superego', also traces the concept of the superego back through Freud's earlier formulations of it. In addition, this historical tracing analyses similarities between Klein's and Freud's views on the superego, and suggests how the metapsychological inconsistencies of the former might be resolved. Critical here is the notion that the death drive and its accompanying aggressiveness are not, in the masochistic femininity of men and women, directed outwards. Both feminine psychical structure, and the impact of the masculine other, turn aggression inwards.

While this means that women are more likely to feel the effects of inertia, it would be a mistake to identify the impact of the other with masculinity as such. In fact to do so would be to let the solution to the riddle escape. The extent to which femininity, and an identity which is formed by feminine means, dominates in a person's psychical life is determined by an underlying force: in part, this force consists of the hallucination that founds the initial inertia. But this force also interlocks with something else. The problem with clarifying the nature of this underlying force is that both the feminine and masculine parties depend on it for their familiar identities. They are reluctant to investigate it, because understanding it means understanding the full implications of the impact of the other. The familiar masculine and feminine identities lead to the conviction that subjects are physically self-contained, but this conviction is essential to maintaining the security of these identities as we know them. Any logic or investigation which runs counter to this conviction is liable to be censored by gaps in the material chain of reasoning.

Chapter 2

The riddle's repression

INTRODUCTION

The 'gaps in the material' Freud attributes to the 'specially inexorable repression' to which a girl's attachment to her mother is subjected have been referred to in the two major debates generated by Freud's second and better known theory of femininity. But they have not been discussed in the economic, physical terms that frame Freud's view of repression. Nor has the economic riddle of femininity. In the debates the key issues have been quite other. In the first debate, the 'great debate' on female sexuality and femininity conducted amongst psychoanalysts in the 1920s and 1930s, the central issues were: (i) the attachment to the mother as such; (ii) the priority given penis-envy and the castration complex in female sexuality; (iii) whether penis-envy was a reaction-formation to a prior attachment to the girl's father; and therefore (iv) whether there was a natural attraction to the father on the girl's part; and – closely related – (v) whether there was an early unconscious knowledge of the vagina and vaginal sensations in little girls. The last-mentioned point was counter-posed to Freud's insistence that in early childhood both sexes knew only one organ: the penis or phallic clitoris. In addition, there was the question of how far cultural considerations resulted in phenomena such as women's masochism (or inward-turned aggressiveness), and of course how far Freud's theory was distorted by an 'unduly phallocentric' view.

In the second debate on Freud's theory, conducted amongst feminists influenced by psychoanalysis and feminist psychoanalysts in the 1970s and 1980s, the issues canvassed have been remarkably similar to those of the great debate, except for three important additions. The first is more tacit than explicit: it is the problem of how identity is founded, and the relation of identity to sexuality. The second is the interplay between psychical and material reality. The third is the question of psychical reality and its relation to language. This question entails the matter of repression, even the repression of the maternal attachment, but it has been recast in Lacanian terms.

Repression is made contingent on language, whose effects bring a repressed psychical reality into being. The fact that repression features at all may seem an advance on the first debate. For while psychical reality had also featured, especially for Melanie Klein, at the tail end of the first debate, it was not tied to the question of repression. On the other hand, the second debate's stress on signification and symbolization takes us ever further away from the economic heart of the matter. The first debate is closer to it, in that Freud's quantitative physical concerns are mentioned occasionally. But in neither debate does repression, or the real riddle of femininity, receive the attention it deserves. We have seen that Freud's riddle was, in the first instance, also an economic or quantitative problem concerning the direction of psychic energy. We will see here that the neglect of Freud's real 'riddle' of femininity is consistent with the neglect of the quantitative matter of repression.

Freud is complicitous with this neglect, as is evident if we turn to the three papers Freud wrote on female sexuality when he finally focused on the topic in 1925. Their key, undiscussed internal contradiction concerns the nature of the repression involved not only in the resolution but also the constitution of the girl's Oedipus complex. These three papers (Freud 1925c, 1931b, 1933a) were written as the context for and during the first debate.

The next section (pp. 39–65) discusses them, together with the writings of those analysts with whom Freud specifically engaged.[1] One advantage in surveying Freud's three papers is that it enables us to distil further Freud's riddle of femininity; it will be clear that in addition to the economic problem of femininity, Freud had other precise questions about this psychical state. More negatively, the key internal contradiction in Freud's theory of femininity concerns the fact that women are more prone to repression, yet possess weaker superegos. This contradiction is not explicated in the three papers. What does emerge is that the defence mechanisms favoured in femininity involve the vicissitudes of the drives that Freud studies in the *Three Essays* and his Metapsychological papers; the defence mechanisms, especially projection, are also closer to those found in the psychoses. On the negative side again, it will be clear that one of the remarkable features about these three papers is their relative lack of theoretical innovation. Another is their uncharacteristic confusion; the forgetfulness evident in Freud's slow steps away from the analogy theory also characterizes the new theory. The 'gaps in the material' which marred Freud's understanding of femininity also infect the theory itself. Yet if we ask what produces forgetfulness and 'gaps in the material', we are returned to the ego and superego, and of course repression. By Freud's account it

1 I shall not be discussing the contributions to the first debate with which Freud did not engage in any detail, partly because they have been discussed elsewhere. See Mitchell (1982), Brennan (1988), Chodorow (1989).

is the (super)ego's censorship that is responsible for forgetfulness, itself a symptom of repression.

In the third section of this chapter (pp. 65–6), we turn to developments following the great debate (there were very few), then to the second debate, and to the object-relations, Kleinian and Lacanian theories that have influenced it. The repression of the riddle of femininity that begins in the first debate continues in the second (pp. 66–81). Despite the emphasis on psychical reality Lacan shares with Melanie Klein especially, we are left with the question as to why the riddle is bypassed, in fact, positively outcast, in the second debate. But the second debate's implicit concern with identity and its relation to sexuality, together with its attention to the interplay of psychical and material reality, will help reformulate the riddle of femininity. So will Freud's real 'last words' on the subject of femininity, which also return us to the ego by a different route.[2] These last words are discussed in the fourth section (pp. 81–2). In 'Analysis Terminable and Interminable' (1937) Freud remarked that femininity, unlike masculinity, was not ego-syntonic. He does not amplify this remark, but it indicates why femininity is not a healthy state; like his three papers on femininity, these last words bear on the consequences of the repression of phallic activity in the girl's case, a repression which, one can infer, has consequences for her activity in general.

FREUD'S THREE PAPERS ON FEMININITY, FEMALE SEXUALITY, AND THE 'GREAT DEBATE'

Freud's three papers on femininity and sexuality stand out in his corpus for this reason. In them, he engages more directly, and more critically, with the work of his fellow analysts than he usually does. By the time he published the first paper (1925c), four of his colleagues had already published on the topic (van Ophuijsen ([1916–17] 1924), Abraham ([1921] 1922), Horney ([1923] 1924), and Deutsch (1925). Freud mentions three of them (Abraham, Horney, and Deutsch) in concluding the 1925 paper, and subsequently refers to van Ophuijsen.

Van Ophuijsen introduced the term 'masculinity complex' ([1916–17] 1924: 39), but like his colleagues he overlooked the significance of the mother as the first love-object, even when the logic of his argument demands her recognition (for instance, ([1916–17] 1924: 42). He is however aware of the economic or quantitative dimension. His women patients frequently

  express a wish to take possession of a person, instead of devoting and

2 'Real' in that while the last time Freud addressed the topic of femininity was in Freud 1940a, this address adds nothing to the problems raised by the three papers on femininity, while something new is added in Freud 1937.

subjecting themselves to him; or they have the feeling that they wish to penetrate someone else, instead of themselves being penetrated; or they remark that a state of tension would disappear if they could but give out something instead of taking something in.

([1916–17] 1924: 42)

Abraham's article on the female's castration complex basically elaborates Freud's theory of penis-envy (for which Abraham provides many convincing clinical examples). The paper is otherwise interesting for four reasons. First, it entirely overlooks the significance of the mother as the first love-object. Second and third, it assumes that women have a capacity for sublimation, especially for sublimating hostility, and it notes that the woman is placed in a position where 'she is compelled to adopt a waiting attitude. In a great number of women we find resistance against being a woman displaced to this necessity of waiting' ([1921] 1922: 25). The fourth notable point about Abraham's article is that when his patients gave up the desire to be a man, they replaced it by the desire to be a woman who is unique, a woman like no other woman ([1921] 1922: 26). This clinical observation may be relevant to the difficulties in forging a female social bond, or 'female symbolic': an idea which emerges in the second debate on psychoanalysis and femininity.

Like van Ophuijsen, Karen Horney at least refers to the 'quantitative' factor, although it is incidental to her argument ([1923] 1924: 61). And her arguments have more subtlety than recent summaries of them indicate, although it is certainly true that one gets little sense of the power of unconscious states when reading Horney, as Mitchell suggests, and also that Horney sees penis-envy as a reaction formation to a prior state (Mitchell 1982). But what is at stake in this reaction-formation is more than an assertion of an innate heterosexual drive in women. For Horney, that assertion came later. In this early paper the state prior to penis-envy Horney has in mind is an envy of the mother's having children ([1923] 1924: 59).[3] She also agrees with Freud about the prevalence of penis-envy, and her analysis of it in her patients is informative.

More generally, two of Horney's observations are relevant to the direction of this book. She analyses her patients' penis-envy and desire to urinate like a man in terms of curiosity and scopophilia ([1923] 1924: 52). Scopophilia, the love of seeing, was connected by Freud with the sexual drive and the drive for knowledge. Horney suggests that penis-envy is due in part to the 'ready visibility' of the male organ.

The man's impulse to investigate finds satisfaction in the examination of his own body and may, or must, subsequently be directed to external objects; while the woman, on the other hand, can arrive at no clear

3 Envy of the mother's having children is also noted by Abraham ([1921] 1922), and is an idea that Melanie Klein makes central.

knowledge about her own person and therefore finds it harder to become free of herself.

([1923] 1924: 53)

Another argument to be singled out from Horney's paper prefigures the stress in recent literature on a woman's difficulties of separating from or 'disidentifying' with her mother.[4] Horney does not make a particular point about this; she says very little about an 'original identification with the mother' ([1923] 1924: 55), which she mentions in passing. But her discussion of rape phantasies featuring father-figures or actual fathers is especially illuminating. One patient 'who till late in life felt herself one with her mother, had experienced with her the father's act of complete sexual appropriation. It is noteworthy that this patient, who in other respects was perfectly clear in her mind, was at the beginning of the analysis strongly inclined to regard these phantasies of rape as actual fact' ([1923] 1924: 55). Horney explains this as an ontogenetic repetition of a phylogenetic experience. She uses Freud's (1913c) phylogenetic appeal to the memory of a primal father, an appeal he makes to explain Oedipal guilt. This primal father possessed all the women. He was murdered by his sons for these women, but the guilt over this crime lives on in race memory. (Which, incidentally, led Malinowski to wonder if there was only one primal father or several: if there was more than one, they must have been simultaneously disposed of, in 'a mass outbreak of crime' (Malinowski 1922).)[5] For Horney, this race memory will account for

> numerous unmistakable observations [where] the child constructs, on the basis of a (hostile or loving) identification with its mother, a phantasy that it has suffered full sexual appropriation by the father; and further, that in phantasy this experience presents itself as having actually taken place – as much a fact as it must have been at that distant time when all women were primarily the property of the father).
>
> ([1923] 1924: 56)

While this early Horney adheres to Freud's phylogenetic argument, her argument silently suggests an alternative explanation for the case material that led Freud to the seduction theory, and subsequently to the notion of psychical reality. It suggests it because Horney writes that the child's phantasy is constructed on the basis of an *identification* with its mother. The difficulty with her suggestion is that there is no explanation for how this 'original identification' is formed. It may be on the basis of conscious knowledge, but this seems improbable. Yet if this 'identification' is

4 Separating and 'disidentifying' are not, necessarily, the same thing, in that the latter presupposes an identification, the former a connection. The recent literature on this topic is discussed on pp. 68ff below.
5 Malinowski was engaged in a debate about whether psychoanalysis was culturally specific by Ernest Jones. See Safouan (1974).

attributed to an unconscious tie with the mother, in which the child's and mother's experience are not differentiated, the difficulty with Horney's suggestion disappears.

The most important, and the most difficult to summarize justly, of the early psychoanalytic contributions on femininity is Helene Deutsch. I shall confine myself here to a few limited comments, but will refer to her subsequent major work (1944) as well as the 1925 paper. Roazen remarks, in a fine defence of Deutsch, that her 'encyclopaedic' book established her as 'the leading proponent of the Freudian outlook on femininity' (Roazen 1985: 27; also Roazen 1992). He adds that it is easy to reduce her work to a crude reiteration of three of the characteristics that mark femininity for Freud: masochism, narcissism, and passivity, without appreciating the different nuances Deutsch gave to each term. This is right, but the nuances work in two ways. On the one hand, Deutsch finds a biological foundation for masochism in the menses, defloration, and childbirth, which takes one further away from Freud's riddle of how feminine masochism is found in men. On the other, she describes feminine passivity as 'activity turned inwards', and contrasts this with the external direction that marks masculinity. One of her main arguments, that 'the man attains his final stage of development when he discovers the vagina in the world outside himself and takes possession of it sadistically' (1925: 51), prefigures an emphasis on external direction in masculine sexuality which I shall discuss below. Deutsch does not develop this contrast between inward- and outward-turned sexuality, or explore its metapsychological implications, but, in 1944, she points to its existence through numerous case histories. She also sees feminine narcissism as a protection against the worst effects of feminine masochism, and stresses that the latter

lacks the cruelty, destructive drive, suffering, and pain by which masochism manifests itself in perversions and neuroses ... what most contributes to the overflow of feminine masochism and gives it its self-destructive character is moral masochism, that is, the sense of guilt and its effects.

(1944: 191 and 271)

We return to the theoretical implications of the 'overflow' of feminine masochism, the notion that narcissism is a protection from it, and its difference from moral masochism in chapter 5. There are two other points about Deutsch's two-volume study that need to be recorded now. She begins, oddly, not with infancy and early childhood (which she does not study in depth) but with girls of 10 and 11. The omission is the closest she comes to admitting what is often implicit in her argument: that the effects of femininity do not take hold until puberty, and that any impact they have at the time of the traditional Oedipus complex is brief and transitory. In 1925, despite the requisite references to the Oedipus complex, she effectively assigns the girl's 'hatred' of her mother not to the Oedipus complex but to 'her anger that her mother prevents her from being a grown-up' (1925: 54).[6] The girl's capitulation to the loss of initiative happens only at puberty, which represents the 'decisive last battle fought before maturity' (Deutsch 1944: 91). That 'maturity' involves accepting the loss, and seeking sublimation of the capacity to act on the world through motherhood, does not detract from Deutsch's detailed clinical analyses of the astonishing differences between pre-pubescent girls and their post-pubescent counterparts in terms of the activity, intelligence, and initiative of the former. Either the biological differences of puberty have a large part to play in the change, as Deutsch concludes. Or is there another factor that comes into play at this point, which we have yet to identify? It would be right, but premature, to identify it as social, for it is the psychical way the social force operates that has special significance. Here the other side of Deutsch's analysis is pertinent. Her notion of passivity as 'activity turned inwards' fits with what, in chapter 4, we will discuss in terms of how the 'involution of the drives' contributes to femininity. Also relevant here is her discussion of the extensive, burdensome, and completely preoccupying phantasy life and world of daydreams occupied by the adolescent girl (1944: 127ff).

Another point about Deutsch. While she leaves out a study of early childhood, she details at length the manner in which female sexuality replays the dynamics of mother and infant. The vagina takes over the oral and passive function of suckling, while coitus helps overcome the trauma of weaning. The male partner represents not only father but mother, and moreover, in a further substitution, the child in the womb represents the woman's paternal ego-ideal. The notion that the masculine partner replays a maternal role not only makes the penis a substitute for the breast, it also prepares the way for the realization that the mother was the first object for both sexes. Deutsch, in 1925, was not the only author to anticipate Freud's eventual realization in this respect, but most of the groundwork was hers.[7] To Freud's realization, and the second theory of femininity, we now turn.

6 Freud in fact mentions the impact on the girl of the real restrictions imposed by her mother.
7 By the time Freud published the 1925 paper, Starcke (1921) and Alexander ([1922] 1923) had also published articles on the castration complex, which, while more concerned with its manifestations in men, are relevant in that they argue for an oral primary castration (loss of the breast) which prepares a person for the castration complex (Alexander [1922] 1923: 22). Starcke is interesting for a number of additional reasons. While adhering loyally to Freud's distinction between 'ego-impulses' and object libido, he writes that both 'during sucking are active and are gratified in one and the same act' (1921: 189). He introduces and stresses the importance of the infant's 'little hands' in its finding its place in the world through the sense of touch (1921: 198). Moreover he anticipates two Kleinian ideas. Both bear on the confusion on the infant's part between what belongs to itself and what belongs to its mother and the distinction between the internal and external world. Starcke believes that the infant thinks the nipple belongs to it (1921: 200) and also suggests that the infant first locates the experience of pain in the external world; that is to say, that pain's origin

'Some Psychical Consequences of the Anatomical Distinction between the Sexes'

When for the first time Freud announces that the girl's first attachment is to her mother he does so without fuss, almost in passing, as though there is nothing novel in the statement. In one respect he is right to do so: the notion that the mother's breast is the first sexual object has been there in the background since 1905, together with many other elements in his revised theory of femininity.

In the earliest of his three papers on femininity and female sexuality, Freud simply says that the mother is the first object for boys and girls. The girl's choice of her mother as her first object is not considered in any detail until the next paper of the three, 'Female Sexuality'. In the first paper outlining the second theory of femininity, Freud asks only how the little girl comes to change objects, from mother to father. As discussed, penis-envy (*Penisneid*) is Freud's answer to this question; an answer that was set long before the question was posed.[8] Freud, like Horney, writes that the envy results from a visual, quantitative comparison with the boy's penis. In asserting this, Freud is relying on his theory of the drives. For both sexes, genital masturbation was originally without any psychical content. But while the boy ties phallic masturbation to the object-cathexes of the Oedipus complex, the girl does not. The 'first step' in her Oedipus complex is penis-envy. In other words, here Freud believes that the girl's clitoridal excitation is not tied to her attachment to her mother: the tie to her mother is not a phallic one. Such a tie is pre-empted by the advent of penis-envy (cf. 1925c, *GW*: 23, *SE*: 252). Subsequently, Freud revised his belief that the girl is not phallically attached to her mother, arguing that the mother is the object of the girl's phallic libido. Here again, the full implications that the mother is the girl's first sexual object were accepted slowly and piecemeal.[9]

---

is felt as external rather than internal (1921: 201, n. 1). The mother figures throughout Starcke's paper. While he does not say explicitly that she is the first love-object, he adds considerably to the clinical evidence that leads to this conclusion through concentrating on how weaning and the loss of the mother's nipple might be considered the prototype of castration (1921: 182 and 189).

8 Freud introduced the concept in 1908c, *GW*: 180, *SE*: 218.

9 Retrospectively, this reluctance to make the girl's maternal tie phallic and sexual is suggestive. It may account for why Freud did not dwell on a possible explanation for penis-envy that caught the eye of one psychoanalytic feminist: Gayle Rubin argued that the girl envies the boy his penis because it makes him hypothetically better equipped to satisfy her mother than she is. Cf. Rubin (1975). This suggestion is echoed by various contemporary writers on Freud's theory of femininity; it is repeated at several points in the collection edited by Chasseguet-Smirgel ([1964] 1981). This is not to say that the physical limitation on the girl's phallic drive where her mother is concerned is a sufficient explanation for penis-envy, but that it is undoubtedly a factor is borne out by Freud's adoption of Ferenczi's (1926) suggestion that 'the high degree of narcissistic value which the penis possesses can appeal to the fact that that organ is a guarantee to its owner that he can be once more united to his mother – i.e. to a substitute for her – in the act of copulation.

Freud lists six consequences of penis-envy. Two are broad consequences, four are more specific. Broadly, penis-envy can result in a masculinity complex,[10] in which the girl may go so far as to disavow the fact that she does not possess a penis.[11] Subsequently, she may be 'compelled to behave as if she were a man' (1925c, GW: 24, SE: 253). The other, more specific consequences of penis-envy are, first, a sense of inferiority. This results from a narcissistic wound brought about by the unflattering comparison with the boy's organ. The girl will come to extend this inferiority from herself to all women.

> When she has passed beyond her first attempt at explaining her lack of a penis as being a punishment personal to herself and has realized that that sexual character is a universal one, she begins to share the contempt felt by men for a sex which is the lesser in so important a respect, and, at least in holding that opinion, insists on being like a man.
>
> (1925c, GW: 24, SE: 253)

The second specific consequence of penis-envy is the character trait of jealousy, which Freud thinks plays a more active part in the mental life of women than of men. The third consequence is a 'loosening of the girl's relation with her mother as a love-object', in that the girl usually blames her mother for her lack of a penis (1925c, GW: 26, SE: 254). A fourth result, 'undoubtedly the most important of all [is] an intense current of feeling against masturbation' (1925c, GW: 24, SE: 255). It is undoubtedly important because of its quantitative effects; there is no place for phallic activity to go. Freud thinks this current of anti-masturbatory feeling can only be explained by penis-envy, and a turning-away from clitoridal satisfaction. In detailing its appearance, he is relying on clinical material in which there was a conflict between the wish to masturbate and the wish to stop. In this last consequence of penis-envy, as with the first, narcissism is an underpinning factor. In that masturbation reminds the girl of an unflattering comparison between penis and clitoris, she stops.

These narcissistically inflected responses are critical in preparing the girl for her feminine reproductive role. They turn her away from masculinity, and constitute 'a necessary precondition for the development of femininity' (1925c, GW: 27, SE: 255–6). They usher in the castration complex which, as discussed in the Introduction, leads to the wish for a child replacing

---

Being deprived of it amounts to a renewed separation from her, and this in its turn means being helplessly exposed to an unpleasurable tension due to instinctual need, as was the case at birth' (Freud 1926a, GW: 169, SE: 139).

10 This term has echoes of Adler's concept, masculine protest. Freud himself notes the woman's masculinity complex as the core of truth in Adler's theory (1914b, GW: 98–9, SE: 54–5).

11 Freud thinks that 'disavowal' is common in children, but that in an adult it would mean the onset of psychosis (1925c, GW: 24, SE: 253). Boys also disavow the fact that women lack a penis (Freud 1923d, GW: 295–6, SE: 143–4).

that for a penis, and the consequent substitution of father for mother as love-object. Thus from the fact that boys possess a penis, and girls do not, Freud argues that the different forms of the castration complex in boys and girls are an intelligible psychical consequence of the anatomical distinction between the sexes.[12] He goes on to discuss the consequences of the castration complex founding, rather than terminating, the girl's Oedipus complex. Given that the motive for demolishing the Oedipus complex and establishing a superego is lacking,

> the Oedipus complex escapes the fate which it meets with in boys: it may be slowly abandoned or dealt with by repression, or its effects may persist far into women's normal mental life. I cannot evade the notion (though I hesitate to give it expression) that for women the level of what is ethically normal is different from what it is in men. Their superego is never so inexorable, so impersonal, so independent of its emotional origins as we require it to be in men. Character-traits which critics of every epoch have brought up against women – that they show less sense of justice than men, that they are less ready to submit to the great exigencies of life, that they are more often influenced in their judgements by feelings of affection and hostility – all these would be amply accounted for by the modification in the formation of their superego.
>
> (1925c, *GW*: 29–30, *SE*: 257–8)

Aside from reiterating that the majority of men are far behind the 'masculine ideal' and that 'all human individuals, as a result of their bisexual disposition and of cross-inheritance, combine in themselves both masculine and feminine characteristics, so that pure masculinity and femininity remain theoretical constructions of uncertain content' (1925c, *GW*: 30, *SE*: 257–8), in this paper Freud says little more. But the paper generated several responses.

It was Ernest Jones who wrote, 'There is a healthy suspicion growing that men analysts have been led to adopt an unduly phallo-centric view of the problems in question, the importance of the female organs being correspondingly underestimated' (Jones 1927: 32). Aside from Jones, the other main contributors to the first psychoanalytic debate on female sexuality were Karl Abraham, Karen Horney, Marie Bonaparte, Marjorie Brier-

---

12 Given the assumption that only the male genital is known, and its importance to the entire theoretical edifice that follows, it is understandable that so many of Freud's psychoanalytic critics have defended women on the grounds that vaginal sensations are present, and the vagina known in early childhood. None of these contributions (which are discussed below) allows that Freud ever admitted any vaginal sensations in childhood, apparently overlooking an admittedly scanty finding. 'If I am to credit a single analytic instance, this new situation [where the girl has taken her father as her love-object] can give rise to physical sensations which would have to be regarded as a premature awakening of the female genital apparatus' (1925c, *GW*: 28, *SE*: 256).

ley, Helene Deutsch, Otto Fenichel, Sandor Ferenczi, Melanie Klein, Jeanne Lampl-de Groot, Josine Muller, and Ruth Mack Brunswick. Freud's most significant opponents were Jones, Horney, and Klein. Horney is the most committed of the culturalists. All Freud's opponents argued, as did Muller subsequently, that the vagina is known in infancy or early childhood and constitutes an alternative source of female sexuality to that stemming from the clitoris. Freud's most significant supporters were Abraham, Deutsch, and Lampl-de Groot, who, like Deutsch, anticipated some of Freud's formulations. If there is common ground between opponents and supporters, it lies especially in an emphasis on orality and its derivatives in female sexuality and a general recognition of penis-envy. The disagreement over penis-envy concerns its genesis.

'Female Sexuality'

Freud is evidently responding to some of his critics in 'Female Sexuality', the second paper of the three on femininity. Yet despite Freud's evident discontent with his own findings on female sexuality, and despite the requisite compliments to his psychoanalytic colleagues, he does not appear to think that any of them have done any better on the subject of femininity. At the end of 'Female Sexuality' he reviews their writing on the topic, which partly consists of responses made to his first (1925) paper on femininity.[13] He is in qualified agreement with some and disagrees with others, but he seems to gain nothing from them. Freud adds that he specifically excludes some of the papers published on femininity by his colleagues (because they obscure his finer points): namely, the 'problems of the superego and the sense of guilt' (1931b, *GW*: 534, *SE*: 241).[14]

In the literature Freud reviews, the lines in the psychoanalytic debate on femininity and female sexuality have already been laid down and are beginning to harden. Both Horney and Jones believe that the phallic phase in girls is secondary; it is a reaction generated by an original threat to a primary feminine attitude towards the father.[15] As I have already indicated,

13 Freud reviews papers by Karl Abraham ([1921] 1922), Jeanne Lampl-de Groot ([1927] 1928), Helene Deutsch (1930), Otto Fenichel ([1930] 1931a), Melanie Klein (1928), Karen Horney (1926), and Ernest Jones (1927).
14 The papers Freud has in mind here have to be Jones (1926) and Sachs (1929). His review of the literature is not comprehensive, however. He excludes a paper by Mary Chadwick (1925), who argues, as did Klein (1926 and 1928) that the man's 'narcissistic' over-estimation of the penis and intellectual rivalry with women are a displacement of his frustrated wish for a child (Klein 1928: 191).
15 There is a similar argument in Müller-Braunschweig (1926), who makes the primary feminine attitude completely biological (p. 361). Where this paper is interesting is in its stress on the differences between the relation between ego and id where the sexes are concerned: 'the ego, in its concern for activity, can find in a masculine sexual striving which has as an active purpose a support, a trend in the direction of its own aims; while in the feminine trend which is directed toward a passive aim it must see an opposing force, a danger, and not a support ... a girl, by establishing the reaction-formation of

Horney's position is more complicated. She believes in a primary penis-envy, followed by a feminine heterosexual attachment to the father, which is in turn followed by a secondary penis-envy. For Horney, it is far more forceful than the primary penis-envy she discussed in her 1923 paper. Secondary penis-envy is related to a dread of injury due to 'the disproportion in size between father and child'. In other words, the vaginal sensations that she (like Klein and Jones) believes are present in early childhood 'are related to Oedipus phantasies and . . . the logically ensuing dread of an internal, i.e. vaginal injury' (1926: 334).[16] It is secondary penis-envy that Horney will later interpret in cultural terms, arguing that it represents a realistic response to the denial of cultural and creative opportunities to women. In her cultural period, Horney will also elaborate on men's envy of women, a theory whose germ lies in her 1923 observations concerning the ability of the woman to have children.[17]

Lampl-de Groot insists on the girl's active phallic phase in relation to the mother. As I noted, her paper in many respects is an anticipation of, and runs parallel with, Freud's findings in 'Female Sexuality'. By 1930 Deutsch also lays stress on the girl's phallic activity in relation to her mother, and Freud commends her for interpreting it as more than 'an identification with her father', as she had done in 1925. But I suspect that, with the possible exception of Lampl-de Groot,[18] Freud's principal if hidden interlocuters in 'Female Sexuality' are Fenichel and, to a far greater extent, Melanie Klein. Both are concerned with the pre-Oedipal phase. More accurately, Klein's theory does not elaborate on a 'pre-Oedipus' period but rather shifts the Oedipus complex back in time, locating its origin in the first year. Fenichel opposes Klein's relocation of the Oedipus complex on the grounds that it is difficult to distinguish between the original content of the pre-Oedipal phase, and its distortion through regression. The main difficulty Klein poses for Freud is that her argument for an earlier dating of the Oedipus complex is based on extensive analyses of very young children. He attempts to explain her findings in terms of accidental factors (for instance, seduction) and, aside from that, notes only

the superego, finds protection against the incestuous trend that also appears as a danger to her ego because it involves her being overpowered' (1926: 360). This argument, while it is not developed, anticipates Freud's argument that femininity is not 'ego-syntonic'.

16 Horney's argument here is founded on the 'plastic concrete thinking of childhood' (1926: 334), and loses the emphasis on unconscious phantasy and the identification with the mother in Horney (1923).

17 Especially Horney (1932), (1933), and (1967). The male envy of motherhood is also discussed in her 1926 paper (p. 328).

18 It seems to be Lampl-de Groot who says that the girl's negative Oedipus complex (that is to say, her attachment to her mother) ushers in her castration complex ([1927] 1928). Here she distinguishes herself from Freud, yet this notion is critical in Freud's 1931 paper. Lampl-de Groot also mentions the relation between beating phantasies and masochistic daydreams ([1927] 1928: 343), as does Anna Freud (1923), a theme to which we return in chapter 5.

that her findings do not agree with his on the long duration of the pre-Oedipal phase in girls. What he omits is any mention of Klein's theory of the femininity phase. This is found in boys and girls at an early age: 'it consists of a very early identification with the mother' (1928: 189), where the boy relates passively to the father or phallic mother. This femininity phase in boys precedes the boy's active sexual drive towards his mother, and his reaction against it exacerbates his subsequent fear of castration. The 'femininity complex' in boys also involves a desire for a child, which comes to be amalgamated with the 'epistemophilic impulse' (1928: 190–1). Both the desire and the impulse are present in the wish to rob the mother's body of its contents, to get inside it, cut it up, devour and dismember it. In turn, these sadistic, epistemophilic drives lead to guilt and a fear of retaliation.

In fact, one of Klein's main arguments for the early dating of the Oedipus complex is that guilt is present in very young children and guilt is associated with the formation of the superego. In the different identifications out of which the superego is composed 'excessive goodness and excessive severity [exist] side by side' (1928: 187). Klein argues that

> in a child of about *one year* old, the anxiety caused by the beginning of the Oedipus conflict takes the form of a dread of being devoured and destroyed. The child himself desires the libidinal object by biting, devouring and cutting it, which leads to anxiety, since awakening of the Oedipus tendencies is followed by introjection of the object, which then becomes one from which punishment is to be expected. The child then dreads a punishment corresponding to the offence: the super-ego becomes something which bites, devours and cuts.
>
> (1928: 187)

Later, Klein will stress the significance of phantasy and projection in early psychical life, and argue that the pressure of the death drive operating within leads to anxiety, and that this anxiety leads an infant or a very young child to project its destructive, death-driven urge on to the other. It accomplishes this through the defence mechanism of *splitting*. It splits a 'good breast' from a 'bad breast' and the introjection of both these phantasmatic objects constitutes the core of its superego. Klein also later detaches the formation of the superego from the Oedipus complex, claiming (although she never argues why) that the Oedipus complex is predated by the superego. Had she dissociated Oedipus complex and super-ego sooner, Freud's disagreement with her about the long duration of the pre-Oedipal phase in girls might have had a more productive outcome.[19]

But it is to the duration of the girl's pre-Oedipal attachment to the mother that we now turn. A discussion of this, and a consideration of the

19 Also discussed in chapter 5, below, pp. 190–2.

phallic phase in girls, are the main ways in which 'Female Sexuality' adds to Freud's first paper on femininity. By discussing the attachment to the mother, 'Female Sexuality' thus adds to the attempt at understanding what Freud now numbers as the girl's two sexual tasks: changing her leading genital zone, from clitoris to vagina, and changing her love-object, from mother to father. Both are necessary if she is to make the 'transition' to femininity.

For Freud, the girl's attachment to the mother now extends from the foundations of object choice to the fourth year. This extension has many ramifications. One has the impression, from Freud's account, that the girl's subsequent attachment to her father is nothing more than an overlay, a kind of cover-up. The psychical dynamics established in childhood are revealed by the patterns and course of a woman's relation to men, but they were actually first established in relation to her mother. There are two related arguments to this effect. One is that a woman will often repeat, in bad, or at any rate conflictual, relations to her husband, the patterns established in relation to her mother.[20] The other is that the period of the girl's attachment to her mother becomes the period when the various neuroses are established. That is to say, given that the attachment to the mother often lasts well into the fourth year, Freud suggests that this period is sufficient 'for all the fixations and repressions [alle Fixierungen und Verdrängungen]' (1931b, GW: 518, SE: 226) out of which the neuroses are born. Accordingly,

> it would seem as though we must retract the universality of the thesis that the Oedipus complex is the nucleus of the neuroses. But if anyone feels reluctant about making this correction, there is no need for him to do so. On the one hand, we can extend the content of the Oedipus complex to include all the child's relations to both parents; or on the other, we can take due account of our new findings by saying that the female only reaches the normal positive Oedipus complex after she has surmounted a period before it that was governed by the negative complex.
>
> (1931b, GW: 518, SE: 226)

Subsequently in this paper, only four pages further on, Freud seems to forget this caveat. In all simplicity, he says 'the phase of exclusive attachment to the mother may be called the pre-Oedipus phase' (1931b, GW: 523, SE: 230). If he is to be consistent, the period for the girl's fixations and repressions thus encompasses the pre-Oedipus phase. Yet a few pages before, Freud felt strongly enough about keeping the Oedipus complex

---

20 There is an earlier argument to this effect in Freud (1918b). In this paper he explains a wife's hostility to her first husband by his deflowering her. Any connection between this explanation for the woman's hostility, and that based on the woman's repeating her relation to her mother in her relation to her husband, is not addressed.

the core of the neuroses to more or less abolish the specificity of the pre-Oedipus phase in girls. He is, as it were, having it both ways. The Oedipus complex remains the locus of repressions and fixations in girls, but Freud continues to speak of their pre-Oedipus period, also characterized by these fixations and repressions. Why is this? Some of the significance of the inconsistency emerges when one considers why the Oedipus complex is tied to the neuroses.

First, the Oedipus complex is tied to the neuroses *as distinct from the psychoses*. The diagnostic distinction between these two main bodies of mental disorders is generally accepted within mainstream contemporary psychiatry. It did not originate with Freud, but his use of it is consistent with the mainstream: the same nosologies are found in psychoanalysis and psychiatry.[21] When it comes to the descriptive diagnoses of disorders, there is general agreement that schizophrenia, paranoia, manic-depression (or melancholia) all constitute psychoses, while hysteria, obsessional neuroses, phobias, and a variety of anxiety states constitute neuroses.[22] Where Freud was original, and it has been argued that this is his most enduring contribution to psychiatry, was in proffering a dynamic explanation of why the disorders constitute exclusive, opposed categories. On the basis of the metapsychology of *The Ego and the Id*, he argued that

> *neurosis is the result of a conflict between the ego and its id, whereas psychosis is the analogous outcome of a similar disturbance between the ego and the external world.*
>
> (1924a, *GW*: 387, *SE*: 149)

Briefly put, in neuroses the ego represses a demand from the id for the satisfaction of a drive (say, a drive with a perverse aim) without providing

21 Freud is using the distinction between neuroses and psychoses by January 1894 (draft H to Fliess), and in a paper on the 'Neuro-Psychoses of Defence' written the same year (1894, *GW*: 72–4, *SE*: 58–61). By the end of the nineteenth century, both terms had wide currency. Hunter and Macalpine believe the term 'psychosis' was introduced by Feuchtersleben in *Lehrbuch der ärztlichen Seelenkunde* who distinguished it from neurosis in 1845. According to Feuchtersleben, psychosis means mental illness [*Seelenkrankheit*] (Hunter and Macalpine 1955: 16); neurosis [*Neurose*] means of, or affecting, the nervous system. Traces of the more somatic connotations of the term are to be found in Freud's division of neuroses into two types: actual neuroses (neuroses with a constitutional origin) and psychoneuroses (with a psychical origin, as the term implies) (1898a, *GW*: 509, *SE*: 279).

22 Which is not to say there is uniformity. For instance, paranoia is a distinct clinical entity in France. In Britain paranoia is recognized only in a type of schizophrenia: paranoid schizophrenia. Of more note perhaps is the manner in which taxonomies of neuroses have proliferated since Freud; in particular, there is a stress on narcissism as a factor in neuroses (notably in H. Kohut (1978)). J. Chasseguet-Smirgel claims that according to most analysts, narcissistic disorders have taken over from sexually based ones (Chasseguet-Smirgel 1984). This poses an interesting problem. While Freud used the term 'psychoses' for most of his working life, at one point he attempted to modify it, introducing the term 'narcissistic neuroses' to replace 'psychoses' (1914c). Subsequently, he used the term only for melancholia (manic-depression) (1924a, *GW*: 390, *SE*: 149–52). These diagnostic shifts all implicate the superego and, it is argued here, femininity.

another 'motor outlet'. The ego does this because the demand is unaccept-able to its reality sense. It is subject to social prohibition. But as a consequence of this repression, the id fights back; the damming-up of libido produces a symptom instead of satisfaction.[23]

> In undertaking the repression, the ego is at bottom following the com-mands of its super-ego, commands which, in their turn, originate from influences in the external world that have found representation in the super-ego.
>
> (1924a [1923], *GW*: 388, *SE*: 150)

In a psychosis, by contrast, the ego refuses the limitations of reality. In the extreme case, it refuses new perceptions – perception is the ego's normal channel of commerce with reality – and sides with the id to constitute a more acceptable reality by means of hallucinations. Instead of joining forces with reality against the id, in a psychosis, the ego joins the id and opposes reality.

There are several weak points in this account, some of which Freud remarked on. One would expect that if the psychotic is re-creating a new world because the real one is unbearable, then the new hallucinatory world would be a pleasant place to inhabit. This is manifestly not the case. Freud attributes the 'unpleasant' aspect of the psychotic's world to the idea that the new world is not created without a struggle with the reality-oriented ego. But aside from this, the nature of the struggle is unspecified. In addition, some psychoses implicate the relation between the superego and ego, rather than, or as well as, the ego and reality. This is the case with paranoia and melancholia. In melancholia, it is the superego that hammers at the ego. In paranoia, it is the superego that is projected outwards, and is thereby returned to the external world from which it was originally internalized. It returns as a persecutor but its persecutions are meant to be the transformed reproaches of conscience.

Other weak points in Freud's account of psychoses and neuroses are pertinent to the Oedipus complex and femininity. The superego evidently has a critical role in dividing neurosis from psychosis. It is cast on the side of reality and the ego, and one can infer that its influence is significant in deciding whether repression or psychosis is the outcome. This is not to say that the superego's strength is the immediate issue in repression. Putting the issue at its most exact, the strongman in the act appears to be the ego. The superego is a force to the extent that the ego listens to it. However, one can surmise that the issue of the superego's strength re-enters in a different guise, to the extent that the stronger it is, the better able it is to get the ego's ear. Yet if this is so, in view of Freud's belief

---

23 This is why, incidentally, Freud insisted on perversion as the opposite of neurosis. If a perverse aim is realized, there is no symptom-inducing repression. See the discussion in chapter 4, and p. 198.

that the superego in girls is not as strong, one could conclude that women are more prone to psychosis than repression.[24] But according to Freud, women are also more prone to repression.

Let us tie this discussion back to 'Female Sexuality'. At one point in that paper Freud, in effect, gives two instances of 'fixations' formed in the phase of attachment to the mother. He says the phase is 'especially intimately related to the aetiology of hysteria' and that the 'germ of paranoia' also lies in this early relation to the mother (1931b, *GW*: 519, *SE*: 227). Paranoia is classified among the psychoses, hysteria among the neuroses or psychoneuroses. The psychoses and femininity were the two areas which Freud thought he knew least about. And he assigns the psychoses, like femininity, to the pre-Oedipal period. With this in mind, the collapse of the barrier between the pre-Oedipal period and the Oedipus complex poses a problem, which returns us to the question of repression. The 'germ of paranoia' is associated with

> the fear of being killed (? devoured) by the mother. [And] It is plausible to assume that this fear corresponds to a hostility which develops in the child towards her mother in consequence of the manifold restrictions imposed by the latter in the course of training and bodily care and that the mechanism of projection is favoured by the early age of the child's psychical organisation.
>
> (1931b, *GW*: 520, *SE*: 227)

This is Freud's only reference to projection in this paper. Later he will add that the girl's aggressive wishes to her mother 'often only come to light after being changed into anxiety ideas' (1933a, *GW*: 128, *SE*: 120). This changeover also implicates the defence mechanism of projection, rather than repression.

As his metapsychology changed, Freud confined the usage of repression [*Verdrängung*] to a specific mode of defence [*Abwehr*] on the ego's part.[25] As we noted in the Introduction, repression was uncovered in the study of hysteria. For Freud, it remained the defence characteristic of hysteria, the typically feminine neurosis. Further, in the Metapsychological paper devoted to repression, Freud distinguished between 'primal repression' [*Urverdrängung*] and 'repression proper'. Primal repression is introduced as a concept in Freud's case study of Senatspräsident Schreber's memoirs (1911b), where Freud referred to three phases of repression when attempting

24 This has been a major issue in the second debate on psychoanalysis and femininity. See the discussion in Brennan (1988).

25 Strachey (Freud 1915d: 144, edit. n.) believes Freud used *Abwehr* and *Verdrängung* interchangeably until 1926, when he restricted the use of the latter to a specific mode of defence (1926a). Other commentators argue that Freud was using repression in a specific sense from early on, even though the distinction was not elaborated (Laplanche and Pontalis 1983: 391–2). Freud elaborated the distinction in his 1926a and 1937.

to define the nature of defence in psychosis (1911c).[26] In the same paper, he discusses projection as a particular form of defence. Yet throughout the papers on femininity, there is no indication that Freud had primal repression in mind. Despite his distinction between primal repression and repression proper, he uses the term *Verdrängung* without qualification, and given that the Oedipus complex is the focus of discussion, it seems reasonable to assume *Verdrängung* refers to repression proper. He does not indicate that the girl's use of projection is tied to primal repression, or discuss projection as a pre-Oedipal mechanism.

Elsewhere (1926a, 1937) Freud mentions the relation between the various defence mechanisms and different phases of psychical development, a reference developed by Anna Freud and Melanie Klein in very different ways.[27] Klein developed Freud's hints that other defence mechanisms preceded repression, especially the defence mechanism of projection. Freud had indicated that the fixation points for the psychoses were established before those for the neuroses. He also, at some points, argued that projection was a primitive defence mechanism, and consistently argued that it was favoured in paranoia (1911b). For that matter, he connected projection to judgement, a faculty he assumed was initially 'oral': judgement was derived from the desire to keep something in, or spit something out (1925b). And while Freud did not make much of this, it is precisely judgement (and hence projection in some way) that is disordered in psychoses: whether or not a perception is real or imagined cannot be judged correctly.

Klein, in developing Freud's views on primitive defence mechanisms, especially projection, argued that the neuroses, and neurotic defence mechanisms, especially repression, bound psychotic anxieties and separated psychotic defence mechanisms from subsequent neurotic ones. As Freud also

26 See especially 1911b, *GW*: 303–5, *SE*: 67–8. Freud refers to his earlier opinion (expressed in 1905b) that 'each stage in the development of psychosexuality affords a possibility of "fixation" and thus of a dispositional point' (1911b, *GW*: 298, *SE*: 61–2). If the sublimation of the homosexuality Freud ties to narcissism breaks down, it no longer contributes to social feelings, and may lead to paranoia. 'This result may be produced by anything that causes the libido to flow backwards' (1911b, *GW*: 298, *SE*: 62). Freud's general presupposition throughout the discussion of Schreber is that in paranoia the homosexual sentiment 'I love him' is transformed into 'I hate him' and thence into 'He hates me'. In turn, this transformation can lead to 'I love no one, I love only myself'. In Schreber's case, Freud implies that this stage of loving only oneself fits with one of Schreber's delusions, in which the world had been destroyed, and he alone was living. It is a delusion which corresponds with the megalomania that so often accompanies paranoia, where the libido completely returns to the self, to infantile narcissism, and thus megalomania results. However, as Freud has to observe, in the Schreber case, the stage in which there was no one else in the world (a variant of infantile narcissism) preceded the stage in which he believed he was being persecuted. And this Freud cannot really explain, falling back on the idea of a partial detachment of the libido (1911b, *GW*: 310, *SE*: 73). I will return to this difficulty in the next chapter.

27 Anna Freud (1937) lists ten mechanisms of defence, viz. repression, regression, reaction-formation, isolation, undoing, projection, introjection, turning against the self, reversal into the opposite, and sublimation.

indicated, 'repression proper' is the defence mechanism associated with the Oedipus complex itself, and, as noted above, Freud thought this defence mechanism generally presupposed the superego established by that complex. While he thought that the ego was the agency of repression, it none the less acted as a rule at the behest of the superego.

So here is the problem. Once the Oedipus complex is either extended back in time or ceases to be the nucleus of the neuroses, what is there in the girl child's development that explains the transition from one set of defence mechanisms exemplified by projection, to another set founded on repression? If it is remembered that the alternative to extending the Oedipus complex back in time was that it ceased to be the 'nucleus of the neuroses', then the problem takes a slightly different but related form. What is it that makes the fixation point for the psychoses (and psychotic defence mechanisms) any different from that for the neuroses (and neurotic defence mechanisms)?

In one respect Freud signals that the boundary lines are thoroughly blurred here by his use of the term 'repression' in relation to the girl's attachment to her mother. In addition to speaking of 'fixations and repressions' in this 'pre-Oedipal phase', it is here he says his impression is that the first attachment to the mother succumbs 'to an especially inexorable repression [*Verdrängung*]' (1931b, *GW*: 519, *SE*: 226). At this point the question becomes, Why is the girl repressing? For that matter, how exactly is she repressing? When Freud allowed that the ego can do the repressing of the Oedipus complex 'although normally we speak of repression in connection with the superego, which is only just being formed', he none the less tied the advent of repression to the period of the dissolution of the complex. But these references to repression in girls carry no such temporal qualification, which means that in her case, there is no evident tie between the dissolution and the defence mechanism. In other words, repression has lost its specific locus. This is not a problem if one makes repression operative throughout psychical life, before the Oedipus complex, but what grounds, if any, does Freud give for doing so? And in fact this solution would only make the problem more acute. How or why does the ego repress alone, without the social sanctions of the superego?

Yet in one way, Freud's observations about the girl's Oedipus complex are consistent with his remarks on repression. Repression is a response to social sanctions embodied in the superego. The girl relinquishes her Oedipus complex because of social forces, more than anything else. For her, breaking off the Oedipus complex and setting up a superego are 'far more than in the boy . . . the result of upbringing and intimidation from outside which threatens her with a loss of love' (1924c, *GW*: 401, *SE*: 178). This stress on the 'outside' might also be a means for handling Freud's view that women are more repressed than men. That is to say, his view here is contradictory to the extent that repression is contingent on the superego and the Oedipus complex, but consistent to the extent that repression is a socially based phenomenon. We shall return to this.

Leaving aside repression, in other respects 'Female Sexuality' is more definite about the course and outcome of the girl's Oedipus complex. In this paper Freud outlines three paths out of her castration complex. The first leads to a complete turning against sexuality. After comparing clitoris and penis, the girl gives up not only her phallic activity but all sexual activity 'as well as a good part of her masculinity in other fields' (1931b, GW: 522, SE: 229). The second response is the masculinity complex.

> Only if her development follows the third, very circuitous, path does she reach the normal female attitude, in which she takes her father as her object and so finds her way to the feminine form of the Oedipus complex.
>
> (1931b, GW: 522, SE: 230)

There is no doubt that Freud thought the twofold transitional task difficult.[28] Nor did the difficulties of the twofold task end with its accomplishment. Freud reiterates that because the girl was left in an Oedipus complex without a good reason for leaving it, 'it escapes the strongly hostile influences [den starken feindlichen Einflüssen] which, in the male, have a destructive effect on it' (1931b, GW: 522, SE: 230) and as indicated this, for Freud, has consequences for the girl's social being and ethical life.

If the girl has little reason, other than prolonged disappointment, for giving up her attachment to her father, her reasons for giving up her maternal attachment are also less than forceful. In 'Female Sexuality' Freud returns to the cessation of this first attachment. Some of the factors he adduces to explain that cessation are, as he points out, also true for boys. Significant among these is the hostility generated by jealousy of rivals, and by the insatiability of the love itself. Lacking a precise aim, it can know no satisfaction. But the girl has an additional, by now familiar complaint to direct against her mother: she blames her for sending her into the world without a penis: 'insufficiently equipped'. She may also

28 When pre-feminist psychoanalysis turned to the implications of the 'changeover', of the fact that the woman goes from mother to father, it made this into a difficulty not for the woman, but for the man. Thus Greenson (1968), of the Stoller school, has argued that the boy's uninterrupted choice of the mother makes it difficult for him to 'disidentify' from her, meaning to establish an 'appropriate gender identity'; i.e. to identify, sexually speaking, with the father. Now Greenson notes that when the boy does cease identifying with his mother, and identifies with his father, this interruption also helps him establish a psychically separate sense of self. He concludes his article with the remark that the girl does not confront the same difficulty in 'disidentification': being of the same sex as the mother, she is identifying with the gender-appropriate parent from the outset. Blithely, Greenson overlooks the implications of this 'advantageous' continuity for the girl's separate sense of self, even though by his argument there is no occasion for her to establish it, as there is no occasion for her to 'disidentify'.

blame her mother for not giving her enough milk. Freud thinks this might have some truth, but not enough to warrant the frequency with which it is heard in analysis. He is inclined to attribute this complaint, too, to insatiability. Finally, the girl may rebel against her mother when the latter attempts to impose a prohibition against masturbation, the most significant of a series of prohibitions that child-rearing makes inevitable – each one an occasion for rebellion, resentment, hostility.

The preceding paragraph sums up Freud's candidate explanations for why the girl turns from her mother. When Freud recapitulates his own account (1931b, *GW*: 527–8, *SE*: 234) he leaves one of these candidates aside; he fails to include insatiability in the summary. He then states that all the motives adduced to explain the girl's hostile turning from her mother, *including the mother's failure to provide her with a penis*, seem insufficient to account for the hostility involved (1931b, *GW*: 527, *SE*: 234). He persists, seeking a more satisfactory explanation. In seeking it, he refers to the unavoidable disappointments of intense love. This is very similar to the thing Freud failed to mention in recapitulating: namely, insatiable love, which can never be satisfied both because it wants everything, and because it does not know what it wants.[29]

Once more in 'Female Sexuality' we see Freud forgetting what he had said within the space of a few pages, and this time, repeating it as if it were new. Not that Freud is unaware that this text is riddled with contradictions. He writes as much when he concludes it. But he ascribes the contradictions to the contradictions inherent in the dynamics of femininity. However in the example just given, what we meet with is not a contradiction in the dynamics, but forgetfulness and confused repetition in the exposition. Together with his forgetfulness in other instances, this suggests that something is going wrong, as if the whole question of femininity were a stumbling block for the reasoning process.

Nor is Freud happy with this 'new' explanation for why the girl turns from her mother. He bolsters the effects of doomed insatiable love by referring to the ambivalence that can characterize strong love. It is ambivalent in that it is accompanied by a hatred that may be as strong. Ambivalence is an archaic feature of mental life; normally it is superseded by the ability to love one's lover and hate one's enemy without apparent equivocation. Almost *faute de mieux*, Freud suggests that it is the ambivalence in the girl's primary attachment that forces her away from it. And when he asks himself why the same should not be true of boys, as there is nothing in this ambivalence that could make it specific to the girl, he answers that 'boys are able to deal with their ambivalent feelings towards their mother by directing all their hostility on to their father' (1931b, *GW*:

29 That Freud himself saw these explanations as very similar is borne out in 'Femininity' (1933a), when he refers to an inevitably unsatisfied insatiable love as the best explanation for the girl's 'turning away'.

528–9, SE: 235).[30] This points to an interesting contrast. The boy transfers his hate from mother to father, while the girl, as Freud writes elsewhere in the same paper, transfers her love from mother to father (1931b, GW: 523, SE: 231). In other words, there is a difference between the origin of the boy's and girl's love for the parent of the opposite sex, and hostility to their parent of the same sex: the girl's love for her father originates in the Oedipus complex, the boy's love for his mother in the pre-Oedipus phase. The girl's hostility towards her mother originates in the pre-Oedipus phase, the boy's for his father in the Oedipus complex (1931b, GW: 524, SE: 231). But keeping to the main thread: one wonders here, if the girl's hostility was not strong enough to smash her Oedipus complex, how was it sufficient to turn her against her mother? The query sharpens when one also notes that Freud believes that the girl's Oedipus complex 'escapes the strongly hostile influences which in the male, have had a destructive effect on it' (1931b, GW: 522, SE: 230). How is it that his hostility to his father helps him smash his desire to do away with him?

'Female Sexuality' ends with a discussion of the sexual drives and their active and passive aims, which adds a new dimension to the relation between activity and passivity in both sexes. This is the child's desire to repeat in an active form that which is done to it passively. 'This is part of the work imposed on it of mastering the external world and can even lead to its endeavouring to repeat an impression which it would have reason to avoid on account of its distressing content' (1931b, GW: 529, SE: 236). Freud describes this as interesting, and it is even more interesting when one considers how it evokes the death drive, which however is not mentioned in this paper. The compulsion to repeat a distressing experience, for instance, reliving the traumatic experiences of war in the form of shell-shock, was one of the things that led Freud to postulate the death drive in the first place (1920a). In the context of female sexuality however there is a difference. The child repeating an experience, distressing or otherwise, is repeating it to transform its passive role into an active one. The fact that it does so shows an 'unmistakable revolt' against passivity. This revolt is more evident in some children than others. Significantly, Freud takes the extent to which it is evident as an index 'to the relative strength of the masculinity and femininity that [the child] will exhibit in its sexuality' (1931b, GW: 530, SE: 236).

That remark also suggests that the correlation between masculinity and activity, and femininity and passivity is unproblematic.[31]

---

30 As with so much else in the theory of femininity, in this reply Freud is borrowing from his earlier work. The boy's Oedipal redirection of hostility from mother to father was elaborated in Freud 1913c.

31 But one instance of this transformation of passivity into activity complicates that correlation. This is a girl's play with dolls. Freud sees this as an indirect reversal of the mother/child relation, and 'evidence of the exclusiveness of her attachment to her mother,

'Femininity'

The correlation between activity and masculinity, passivity and femininity becomes problematic in the last of the three papers, 'Femininity', which begins by explicitly questioning that correlation.[32] This is the paper which Freud began by declaring femininity a riddle against which heads have knocked throughout history. In it, he writes as if the problematic nature of the correlation between activity, passivity, and sexual identity is as critical to the riddle as masochism in men.

At the outset, he declares that biology can be of almost no help in understanding this correlation; even if sperm are active and ova passive, even if the male 'seizes' and penetrates the female, to concentrate on this is only to 'reduce ... the characteristic of masculinity to the factor of aggressiveness so far as psychology is concerned' (1933a, GW: 122, SE: 115). He also discards the idea that the active and passive meanings of masculinity and femininity are their psychological meanings.

Apparently, Freud is still working in relation to the three meanings of masculinity and femininity outlined in the Three Essays: a biological, psychological, and social sense (1905b, Studien: 123, SE: 219–20). That is to say, tacitly, these meanings frame the paper: after considering the provinces of biology and psychology, he briefly mentions that of sociology. The context is the significant observation that while the psychological characterization of femininity as passive is unfruitful, we might consider that 'it gives preference to passive aims. This is not, of course, the same thing as passivity. To achieve a passive aim may call for a large amount of activity' (1933a, GW: 123, SE: 115). But if we think this, 'we must beware ... of underestimating the force of social customs, which similarly force women into passive situations' (1933a, GW: 123, SE: 116). Yet Freud gives little attention to that social realm. His main concern remains the problematic psychological definition. It is in exemplifying why it is that passivity, femininity, and women do not always go hand in hand that Freud considers masochism, the passive feminine trait, which because it is also found in men constitutes Freud's real riddle of femininity, one that 'psychology [like biology] is unable to solve' (1933a, GW: 123, SE: 116).

---

with complete neglect of her father-object' (1931b, GW: 530, SE: 237). What is at issue here is not femininity as passivity, which characterizes the relation to the father. This mothering reversal represents the 'active side of femininity' [die Aktivität der Weiblich-keit]. In 'Femininity' Freud's formulation of the same phenomenon is rather different. The girl's play with dolls 'was not in fact an expression of her femininity; it served as an identification with her mother with the intention of substituting activity for passivity' (1933a, GW: 137, SE: 128).

32 Written for the New Introductory Lectures Freud was unable to deliver, but which he wrote as if he was addressing an audience. Both Naomi Segal (1988) and Jane Gallop [1982] have pointed out that Freud in fact changes to the third person plural when referring to the women in the audience. Strachey, politely, translates an ambiguous 'sie' as 'you' (Segal 1988: 241–2).

sexual identity emerge in some remarks Freud makes on development. He does not make these explicit, but they are there. Consider the following three observations, offered within the space of two (admittedly long) paragraphs.

1 Differences emerge ... in the instinctual disposition which give a glimpse of the later nature of women. A little girl is as a rule less aggressive, defiant and self-sufficient; she seems to have a greater need for being shown affection and on that account to be more dependent and pliant ...
2 One gets an impression, too, that little girls are more intelligent and livelier than boys of the same age; they go out more to meet the external world and at the same time form stronger object-cathexes ...
3 Both sexes seem to pass through the early phases of libidinal development in the same manner. It might have been expected that in girls there would have been some lag in aggressiveness in the anal-sadistic phase, but such is not the case. Analysis of children's play has shown our women analysts that the aggressive impulses of little girls leave nothing to be desired in the way of abundance and violence.

(1933a, *GW*: 124–6, *SE*: 117–18)[33]

To assert the last point in view of the first is courageous. But in fairness, I have to note that the contradiction between these points is softened a little if one takes account of how the first is a developmental observation, the last an observation drawn from analysis. The lesser aggression could either develop later than the anal-sadistic phase, and/or it could overlay that phase in a repressive series of prohibitions about what girls do and do not. However this softening only returns us to the harsh matter of repression. And the issue of the girl's possibly greater liveliness, intelligence, and orientation to the external world remains, though this too could be sacrificed to repression, and by Freud's account of the stunting of curiosity and the drive for research in girls, so it is. That is to say, Freud had ascribed woman's comparatively lesser urge to research and intellectual capacity to the catastrophe of the Oedipus complex.[34] Yet what the passage quoted above suggests is that possibly the boy lags behind the

33 A reference to Melanie Klein, perhaps.
34 In two passages the penis and castration complex are directly associated with intellectual capacity. 'The wish to get the longed-for penis in spite of everything may contribute to the motives that drive a mature woman to analysis, and what she may reasonably expect from analysis – a capacity, for instance, to carry on an intellectual profession – may often be recognized, as a sublimated modification of this repressed wish' (1933a, *GW*: 134, *SE*: 125). And the absence of a penis in women can be associated with 'feeble-mindedness'. 'I learnt from the analysis of a young unmarried woman who had no father but several aunts that she clung, until quite far on in the latency period, to the belief that her mother and her aunts had a penis. One of her aunts, however, was feeble-minded; and she regarded this aunt as castrated, as she felt herself to be' (1923d, *GW*: 298, n. 1, *SE*: 145, n. 1).

girl initially, which means that the resolution of the Oedipus complex represents a comparative gain in intelligence and curiosity for him.[35]

Much of 'Femininity' repeats points made in Freud's earlier two papers on the subject. For instance, Freud mentions narcissism again, this time in a way that links it to his findings in the metapsychological paper 'On Narcissism'. In that paper, Freud distinguishes between two modes of choosing an object: one is anaclitic, i.e. based on an attachment formed in relation to needs that were real enough; the other is narcissistic: the object chosen is a reflection of one's ego or ego-ideal. If one loves in the anaclitic mode, one loves 'a woman who tends [one's needs]', a woman like the mother who fed one, or 'a man who protects [from harm]'. Alternatively, one may love according to the narcissistic mode, in which case there are three options: one may love an object based on (i) the person one wants to be, (ii) the person one is, (iii) the person one once was. Freud styles the anaclitic mode of loving as masculine, and active; the narcissistic mode as passive, and feminine; in the first, one loves, in the second, one needs to be loved. As he does so he emphasizes especially that masculinity and femininity are not tied to biological sex; a point exemplified in this instance by a discussion of narcissistic object-choice in some male homosexuals. Underlying the theory of narcissism is the theory of ego and object-libido. A detailed discussion of this, and further elaboration of narcissism, has been held over to chapter 4. What needs to be recorded here is that in referring to feminine narcissism, Freud is tying the narcissism involved in penis-envy to the theory of narcissistic object-choice, which is 'often made in accordance with the narcissistic ideal of the man whom the girl had wished to become' (1933a, GW: 142, SE: 132–3).

Freud also amplifies his earlier papers in a discussion of the 'three paths' the girl follows in response to her castration, a remark that makes it plain that the difference between the first path (sexual inhibition or neurosis) and the third (normal femininity) is merely one of degree. It seems in

35 This question of the respective development of boys and girls (although I have expressly excluded developmental research from this study) raises the further question of what happens in their differential development at puberty. The issue of the diphasic onset of sexuality, which constituted Freud's second major discovery, according to him (the unconscious and the interpretation of dreams being the first), does not figure in any of the three late papers on femininity. At least, it only figures in so far as Freud revises his earlier belief (in 1915) in the idea that the genital organization only came into being at puberty. The significance of the latency period vis-à-vis her changeover from masculine activity and curiosity to feminine intellectual inhibition is not discussed. However the developmental indications are that it is only at puberty that an intellectual difference between boys and girls appears in certain fields. From Freud's perspective, this would probably count as a kind of confirmation: it ties the girl's intellectual state to her sexual difference. On the other hand, the latency period is explained by the repression of the Oedipus complex, and, with it, all sexual desire. As the girl's feminine inhibition is also tied to repression, we are left here with a situation where she continues (assuming the developmental evidence to be right and Freud to be right as well) to function on an intellectual par with boys through a repression of the repressed!

both cases, 'Passivity now has the upper hand, and the girl's turning to her father is accomplished principally with the help of passive instinctual impulses' (1933a, *GW*: 137, *SE*: 128). In both cases, what is lost is phallic activity. 'If not too much of it is lost . . . through repression, this femininity may turn out to be normal' (1933a, *GW*: 137, *SE*: 128). Given that the passive impulses are present in the preceding anal phases, and as an aspect of other drives, this raises the question of whether there is a pre-existing relation between repression and the constitution of these impulses. It is a question that would demand more explanation of how the passive impulses are formed before it could be answered. For instance, are passive impulses formed through passive experiences? Freud's discussion of toilet-training as the exemplary experience of a passive experience might imply this. In fact it is noteworthy that in this paper, as in 'Female Sexuality', one of the contrasts between activity and passivity is expressed in terms of the child's desire to repeat what has been done to it in an active form.

In the end the discussion of the correlation between sexual identities and passivity and activity does return to the biology Freud discounted at the outset. When Freud asks what can decide in favour of the second path, the masculinity complex, his only answer is that the identification with the phallic mother or father presupposed in that path is 'a constitutional factor, a greater amount of activity, such as is ordinarily characteristic of a male' (1933a, *GW*: 139, *SE*: 130).

'Femininity' terminates with a tabulation of femininity's deficiencies. Freud has by this point again mentioned envy, this time as a general characteristic, and a weaker sense of justice. The weaker sense of justice had been mentioned previously in Freud (1925c) in connection with the notion that the motive force for woman's establishing a superego was not as strong. In other words, the weaker sense of justice was contingent on the weaker superego. In the paper under discussion, Freud writes that: 'The fact that women must be regarded as having little sense of justice is no doubt related to the predominance of envy in their mental life; for the demand for justice is a modification of envy and lays down the condition subject to which justice can be put aside' (1933a, *GW*: 144, *SE*: 134). That is all he says on this count. What is the process whereby envy is modified into a demand for justice, or by which any one emotion is modified into another? Freud has an answer to this question in the concept of reaction-formation. But reaction-formation (i) presupposes that a given emotion, such as sadism, is present in order for it to be transformed, and (ii) has a quantitative dimension: the greater the sadism then (potentially) the greater the compassion. The difficulty with the foregoing observation on envy and justice (presuming it is right to suppose that modification takes place via the mechanism of reaction-formation), is that envy would have to be present in order for any sense of justice, weak or strong, to develop. Moreover the possessor of a strong sense of justice must once have known envy. Freud has already said that the sense of justice in the ideal masculine case is strong. It results from the superego's formation. But it must once have had a basis in envy. The predominance of envy in the mental life of women has been assigned to penis-envy. In which case, we must ask: where did this envy in men come from, what was its object?

In 'Femininity's final tabulation, Freud says that women are 'weaker in their social interests and have less capacity for sublimating their drives than men'. Both points have been made before. What was absent in their making was the failure to draw the implication that because the capacity for sublimation is less, there is more potential for pathology. This pathology is evoked in his concluding remarks in 'Femininity'. It is here that Freud refers to a woman of 30's 'psychical rigidity' and unchangeability. Rigidity is a mark of pathology, as Freud shows in the case study of the Wolfman (1918a, *GW*: 151, *SE*: 116). Moreover, it is a mark of pathology that he expressly ties to the resistances of the ego,[36] and to a kind of 'psychical entropy', an expression Freud uses at least twice (1918a, *GW*: 151, *SE*: 116; 1937, *GW*: 88, *SE*: 242). One of the passages in which he discusses rigidity in the context of pathology is worth quoting at length, precisely because it echoes (without referring to femininity) the description of the woman of 30, whose 'pathways to further development' appear to have been closed. In 'Analysis Terminable and Interminable' (1937), Freud writes that with some patients

> we are surprised by an attitude . . . which can only be put down to a depletion of the plasticity, the capacity for change and further development, which we should ordinarily expect. . . . When the work of analysis has opened up new paths for a drive's impulse, we almost invariably observe that the impulse does not enter upon them without marked hesitation . . . with the patients I here have in mind, all the mental processes, relationships and distributions of force are unchangeable, fixed and rigid. One finds the same thing in very old people, in which case it is explained as being due to what is described as force of habit or an exhaustion of receptivity – a kind of psychical entropy. But we are dealing here with people who are still young. Our theoretical knowledge does not seem adequate to give a correct explanation of such types. Probably some temporal characteristics are concerned – some alterations of a rhythm of development in psychical life which we have not yet appreciated.
>
> (1937, *GW*: 87–8, *SE*: 241–2)

Let us sum up before bringing this discussion of Freud's three papers on femininity and the 'Great Debate' to a close. Whatever the 'temporal

---

36 Cf. also Freud 1915e, where rigidity on the ego's part is given as the explanation for sleeplessness: the ego is so resistant to the unconscious that it cannot permit itself to sleep, in case it dreams.

characteristics' Freud has in mind in the passage just quoted, they are not tied, nor is there any reason for implying that he thought they should be tied, to the obvious temporal difference between the boy's and girl's Oedipus complex, in which the boy defers his desire for the mother, and achieves a full or partial sublimation of the libidinal drive involved, while the girl stays attached to the father in phantasy, lingering in the Oedipus complex. But the tie between temporality, and psychical entropy and rigidity should be borne in mind.

Meantime, this argument has reached a point where it is possible to distil further precise questions concerning the riddle of femininity. Three of these questions are Freud's. Two are mine, although they arise directly from his enquiry. Freud's explicit questions are: (i) (the question with which we began, the quintessential riddle of femininity) Why is passivity (as a mark of femininity), and why are the marks of passive femininity, such as masochism, not confined to women? In other words, how is it that men are feminine? (ii) Why does the girl turn away from her mother in hate? Is penis-envy sufficient to explain this? (iii) How do masculinity and femininity differ from activity and passivity?

The following questions also arise, although Freud gives them less attention: (iv) Why is it that women may become rigid, and/or why does 'the difficult development to femininity' exhaust 'the possibilities of the person concerned'? (v) By what means does the girl repress more than the boy, given that her superego is weaker? Is the social force of repression sufficient to account for this, and if so, how does it work psychically? Finally, the fact that Freud either avoids, or is blind to the implications of, the contradiction concerning repression needs to be noted. This contradiction means that femininity verges on pathology, but the pathological implications of the idea that the girl represses by some indeterminate means without the option of sublimation are not explored.

In sum, the burden of my argument so far is that as the repression as distinct from the sublimation of the Oedipus complex may lead to pathology, and as the girl's Oedipus complex is repressed rather than sublimated (although how it is repressed is unclear) then femininity has to be tinged by pathology. It is an obvious option to pursue, a link that is almost made by Freud, and yet it is not. Which leads to a further question: Why, given the claims that women have less capacity for sublimation, given that he gives a description of a pathological state immediately after referring to that lesser capacity, and given that he has elsewhere insisted on the pathological consequences of the repression, rather than the sublimation of the Oedipus complex, why does he not investigate the pathological implications of femininity as he describes it? Is this another instance of 'gaps in the material'? Missing links which mean that the description of femininity can be read as other than a description of a pathological state?

For as things stand, the enduring image of Freud's theory of femininity is of a negative characterology, rather than a state to be overcome.

SUBSEQUENT DEVELOPMENTS

In part, the dogmatism that has affected subsequent psychoanalytic discussions of femininity is due to the fact that while Freud reiterates his dissatisfaction with his explanations of femininity, he manages to insist on them. In the beginning, he is always careful, qualifying the universality of his findings. The whole of 'Some Psychical Consequences' (1925c) is qualified at the outset by the statement that its findings 'would be of great importance if they could be proved to apply universally' (1925c, GW: 20, SE: 248; see also 1924c, GW: 401, SE: 179) and concludes with the reminder that the findings are based only 'on a handful of cases' (1925c, GW: 30, SE: 258). Similarly, Freud doubts that his description of the processes involved in the Oedipus complex is the only possible one (1924c, GW: 401, SE: 179) and asks, regarding the prehistory of the complex (in boys), 'whether a great variety of different preliminary situations may not converge upon the same terminal situation' (1925c, GW: 22, SE: 251). In fact he is generally dissatisfied with the information on the pre-Oedipus phase in boys: for instance, he says we need to know more about this phase to be sure why the boy's hostility to his mother is surmounted (1931b, GW: 529, SE: 235). But after the last of the papers devoted to femininity, he has little to add to his concluding observations on the rigid woman of 30, whose difficult development to femininity had exhausted her possibilities. And there are no more qualifications; Freud is claiming for the second theory of femininity the full authority of 'observation' without the benefit of 'speculative' additions (1933a, GW: 120, SE: 113). We might say that in the end, he is almost rigid, as if the problem of femininity had exhausted the possibilities of the theory concerned.

Apart from very occasional byplays in his footnotes, Freud ceased to engage with his colleagues' views on femininity after 1931. However the lines of difference about female sexuality that had been laid down by 1931 continued to be reinforced by his colleagues, to the extent that in the mid-1930s, a series of talks was planned to clarify the disagreements between the London and Vienna psychoanalytic societies; the first and main disagreement centred on female sexuality. In the end, the only talk given was by Ernest Jones (1935). It reiterated the fundamental disagreement with Freud referred to above: viz. that there was early knowledge of the vagina, that girls were naturally drawn towards their fathers, that penis-envy was a secondary phase, and that Freud was unduly phallocentric. It also emphasized a new dimension in the differences between London and Vienna, concerning psychical reality, of which more in a moment. Freud's supporters continued to draw attention to evidence for a primary and long-lived first attachment to the mother. In Deutsch's case, this evidence was amplified by studies of female homosexuality, showing how the mother/infant relation and its oral associates were recapitulated in homosexual relations between women (1932, 1933a). But apart from many illuminating clinical illustrations, little that was new was added to the positions already described.[37] Nor was much added thereafter (Mitchell 1974: 121), until the second debate, a product of the second women's movement, began.[38]

THE SECOND DEBATE

One of the remarkable features of the second debate is the extent to which its preoccupations parallel those of its predecessor.[39] The critique of phallocentrism (or phallic monism: 'only one sexual organ is known'), the biological and cultural arguments against Freud's theory are repeated in

37 Although new protagonists joined or had joined both sides, notably Muller (1932), Brierley (1932, 1936), Bonaparte (1935), and Brunswick (1940).
38 The interregnum between the first and second debates was marked by further interventions by Deutsch (1961) and Clara Thompson (summed up in Thompson 1950). It reached a high point with Beauvoir [1949] who recognized narcissism (amongst other marks of femininity), treated Deutsch's analyses with respect, but pointed to the cultural induction of the phenomena Freud and Deutsch described. It reached a low point with Bonaparte (1951), who argued both that women had less libido biologically and that the clitoris was a supernumerary organ. Reviewing the psychoanalytic literature in the two main journals, the *Psychoanalytic Quarterly* and the *International Journal of Psycho-Analysis*, one finds that the articles on the subject of femininity and female sexuality are relatively few. In the *Psychoanalytic Quarterly* there are twelve articles on female sexuality between 1935 and 1966. Interestingly, the category of 'female sexuality' disappears from the index to the *Quarterly* in 1967 and is replaced by 'female psychology' and female development. I surmise that these new categories reflect the move away from sexuality, and towards a developmental sociology of psychoanalysis, a move that aroused Lacan's antagonism, and that has been thoroughly criticized by Mitchell (1982). But even within these tamed categories only four articles appear between 1967 and 1976. By way of some form of compensation, two articles appear under another, the new category, 'feminism'. After 1977 there are more articles under 'feminism' but only two in the psychology and development categories prior to 1986. Of these, Wimpfleimer and Schafer (1977) is interesting for its criticisms of Helene Deutsch's methodology, which it characterizes as scientistic and dualistic. The *International Journal of Psycho-Analysis* published a total of twelve articles directly on the topic of Freud's theory of femininity in the fifty years between 1940 and 1990. Leaving aside the journals, the debate on femininity and female sexuality opened out again with Chasseguet-Smirgel ([1964] 1981), and the numerous feminist critiques of Freud analysed in Mitchell (1974), which, while they took Freud as the 'enemy', still prompted a more 'woman-friendly' reconsideration of the question of femininity in the psychoanalytic literature thereafter. However the psychoanalytic reconsiderations of femininity in the late 1960s and 1970s (see especially Miller 1972) were more concerned with the cultural factors in femininity and cultural biases in Freud. His own riddle of femininity remains unaddressed.
39 Rose (1982) argues that an appeal to a natural source for female sexuality is a backward and 'essentialist' step; this backward step is meant to be repeated by more recent feminist opponents of Freud's views, such as Chodorow (1978) and Irigaray [1974 and 1977]. Rose, and Juliet Mitchell, occupy a position similar to that taken by Freud's supporters in the first debate.

the second debate. Freud's feminist defenders also repeat arguments from the first debate, in so far as they insist on the importance of the father and castration in founding masculinity and femininity. In these respects, only the dramatis personae have changed. But both the critiques and the defence in the second debate interweave with other currents of thought which add massive new dimensions to how femininity is conceived. Amongst these currents, two stand out. The first is the object-relations theory that devolved from Melanie Klein, and which veered into two tributary streams: one about the sociology of family life (non-Kleinian), the other about the 'inner world' of phantasy (Kleinian). The second current flowed out of the Seine; it consists of theories about language, signification, and the symbolic order, theories propounded by Lacan in the first instance. Both streams in the object-relations current make the mother the most significant factor in psychical life. The Lacanian current insists on the importance of the (symbolic) father, and the role of the phallus in symbolic castration. In this section I will try to show how these currents converge over the question of identity. This convergence emerges only once identity is defined: it is central, but underformulated, in the second debate.

In more detail: the object-relations current begins with Dinnerstein [1976] who is indebted to Klein, and Chodorow (1978), who is indebted to the object-relations stream that focuses on the social or material realities of parenthood (the Balints (1939 and 1968), Mahler (1968), Winnicott (1965), etc.). Chodorow's theory more than Dinnerstein's has attracted followers who have applied and developed it, and also attracted more criticism. As Chodorow gives a completely comprehensive and excellent introduction to the object-relations theories she draws on (as does Hamilton 1979), there is little point in a summary exposition of object-relations, except for two points which are salient here. The first is the object-relations assumption that mother and child are a unit from which the child has to emerge with a distinct sense of itself. It has to go through a phase of individuation-separation from the unit of which it was once part. In this process, its psyche is shaped by the object-relations it internalizes. It has to give up its mother; it then, as with Freud's ego in 'Mourning and Melancholia', takes on the shape of the object it has lost; and the ego will continue to be shaped by later losses. The object-relations canon begins with Freud's observation that 'the ego is a precipitate of abandoned object-cathexes'. The wonderful thing about the German word *Besetzung*, which Strachey translates (with apologies) as cathexis, is that it connotes both an emotional state (being occupied or taken over), and an energetic one (being 'charged').[40]

40 In more detail, Strachey's translation of *Besetzung* as cathexis is contentious, because cathexis conveys the idea of an energetic attachment or investment in an object, phantasy, or memory, but it loses the connotation of occupation, of being occupied, being engaged, also conveyed by the German term. *Besetzung* connotes both the act of becoming occupied or attached to an idea, object, etc., and the quantity of energy or quota of affect involved in that attachment.

The energetic connotation is lost in object-relations theories, which brings me to the second point about them. Object-relations theories have counterposed themselves to Freud's theory of the drives, in a not very interesting dispute about whether the drive comes before and exists independently of the object, or the object induces the drive (one is driven to regain what one has lost, or a substitute for it). This means that in general, object-relations theory ignores the drives, or energetic dimension. Michael Balint remarked, notoriously, that he got lost in Freud's plumbing.[41]

Chodorow's point of departure, in one sense, is the question of individuation-separation. And in her early work, like the object-relations theories she draws on, she focuses on how the relation to the mother (as object) is internalized by the child. Girls identify with, or internalize, a mother from whom they have never, in a sense, taken their distance. They never take their distance because women in general mother (at home), while men are more distant as fathers (in the workforce). While the boy has to break with the mother and identify with a parent who is absent, a girl does not. Hence she is more likely to stay in a relational, less differentiated mode, in which emotional intersubjective connections are more important. The boy, on the other hand, does have to take his distance, identify with a parent who is out there, and make a break with the mother which makes him less relational and more objective.

Whatever the criticisms of Chodorow's theory, which I mention shortly, it has evident experiential appeal. It leads to the conclusion that 'masculinity is damage', which appeals to some. Also, the idea that connectedness and lack of individuation figure more in women, and the idea that relationships are more important to women, resonates with experience to the extent that Chodorow's theory has helped generate two major strands of feminist thought: (i) an outstanding critique of science and the subjective/objective values encapsulated in it (Keller 1985); (ii) a critique of impartial ethics, arguing that the values of relatedness and empathy are cardinal in a different, rather than a weaker, sense of justice in women (Gilligan 1982). Chodorow's work has also generated, or interweaved with, an object-relations investigation of masochism (in terms of the desire for domination) and femininity (Benjamin 1988).[42]

Chodorow's is a cultural or social theory. Like the culturalists in the first debate, she attributes the disabling effects of femininity to sociological facts or assumptions: her theory hangs on the idea that women do the mothering at home, and men work outside. If that changed, so would feminine and masculine identities. It is Chodorow's concern with social

---

41 The object-relations neglect of the drives does not mean that the body is ignored altogether. Winnicott (1975: 247) discusses the psyche–soma split in terms of its potential pathology, and from a feminist object-relations standpoint, Flax (1990) draws attention to the fight over energy and objects. The neglect of the flesh is more pronounced in the secondary literature than it is in the originals.
42 Benjamin (1988) overlaps with this argument on masochism.

realities that has been criticized by defenders of Freud, on the grounds that her argument sacrifices or bypasses psychical reality (Mitchell and Rose 1982, Adams 1983), as other feminists before her have sacrificed the unconscious (Mitchell 1974). In essence, the critique of the neglect of psychical reality comes down to this: social or material realities do not simply hop across to the psyche, nor does the psyche merely reflect the realities in which it lives. The psyche is structured according to certain processes which are essential to securing an identity capable of *being socialized*. That entity is not pre-given, but constructed. The defenders of Freud see the (symbolic) father's role and castration as critical in bringing this psychical reality, and the identity it founds, into being. But while the defenders' arguments resonate with those of Freud and his allies in the first debate, their dependence on Lacan changes the grounds for the defence in other ways. In addition, 'psychical reality' is an issue not only for Lacan, but for Klein. Klein also argues that a psychical reality, formed in relative independence of material reality, interacts with social familial circumstances. But before I discuss Lacan's theory, and Klein's in more detail, I want to point to how both the sociological object-relations current and the symbolic linguistic one make identity central albeit in different ways.[43]

Identity and its formation became an issue in psychoanalysis only after the Second World War. But it did so obliquely. The term 'identity' entered into psychoanalytic currency by a variety of paths, without ever being defined, just as it has largely ecaped definition in feminist writing.[44] In part, identity began to figure in psychoanalysis on the basis of an elaboration of Freud's theory of how the ego takes on its distinctive character through the relations it internalizes. As I have indicated, developments here led to the object-relations schools of psychoanalysis, and brought the question of individuation to the fore. For some object-relations theorists, especially Winnicott, the critical issue is how the subject comes to have a 'space' of its own and an identity that is separate from its mother's (an idea which, while it partakes of the presupposition that the infant is originally one with the mother, leaves the exact nature of the connection unspecified). In part, identity became an issue because of the way the ego was

43 But while the emphasis on psychical reality appears to mark one difference between the first and second debates, this difference is more apparent than real. Psychical reality also figured at the tail end of the 'great debate'; the context was a disagreement between Melanie Klein (and her followers) and Anna Freud (and hers) over how psychical reality (and with it, the Oedipus complex and the unconscious) is formed. For Melanie Klein especially, the significant thing about psychical reality is its relation to phantasy. Klein also emphasized the role of projection and anxiety in the ego's development, and suggested that repression is a subsequent defence mechanism, tied to the 'genital' Oedipus complex. In this, she is in effective agreement with Lacan, and the Lacanian-influenced contributors to the second debate. For a more detailed discussion see Brennan (1988).
44 Although 'the politics of identity' is now foregrounded because of an increasing awareness of ethnic and racial differences, and differences in sexual orientation. See Fuss (1989) on the lack of definition of the term, and Strathern (1988) for an attempt at one, in a context that argues against 'self-contained' identity as the only form 'identity' can take.

emphasized by the aptly named 'ego psychology' school of the United States, to the extent that the 'ego' and 'identity' can be conflated. Identity also came to matter because of the increasing incidence of what the diagnostic manuals defined as narcissistic personality disorders. 'By the 1970s, narcissism became the single most-discussed psychoanalytic topic in North America' (Roazen 1985: 29).

But the concern with the ego, and to some extent the concern with narcissism in North America, were concerns about making the ego 'strong' or encouraging the development of a healthy narcissism in childhood in order to protect the self against the development of a narcissistic over-compensation in adulthood (Kohut 1978). The idea that one should strengthen the ego was psychoanalytic anathema for Lacan. Paradoxically, Lacan's attacks on ego-psychology have obscured his own concern with the formation of identity. Lacan did not only believe that identity was a fiction, a constructed rather than a given thing, and that the idea of a fixed identity was illusory. He also stressed that the construction of this fiction is how psychical reality is founded, and that the construction was a protection against psychosis.[45]

The construction is a two-stage process. The first stage is the imaginary mirror stage, in which the child perceives itself in a mirror as a whole, or it perceives itself as a whole through the mirror of itself that its environment provides. This *Gestalt* image is opposed to the child's experience of itself as a disconnected bundle of parts. In this mirror stage, however, the child is still connected with its mother in an imaginary dyad. It is not sure where it ends and the other begins. The nature of the connection between the infant and the other is not something that Lacan, like the developmental theories he criticizes, makes clear, although he intimates that it originates in shared phantasies (see pp. 228–9 below).

The infant's relation to the 'ideal-I' constructed in the mirror stage is problematic for another reason. This relation is fraught with aggressiveness. The infant perceives its mirror-image as something that constrains and 'passifies' it, as well as something that gives it an image of itself. This feeling of constraint leads to anxiety on the infant's part, which in turn leads it to project its aggression on to another in the real world. Both the dynamics of projection and aggression, in the infant's understanding about where it ends and the other begins, are resolved or potentially resolved with the intervention of the 'symbolic father' of language. The existence of the third term encapsulated by the idea of the symbolic father is necessary for the second stage in the process of identity-formation, and for the foundation of psychical reality. This third term enables the subject to represent its difference from the mother, and to repress the connections that otherwise interfere with its sense of its boundaries.

45 See Brennan (1988) for a more developed account.

Language breaks these connections. It effects a break in a way that parallels the actual intervention of the father between mother and child. It is because language parallels the role of the father in breaking a connection that Lacan is able to reread Freud's phylogenetic explanation of the Oedipus complex in symbolic terms: regardless of the realities of the actual familial constellation, language will always effect separation. Language founds psychical reality through repressing connections in a related act of separation, an act that relies on difference. The difference between linguistic signifiers is the condition of speech and language. But by repressing connection, these signifiers always leave something unsaid. This something lives on in the unconscious, which gives rise to the desire that can never find exactly what it wants. Because, by definition, what the infant really wants (its need) escapes definition. More to the point, the unconscious is born through this act of repression; the psychical reality of wishes which cannot be expressed lives on, and will seek access to expression through the only channel of expression available to them. This channel is the chain of signification, which wends its way, through puns and other non-linear forms of expression, around the fixed meanings attached to objects through words. But this disruptive process, however truth-revealing and enlivening, does not dispense with the necessity for fixed meaning. In fact the fixing of meaning is essential to identity.

In a sense, the first fixed meaning, for Lacan, is the mirror-image the subject has of itself. This mirror-image captures it, while giving it the preliminary definition it lacked hitherto. Given my overall spatio-temporal concern, it should be added here that the mirror stage is, for Lacan, a spatial phenonemon (the body-image is formed at a distance, through the eye of an imagined other). Language on the other hand is temporal; in the psychoanalytic situation, it takes the subject beyond its present fixed meanings into a new time. And given the question of identity, it should also be added that the imaginary continues to be the place in which identity is fixed, while the symbolic path is the means for shifting a fixed identity into one that is less fixed, more productive and truthful. The imaginary continues to be the place in which identity is fixed because it is the place in which the different identifications out of which the ego is composed cohere. For Lacan continues to suppose, as did Freud, that the ego is formed through identifications (some stemming from 'abandoned object-cathexes'). At the same time, in order to feel that it is *one* self, these different identifications have to be united. For Lacan, the mirror stage gives the subject-to-be one image of itself as whole. For Freud, the ego is the principle of synthesis or coherence. In the interests of synthesis, it moulds often conflicting identifications into a unity, although the price of this unity is (usually) the suppression of any contradictory implications of diverse identifications. In the process of analysis, these suppressed implications are drawn out and the existing fixity broken down. It is broken down not in order to leave the subject broken and unfixed, although such a breakdown is meant to be a good thing in the postmodern vernacular, and Deleuze's invocation of a 'schizophrenic flow' (Deleuze and Guattari [1972]).[46] Fixity is broken in order that the suppressed and contradictory implications be woven into a new history of the subject. This new history changes its identity, which, ideally, should incorporate more of the truth that it has hitherto relegated to its unconscious. This symbolic recovery and reweaving of another history, and composition of a richer identity, can in turn lead to further fixity if it becomes complacency. Which is why, perhaps, Freud recommended that one re-enter analysis every five years.[47]

That much said: one difficulty with Lacan's account is, as I indicated, that the connections broken through the intervention of language are ill-defined, and the nature of the unrepresentable need is of course unrepresented. This leaves his theory at a level of abstraction that accounts for much of its obscurity. A far better-known problem with Lacan's account is that language is tied not only to the father, but to the phallus. The difference or empty space which is the condition of differentiation between words and phonemes is marked by the phallus, as 'signifier of lack'. This means that the phallus marks the difference which can never in itself be expressed. If it was, the gap or difference, ostensibly, would be erased. From this perspective, the phallus is a neutral signifier. The problem is that, in order that the subject maintain a fixed identity, this neutral signifier has to be tied to the body. So that while the symbolic is the path beyond fixity, it depends, paradoxically, on the fixity of sexual identity.

For the embodied subject, difference can be represented only on the *visual* basis that father and mother are different; it depends on the recognition of the visual anatomical difference between the sexes. Because of this, the neutral phallus is tied to the male penis. This core Lacanian idea has been so extensively discussed[48] that any additional detailing of it seems almost superfluous, except that it is an idea that we will reinterpret, or rather re-read from the feminine side, in chapter 4. What is immediately relevant about it here is that the Lacanian emphasis on the visual anatomical difference in situating the subject entails that the relative ease with which the subject will find itself situated will vary for boys and girls. It is easier for the boy to recognize and represent his difference from the mother, because of his possession of a penis. This is his means of representing 'lack', where 'lack' means that he is separate from the mother and therefore lacking the omnipotence he phantasized he possessed in the original dyad. Without the recognition of this lack, he is subject to a

46 Deleuze does however stress the significance of energetic connections. The difficulty I have with him is that he assumes that the only one way of thinking those connections is in the psychotic terms in which they present themselves. See the next chapter.
47 For more discussion of the process of combining conflicting identifications into an artificial unity see Brennan (1989).
48 For instance, see the discussions and reviews in Ragland-Sullivan (1986) and Grosz (1991).

number of psychotic disorders, uncertainties concerning what his specific identity is, of which the delusion of omnipotence is only one. It is because she lacks this means of representing 'lack' that the girl is more prone, by this Lacanian argument, to psychosis at worst, and narcissism at best.

Irigaray has argued that the grain of truth in Lacan's theory lies in the ability to represent one's relation to one's origin ([1974] 1985a, [1977] 1985b).[49] The boy is better equipped in this respect: the penis enables him to acknowledge his difference from the mother because it guarantees that he may one day be united with a substitute for her. At the same time, his origin is guaranteed in that he is made in his father's image, and carries his father's name. Both the father/son and the mother/son relations are extensively documented in cultural symbolism. The girl, on the other hand, has no means of representing her relation to her maternal origin, and the lack of the cultural symbols that would enable her to do this is the real cause, for Irigaray, of the girl's identity-doubts, her narcissism, and her melancholia.

This reference to Irigaray's argument signals how the two currents in the second debate overlap. The object-relations' preoccupation with the mother, and the symbolic concentration on the father, overlap in that the *mother's* relation to signification and symbolization is also a major issue in the second debate (thus Flax 1990). Kristeva, like Irigaray, and Cixous (Cixous and Clément [1975] 1986) (to name the eternal triad, amongst others), is concerned with the mother's relation to signification.[50] At least, Kristeva ([1980] 1982, [1987] 1989, and 1980: 239 especially) is concerned with the mother's relation to signification; and what signification means in relation to the mother's body. She is also concerned with the nature of the connection between mother and child, and is remarkable in writing of it in driven, energetic terms. 'Drives involve pre-Oedipal semiotic functions and energy discharges that connect and orient the body to the mother' ([1974] 1984: 27). Note however that it is 'the body' (of the pre-Oedipal subject) that is connected and oriented to the mother; the nature of the mother's connection to the body is another question.[51] The semiotic is an energetic rhythmic process unbound by ordered space-time as we experience it. Yet Kristeva also assumes that while the semiotic process is unbound, the semiotic 'quantities of energy [which] move through the body' are 'discrete' (ibid.: 25), even before the subject is constituted by the symbolic law. In this Kristeva is true to Freud, even when she seeks to go behind him in postulating a pre-Oedipal semiotic process. Freud also assumed that the subject's energy was discrete, in the sense that it is limited and self-contained.

49 The point is drawn out in Whitford (1986).
50 On Irigaray, Cixous, and Kristeva, see Moi (1985) and Grosz (1989).
51 When Kristeva (1986) does discuss the mother's connection to the infant, the discussion takes another turn from that outlined in chapter 4. See pp. 171–3.

The notion that the semiotic is connected to the mother lends itself to the idea that the semiotic drives and rhythms are feminine. Kristeva's famous thesis loosely identifies this feminine force with the poetic pulsion which disrupts the symbolic law of language. She also identifies the symbolic law with logic, and makes it paternal (in this, she is true to Lacan). In brief, the maternal, or feminine, semiotic, poetic force is the *antithesis* of logic. This force underpins and yet resists a restricting, 'logical' symbolization, but can never supplant it. It can only disrupt, which leaves logical and social power (the two are identified by Kristeva) in the hands of a rigid paternal structure.

As I indicated, Irigaray is concerned with the failure to symbolize the mother: thus she challenged the idea that only one sexual organ is known. She challenged it not in terms of arguments about vaginal sensations, but by an attempt at symbolizing the vagina (and the multiplicity of female sexual parts). However until Whitford (1986, 1989, 1991) made the effort to piece Irigaray's multiple but scattered insights into a coherent argument, Irigaray's references to actual bodily parts were frequently read as an essentialist appeal to the female body, which echoed the arguments about an essential, primal experience of one's natural female sexuality in the first debate (Rose 1982). I am convinced that the only way to move the debate over essentialism forward is to change its terms (cf. de Lauretis 1989) but I will not engage with it further here as my main focus in this brief survey of the second debate is the debate's relation to the real riddle of femininity.

In a sense, the real riddle of femininity is touched on in that the importance of repression is stressed. It is stressed in terms of how symbolization, language, and signification (the symbolic) bring the unconscious and psychical reality into being, and how identity is formed in this process. The usefulness of this redefinition will not be disputed here, but its limitation must be noted; it avoids, or it regards as wrong or irrelevant, the quantitative problem that led Freud to knock his head against the problem of femininity. Similarly, while 'the specially inexorable repression' of the girl's attachment to her mother features in the second debate, it does so largely in terms of symbolization and signification. Hence Irigaray's placement of the cultural failure to represent or symbolize the girl's relation to her mother at the heart of the problem of femininity. For her, this failure results in the difficulties with sublimation experienced by the girl and many of the stigmas, the marks of femininity to which Freud drew attention. Other feminist commentators have also discussed these stigmata; and, in that the death drive and melancholia are beginning to feature in these discussions, one might expect that masochism, the heart of the riddle, would creep back in energetic terms.[52] But although the

---

52 See the essays by Rose (1989) and Ragland-Sullivan (1989); also Silverman (1988).

question of libidinal economy features in the second debate, it does so in a manner that I can only style as utopian. Irigaray ([1977] 1985b) and Cixous (Cixous and Clément [1975] 1986) write of an economics of plenty, and contrast it with Freud's economics of scarcity. Both, especially Cixous, invoke an economy of generosity,[53] in which a maternal or female economy is unlimited in what it draws from or passes on. There probably is such an 'economy'; but it will not come into being merely by invoking it as an ideal, or writing as if it already exists. That much said, Irigaray is also concerned with physics. This, as much as any notion she has of economy, needs more attention. The difficulty here is the relation between Irigaray's use of the term 'economy' and her references to 'physics'. Economy is used at times symbolically ('the economy of truth' (1975: *passim*)); at others, economy might be being used as an energetic term ('the economy of the death drives' (1975: 54)). These shifts are reflected in Whitford's (1991) important book on Irigaray, where 'economy' figures as a synonym for 'system', less *passé* perhaps, but just as general.[54] Yet while it is clear that Irigaray's economy is not identical with the energetic level, energetic psychodynamics are invoked in her references to physics, and although the relation between economy and physics is unclear in her work, Irigaray clearly has some relation in mind. Moreover the importance of physics in Irigaray's thought has been underestimated. As far as I am aware, only Grosz (1988) and Schor (1989) have drawn attention to it.

But we are left with the questions, what kind of 'physics' is Irigaray using, and how does it bear on her project overall? On the first question: Irigaray levels a criticism against 'science' (*tout court*) on the grounds that it has failed to develop a theory of fluids (cf. Schor 1989). Fluids, the mark of the indefinable feminine, as distinct from the hard cut and dried masculine, are significant for Irigaray because they cross boundaries and are not, she thinks, isolable, objectifiable and definable. This in some ways appealing argument is undercut by the fact that fluids are just as measurable as anything else. Nor has 'science' ignored 'fluids'. The importance of fluids and their measurement in Victorian thermodynamics and subsequent physical theories cannot be underestimated (cf. Bunge and Shea 1979, Keller 1983, Schaffer 1992). Yet although Irigaray's condemnation of science is not justified, the idea of crossing boundaries is vital. It is a pity that Irigaray does not elaborate on it herself very much, and that when

53 Morag Shiach's (1991) analysis stresses the importance of generosity in Cixous's thought.
54 Whitford rigorously notes this shift in meaning, but thinks possibly it has a point on the grounds that every time the term 'economy' is used, this, as with Irigaray's similar general use of other terms, means that 'more or less the whole field of the symbolic is evoked each time' (1991: 187–8). The problem with such a general evocation is that anything can mean anything. One may counter that the omnipresence of the symbolic has to be stressed. But this is the symbolic we live in and have to use in order to find a way beyond it. Invoking it as a mutually supporting structure with no open doors or cracks means that the very contradictions and inconsistencies within it are not revealed.

she does, the theory she calls on, that of the physicist Ilya Prigogine, is problematic. Very briefly, Prigogine has hypothesized the existence of non-entropic energy systems which cross boundaries, and which exist alongside the energy whose entropy, by Newtonian law, increases. As I have indicated, Prigogine's argument is a controversial one, dismissed altogether by many physicists.[55] Yet even if it were indubitable, there is nothing in it which could lead one to equate non-entropic energy systems with 'feminine sexuality' on the face of it, as Irigaray does when criticizing Freud's principle of 'equilibrium' on the grounds that it is 'masculine sexuality' which is governed by 'thermodynamic principles'.

> 'Feminine sexuality' could perhaps better be brought into harmony –
> if one must invoke a scientific model – with what Prigogine calls
> 'dissipating' structures that operate via the exchange with the external
> world, structures that proceed through levels of energy. The organiz-
> ational principle of these structures has nothing to do with the search
> for equilibrium but rather with the crossing of thresholds. This would
> correspond to a 'surpassing of disorder or entropy without discharge'.
>
> (Irigaray 1989: 62)

It is one thing to accept, like Spinoza, or like that fellow traveller Deleuze, that there are forms of motion and energy which surpass boundaries in a life-enhancing way. It is another to equate that which surpasses boundaries and entropy with 'feminine sexuality'. Overall this book is an argument against the idea that the boundaries which construct limits are pre-set, and it is also, to an extent, an attempt at understanding their construction in spatio-temporal terms. But the very point of this argument is that one cannot dispense with the real physical effects of that construc- tion by wishing them away, without knowledge of how they are produced. If a generous economy can come into being, it will be by understanding what prevents it from existing now. Unless the present restrictions on this hypothetical economy are understood, any reference to it remains utopian because the nature of the restrictions remains unspecified. Unless they are specified, they cannot be changed. The next chapter's argument on how Freud's self-contained energetic model of the psyche is constructed can

---

55 Prigogine's earlier work won him a Nobel prize. Yet even in Prigogine and Stengers (1979) and certainly by Prigogine (1988), he tends to proceed by inspired intuitions whose relation to one another is assumed rather than detailed. In enquiring into how far Prigogine is used or taken seriously amongst physicists today, I had a useful conversation with Simon Schaffer, who works (amongst other things) on how science elects some while considering others regrettable. This process of election and dismissal is not based on argument, as we have known since Kuhn (1966). It is a process that can be effected by a raised eyebrow, and Prigogine, amongst Anglophone physicists raises sceptical eyebrows in the way that Lovelock does. However unjust the eyebrows, they have more licence in their elevation when they are responding to ideas which are unsupported by an argument, ideas which, however interesting and significant, are unconnected and often appear contradictory.

also be read as an argument about how 'an economics of scarcity' is constructed. But the condition of this reading is that the phenomenon of energy be taken into serious account, together with the notion that this economic construction secures masculine as well as *feminine* identity. It is not the case that 'feminine sexuality', of itself, surpasses 'disorder or entropy'. It is rather that the construction of femininity and masculinity is simultaneously the construction of an inertia and an entropy which afflicts the feminine party more than the masculine. In fact, I will argue that a notion of constructed inertia presupposes a form of living motion which is not entropic. But this contrasting living motion is in no way identical to 'feminine sexuality'. The contrast has to be experienced by both sexes, by all human beings. The thing is that masculine sexuality appropriates more of that motion, at the expense of a femininity which is 'slower'. Which returns me to some of the underdiscussed energetic aspects, such as they are, of Lacan's theory.[56]

The visual recognition of the anatomical difference between the sexes can also be a kind of narcissistic short-cut to a secure identity for the boy. It is this because it is a way of disposing of the aggressive drive that endangers identity in the mirror stage. The idea that any subject needs to dispose of this aggression before it can secure its identity is implicit in Lacan's theory, but the implications are not explored by him. He does however conclude, like Freud, that hostility to the father and the psychical phantasy of woman (in which the subject splits women into two types – good and bad, mother and whore) are necessary adjuncts of the subject's successful resolution of the Oedipus complex; or, as Lacanians have it, 'entry into the symbolic order'. Both hostility to the father, and a libidinally imbued hostility to the 'bad woman', dispose of the aggression which is threatening to identity, because the subject fears the retaliation of its own ego-ideal until it has found a way of bringing ego-ideal and ego together. It can find this way only if aggression and the anxiety related to it are projected outwards, and are, therefore, no longer a part of the subject's intra-subjective psychical relations.

I have described the visual anatomical difference as a narcissistic short-cut to securing identity because I have Klein's explanation of how aggression and anxiety are resolved in mind. In her theory the subject also splits its objects into good and bad categories. It does so under the pressure of anxiety, which Klein attributes to the death drive operating within, rather than the constraining effects of the subject's own ego-ideal (Klein 1946 and 1957). But the genesis of the anxiety is not the issue here or, rather, now. The issues are: (i) how Klein's account is also an account of a psychical reality; and (ii) what the subject does with the aggression the anxiety results in.

56 Some of Lacan's neglected discussions of psychical energy are detailed in Brennan (1990) and Boothby (1991).

Klein's theory that the infant splits its objects into two types relies on the assumption that the infant phantasizes. In phantasy and hallucination (Klein did not distinguish between these terms), it creates a good and bad breast, and a good and bad mother. These are not real objects that the infant imports from its social surroundings. More exactly, the breast and mother are (often) real. But the infant's construction of their good and bad nature is a psychical reality, in which badness is projected on to the breast, which becomes a persecutor, a source of pain. This psychical reality can be reinforced or countermanded by material reality.[57] Now the idea of an interplay between psychical and material reality has been neglected by Klein's critics, and many subsequent Kleinians. It mattered to Klein, and had it mattered more to others, the split in the object-relations schools that developed, post-Bowlby and post-Winnicott, might not have been so great.

Of course, what the more sociological or developmental object-relations theorists resist is the premiss that underpins the bad-breast concept. The concept rests on the assumption that the infant is aggressive in inclination. It has initially directed its own death-driven aggression on to the breast, cutting it up, devouring it, etc., in phantasy. The infant then phantasizes that the breast will retaliate in kind. These considerations return us to aggression's origins.

For Klein, if the subject splits its objects into good and bad categories, it also splits its ego (Klein 1946). It is only able to overcome this split by recognizing that good and bad can coexist in the same object and, therefore, that they can coexist within the subject itself. Any resolution of the dynamics of aggression and anxiety which avoids recognizing that good and bad coexist in the same object is a short-cut. It is a short-cut because bringing good and bad together entails what Klein terms 'reparation'. Putting it at its simplest, 'reparation' is creative labour. Bringing good and bad together is both its condition and its consequence. It is its condition because it is only when the subject recognizes its own aggressive wishes towards the other on to whom it projects aggression that it can wish to repair the damage done (in phantasy or reality). It is its consequence because as long as the subject continues to split good and bad, it splits its own ego and its own capacities to act creatively.

Although Klein did not develop this theory in terms of its implications for identity-formation, she puts a special stress on the intimate connections between splitting, anxiety, and psychoses. In another context, it would be worth exploring the parallels between her theory and Lacan's in these respects in more detail. Klein's psychical reality features in infancy. So does Lacan's, but it recurs in the masculine Oedipus complex. But the split into good and bad types is common to both. Yet enough that to the

57 See Brennan (1991b) for a poorly written but basically sound argument about psychical and material reality.

extent that a person with a securely formed identity is less likely to be psychotic, Klein's theory points the way to another account of how such an identity is formed. In fact, some such account is absolutely required by Lacan's stress on sexual difference as the key to representing 'lack'. If women are more prone to psychoses because they cannot represent 'lack', how do women avoid psychoses at all? Klein's theory suggests women avoid them by creative labour, and necessarily suggests that men may avoid them by this means as well. In other words, the man may secure his identity by means other than the narcissistic short-cut and its projection of hostility on to the other, especially the other woman. If Klein is right, Irigaray's stress on a cultural 'female symbolic' represents only one half of the conditions under which a woman's identity could be formed differently. The other half would consist in the outlets for creative labour available to women – outlets which of course have been economically and socially blocked, and/or restricted to those provided by motherhood and lower-grade occupations.[58] To consider these outlets is to add another (hitherto ignored) dimension to the interplay of psychical and material reality. I will return to this consideration, which will figure as this argument develops. The notion of creative labour is necessarily an energetic notion. That is to say, it involves the deployment of psychical energy. Ultimately, it bears on how the contemporary concern with identity and its relation to sexual identity can be connected to Freud's real, quantitative riddle of femininity. But in the literature thus far, this connection has not been made.

In sum, the new concerns the second debate over Freud's theory of femininity adds to the first are: (i) individuation from a mother/child unit, and how this bears on a relational or connected female, as distinct from a dispassionate male, standpoint; (ii) the relation between sexual identity, psychical reality, and language; (iii) the interplay between social and psychical reality. These are not the only concerns of the second debate, whose preoccupations I have discussed elsewhere.[59] But it is these concerns that bear on the riddle of femininity. Or rather, as already indicated, they cut both ways. On the one hand they take us further away from Freud's own riddle. On the other hand, these concerns are also ours. The undifferentiated mother/child connection is critical in what follows, provided it is treated as an energetic connection. Psychical reality and the symbolic father's role in founding identity is critical too, provided its spatio-temporal dimensions are drawn out, for it is these that break energetic connections and remake them through identities.

If my treatment of the second debate literature seems cursory, this is because I would rather proceed by developing an argument about the

58 Irigaray herself does not ignore the socio-economic dimension [1977]. But, as with Virginia Woolf, this dimension disappears in most of the commentaries.
59 See Brennan (1989).

riddle of femininity, than by criticizing the existing literature for its short-comings. It seems more practical, and possibly more profitable, to signal where there are overlaps between this argument and that literature. The procedure of detailed exposition and critique might have led to the same conclusion that I reach in this book, but it would have involved many detours and taken that much longer. Also, there is always the risk of losing the thread in other frames of reference. My main critical observation on the second debate concerns its utopian aspect; to go beyond femininity, we have to understand how it is tied to identity, and understand how identity is constructed, before any reconstruction of it can be attempted. By mentioning Klein, I have indicated that the exercise of this understand-ing is work in itself; it involves shifting the boundaries of the identities we have.

By all the psychoanalytic theories discussed here, identity is something that: (i) requires a boundary, and therefore (ii) requires separation of self and other. It requires (iii) that this boundary is in some way fixed, and (iv) that the different identifications out of which the subject is composed cohere to some extent. In all accounts (excepting the Kleinian), *sexual* identity and the difference between masculinity and femininity depend on the identification with the father, which suppresses connection. Where the accounts vary is in their understanding of the nature of this identification, and whether they allow for the fact that the projection of aggressive drives on to the other is also essential to securing identity. For Klein, the consequences of this projection can be overcome by labour (a remarkably Kojève-like conclusion). Lacanians have insisted that *any* identity is always a sexual identity; there are no boundaries unless a paternal symbolic has suppressed connections. This leaves women with less fixed identities, in that women are less able to represent their separateness or project their aggression. In object-relations feminism, women also have less fixed identi-ties. The boy's identification with the father means more distance, more suppression of connectedness. It is worth adding that, once identity is made central, there is another point of commonality in diverse psychoana-lytic theories. It is space. It figures for Lacan, and for object-relations feminism in a less explicit way. The transitional space that established a distance between mother and infant extends further in the masculine case, as the father supposedly holds sway over a distant social sphere.

But I have anticipated too much on the direction of this argument. Enough for now that the second debate has, I have implied thus far, effectively reformulated the relation between masculinity and femininity in terms of identity. A similar reformulation is demanded by, although the discussion of it was neglected in, Freud's own theory of femininity.

FREUD'S LAST WORDS

In the context of Freud's own corpus, the connection between identity and his riddle of femininity needs to be established more carefully. We have help in making this connection in some of Freud's last words on the subject of femininity. In them, he refers to masculinity as 'completely ego-syntonic' [*ichgerecht*] in a way that femininity is not (1937, *GW*: 97–8, *SE*: 250–1). He makes this observation shortly before embarking on a discussion of why it is that the wish for a penis persists in women, and why the fear of taking a feminine, passive position in relation to another man should be so ineradicable in men. In a softening of earlier criticism of Adler, Freud writes that the man's fear is perfectly described by Adler's term, 'masculine protest'. He then makes the remark that has been so much quoted in contemporary discussions of Freud and femininity.

> We often have the impression that with the wish for a penis and the masculine protest we have penetrated through all the psychological strata and have reached bedrock. . . . This is probably true, since, for the psychical field, the biological field does in fact play the part of the underlying bedrock. The repudiation of femininity can be nothing else than a biological fact, a part of the great riddle of sex.
>
> (1937, *GW*: 99, *SE*: 252)

But in this context, that remark is not only interesting for the reasons it is usually quoted (viz. to illustrate Freud's ultimate appeal to biology). It is also significant because of the reiteration of the real riddle of femininity it contains. It is femininity in men that is the problem, whether it is their fear of femininity, or their penchant for its masochistic derivative. Moreover, and this returns me to the main thread, the discussion of the bedrock is preceded by one on the relation of sexual identity to repression, and of repression, as a quantitative concern, to the ego. Freud had always rejected Adler's (and as well, Jung's and Fliess's) attempt to 'sexualize' repression. By 'sexualizing repression', Freud meant making the motive force of repression the drive to repudiate one's femininity, in the man's case, and masculinity, in the woman's. As he argued at other points (especially 1919b) this logic does not explain masculinity in women, amongst other things. To sexualize repression is 'to explain it on biological grounds instead of purely psychological ones' (1937, *GW*: 98, *SE*: 251); it is to abandon the question of the psychical construction of masculinity and femininity, together with the relation of repression to the ego. Yet given Freud's belief that the biological grounds of the 'repudiation of femininity' are the ones that psychoanalysis cannot uproot, his emphasis falls on the actual difference between the sexes, as well as on the relation of repression to the ego.

To grasp why masculinity is 'completely ego-syntonic', we have to turn back a few chapters in 'Analysis Terminable and Interminable'. Freud is discussing the aim of psychoanalytic therapy, which is 'to replace repressions that are insecure by reliable ego-syntonic controls' (1937, *GW*: 73, *SE*: 229). In turn, this replacement is meant to put an end to the dominance of the quantitative factor: the strength of the drives and the strength of the ego's resistance to them. The ego that erects the repressions is involved in a permanent expenditure of energy, for its repressions 'behave like dams against the pressure of water' (1937, *GW*: 70, *SE*: 226). The water is the drives, the pressure their strength, and the ego's spending ability is restricted or enhanced by the factors we discussed in the Introduction (accidental shocks, other traumas, the constitutional strength of the drives). Masculinity is ego-syntonic because it does not involve a passive attitude. That is almost all Freud says. But the implication of his observation, i.e. that a passive attitude is not ego-syntonic, is that an active attitude is so. An active attitude is one in which the drives, as we shall see in more detail in the next chapters, are externally directed. In females, and this is where Freud implicitly turns to identity, it appears that 'the striving to be masculine' is only ego-syntonic

> at a certain period – namely, in the phallic phase before the development to femininity has set in. But it then succumbs to the momentous process of repression whose outcome, as has so often been shown, determines the fortunes of a woman's femininity.
>
> (1937, *GW*: 97, *SE*: 251)

As Freud has devoted a great deal of space in this particular text to demonstrating that an ego-syntonic attitude is the obverse of a pathological one, this means that femininity is indeed pathological. It also means, if the striving to be masculine is only ego-syntonic before 'the development to femininity has set in', that there is a conflict between a woman's ego and her active striving. We might say that to maintain her feminine identity psychically, she has to repress her activity. The next chapter will reveal that this conclusion marks the return of an old phantom. The notion that women had to repress activity to secure feminine identity was precisely the conclusion that Freud reached in his early work with Breuer on the pathology of hysteria, the quintessence of femininity. But this, once again, he appears to have forgotten.

Chapter 3

The division of attention

INTRODUCTION

Close to, or at, the point where a question on Freud's theory of femininity is being formulated, the discussion or debate which produced it folds or shifts its focus. The second debate had a brilliant beginning with Juliet Mitchell's *Psychoanalysis and Feminism*, which looked to Freud precisely for a theory of how a lady is made, and how her active strivings and intelligence are suppressed. It had major contributions from Nancy Chodorow and Luce Irigaray who, while they missed the riddle, did attempt to explain much of the phenomenology of disabling feminine characteristics. But the responses generated by their attempts usually took the form of criticism, which, however well-warranted, focused on theoretical unorthodoxies, rather than the need to explain femininity. This is not absolutely true; one thinks of the insights of Jessica Benjamin (1988), Jane Flax (1990), and the stunning explorations of Julia Kristeva (especially Kristeva [1987]). But it is generally true that the minute the real riddle of femininity is approached, the debates digress. The digression can take the form of invective against the *Penisneid* of Freud's critics; or polemic against Freud's patriarchal bias. It can take the form of apparent forgetfulness. Either way, the logical direction of the enquiry is diverted; attention is directed elsewhere.

At this point, one might well wonder if there is something in the nature or subject-matter of femininity that prompts the tendency to digress. This consideration might lead to a digression of our own, concerning the process whereby attention or direction are sustained, or diverted. But perhaps it is not, after all, much of a digression: the only moment when Freud concerned himself with the nature of attention is also the period when he was preoccupied with hysteria, when he believed in the analogy theory, and when psychical reality first became an issue. Freud turned to attention in the unpublished *Project for a Scientific Psychology*, the work written to address problems raised by the *Studies on Hysteria*.

According to Strachey, while 'attention' as a concept receives only a passing glance after its genesis in the *Project*, it resurfaces under the guise of reality-testing (1950b [1895]: 393) in Freud's 1911 theory of the ego. But it is worth retracing that genesis in detail, for the sake of understanding the concept of attention more clearly, and for other reasons besides.

First, perhaps it was less that Freud forgot about how active strivings were suppressed in hysteria, and more that he ceased to attend to the implications of his own early theory, especially that theory he wrote in collaboration with his early mentor, Josef Breuer. As I have indicated, Freud wrote the *Project* in order to explain the mechanism of repression in hysteria. This initial explanation was based on psychophysics, especially Fechner's psychophysics.[1] Despite the reduction of Freud's physicalist thinking to biologism (a reduction in which Freud also partook), his thinking about repression continued to be cast in physicalist terms. Repression, after all, involves an expenditure of energy; it is precisely a repressing force. In addition, it was in the *Project* that Freud made his

1 Freud's debts to Fechner's psychophysics have been credited, beginning with Freud himself (1925d, *GW*: 86, *SE*: 59). Freud referred to Fechner in the *Project*, where he mentions 'Fechner's Law' on the mathematical relation between the intensity of stimulation and the resultant sensation. Fechner's influence on Freud has been discussed by Jones (*Life*, vol. 1), Ellenberger (1970), and Sulloway (1979). Sulloway argues that Freud's debt to Fechner is less problematic than his debt to the so-called 'Helmholtz School' with whose 'mechanic materialism' Freud had to break (Sulloway 1979: 65ff). Sulloway also infers that 'perhaps most *directly*, the Breuer-theory of hysteria reflects the "Fechnerian School" of psychophysics far more than it does the long-since defunct "Helmholtz School" of biophysics' (Sulloway 1979: 67). Sulloway goes on to argue that Freud's original debt to a physicalist approach is displaced on to 'an organismic evolutionary or "biological" one': the latter approach was also evident at points in the *Project*, which Sulloway thinks contains the seeds of the biological, developmental point of view he discerns in Freud's theory (Sulloway 1979: 131 and *passim*). Two things need to be noted here. The first is that while Freud felt he could not make the *Project* explain repression in terms of quantities of energy and laws of motion (8 October 1895, *Letters*) the force of physicalist approaches continued to make itself felt, especially in Freud 1920a. The second point is more a reiteration of the suggestion made earlier: that psychophysics lent Freud the physical dimension he needed (quantity as an inescapable datum of psychical facts) without the evolutionary connotations of the biological model. As I have stressed at various points, the fact that so much of Freud's metapsychology relies on spatio-temporal considerations (the spatial topography, deferral in reality-testing, and the masculine Oedipus complex, deferred action, the timelessness of the unconscious and the fact, perhaps the main fact, that pathology is tied to the inability to extricate oneself from the past) cannot all be coincidence, but its formulation in terms of contemporary physics has not to my knowledge been attempted. However there was an early discussion in the *Psychoanalytic Quarterly* between Rado and Reiner on the idea that causality is a psychical construction. I return to this in my *History After Lacan*. The main point is that my discussion now is speculative. It trenches on territories in which there are substantial literatures, and comes to conclusions which could only be borne out through an evaluation based on those literatures. This chapter's argument on constructed inertia should return us to the physics of today, rather than Freud's day, but this is not something I can pursue at length. What I can do is point to how a re-evaluation is demanded by Freud's hidden logic, while noting that the conclusions Freud himself drew from psychophysics are a little like the old wishes of the unconscious that make themselves felt in the manner they were first experienced; his psychophysical conclusions continue to exert their time-bound influence, and their full bearing on the logic of his theory can be apparent only when they are examined.

most sustained attempt at thinking through the nature of psychical energy itself. It is now generally accepted that psychical energy cannot be the same thing as physical energy, in so far as the attributes of 'physical energy' and 'psychical energy', as Freud and his successors have described it, appear incommensurate (Shope 1971).[2] But this general acceptance does not dispose of the fact of psychical energy. 'Theory is all very well', as Freud said in one of his favourite, often repeated quotations from Charcot, 'but it does not stop things from existing' (for example, Freud 1905a: 115). It does not stop the fact that depression is tiring, or that an analytical insight can produce exhaustion, or that the ego's rigidity can produce sleeplessness, or that one's temper can explode. The fact that psychical energy exists and has physical effects remains to be explained.

I would hazard that without exception, all the attempts at theorizing psychical energy are constrained by the notion that this energy is contained within the boundaries of the subject. They make no allowance for the possibility that psychical energy is something that works between as well as within distinct individual beings. If that possibility is allowed, the internal inconsistencies in the attempts at theorizing psychical energy and its relation to physical energy begin to be resolved. Some of the reasons for this should be clearer by the end of this chapter.

In addition, although attention, thinking, and intellectual judgement matter in Freud's later work on reality-testing ('thinking', wrote Freud, 'is a kind of experimental action') these are not the features of reality-testing that spring to mind when that controversial concept is evoked. This is not to say that Strachey is wrong about the connection between attention and reality-testing. I think he is very right. But what needs to be drawn out is that attention itself is a form of psychophysical energy, and this, together with an elucidation of Freud's early theories concerning the suppression of women's activity, can best be done by returning to Freud's early work, and to his collaboration with, and divergence from, Josef Breuer.

In the next section (pp. 86–101) I turn to the *Studies on Hysteria* (focusing on Freud and Breuer's collaboration, and Breuer's famous case study of Anna O.). This discussion will draw out the significance of visualization in relation to symptom formation, and suggest how visualization is tied to the 'freezing' of affect and paralysis that can characterize hysteria through the mechanism of attention. It will draw these things out in a discussion of the interplay between phantasy, especially conscious phantasy or daydreams, and a material reality that may or may not allow

2 Shope's article, which is the best I have found on the energy question, is limited because it takes a 'one-body' psychology as its point of departure. It does not consider the psychical energetic interaction between individuals as a possible means of resolving some of the inconsistencies it points to between the concepts of psychical and physical energy. In an extended discussion, the suppositions in this chapter could be shown to constitute a critique of Shope.

for creative outlets for activity. The third section (pp. 101–7) focuses on Freud's divergence from Breuer; the fourth (pp. 107–19) turns to the *Project*. Discussion of the *Project* shows how the illusion of a self-contained boundaried identity, cut off from psychophysical energetic connections, comes into being through a peculiar construction of inertia. Other common threads in this discussion are the role of language in symptom formation, and how Freud's later theory of anxiety and its relation to repression was anticipated in his early work. However, the critical contribution of this, and the preceding section, bears on the physicality of ideas, and physics, as Freud did and did not understand it.

The fifth section (pp. 119–34) takes Freud's Metapsychological paper on repression as its departure point. This leads into further discussion of language, and the different roles played by different forms of attention in masculinity and health, and femininity and pathology. It also leads to a reconsideration of the excessive repression that characterizes femininity, and its connection with the defence mechanisms that characterize the girl's relation to her mother. The concept of phantasy, critical in hysteria, helps make this connection. Phantasy is the key to how the repressed activity that characterizes femininity is 'turned back against itself', to borrow a phrase used by Freud to describe one of the drives' vicissitudes. The nature of this turning-back will have been clarified in the section on attention, phantasy and hysteria, where the direction of attention is discussed. I will also suggest that the point to this backward-turning is a kind of 'secondary gain' for the subject in terms of maintaining identity. Nor is it only feminine identity that benefits. Masculine identity also finds its bearings in terms of what it projects on to the woman in phantasy, and it is this gain and all it entails that makes it prone to forgetfulness.

THE *STUDIES ON HYSTERIA*

The *Studies on Hysteria* consists of a 'Preliminary Communication', written jointly by Freud and Breuer, five case histories (four of them Freud's), and two theoretical addenda, separately written by Freud and Breuer. In their joint communication, they explain hysteria mainly in terms of a forgotten 'psychical trauma' and the failure of abreaction following it. Abreaction, the discharge of an emotional affect by some fitting means (for instance, tears for grief; or anger, in the form of a physical blow, or a satisfying verbal rejoinder in the case of insult), allowed the otherwise 'strangulated affect' to be released. Affect could also be dealt with by means of the wearing-away afforded by speech (confiding and confessions) in critical association. The last named is the process whereby an idea is brought into conscious association with other ideas, and, with the aid of the 'critical' faculties, modified accordingly. (Actually Freud and Breuer term this process 'association' or 'associative communication'. I have attached the adjective 'critical' because 'association' in psychoanalysis has come to mean free association.)

By critical association, a mortified man can re-establish his self-respect. He can contrast the occasion of his mortification with others which affirm his worth. But if he is unable to do this, or, more generally, if none of the wearing away processes occurs, or occurs adequately, an hysterical symptom may result. In short there are two main means of wearing away the affects and effects of the memories and phantasies that lead to the formation of symptoms. The first is speech. The second is some form of emotional release or energetic, quantitative discharge.

It may be significant that Freud and Breuer imply in passing that the action of time in wearing away feeling is not due to any inherent property of time, but to the fact that the passage of time allows for more abreaction (see Freud with Breuer 1895b, GW: 87, SE: 8). Yet it should be added that when there is no abreaction, one stays in the past in so far as one remains unconsciously attached to the memory that otherwise fades. That memory (or phantasy) continues to attract a cathexis to itself. The concept of cathexis (*Besetzung*) (see p. 67), which makes its published debut in the *Studies*, is critical to Freud's economic theory.[3] In fact Freud's economic thinking is basic to the whole conceptual armature of the *Studies*, although the concept of abreaction itself drops from Freud's, and most subsequent, psychoanalytic thinking.[4]

Freud and Breuer adduced that the failure of abreaction, or the 'abreaction' consequent on talk or critical association, was at issue in hysteria by reasoning backwards, from the circumstances under which they were able to make hysterical symptoms disappear. They found first, that the symptoms were prompted by memories which retained their full affective and sensory force because they had not been abreacted. Second, that the symptoms disappeared when the memory of the unabreacted event or feeling which prompted them had come to light, and 'when the patient had described that event in the greatest possible detail and put the affect into words' (1895b, GW: 85, SE: 6). This was the 'cathartic method'.

Freud and Breuer outline two sets of conditions in which a memory persists due to the failure of abreaction, acting 'like a foreign body' in the system. In the first set, elaborated by Freud, the memory itself is significant; the trauma can be 'intentionally repressed' (1895b, GW: 89, SE: 110–11). In the second set, promulgated by Breuer, the memory or idea matters less

3 It also appears in the *Project*. While Freud first developed the concept in the context of the neurone system he put forward in the *Project*, he retained it after he abandoned his attempts to locate psychical energy in the *Project*'s anatomical terms.

4 This is probably because the concept of abreaction was taken out of context and made the cornerstone of Wilhelm Reich's orgasmic version of psychoanalysis (Reich 1970). Unfortunately, Reich's biological theory obscured the significant grains of truth in Freud and Breuer's original account: that is to say, it obscured the idea that emotional discharge has a beneficial effect.

than the affective circumstances in which it occurred. Ideas may persist because 'they originated during the presence of severely paralysing affects, such as fright, or during positively abnormal psychical states, such as the semi-hypnotic twilight state of daydreaming, auto-hypnoses, and so on' (1895b, *GW*: 89–90, *SE*: 11). These memories are not significant in themselves, but become so because they originate in a 'hypnoid state' which precludes abreaction, and thus they retain their intensity.

While the key concept in the first set of conditions, repression, was to become the foundation stone of Freud's theory, the second set of conditions, the 'hypnoid state', from which Freud took his distance even in the *Studies*, has been relegated to the archive of dead ideas. From there I wish to resurrect it. Not because it is in any sense a better or, for that matter, coherent explanation of hysteria, but for these related reasons. First, paradoxically, the hypnoid state theory will cast light on the workings of repression. It will do this through a somewhat discursive discussion of attention, for which I enjoin the reader's patience in advance. Second, two vital ingredients of the hypnoid state theory survive in Freud's corpus. One is the role of anxiety in freezing motion or activity. The other critical ingredient is daydreaming, which I shall discuss first, as it brings the economy of attention to the fore.

The idea that daydreaming is harmful, and a potential index of pathology, survives in more substantive if underappreciated forms in Freud's thought.[5] It survives in spite of Freud's subsequent thorough repudiation of Breuer's hypnoid state theory.[6] There are references to 'harmful daydreaming' in *The Interpretation of Dreams*, where Freud published his 'first topography'. And daydreaming is opposed to intentionally *directed* thinking as late as 1921. In his preface to Varendonck's *The Psychology of Daydreams*[7] Freud argued that daydreams should be counterposed to

5　Perhaps Freud's stress on the idea that daydreaming is harmful is nowhere better borne out than in his letters to his daughter, Anna, in which he tells her she daydreams too much, and advises her to desist. See Young-Bruehl (1988).

6　A year after the *Studies* he 'definitely repudiated' the concept of hypnoid states; 'by 1900 it had become "that unfortunate idea that had been forced on me"', and in the next year a "superfluous and misleading idea" ', *Life*, vol. 1: 301.

7　Dr J. Varendonck's *The Psychology of Daydreams* meticulously records a series of the author's daydreams, miming Freud's recording of his own dreams in *The Interpretation*. The story of this book, which the author wrote in the trenches during the First World War having lost an earlier thesis, is fascinating in itself. 'The post [as an interpreter] for which I had volunteered in the army allowed me to remain most of the time at a distance of a few miles from the firing-line, so that I could devote all my leisure to writing another thesis' (Varendonck 1921: 26)(!). The book is a rare contribution to a neglected topic. It was translated into German by Anna Freud in 1922, a year before she published an article, 'The Relation of Beating-Phantasies to a Day-dream', to which we will return. Anna Freud's article acknowledges a debt to Lou Andreas-Salomé, also interested in the topic of daydreams. It seems this topic concerned the first generation of women analysts more than their publications indicate (cf. Young-Bruehl 1988). Karl Abraham also discussed daydreams in his *Ueber hysterische Traumzustände*. Incidentally, Freud first used the word *Phantasien* in the *Studies on Hysteria*.

intentionally directed reflection (1921b, *GW*: 440, *SE*: 272).[8] Conscious daydreams or phantasies also figure in Freud's 1911 theory of the ego. There,
daydreaming represents the retreat from painful reality; it is the recourse
of the subject who is unable to change reality by acting upon it.[9]

Here, we can note one aspect of that retreat from reality which is lost
in the 1911 theory, but which features in the *Studies on Hysteria*. This is
the role played by social circumstance. Before proceeding to discuss this,
I should stress that I do not want to reduce either femininity or hysteria
to those social circumstances. The object in showing how daydreams
facilitate hysteria is to draw out certain aspects of Freud's early theory
which present us with a prototype of a pathological femininity which can
either be reinforced or negated by social realities. It is not intended to
disguise or obscure the internal psychical dynamics by which any ego can
linger in phantasy. Rather, it is intended to contribute to understanding,
without claiming to explain on social grounds alone, Freud's observation
that women's sexuality 'lingers' in phantasy in a way that men's does not
(1912d). Indeed, the fact that the psychical and social picture is more
complex will also emerge from this discussion of the *Studies*. It will do
this when we come to the significance of attention and visualization in
the formation of symptoms, for it is this that casts light on the 'failure to
abreact' as a tie to the past.

In the first instance, social reality features in the 'Preliminary Communication' in the *Studies* in an aside on the origin of hypnoid states. For
the purposes of the 'Preliminary Communication', despite his subsequent
repudiation of the hypnoid state idea, Freud is in temporary agreement
with Breuer. They write:

8 Apart from the implications of 'intentionally directed reflection' for this book's argument
  on the significance of direction in femininity and Freud's metapsychology, Freud's remarks
  on Varendonck are also interesting because they are consistent with another idea: daydreams as conscious phantasies and unconscious phantasies are closely connected, separated
  only by the fact that the contents of the former are thinly disguised versions of unconscious
  phantasies. When Freud discussed unconscious phantasy he described it as closely connected to daydreaming, or conscious phantasy (Freud 1908a). Conscious and unconscious
  phantasies can follow the same logic; the point is that neither is intentionally directed.
  However we shall see later in this section that this demarcation between intentionally
  directed reflection and daydreams is insufficient, for daydreams can be intentionally
  directed. At the same time, the fact that the distinction between consciousness and unconsciousness is largely irrelevant where daydreams are concerned fits with this argument, as
  does Freud's belief that unconscious thought can also be intentionally directed, a belief
  that accords with the notion that repression is intentional. According to Laplanche and
  Pontalis, Freud (1900) shows that the structure of daydreams is comparable to that of
  dreams in that both are compromise-formations. They write: 'Freud presents phantasy as
  a unique focal point where it is possible to observe the process of transition between the
  different psychical systems in vitro – to observe the mechanism of repression or of the
  return of the repressed in action' (Laplanche and Pontalis 1983: 316–17). This is their
  interpretation of Freud's remark that 'Phantasies draw near to consciousness and remain
  undisturbed so long as they do not have an intense cathexis, but as soon as they exceed
  a certain height of cathexis they are thrust back' (1915e, *GW*: 290, *SE*: 191).
9 See chapter 4, pp. 158–69.

[Hypnoid states] often, it would seem, grow out of the day-dreams which are so common even in healthy people and to which needlework and similar occupations render women especially prone.

(1895b, *GW*: 92, *SE*: 13)

For Freud, these 'similar occupations' include simple boredom. Freud agrees with Breuer that daydreaming is harmful to the extent that he avoids a Weir-Mitchell[10] 'rest cure' for one of his patients, as daydreams afflict those who are bored (1895b, *GW*: 266, *SE*: 267). Breuer's own account of 'similar occupations' and their relation to hypnoid states is far more developed, which is appropriate, given that daydreams are essentially his concern. He writes that daydreams occur especially in those looking after someone close to them who is ill, and those in love (1895b: 233–4).

Of course the question that comes to mind is this: If daydreaming is exacerbated when sick-nursing or in love, is there a factor common to both occupations which predisposes one towards daydreaming?[11] On the face of it, sick-nursing and the state of being in love have in common the fact that in both one is preoccupied with another, without this preoccupation involving commensurate action, or the full concentration of attention. We will return to this, concentrating for now on the 'social reality' of sick-nursing, which figures largely both in the case of Fräulein von R., and in the most famous of the case histories, that of Anna O. Like Freud's patient, Elisabeth von R., Breuer's celebrated patient, Anna O. (whom Freud credited with the invention of the 'talking cure' and who under her real name, Bertha Pappenheim, was to be a women's rights campaigner) acquired her hysteria nursing at her father's sick-bed. In fact, of the five case studies, I concentrate on these two. For my purposes they are the most interesting. Both Elisabeth von R. and 'Anna O.' lived lives which in Bertha Pappenheim's words were 'typical of a *höhere Tochter*' (a middle-class daughter of marriageable age). Pappenheim's mentor, Alice Salomon, who preceded the former in social work in Germany endured a similar upbringing. She described it thus:

The unhappiest years of my life were between the ages of fifteen and twenty.... I danced a lot.... We were among the first ... to play tennis ... but there were twenty-four hours in a day ... the life of a *höhere Tochter* was unbearable.[12]

10 Weir-Mitchell was a popular nineteenth-century psychiatrist whose 'rest cure', prescribed, amongst others, for Charlotte Perkins Gilman, consisted of sleeping a great deal, eating as much as possible, and reading and thinking not at all. See Ellenberger (1970) for a less tendentious account.

11 The state of being in love features in only one of the five women studied (Miss Lucy N.) although repressed love is inferred in the case of another, Fräulein Elisabeth von R.

12 Quoted in Kaplan (1984: 105). As Kaplan notes, it was Salomon who founded the field of modern social work in Germany. Accordingly, Jones is wrong in stating that Bertha Pappenheim was the first German social worker. But she was a first in one respect, in founding the *Jüdischer Frauenbund*, and certainly an active leader in the social work field; the *Frauenbund* established homes for young Jewish women in need of refuge.

Both Anna O. and Elisabeth von R. were unable to develop their executive capacities in reality; in this respect their case histories bear on the question of the ego's relation to reality and the effects of being unable to act on it. Yet only in Anna O.'s case is this limitation associated with daydreaming, even though sick-nursing is prominent in both aetiologies. In fact if we turn to the analysis of the genesis and course of the two hysterias, we can find a significant divergence. Where Breuer focuses on daydreams, Freud focuses on sexual affect. Where Breuer focuses on the implications of being unable to act on reality for psychical structure (we could say, for the ego, or identity as we will eventually define it), Freud focuses on the implications for sexuality. In one respect this divergence reflects their different emphases on repression and the hypnoid state; Freud's position follows on logically from his distinctive argument in the *Studies*. In another respect, Freud's focus on sexuality is the first instance of what is to become a pattern, in which he consistently analyses psychical conflicts in women in terms of their sexuality, as distinct from their ego structure. This is so despite the fact that in addition to the role of the daydream, many of the terms and concepts employed by Breuer return in the *Project* and enter into Freud's theory of the ego.

Here, let us stay with the first of the two case histories. As Breuer describes it, Anna O. manifested two distinct personalities. One was coherent. The other was dissociated with symptoms that would today be called psychotic. One was kind, sympathetic, and very intelligent. The other was emotionally impoverished and mean. With the desire to explain this dual personality in mind, Breuer begins by stressing that Anna O.'s 'powerful intellect' was without the food it needed. This 'absence of adequate intellectual occupation' together with her monotonous family life led to daydreaming, her 'private theatre' (1895b: 21 and 1895b: 41). When Breuer elaborates on why Anna O.'s monotonous family life and inadequate intellectual occupation led to daydreaming, thence to hypnoid states and hysteria, he does so in terms of her 'surplus of mental liveliness and energy' (1895b: 41). The link is made in terms that Freud will subsequently style 'economic'. Actually two links are made here. The first is a general one, made in terms of energy. The second concerns mental liveliness. The notion that intellection itself works on an economic model has not been remarked, but it becomes more remarkable and more comprehensible if attention itself is understood as a form of psychophysical energy.

Turning here to the more general argument on energy. Anna O. has a surplus of energy, but the reason for this, according to Breuer, is that less energy is used in daydreams. His argument is complicated.

A great variety of states lead to 'absence of mind' but only a few of them predispose to auto-hypnosis or pass over immediately into it. An investigator who is deep in a problem is also no doubt anaesthetic to a certain degree, and he has large groups of sensations of which he forms no conscious perception; and the same is true of anyone who is using his creative imagination actively (cf. Anna O.'s private theatre [p. 22]). But in such states energetic mental work is carried on, and the excitation of the nervous system which is liberated is used up in this work. In states of abstraction and dreaminess, on the other hand, intracerebral excitation sinks below its clear waking level. These states border on sleepiness and pass over into sleep. If during such a state of absorption, and while the flow of ideas is inhibited, a group of affectively-coloured ideas is active, it creates a high level of intracerebral excitation which is not used up by mental work and is at the disposal of abnormal functioning, such as conversion.

(1895b: 218)

But for daydreams to use less energy in a way that is counter-productive three things need to happen. The daydream needs to be charged with affect, either sexual affect or the care and sorrow (leading to anxiety) accompanying sick-nursing. Second, the flow of ideas involved in the daydream needs to stagnate. Because Breuer assumes a zero/sum quantitative theory in arguing it (see, for example, 1895b: 238) he is able to tie the notion that less energy is used in a daydream to the formation of pathology in the form of the hysterical symptom. It is fuelled by the energy aroused by the subject-matter of the daydream, energy that is unemployed in the motor activity accompanying it. Third, there has to be a duplication of psychical functioning, although Breuer is confusing when it comes to saying precisely what the duplication of psychical functioning involves. He wishes to argue that it results in a split consciousness, or dual consciousness, and thereby to explain the two distinct personalities Anna O. manifests. It is this wish that led to his insistence on the priority of hypnoid states in the formation of hysterical symptoms, and ultimately, to his divergence from Freud.

But consider the reason Breuer gives as to why sick-nursing and being in love predispose us to daydreaming. It is the intensification of preoccupation, and the 'simultaneous existence of changing impressions and reactions from external life on the one hand, and an affectively-coloured group of ideas on the other' (1895b: 234). If one asks, once more, what this 'simultaneous existence' involves, it has to involve attention *to* something, rather than consciousness in general. More precisely, it has to involve some attention to visual, auditory, and other sensory phenomena in reality. It also has to involve attention to auditory or linguistic representations and visual images in phantasy.

Anticipating a little, and reading between the lines, the duplication of psychical functioning consists of a duplication or a division of *attention*, rather than consciousness. If I am privately attending to one thing, but observably doing another, which I attend to only as much as I have to, then at one level my mental capacity for action and my capacity for thought are divorced. In Freud's theory my capacity for thought is part of my equipment for testing reality. My mental capacity also helps me test it, and it can help me change it, in conjunction with my capacity for action. In the duplication of psychical functioning, it appears that a large part of thought is divorced from action. Yet this appearance may be misleading. What if it is the case that the capacities for thought and action are so intertwined that one always implicates the other (an idea that ultimately bears on the physicality of ideas, although this is not the immediate concern)? It is part of the received wisdom of psychoanalysis that no action is accidental. Action has some thought, however unconscious, in its parapractic train. By the same token, if we suppose that thought has some part of the capacity for action in tow, then in the case of daydreams it would not only be attention that turns inwards, towards a private theatre. It would also be some part of the capacity for action. One can then suggest that if this inward-turning of attention is part of the capacity for activity in general, it would result in a diminution of that capacity. Or rather, one can say, if that capacity is turned inwards, if it is an act of force in itself, its effects will make themselves felt energetically, in anything from depression through to paralysis. These suggestions can be kept in mind while more arguments for them are laid out.

Returning to Breuer's thread of reasoning, the word 'attention' is avoided by him, except where it is completely unavoidable.[13] This may be due to Breuer's (and Freud's) desire to distance themselves from Janet's notion of an *insuffisance psychologique* (Janet 1901: 230). Janet himself, although Breuer does not refer to this, formulates the phenomenon in question as a disorder of attention. The *insuffisance psychologique* leads to a splitting of consciousness because the ideas which are not attended to by the patient accumulate in another stratum of the mind. According to Breuer, Janet sees hysterics as suffering from a basic psychological weakness in which 'Every idea takes possession of the whole of their limited mental activity' (1895b: 230). Now it is one thing to say, as Janet does, that 'the splitting of consciousness occurs because the patients are weakminded', and another to say with Breuer that 'they appear to be weakminded because their mental activity is divided and only a part of its capacity is at the disposal of conscious thought' (1895b: 231). But the second proposition would be enhanced by the formula that it is their attention that is divided. Even if this brings one close to Janet's formulation, it remains true that for Janet a psychological insufficiency causes the division, while for Breuer the division causes the insufficiency. In sum, both here and elsewhere, if one enquires as to what 'divided mental activity' consists of, attention has to be a large part of the answer.

13 As for instance in a reference to Exner (1895b: 195).

There is another point that needs to be made about Breuer's analysis. I noted that the daydream needs to be charged with affect leading to anxiety. Yet while the 'Preliminary Communication' gives severely paralysing affects and semi-hypnotic twilight states as alternatives, in the relevant case study itself, that of Anna O., the semi-hypnotic twilight state of daydreaming and a severely paralysing affect coincide.

> It seems certain that with her the auto-hypnosis had the way paved for it by habitual reveries and that *it was fully established by an affect of protracted anxiety*, which, indeed, would itself be the basis for a hypnoid state. It seems not improbable that this process holds good fairly generally.
>
> (1895b: 217–18; emphasis added)

The unclarity here – is it the hypnoid state or the affect that does the freezing? – should be noted. So should the fact that in Freud and Breuer's temporary agreement on a hypnoid state, its defining characteristic is that because either the hypnoid state or the affect associated with it freezes abreaction, ideas or images concurrent or contiguous with each other in a hypnoid state become significant. So that if an image of a tree coincides with an intense emotional experience, trees may figure in a later symptom not by virtue of being trees, but by the sheer proximity to the significant experience.

Analysis by contiguity can be read as a survival of nineteenth-century associationist psychology. It fits the model or underlying assumptions that gave birth to the hypnoid state theory, and (this is especially interesting) as it does so, it shows that a memory becomes significant as a symptom because it is contiguous with something that focuses attention on a part of the body. To take a further example, Anna O.'s right arm becomes rigidly extended when she sees some object, for instance, a tree branch, with a more or less snake-like shape. Breuer explains the origin of her symptom this way:

> She fell into a waking dream and saw a black snake coming towards [her sick father] to bite him. . . . She tried to keep the snake off, but it was as though she were paralysed. Her right arm, over the back of the chair, had gone to sleep and had become anaesthetic and paretic.
>
> (1895b: 38)

In Breuer's and Freud's terms, the waking dream (presumably a hypnoid state) would be significant if it curtailed the affective response to the snake hallucination. But once again, the hypnoid state and anxiety, or an emotion belonging to the same family, coincide. In this instance Anna O. was frightened, and fright (a member of the anxiety family) was included in the list of affects that precluded abreaction. But in this case, the process of symptom formation in the form of hysterical paralysis also involves catching two contiguous happenings in the same frame of association.[14] And when they are caught, I have inferred that the capture is effected by attention, a form of attention that is allied with fright.[15] Breuer, as we have seen, numbered anxiety amongst the paralysing affects. ('Fright paralyses outright *the power of movement* as well as of association [of ideas], and so does anxiety if the single useful reaction of running away is excluded by the cause of the affect of anxiety or by circumstances' (1895b: 202 emphases added).)

What this means, in Breuer's example, is that the alliance between attention and fright depends on visualization. In fact, both real visual observation and sensory visual hallucination are involved in the contiguous freeze-frame. It is the attentive capacity to see and the capacity to imagine (another, more self-directed form of attention) that effect the contiguous capture. So we can say more than that the capture is effected by attention. We can say it is effected by two forms of visual attention, one being the moving attention to the present, the other being the attention frozen in hallucination. Moreover the attention frozen in hallucination, while it may move into its fixed position along the path of a daydream, becomes unconscious: the frozen hallucination has to be brought back to consciousness via the route of recollection.

How is it then that attention takes these different forms? And really, if we take account of the type of attention that is diverted in daydreams, we have to consider three forms of attention. But is it right to give these three 'forms' the name of attention? Why not, indeed, reserve the name consciousness for the attention split in daydreams and the attention directed towards the moving present, and unconsciousness for what I have described as fixed or frozen attention? For instance, Breuer, when he talks of the result of the duplication of psychical functioning, speaks of a splitting of consciousness, and uses this to account for Anna O.'s two personalities. The answer is that attention, at least in the reading I have given it here, allows for more conceptual flexibility. It allows one to think of psychophysical energy in terms that follow similar unconscious and conscious paths. Just as Freud insisted that there was a structural homology between unconscious phantasies and daydreams, I want to argue that there

14 The question of how hysterical symptoms are formed by contiguity was one Freud himself tackled in a subsequent paper on hysteria (cf. Freud, with Breuer, 1895b: 241). On a symbolic reading, Anna O.'s arm might refer to a conflict over sexual identity in which it expressed her own claims to a masculine potency at the same time as it protested her feminine impotence. The snake crawling to bite her father is also loaded with clichéd phallic symbolism, but may none the less be relevant for all that. (Not only did Breuer note that the 'sexual factor' was underdeveloped in Anna O.; Freud lamented the fact that any sexual bearing of her aetiology was never explored.)
15 One can even wonder if the anxiety family consists of varying degrees of paralysing attention. Cf. Cannon [1929] who discusses this in one of the last great syntheses in biology, before that science collapsed, like psychology, under the weight of accumulated discrete experiments.

is a similar structural homology in the workings of attention at the conscious and unconscious levels.

But before that, let us consider why conscious attention is preferable to consciousness as a concept. While consciousness, as a form of psychical energy, is neither active nor passive in its connotations, attention connotes an active deployment of psychophysical energy, or rather is an act of deployment of that energy. If I attend with all my being, when I am engaged in 'consciously directed thought', inexorably I grow more tired. Yet this notion of active deployment is not quite accurate, in terms of the two types of conscious attention sketched thus far. Active deployment is associated with the moving observation and motility that are dissociated from daydreams, precisely because activity is associated with externality. On the other hand, as Freud put it in discussing femininity, 'a great deal of activity can be directed towards a passive aim' and it will be recalled that Helene Deutsch characterized femininity as activity turned inwards. Presumably, she meant that it could be turned inwards consciously as well as unconsciously.

Here we have our clue. It is the *direction* of attention, the fact that attention is inevitably directed somewhere, that properly differentiates it from consciousness. (Not for nothing did Freud advise analysts to suspend their attention, rather than their consciousness(!), in order to conduct analysis (Freud 1913d, 1914a).) The notion that direction differentiates attention from consciousness becomes more significant when we take account of the five senses. If we ask, How are we conscious? or, How do we attend?, the answer is through smelling, touch, hearing, taste and sight. This answer, of course, means that the difference between how we attend and how we perceive also becomes an issue, for the five senses, traditionally, are means for sensory perception. But the question of perception raises identical problems to those raised by the question of consciousness; that is to say, it raises the question of whether perception is active or passive, and to raise this question is once more to single out direction as the key factor, and to single out attention as the faculty that embodies it. In fact, that last sentence is revealing in itself: it is precisely attention that embodies direction, for it is this that can be turned inwards, turned outwards, fixed, or abstracted.

In support of the idea that it is the direction of conscious attention, or the fact that it is the direction embodied in attention, that properly differentiates it from consciousness, we can note something that will not have escaped the reader who is an inveterate daydreamer, or a careful student of Anna O. This is that the construction of a 'private theatre' involves a great deal of consciously directed thought, and that Freud's characterization of daydreams as lacking direction is therefore insufficient. Daydreams do indeed flourish in a climate where there is little outwardly directed conscious attention, but daydreams can also be consciously directed internal theatres. It is simply that attention is directed inwards, and is emotive and affective, not detached. But the question as to why direction goes different ways, or how attention is directed one way or the other, remains.

Yet we may already have begun to answer this question. If attention is also deployed unconsciously in a frozen contiguous event, an imaginary hallucination, this attention is fixed, precisely because the hallucination is frozen. It does not move from its anchorage in the past; it is divorced from the associative connections between ideas. If one thinks about it, a fixed point of reference is essential to establishing any direction; there can be no direction unless it is direction to or away from something, and that 'something' has to be fixed. The attention frozen in unconscious hallucination would constitute this fixed point, from which attention could be directed either way.[16] However the premiss of this fixity is precisely that the hallucination stays unconscious. In Freud's terms, this means it stays repressed. Anticipating more discussion, I posit that the first frozen or repressed hallucination constitutes the joint foundation of the unconscious and psychical reality. In other words, it constitutes the first fixed still point from which the subject-to-be gets its directional bearings, from which attention can flow inwards (in subsequent repression and day-dreams), or in the moving forms of directed thought and outward motility.

But having introduced this reference to hallucination in relation to a discussion of daydreams and the direction of attention, both the similarities, as well as the differences, between *conscious* hallucinations and day-dreams should now be discussed. This will enable us to begin elucidating some of the critical spatial and temporal factors in psychical life. Conscious hallucinations, and daydreams (as described by Breuer) have three things in common. First, daydreams, like hallucinations, provide instant

16 If directed attention works unconsciously as well as consciously, we have solved the problem as to what constitutes the force of repression (see pp. 107, 113), as distinct from the motives for repression. Freud is explicit about motives, in that his list of the 'repressive forces' as disgust, shame and morality in Draft K (1896) of Freud 1950a [1892–9] (Extracts from the Fliess Papers) reads like a list of motives, rather than energetic forces. Yet even this may be only a superficial difference. This paragraph began with a discussion of the five senses, and two of the motive forces for repression listed by Freud are tied to these senses: disgust has an oral/gustatory connection; shame is notoriously tied to sight. In turn, this raises the question as to how far the senses themselves are shaped by directed attention (and vice versa) a question that can be best discussed after the dissection of Freud's theory of the drives (chapter 4), drives that are well known as oral, anal, phallic, and scopophilic. How paralysing these are is a question that can also be better considered after discussing Freud's *Three Essays* in chapter 4. Meantime, what I have argued about the equivalence of active, directed perception and attention (and the idea that attention is direction) is confirmed in Freud's discussion in the *Project* of how the sense organs that are capable of being closed are closed in sleep. 'Perceptions should not be made during sleep, and nothing disturbs sleep more than the emergence of sense-impressions. . . . This seems to indicate that during day-time a constant, even though displaceable, cathexis (attention) is sent into the . . . neurones which receive perception' (1950b: 337).

gratification. Second, daydreams, like hallucinations, lead to an unproductive accumulation of excitations (as Freud will argue in the *Project*). Third, daydreaming, like an hallucination involves a disorder of attention, although this likeness between daydreams and hallucinations is not as obvious as the first two. It needs to be drawn out.

We have seen that daydreaming involves a duplication of psychical functioning, in which attention is divided. Attention works by way of the senses, and in this, cannot be distinguished from perception in an active sense. That is to say, while perception, like consciousness, can be undirected (or 'passive'), when one actively focuses or actively listens, one is directing attention to seeing or listening. In a daydream, there is no disorder of attention in the way there is when an hallucination is taken for reality, in that there is no disorder of perception. One knows a daydream is not real. It is not confused with present reality, in the way that a conscious hallucination can be. Daydreams have the psychical advantage over hallucinations in that they are aware of what is and what is not present. They have acquired, so to speak, a sense of time.

Yet in that they involve more than a straightforward distinction between memory and anticipation (the recollection of the past and an awareness of the future, or indeed a reasonable, if imagined, prediction of the future), this sense of time is not tied to reality. In fact, it is often the completely unlikely phantasies of the future they entertain that marks daydreams as unrealistic.

Given that daydreams involve more than memory and present perception, given that they have a sense of time, we have to ask by what means do they remove themselves from the present and present perception? The answer has to be, they depend on a capacity for abstraction. This capacity can be deployed in unrealistic or realistic ways, but it is none the less a capacity which knows about time. So the essential difference between the disorder of attention in daydreams, and that in hallucinations, is that the former does not involve a disorder of perception, where a present hallucination is taken for present fact. We might say that the disorder of attention in daydreams is of a different spatio-temporal order. It involves a redirection of attention inwards (or a suspension of or division in active attention directed outwards), away from the present, but not a loss of the sense of what is and is not present in time, although daydreams can also encapsulate the tie to the past of unconscious phantasy. On the other hand hallucination is directed outwards, and does involve a loss of what is and is not the case in present time. Of course, to say that hallucination is directed outwards is also to say that it has a spatial aspect, but the bearing of this spatial aspect is that it abolishes time. Daydreams and abstraction do not. Hallucination also takes over space in a more dramatic way. A daydream occupies a smaller, internal pictorial frame, and leaves the spatial perspective of external reality intact; an hallucination is writ large, out there.

What then of the unconscious version of these processes? I want to propose that when an hallucination is repressed, constituting a fixed point, there is no difference between it and an unconscious phantasy. As a repressed daydream is also an unconscious phantasy, as we have seen, this indicates that there are two levels of unconscious phantasy: one primal, the other secondary.[17] The second level of unconscious phantasy also operates at a different spatio-temporal level, but further discussion of the spatio-temporal factors has to be bracketed for the moment, lest the especial emphasis on visualization in the foregoing discussion is neglected. Hallucinations and daydreams are frequently visual. Even when an hallucination is unconsciously repressed, it is still an image. The thinking in pictures characteristic of the hysteric, 'the visual type', deserves more investigation. This emphasis is by no means only Breuer's preoccupation. Anna O.'s 'private theatre', a pre-eminently visual affair, has echoes throughout the *Studies*. Freud notes at other points in them that hysterics are mainly 'visual types' (1895b, *GW*: 174, *SE*: 119 and 1895b, *GW*: 282, *SE*: 280). They reproduce memories of hallucinatory vividness (1895b, *GW*: 87, *SE*: 9) describing the *scenes* of memories 'vividly and in colours' (1895b, *GW*: 107, *SE*: 35). Nor is Anna O.'s private theatre the only instance of the theatrical metaphor for different forms of visual psychical activity in the psychoanalytic literature. Freud of course spoke of the *andere Schauplatz*, commonly translated as the 'other scene' (and literally, the other showplace) of psychical reality. And in an altogether other context, Jung observed that frequently in the dreams of women there appeared the figure of the cinema-operator, reeling scenes through a camera.[18] The 'other showplace' of dreams is the place where repressed hallucinations are on temporary parole. But the unconscious cinema-operator is remarkably like the impresario conducting daydreams.

In this connection, it is worth noting Freud's paper 'Hysterical Phantasies and their Relation to Bisexuality' (1908a). This has been commented on in recent feminist literature; it is meant to illustrate how the 'subject-position' of the hysteric can shift around.[19] In fact it shows something more precise than this: it shows that there are two positions. In one the hysteric is the visual object of the phantasy. In the other she is the impresario conducting it. The impresario, the subject, has, as indicated already, the capacity for directing the action, but this action is not directed outwards towards reality, as it is in the case of the deferring ego. It is directed inwards. Moreover, more importantly, the cinema-operator has a conscious equivalent in the man whom the woman imagines looking at her. In the interaction between beings, the feminine other is notoriously the object of the masculine gaze. It is as if this gaze overlays her own inward-turning, manifest

17 As Laplanche and Pontalis [1964] have already argued from another perspective.
18 Jung (1944–78), vol. 9: 197.
19 Cowie (1991: 165ff) argues this in a cinematic context.

in her attachment to a visual image of herself in daydreams. In her inward-turning, first, there is a repressed hallucination, a still fixed point. Second, there is a repressed daydream, an unacceptable conscious phantasy. Third, there are the surviving daydreams. All of which constitutes quite a psychical load, even before the gaze of an actual other is taken into economic account. The gaze of the real other will feature again below (pp. 117, 128). There is a more pressing issue. It is the relation between visual images and language, which will also bear on the spatial factor. Language, as discussed in the last chapter, has figured prominently in the contemporary literature on Freud and femininity, so prominently that it has almost effaced the visual image. But language is none the less critical for all that.

In the hysterical patients of the *Studies*, the visual pictures, so significant to the source and course of the illness, fade and fragment when the patient uses language to describe them. '*The patient is, at it were, getting rid of [the picture] by turning it into words*' (1895b, GW: 283, SE: 280, original emphasis). Language through speech, Forrester argues, seems to complete and thereby release the attempt at symbolization represented by an hysterical symptom ([1980] 1985). The talking cure, incidentally, is not the only linguistic means for mitigating the power of visual scenes. Anna Freud writes of a patient with elaborate if monotonous daydreams that once she *wrote* a daydream down as a short story it faded away.[20]

20 Anna Freud's focus on writing may contribute to solving a problem Freud posed at the end of a brief paper on 'Creative Writers and Day-Dreaming' (1908d), where he observed that how some neurotics found their way back from the world of daydreams to the world of reality through creative writing was mysterious. The context for his puzzlement was focused more on the content of daydreams than the way in which daydreams restricted the subject's ability to act on the world. Freud's brief piece on creative writers does not dwell on the antithesis we find in Breuer between daydreams and concentrated intelligent activity, although, as we have seen, Freud retained an antithesis between daydreaming and intentionally directed thought. Yet writing usually involves more energetic expenditure and directed motor activity than talking does. In this, it is consonant with Breuer's observation, and it represents a departure from those features of daydreams which involve an abnegation of the activities Freud elsewhere assigns to the ego. Of themselves, daydreams make no demands of motor activity. The visual production, the private theatre of daydreams, can take place while the impresario, the subject, is entirely still, although as Breuer and Freud observed, daydreams can also coincide with that type and degree of motor activity found in monotonous occupations. They can coincide with it because these occupations do not demand all one's attention. The significant point here is that writing reunites concentrated attention to a consonant motor activity. Anna Freud herself effectively explains the neurotic's way back by ambitious ego tendencies, and the desire to communicate with others. Both matter. Ambition alone is ineffective without the wish to communicate; it was this that led Anna Freud's daydreamer to 'round off the action'. At the same time Anna Freud is evidently formulating the issue in terms of the pleasure principle, which brings me to a second point. Her patient was anticipating future readers. Her goal had shifted from the present pleasure of the daydream to the deferred one of the reader's response. It is this deferral of present pleasure, as stressed in the Introduction, that is problematic in femininity. But the desire to communicate with others is a new factor to be taken into account, in relation to deferred gratification. Lacan stresses the importance of the desire to communicate in arguing for the importance of a distinction between the imaginary ego, and the subject who communicates via the symbolic means of language.

What both talking and writing have in common, when they release the hysterical symptom, is that both are means whereby something that had been held in place is turned outwards, and in that turning, attention and symbol flow in the same direction. Thus far, I have argued, on the basis of Breuer's analysis, that the things that stand in the way of the translation into words, and of motor activity, are a conscious daydream and an unconscious frozen image. Anxiety (or members of the anxiety family) fixes the frozen image (although the path to it may lie through conscious daydreams), and this anxiety-fix, I have suggested, is homologous with unconscious fixed attention: a form of repression. In the rest of this chapter, I argue that this interpretation resonates with, and largely resolves, the difficulties Freud subsequently experienced with the theory of repression. It also suggests that the differences between Freud and Breuer over the power of hypnoid states and repression in causing hysteria are nominal rather than substantial. The fact that Breuer's observations, as distinct from his interpretations, were cast in the context of a 'hypnoid state' theory has obscured their salience. But to draw this out, we need to look at Freud's divergence from Breuer in more detail. Also, now that the role of language in releasing hysteria has been mentioned, and given the pre-eminence accorded its part today, we need to note its actual role for Freud. We begin by following Freud's path through his analysis of Elisabeth von R., tracing the same course from social reality to attention, but interpolating language. I then turn to Freud's and Breuer's disagreement over the respective merits of hypnoid states and repression in explaining hysteria, and after that, to the *Project*. Both the *Project* and the analysis of Elisabeth von R. are invoked today as studies that reveal the agency of the letter, and the power of the word, in repression (Forrester [1980], David-Ménard ([1983] 1989). But, as usual, they do not of themselves resolve the economic, energetic question.

THE DIVERGENCE FROM BREUER

The relation between daydreams and intellectual stimulation does not figure in Freud's discussion of Elisabeth von R. He records that she had a demand for intellectual development, but treats it in a manner that presages his notion of masculine identification in women. He notes that Elisabeth 'wanted to study or to have a musical training' and that she did not want 'to sacrifice her inclinations and her freedom of judgement by marriage' (1895b, *GW*: 202, *SE*: 140). He then ties these ambitions to Elisabeth's being more of a son than a daughter to her father, in whose company she found 'intellectual stimulation' although 'her mental constitution was on that account departing from the ideal which people like to see realized in a girl' (1895b, *GW*: 202, *SE*: 140). In other words, and this deserves more investigation, the antithesis in Elisabeth's case is between intellectual fulfilment and sexual identity. In Anna O.'s it is between intellectual fulfilment and daydreams. All of which has to raise the question, Is there a connection between (hysterical or feminine) sexual identity and daydreams? This needs to be borne in mind, especially given the significance of conscious phantasy, and the conscious equivalent of the 'cinema-operator' mentioned above.

Meantime, it is clear that if Fräulein Elisabeth marries she cannot reasonably hope to act on her ambitions. Given this, we might expect that a conflict between her sexual identity and acting on reality will manifest itself. In which case, the question becomes, If any manifestation of this conflict is to be found, does it take the form of the egoic conflict between acting on reality and retreating from it? As I noted, in this case Freud makes no mention of a retreat into daydreams. But there is another, very direct sense in which the inability to act features in Fräulein von R.'s pathology.

Her presenting symptoms were a difficulty in walking and standing, and pains in her legs. Not only this, but her musculature, that apparatus Freud will later connect with the drive for mastery and reality testing, was affected (1895b, GW: 244, SE: 176). Elisabeth's symptoms first appeared when she was nursing her father, and one may have had a direct physical cause on that occasion. It gathered strength as a specifically hysterical symptom a few months later. Freud pursues three lines of analysis in accounting for it: the contiguous, the erotic, and the symbolic.

One line of Freud's reasoning is contiguous in that it relies on the proximity of one emotion or experience to another. He attributes Elisabeth's difficulty in walking and standing to an association between a physical pain and a psychical pain, both of which were felt during her father's illness. The physical pain was the initially real pain. The psychical pain was prompted by a neurotic conflict. There are also other contiguous associations from that period. For instance, when she was bandaging her father's painful leg, it rested on her own right thigh and part of her own leg pains dated from that moment (1895b, GW: 244, SE: 175). In these instances, Freud in fact refers to conversion by 'associative connection' (1895b, GW: 244, SE: 175) and 'conversion through simultaneity' (1895b, GW: 247, SE: 178), which is more precise than 'contiguity', although its purport is the same. Also, while Freud is clearly focusing on how events are caught in the same time-frame, he is more concerned with the affect that is retained, and not abreacted, rather than visual hallucination, or divided attention. However these figure as asides in other examples he introduces in discussing the contiguous aspect of Fräulein von R.'s symptom formation. He mentions that affect was retained when an analysand was sick-nursing, because this is a job in which an individual 'will soon divert his attention [Aufmerksamkeit] away from his own impressions, since he has neither time nor strength to do justice to them' (1895b,

GW: 228, *SE*: 161–2). In another example, Freud, again comparing Fräulein Elisabeth with another patient, notes that in the latter's symptom, where 'there was no symbolization but a conversion through simultaneity . . . She saw a painful sight which was accompanied by feelings of self-reproach' (1895b, *GW*: 248, *SE*: 178–9). For Freud this event led to defence, or repression. In these examples of contiguity, or conversion by simultaneity, neither the ability to attend, nor the painful sight, are given any prominence by Freud. They are merely mentioned on the way. But these mentions resonate with Breuer's account, at the same time as they lay more stress on the notion that the retention of affect, and repression of ideas, are part of contiguous symptom formation. What is more, the stress on affect indicates how my brief allusion to detachment in an earlier reference to inwardly directed attention (p. 97) might be amplified. In noting that if daydreams pave the way for hysterical symptom formation, they do so not only because attention is inward-turned, but because it is not detached, I had in mind the fact that one can meditate on one's own psychical state in a detached way, with some degree of self-awareness as to what that state is, has been, or might be, and this very act of detachment presupposes a lack of affect as well as of phantasy. The attempt at self-awareness is an attempt to grasp a reality which is not (necessarily) self-serving. And possibly the critical concept here is less 'reality' than it is distance. For distance is presupposed in the conscious thought directed towards outer reality, and so too is distance presupposed in detachment. I mean, a standard synonym for detachment is distance, and perhaps the synonym is less figurative than it appears to be at first.

Turning now to Freud's second line of analysis of Elisabeth von R., in which erotic conflicts as such predominate. Especially, there is a conflict for Elisabeth over her brother-in-law, married to a favourite sister. The sister died soon after Elisabeth's father. To the brother-in-law Elisabeth was, by her own standards, inadmissibly attracted. Some of the occasions when that attraction forced itself home were associated with her legs: a *walk* in which she felt obliquely attracted to her brother-in-law; and *standing* by her dead sister's bedside at the point where she realized her brother-in-law was 'free'. This line of explanation, which seems to have had the largest part to play in removing Elisabeth's symptoms, is evidently also tied to contiguity, or conversion by simultaneity, and moreover it introduces the third line of explanation (by symbolization), for the fact of Elisabeth's 'standing alone' was painful to her (1895b, *GW*: 216, *SE*: 152).

In terms of Freud's explanation by symbolization,

> the patient had created, or increased, her functional disorder by means of symbolization, that she had found in the astasia-abasia a somatic expression for her lack of an independent position and her inability to make any alteration in her circumstances, and that such phrases as 'not

being able to take a single step forward', 'not having anything to lean upon' served as the bridge for this fresh act of conversion.

(1895b, *GW*: 244, *SE*: 176)

Strikingly, the conversion by symbolization is tied to her masculine identification as well as her feminine identification. It thus prefigures what Freud would subsequently identify as the basic bisexuality of hysteria. In terms of her masculine identification, Elisabeth's symptom reflects the fact that her forward action is inhibited ('not being able to take a single step forward'). In terms of her feminine identification that symbolization reflects her lack of a dependable man, or for that matter economic circumstance ('not having anything to lean upon').

At this point this should be noted: while Elisabeth's feminine desires and demands are reflected in symptoms formed by contiguity (as well as symbolization) her masculine desire is only reflected in symbolization by words; *her masculine identification expresses itself in nothing else*. In addition, despite subsequent emphasis on symbolization, language and the 'symbol written in the sand of the flesh' as something that 'resolves itself entirely in an analysis of language'[21] as the true significance of Freud's discovery, Freud, as Bowie (1991) establishes, gave it no particular weight. Freud even wondered if the fact was that hysterical symptoms and the words they reflect (a 'stab in the heart', 'a slap in the face') did not 'alike draw their material from a common source [*gemeinsame Quelle*]' (Freud (1895b, *GW*: 251, *SE*: 181). It is a view he held to, writing subsequently that in 'following the usage of language, neurosis, here as elsewhere, is taking words in their original, significant sense, and where it appears to be using a word figuratively it is usually simply restoring its old meaning' (1908b, *GW*: 208, *SE*: 174).[22]

Moreover Freud clung to the idea that hysteria was contiguous for some time. In a letter written to Fliess, written five years after the *Studies* were published, Freud used a distinction paralleling that between contiguity and symbolization in formulating an early taxonomy of the psychoneuroses. He proposed that in hysteria displacement follows any path of contiguous association; in obsessional neuroses it follows that of association through

21 Both quotations are from Lacan (1953b), 'The Function and Field of Speech and Language in Psychoanalysis', and are cited in Malcolm Bowie's discussion of 'Language and the Unconscious' in Bowie (1991). Bowie's analysis shows how Freud's theory of the unconscious and the symptom is precisely not reducible to language, as the early Lacan alleges.

22 This idea is discounted by Lacanians such as David-Ménard ([1983] 1989). David-Ménard argues against the psychical/physiological dualism she discerns in Freud's theory of hysteria, and does so specifically in the context of an analysis of Freud's interpretations of Elisabeth von R. But this argument only replaces dualism with a theory in which language is monocausal and all-powerful, making itself felt in the body as well as in speech. But the psychophysical effects of language still have their origin in language, and language remains something outside the subject and alien to the subject, something the subject is 'born into'. Below, the hypothetical 'common substance' at the base of language will come into its own, although not quite in the form that Freud inferred.

resemblance of ideas; in paranoia the path is that of causal connections (*Life*, vol. 1: 306). Freud's distinctions here contrast with the links he drew subsequently between the phantasies common to paranoia, hysteria, and perversions.

> The contents of the clearly conscious phantasies of perverts (which in favourable circumstances can be transformed into manifest behaviour), of the delusional fears of paranoiacs (which are projected in a hostile sense on to other people) and of the unconscious phantasies of hysterics (which psycho-analysis reveals behind their symptoms) – all of these coincide with one another even down to their details.
> (Freud 1905b, *GW* 5: 65, n. 1, *SE*: 165, n. 2)

In the early taxonomy, we have distinct pathways, rather than similar phantasies. Yet if Freud is right in both cases, and the same phantasies are revealed in the different illnesses, then *the difference between them is not one of the content of the phantasies, but of the route they follow*. The route they follow reintroduces the question, or the concept, of direction, in so far as these pathways resonate with the distinction I drew earlier between inward-turning attention in daydreaming and hysteria, moving attention, and the attention fixed as a still point in hallucination. But do they resonate that much? The inward-turning of attention in hysteria, and its unconscious fixation, resonate with visual and affective contiguity, but the pathway of causal connection in paranoia, and the association of ideas in obsessional neurosis, are new. I intend to leave aside the pathway of causal connection for now, but the association of ideas is something that has to be pursued, because this 'association of ideas' is equivalent to association along the much-publicized chain of signification.

There is an excellent illustration of how this association works in Freud's analysis of the Ratman. At one point in the analysis, the Ratman interpolates his lady's name into a prayer. The lady's name ends in 's'. In the prayer, it is followed by 'Amen'. The Ratman thus produces a sound, 'Samen', which puns on 'semen' (1909d, *GW*: 443, *SE*: 225). This association by sounds indicates how signifiers are associated with one another, in a punning sequence of sounds, and this association is different from that between the concept or thing that the signifier is meant to represent. It is precisely because sounds and signifiers could be associated with one another by this means, and because psychoanalysis could unravel their meaning on the basis of a similarity of sounds, rather than the traditional connection between word and thing, that the unconscious is meant to be structured like a language.

The Ratman is an obsessional neurotic, who avoids his feelings of hate and guilt by displacing these affects into conscientiousness and obsessive rituals. Obsessional neurosis is the quintessential masculine neurosis, just as hysteria is condensed femininity. It is worth reiterating here that it is

Elisabeth's masculine identification that is expressed by symbolization in words, or 'the association of ideas'. Of course, the fact that association along the chain of signification features both in the archetypal masculine neurosis and Elisabeth's masculine identification does not mean that this form of identification is purely masculine. But the parallels are worth recording, especially given claims that this form of association is the true territory of the unconscious, and given that the visual, contiguous, and energetic dimensions of psychoanalysis are so frequently discounted today. Moreover, once the parallels are recorded, we can ask if there is something in the visual and/or affective 'fixing' in hysterical symptom formation that permits association along the chain of signification to come into being. More of this below. Here, it is necessary to ask about the fate of 'attention', when it comes to following a chain of signification. Presumably, following a signifying chain involves movement rather than fixity. But this movement is not the same as the form of moving attention deployed in perceiving the present. It is a form of movement that is displaced from present perception to signification, and it does not involve conscious attention. And as I said, its relation to unconscious or fixed attention remains to be addressed. We will be better able to do this after the concept of repression, the point of divergence between Freud and Breuer, is analysed.

As I have indicated, Freud was already distancing himself from hypnoid states in the *Studies*. While Breuer does not deny the significance of repression in relation to hysteria, he wants to make repression, as a determinant of failed abreaction, subsidiary to the effects of hypnoid states. Tactfully, he suggests that repression is insufficient to account for the dual personality often found in hysteria. Repression can only account for the fate of specific ideas. On the other hand, Freud even in this collaborative venture suggests that hysteria based on repression (defence hysteria) lies at the root of hypnoid hysteria. In Freud's experience, 'the so-called hypnoid state owed its separation to the fact that in it a psychical group had come into effect which had previously been split off by defence' (1895b, *GW*: 289, *SE*: 286). His argument is the mirror-reversal of Breuer's claim for the psychogenetic priority of hypnoid states. Freud is the more able to claim priority for repression in so far as he had another explanation for failed abreaction, more closely allied with defence or repression. This is the notion of a retention hysteria, foreshadowed in the discussion of Elisabeth von R. It is called a retention hysteria because in it affects are retained, often because the subject fends off, or represses their release. This is done either for ethical reasons, or reasons of social appropriateness. (It is not fair to be angry, or fitting to cry.)

With this in mind, one can ask just how far the concept of a hypnoid state and a hypnoid hysteria differs from that of a retention hysteria. Freud himself had written on three forms of hysteria: defence, hypnoid, and retention hysteria, a year before the *Studies* were published.[23] By the time of the *Studies* the notion of a retention hysteria was preferred. A hypnoid hysteria, it will be recalled, is one in which the abreaction could not take place, not because of circumstances but because the subject was in some way paralysed, either by a peculiarity of the hypnoid state itself, or paralysing affects. In both hypnoid and retention hysterias the consequence is the same (affect is retained) and so is the connection to the formation of an hysterical symptom (the excitation of the affect fuels it). One could argue here that the fact that daydreams can introduce a hypnoid state marks a real difference between the two types of hysteria, except for this: Breuer explicitly argued that daydreams involve the retention of excitation and affect. Given that the retention of excitation and affect is critical to both hypnoid and retention hysteria, is any difference effected by the subject being unable, in the sense of unwilling, to discharge in a retention hysteria, and unable, in the sense of incapable, to discharge in a hypnoid hysteria? Once the problem is posed this way, the concept of hypnoid hysteria begins to resonate with Freud's third type of hysteria, defence or repression hysteria. Daydreams lead to the same end result one way, ethical and social considerations mark out another route. The end result is that in both defence and hypnoid hysterias, the subject is incapable of a certain response. Let us consider the role of the paralysing affect in this connection, remembering here Freud's belief that, at bottom, hypnoid hysterias will turn into defence hysterias.

Paralysing affects prevent the subject from acting on the idea or discharging the emotion. Now there is a sense in which this is precisely what repression does. It prevents the subject acting on the idea or discharging the emotion. It is worth repeating here that Freud throughout his work makes it plain that repression is an economic force in itself. Bearing in mind my proposition that attention, as a form of psychophysical energy, is identical to the repression when that attention is unconsciously fixed, we may have a way of reconciling some of the observations that underlie the hypnoid state idea with the theory of repression. I have already noted the key role played by anxiety (and members of the anxiety family) in 'paralysing affects', and suggested that, in turn, anxiety paves the way for and coincides with the fixing of attention. I am suggesting now that repression involves the same process.

CONSTRUCTED INERTIA

The idea that repression involves paralysing affects is not as implausible as it may first appear from the standpoint of Freud's psychical economies, if we anticipate the development of those economies. Over thirty years

---

23 Freud 1894 and 1896c are the main works here.

after the *Studies*, in *Inhibitions, Symptoms and Anxiety* (1926a), Freud was
to argue against his early view that sexual repression caused anxiety, and
conclude that anxiety caused repression. In *Inhibitions, Symptoms and
Anxiety*, Freud also noted that anxiety is more prevalent in women. But to
make this connection between anxiety and the different forms of hysteria
meaningful, to try to fill in the links between the theory of daydreams
buried in the hypnoid states, the role of unconscious phantasy, and the
pathological implications of daydreams in Freud's later theories of pleasure
and reality in the ego, the development of Freud's economic theories and
the question of repression need to be traced more slowly. In the next
section, we turn to the Metapsychological paper on repression and the
1926 theory of anxiety. In this section, it remains to address the
manuscript Freud wrote specifically to address the relation between
hysteria and repression: the unpublished *Entwurf einer Psychologie*
(*Project for a Scientific Psychology*) (where Freud first addressed at length
the physical, quantitative concerns he would later style 'economic'). In
addition, a retrospective on the *Project* is interesting because in it, Freud
himself had assumed that anxiety causes forgetfulness, itself a form of
repression.

Keeping to the immediate economic point: in the *Project*, Freud wanted
to explain not only the mechanism of repression in hysteria, but with it,
the significance of what, in the *Studies*, he termed the 'retention of large
sums of excitation' (1895b, *GW*: 160, *SE*: 103), sums of psychical excitation
that were converted into motor activity of a symbolic sort (1895b, *GW*:
151, *SE*: 93) in hysterical symptoms. The *Project* is a speculative argument
about how sums of excitations have different meanings, pathways, and
consequences. It is also, suggestively, an argument about how the ego is
formed, an argument that suggests how the ego is a 'giant phantasy'
(Laplanche [1970] 1976) in itself, held together, I think, by attention. We
have already discussed the Lacanian notion that the ego is 'fixed'. We are
now analysing what this fixity means in fact. But to begin finalizing this
analysis, we have to approach fixity by the pathways the *Project* sets up.

And to understand the pathways (which depend on a complicated
system of 'neurones'),[24] one has to begin as Freud did, with the assumption
that quantity, or a flow of excitation (he calls it Q), is the key factor in
how the psychical apparatus works. Q 'distinguishes activity from rest . . .
subject to the general laws of motion' (1950b: 296). Freud adds that any
system will seek to divest itself of quantity or Q: 'This is the principle
of neuronal inertia' (1950b: 296). It is critical that this principle, as Freud

---

24 Freud introduced three classes of neurones. The difference between them need not concern us at this point, but briefly, they are the *phi*, *psi*, and *omega* neurones. The *phi*
neurones do not resist the flow of quantity. The *psi* neurones do to some extent in that
they retain permanent traces of the quantity that flows through them. The *omega* neurones are concerned with perception.

understands it, is a principle of lack of motion, or freedom from excitation. It is critical that Freud also describes this as a principle of constancy. Constancy means (oddly enough) keeping things constant. Whether they are moving or still is irrelevant as long as their velocity or stillness is unchanged. But what Freud did was to assimilate the notion that a body will seek to stay unchanged (keep its motion constant) with the notion that it will seek to divest itself of quantity or motion. The confusion is evident in remarks such as the following which comes in 1920: 'The mental apparatus endeavours to keep the quantity of excitation present in it as low as possible or at least to keep it constant' (1920a: 9).[25] Inertia is equated with lack of motion, rather than unchangingness. In short, although Freud did not realize this, his understanding of inertia is radically different from the laws of motion in thermodynamics. Freud's neurones want to get rid of any quantity or excitation rather than keep it the same. That Freud's assumptions about the general laws of motion and inertia are *prima facie* wrong is also borne out in his discussion of sleep as a '*motor paralysis (paralysis of the will)*', where he assumes that 'The will is the discharge of the total [*psi*] Q*n* [see p. 97, n. 16]': (1950b: 337). While Freud allows that other sources of excitation persist in sleep, the idea that sleep is more inert because it lacks motion is revealing.

In terms of Newton's first and second laws the principle of inertia *is* the principle of constancy. The concept of inertia had a lengthy history in physics before and after Newton.[26] While the concept's history in the late nineteenth century was varied, inertia was not about lack of motion; it is about constancy in the sense that, left to themselves, bodies will continue at the same motion or remain in a state of equilibrium.[27] In short Freud's confusion lies in his equation of inertia with lack of motion, rather than unchangingness. And even if one takes a definition of inertia as the resistance to motion,[28] this is still inconsistent with Freud's theory, as we shall see. At the same time, what we have in Freud is a theory of the construction of psychical inertia as a state of rigidity, a theory that bears on the *construction* of the sense of time and space. This is of far more interest to Einsteinian than Newtonian physics: for Einsteinian physics raises problems for psychology. These problems are: (i) how it is that the sense of time and space are constructed, and (ii) how it is that space and time present themselves as distinct at the same time as

25 See the Editor's Note to Freud (1915c) for a discussion of the difference between the pleasure and constancy principles, and *Life*, vol. 1: 405–15.
26 See Christensen (1981) for a survey of the persistence of the problem of inertia.
27 See Schaffer (1992) on the nineteenth-century interpretation of thermodynamics.
28 '[Kepler] had argued, following the neo-Platonic devaluation of matter, that " . . . opposition to motion is a characteristic of matter; it is stronger, the greater the quantity of matter in a given volume". This property of resistance, not only to the initiation of motion, but to acquired motion, Kepler called "inertia"' (Roche 1986: 44).

space-time is a continuum.[29] So that while Freud's physics are in principle inaccurate, his idiosyncratic notion of inertia may have made a far greater contribution to physics than he could have anticipated, if it is read as I read it here, as an account of how a specific type of inertia is constructed through the constitution of a fixed still point. It might contribute to physics, as well as an understanding of the psychical rigidity that characterizes femininity and the neurotic psyche. Yet the psyche must be the immediate concern, for it is the attempt to deal with quantity while keeping itself alive that determines the shape of the psyche of the *Project*. It is the attempt to deal with quantity that induces the repression of hallucination, founds psychical reality and the unconscious, and brings the first fixed point, the first moment of constructed (anti-natural) inertia, into being.

Having begun with quantity, Freud then wants to make a distinction between two forms of quantity: in addition to Q, there is Qn. What Qn is is unclear. I hazard that it is the amount of quantity the nervous system has acquired internally, while Q includes the excitations or quantities of external stimuli, which the organism may or need not acquire, and which it will seek to avoid. Qn is the amount of excitation the nervous system has to put up with, while seeking to divest itself of Q in general. It has to put up with Qn to deal with the exigencies of life. For although Q comes to the organism from external stimuli, and although it will seek to divest itself of Q through action, it has to know what action to take. And it can only know this through experience and memory, which brings us to the *Project*'s pathways.

The pathways are set up between a particular class of neurones: Freud terms them the *psi* neurones. These neurones store energy, or Qn. They also have 'contact barriers' between them. These contact barriers, equivalent to what neurology later named synapses, act as a kind of censorship apparatus. They either permit or prevent the flow of quantity from one neurone to another. Whether they permit it or not will depend on whether contact between them has been 'facilitated', and a facilitating pathway established. Whether or not it is established will depend on an 'experience of satisfaction', and 'a basic law of association by simultaneity' (1950b: 319), in which the experience of satisfaction is recalled. It can be recalled because the experience of satisfaction lays down a mnemic image (which can be kinaesthetic or motor as well as visual) of the action or object which produced the satisfaction. At the same time, this mnemic image can be misleading. It can 'produce the same thing as a perception – namely a hallucination' (1950b: 319). But hallucination inevitably leads to unpleasure, and this tells us something very important.

29 A third problem concerns how it is that time appears to be an asymmetrical phenomenon. This, together with the question of causality, is discussed in Brennan (1991b).

In order to establish a memory of a real perception, and to distinguish it from hallucination, the organism needs the experience of unpleasure. What is more, it then needs to repress the hallucination, which involves a constant expenditure of energy. In the *Project*, Freud posits that 'if an ego exists it must *inhibit* [meaning delay] primary psychical processes' concerned with wish-fulfilment, and the motor activity which responds to those wishes by excitations (1950b: 324 and *passim*). This inhibition of primary process hallucination is necessary in order for the ego to check out whether the hallucination is real or imagined; if it is imagined it is repressed.[30] In turn, how the ego decides whether an hallucination is real or imagined is tied to the faculty of judgement (ibid.). This is a different derivation for the faculty of judgement than the oral one (p. 54 above), but that is not the immediate issue.

If inertia is the resistance to change, the response to an hallucination would not be to repress it but to dismantle it altogether. Even if inertia is defined as the resistance to motion, the fact that the subject-to-be *keeps* the hallucination is at odds with constancy in that a constant expenditure of energy or motion is necessary to keep the hallucination repressed. Thus any hypothetical psychophysical equilibrium is disrupted by this repression. The subject is not born repressing hallucinations. When it does so, it constructs an inert point, in the common-sense usage of inert. This construction is the keystone in the foundation of the subject's identity in two ways. As I indicated above, it not only gives it a fixed 'subject-centred' point of reference for the directions its psychophysical energy will follow thereafter. It also establishes the beginning of its memory. Memory, or history as it was called in the last chapter, is another constituent of identity. I will expand on these points.

What Freud is arguing, in effect, is that in order to establish a functional memory the subject-to-be needs the experience of hallucination. Freud is quite explicit about the fact that memory is something that is established by facilitations, at the same time as facilitations establish memory. This is a tautological point, but he is insistent about it. The characteristics of memory could not emerge unless some pathways rather than others are preferred. At the same time, 'memory is evidently one of the powers which determine and direct [an excitation's] pathway' (1950b: 300).

In sum, facilitating pathways are fixed on or cathected in order to deal with pleasure and unpleasure, and to distinguish between what is real and what is not. The organism needs to be able to distinguish between what is real and what is not, and to have a certain store of quantity in reserve in order to establish a memory, and to take what Freud calls 'specific actions' in order to deal with 'the exigencies of life' (hunger, survival, etc.). Of course 'At first, the human organism is incapable of bringing

---

30 The point is made more clearly in a discussion of the secondary process in Freud (1900).

about the specific action. It takes place by *extraneous help*, when the attention of an experienced person is drawn to the child's state by dis-charge along the path of internal change [meaning, for instance, screaming]' (1950b: 318).

This is the first mention of attention in the *Project*. It is next mentioned as a property of the ego (1950b: 324). The ego is a mass of constantly cathected neurones or established pathways; it is the totality of psychical cathexes at a given time (1950b: 323). 'Let us picture the ego as a network of cathectic neurones well facilitated in relation to one another' (1950b: 323). In less technical language, what this means is that the familiar path-ways for coping, remembering, and interpreting are connected in a way that produces a coherent structure.

Freud says that this ego network has a permanent component as well as a changing one. By his definition, the permanent component must consist of fixed facilitations or pathways; the changing component of new and/or altered facilitations. The ego, as stated, is also in possession of the faculty of attention. Somewhat surprisingly, in view of the fact that Freud has already established grounds for distinguishing between hallucination and perception in terms of whether satisfaction or unpleasure results, he also makes the faculty of attention a biological property, capable of distinguishing a perception from an hallucination. But this appears to be insufficient. He needs a 'biological rule of attention' to explain why the ego will direct more energy to ('hypercathect') perceptions which may lead to satisfaction. He needs this rule because he cannot explain why the ego should avoid pain 'mechanically', meaning in terms of physical rather than biological events. Such explanation goes against the 'physics' of the original trend towards inertia, on which the entire logic of the *Project* is based. Also the organism likes to follow the old pathways it has estab-lished, for establishing new pathways means expending more quantity; following old pathways means less quantity is expended. Accordingly, the ego likes to repeat what it has done before (1950b: 323) even if its life is at risk through an inappropriate repetition. To make the same point differently, if the organism wants to divest itself of quantity or energy, why should it gather up energy and expend it, simply in order to save itself? Thus Freud had to make life-saving attention a biological necessity, rather than a physical one.

To complicate the question of attention further, the mechanism of atten-tion 'consists, in every case, of the ego *cathecting* those *neurones* in which a cathexis has already appeared' (1950b: 371). Now it should follow from this that as the ego is 'a network of cathected neurones', it also attends to itself. And if the ego has both a permanent and a changing component, its attention has to be in some way split. More precisely, as the cathected neurones are 'well facilitated in relation to one another', and this means that they cohere, this in turn suggests that the permanent component of the ego is the coherent part. Yet this means that some of the ego's attention goes to maintaining its coherence in the first place, despite Freud's assumption that the biological rule of attention only operates explicitly in relation to 'life's exigencies'.

This is consistent with my proposition that the force which represses hallucination consists of nothing less than attention, for this repressing force is also turned inwards. It is also consistent with the idea that this repression is a foundation of the subject's identity. The question then becomes: Does this coherent ego, consisting of facilitating pathways, have the apparent unity of an identity or 'personality'? Freud in fact assumed it did (in a cheerful leap from the ego that repressed hallucinations to the adult ego: a leap that will concern us in a moment).[31]

31 Freud's assumption that the ego has a coherent identity is plain in another of his divergences from Breuer. It will be recalled that the division in consciousness involved in 'preoccupation', where the subject is attending to two things at once, may for Breuer lead to a splitting of the mind (see 1895b: 225). This theory of the split mind parallels Freud's division of the psyche into the conscious and the unconscious, but the parallel also reinvokes the divergence that began with Breuer's emphasis on the hypnoid state (and the divided consciousness that prefigures it) and Freud's on defence or repression. On closer examination, it is plain that the reason Breuer insisted on the priority of hypnoid states was his wish to explain the existence of dual personalities. The idea of a dual personality received so much attention in nineteenth-century psychology that no contemporary theory could neglect it. Freud attends to it, but briefly, and thinks it can be explained by the splitting of the mind that comes into being when the ego represses ideas that are incompatible with others; this is the condition of their subsequent 'inadmissibility to consciousness'. Breuer clearly believes that repression is insufficient to account for a 'genuine splitting of the mind'; repression can account only for specific unconscious ideas. In other words, Breuer is making a distinction between unconscious ideas and the split mind, and, as I indicated, believes hypnoid states are necessary to account for the discrete and in some respects unified entity of the 'other consciousness' or dual personality, sometimes styled the *condition seconde* of the hysteric, manifest in a hysterical or psychotic attack. Such an attack is one where another consciousness, a set of ideas and related behaviour patterns foreign to everyday consciousness, or in extreme cases another personality, takes over the government and behaviour and utterance in a manner observable to others, and even to the sufferer. Breuer notes that Anna O. observed her own hysterical attacks from a corner of her mind (1895b: 228–9; also 46). Freud will make a similar observation on psychotics years further on. Breuer's approach has the merit of raising and addressing the problem of how it is that unconscious ideas and processes come to cohere in the unity presented by a *condition seconde*; what holds it together? Freud is able to explain the existence of the florid second personality only by arguing that two separate sets of ideas appear to exist because the 'correct connections' between them have been repressed and withheld. The fact of resistance means that only some ideas are at the ego's disposal. Others are not. When those not at the disposal of the ego appear, so, deceptively, does an apparent 'second personality' (1895b, *GW*: 291, *SE*: 287). Now this argument tacitly assumes that the withholding of the correct connections also results in (or constructs) the unified appearance of a second personality, and it is not easy to see how this would come about. One possibility is that the establishing of the false connections that substitute for the correct ones involves establishing a synthetic alternative personality. Given that it is the ego that withholds the correct connections, in the interests of repression, and that it is the ego that Freud will later credit with the capacity for synthesis, the ego may be the agency constructing the unified appearance. Freud does not say this; he leaves the specific issue of the unity of the second personality unaddressed. Yet in view of the idea that the ego is a mass of cathected neuronic pathways in turn cathected by attention, the unity or coherence of the second personality could

There are two possible explanations for this unity. One is that the subject gives this unity to itself. This explanation is improbable if it presupposes that the subject has the means to give itself this unity (see pp. 117–18 below). It is also improbable in Freud's own terms in the *Project*. The idea that the subject would be diverting attention to no end other than giving itself an image seems an unjustified physical luxury. The second possible explanation of unity is foreshadowed in Freud's glancing remark that, before the organism can undertake 'specific actions' on its own behalf, it requires the 'attention of an experienced person'. In other words, I am suggesting that the ego may also acquire its coherence through the attention of another, and this is the condition of its 'mirror stage'.[32]

Also the idea that the other's attention has an impact helps solve the problem of where the attention would come from to meet the exigencies of life. The other's attention could endow the organism with more energy for meeting those exigencies. If the attention of the other enhances energy, this might mean that the explanatory approach of the *Project* could remain primarily physical, rather than biological; if attention comes from another, there is a physical force countermanding the trend towards inertia, a force that comes from outside a self-contained system, but which cannot be taken into account when one thinks within self-contained terms. On the other hand, given that the mirror stage is experienced as restricting, as well as enlivening, it should follow that the attention from the other also works in these ways. It enlivens. Or it restricts. What is responsible for this?

Here, it is worth recalling my earlier suggestions: (i) that the repression of an hallucination relies on attention diverted inwards; (ii) that this repressed hallucination was the first still point in founding the subject's boundaries. What I want to suggest now is that the attention from the other interlocks with the first repressed hallucination. It does so at a literally imaginary, or image-ridden, level and is an intermediate stage in the subject's constructed inertia. In that the image from the other and its own repression of hallucination interlock, the subject-to-be confuses the

be explained in terms of attention. Provided, and it is a big proviso, that we allow for two sets of attention, constructing two personalities. Before we can deal with this, we have to ask where the attention that holds the ego together comes from? This is discussed in the text. As a rider, it is worth adding that a 'dual personality' can be a factor in everyday as well as psychotic experience. We are most of us familiar with the experience of becoming a different person in the presence of another, not just through the desire to please, but as if our own personality is displaced by another one.

32 There is a wonderful description in Lacan's *Seminar I* ([1953–4] 1988) of how the infant, when it is checking out its reflection in the mirror, turns to the mother for validation of what it sees. Lacan uses this to show that a symbolic third term, a third party, is present from the beginning, and thereby concludes that his earlier arguments about a dyadic mirror stage *preceding* the symbolic were wrong. We could use the same example to show that the infant is calling for an attentive validation from without, at precisely the moment that it turns its attention inwards.

restrictions it imposes on itself with the image it receives from the other; both conspire to keep it in place. Moreover while the repression of an hallucination entailed a constant expenditure of energy in an immobilizing process, and led to the *temporal* delay involved in checking out whether an hallucination was real or not, the image from the other brings *spatial* factors to bear on the first fixed point. The image from the other is always experienced at a distance (as Lacan, and, in an oblique way, Winnicott argued; p. 80 above). The fact that this image is directed towards the subject helps consolidate the subject-centred perspective born of the con- structed fixed point (the subject is the centre of the other's attention), while it gives the subject-to-be an imaginary unity.

That imaginary unity, as I stressed, is always restricting, even though the attention from the other can be enlivening.[33] Presumably, the attention from the other is more enlivening than any restrictions that accompany the essential unity that the other's image also confers, although this would not pre-empt the nascent subject's blaming the other for the restrictions imposed on it in a confusing interlock. Alternatively, the attention from the other could in principle be identical to, rather than merely confused with, the restricting attention used in repression.

In the context of whether the attention from the other can be enlivening or restricting, it is worth returning to the division of attention in hysteria. This also needs to be tied back to constructed inertia, and the part the division of attention plays in it. The first thing to record is that in hysterical repression, and the part the division of attention plays in it, we are evidently considering a different psychical level from that of the primal repression of hallucination. We are considering a subject who has already become differentiated according to sex, and therefore considering a more formed or even more 'adult' ego, which deserves the name of identity. The workings of this more formed ego are also illuminated by the role anxiety plays in inhibiting appropriate action in Freud's account in the *Project*. His discussion of this will return us to the notion that attention turned inwards is a form of repression, in that it works towards rigidity, and that as it does so, it evokes anxiety.

When Freud is discussing why the ego cannot adapt or alter itself to contend with novel exigencies of life, and why excitations follow an inappropriate pathway, he holds 'a severely paralysing affect' or anxiety (which can be a severely paralysing affect) responsible. Partly, but not only, for the sake of simplicity in the following exposition, I will call this disabled ego neurotic (while acknowledging that the neurosis can be very temporary). Strictly this disabled ego is not the product of anxiety, but of 'strong affects', according to Freud. Yet while Freud holds strong affects responsible, whenever he exemplifies, the specific example of a strong

33 Cf. Callois (1935) who argues that the fusion with the other in mimicry goes with a loss of psychic energy.

affect is a member of the anxiety family. Similarly, in the *Studies*, 'strong affects' are also synonymous with anxiety.[34]

As I indicated, it is plain from Freud's examples that it is a later, formed ego that is at issue, even though Freud makes no distinction between two stages in the formation of the ego, or identity. Consider an illustration of the circumstances in which the attempt to discharge quantitative excitations follows the old pathways. Under the impact of 'a great anxiety' (1950b: 357) Freud follows an old pathway which is unproductive and, under the circumstances, unrealistic. He forgets to make use of the telephone he had installed to cope with emergencies, and does a lot of running around in consequence. He writes: 'this forgetting involves the disappearance of [the power of] selection, of efficiency and of logic in the passage [of thought] very much as happens in dreams' (1950b: 357).[35] In other words, not only does anxiety interfere with memory; it interferes with the capacity to think through, and in this sense, to attend to a new situation. The ego falls back on the past, for it is evident that it is old pathways which the ego reverts to under the impact of anxiety, which in turn suggests that anxiety keeps the ego tied to the past, makes it forgetful, and prevents the organism from orienting itself to the present. Yet the fact that the neurotic ego falls back on old pathways supplies another reason for arguing that, and makes it plain why, attention is a form of psychical energy that can be deployed in repression. Because if one is unable to attend to the present, one's capacity for attention is going somewhere else. In other words, attention has an economy, which, whatever its plenitude before an identity is formed, is restricted after (or by) that identity's formation.[36]

It is understandable why Freud leapt from the *formation* of the ego to the workings of the ego in adulthood and neuroses. He had argued that the ego requires attention to maintain it; it is a mass of neurones cathected by attention, and established on the basis of familiar pathways. In an 'adult' instance where more attention goes to pathways that are familiar, if relatively useless, it therefore goes to the ego. Thus there is a clear parallel between the workings of the early ego and the later neurotic one. But one can also deduce from Freud's telephone trouble that anxiety is the signal that the ego is imperilled, and requires more attention for its maintenance.

As anxiety also leads to fixity in hysteria, the question then becomes:

34 In that while Breuer also holds 'strong affects' responsible for hypnoid states, his exemplifications always refer to members of the anxiety family.

35 The disappearance of selection characterized the disorder of attention. For Janet (1901), this was a hallmark of hysteria.

36 If, when anxiety is felt, the capacity to attend is diminished, it seems reasonable to assume either that attention is diminished because it becomes anxiety, or (which I think more probable) that anxiety is the feeling experienced as one form of attention is converted into another.

Is hysterical fixity also a means for maintaining identity? Given that the attentive image from the other interlocks with the primary repression of hallucination (both fix the subject in place) is there a parallel interlock at work in hysteria and the neurotic ego of Freud's *Project*? We have seen that in the latter the subject diverts some of its attention to the maintenance of the ego, and if it diverts too much through an attachment to an old pathway, it cannot give the energetic attention it needs to give to new realities. In hysteria, the subject also does not give the attention it needs to give to reality, either because that attention is fixed or frozen in a repressed hallucination or because it is split in daydreams. As we have seen too that the daydream has a conscious equivalent in the gaze of the external other, we are now asking if this gaze (and there may be other fixing gazes in pathology) also interlocks with the subject's own inward-turning to maintain, at the same time as it restricts, the ego. If it does, it overlays and interlocks with a particular path to securing identity. In neurosis, hysteria, and femininity, this path goes back to the past.

But to really make sense of this, we have to keep the distinction between the formation of the ego on the one hand, and the neurotic ego, hysteria, or femininity on the other, firmly in mind. It is critical to remember that in both neurosis and hysteria, the subject is (also) producing an inward-turning of its own accord, but at a different level. At this level, as a matter of course, it turns attention inwards in maintaining its identity. Unravelling the workings of pathology was always Freud's key to understanding apparent normality, and identity maintenance is no exception. If the subject diverts more attention towards its own image when it feels itself to be in jeopardy, this means that it diverts some of its attention towards identity maintenance as a rule.

This inward-turning of a subject with a boundaried identity means that there are two levels of inertia. One is the primary constructed inertia which I have provisionally tied to primal repression. The other is a secondary inertia, which also slows the subject down, and makes it less able to act effectively, as in the anxiety of the neurotic ego, or the often literal paralysis of hysteria. I argued that Breuer's hypnoid state theory, in which anxiety and split attention are paramount, is, on analysis, the same as Freud's theory of how hysteria was formed through defence or repression. In turn this should mean that the secondary inertia of hysteria, and sometimes of the adult (neurotic) ego, is equivalent to secondary repression.

The idea that there are two parallel levels of inertia and repression bears on the ego's tie to the past, and hallucination, and the tie to the past in femininity or neurosis. It also helps explain why, in Freud's account of femininity, it is difficult to distinguish between the fixation points for the psychoses, and those for the neuroses (pp. 51ff above). The fixation points for the psychoses are connected to the experience of hallucination, in which a new reality is constructed when the hallucination refuses to stay repressed. The fixation points for the neuroses consist of a tie to the past constructed through phantasy, in which the new reality is only phantasy, and is known to be such, even though it makes the subject less able to act. Of course the fixation points for the neuroses may also lie in repressed hallucination; the analysis of hysteria revealed this. The subject does not dispense with its capacity for hallucination when it represses its initial one(s). But what is significant about the repressed hallucinations of hysteria is that they are the product of a subject, a being whose identity is constructed. They are the product of a being who recognizes distance and externality, of which more in the next chapter. In terms of our earlier discussion of the spatio-temporal difference between hallucination and phantasy, the fixation points for the psychoses abolish time and space; those for the neuroses tie the subject to past time, and slow it down in space. But before these fixations come undone, they are homologous in that both repress activity by diverting attention inwards. By virtue of this homology, but not only this homology, femininity is borderline: on the border between neurosis and psychosis. The homologous overload of repression makes the girl's resentment of her mother for the manifold restrictions imposed upon her (p. 57 above) more explicable.

Part of that overload is self-imposed. Part of it depends on the effects of the other's (or others') attention. Once the subject has a boundaried identity (more on the second stage of this below, pp. 132–4), it is in a situation where its established economic supply of attention can be diminished or displaced. How far this established supply depends on fixed attention from another, and turning one's attention inwards in an apparently similar fix, comes to the same thing at one level: the effects of an identity fearing the loss of recognition will mean it directs more attention to itself, as may happen with lost jobs or broken relationships, although these severances can also enhance energetic attention. Which brings me to the difference between these sources of supply. It is at the economic level that the difference is real, in that another's fixing (or facilitating?) attention has energetic effects that cannot be calculated in terms of the self-contained zero/sum economy that restricted Freud's thought.

The nature of these effects depends, as I have tried to indicate, on the nature of the attention. The attention from another works in two ways, and it seems to work at two levels. At the level of primary inertia, the attention from the other facilitates the ego's synthesis by enabling it to cohere, at the same time as the image it gives is felt as restricting. At the level of secondary inertia, the probability is that the attention from the other can also restrict the subject's motor activity, overlaying the tie to the past that characterizes the neurotic ego and femininity. But if attention can restrict at this second level, it should also be able to facilitate. In support of this idea, we can note this: masculinity is meant to be 'ego-syntonic'. Masculinity, and the non-neurotic ego, are not tied to the past, but oriented to the future. In terms of the physical economy of attention I am proffering, it would appear that masculinity is endowed with an extra dimension of moving attention, a dimension which femininity lacks. The questions are, What is the source of this moving attention, or How is it that attention alleviates the tie to the past in masculinity, but not in femininity? We have to answer these questions before the construction of secondary inertia, the second border for subjects' identities, can be understood. We will be better placed to answer them after a discussion of Freud's 1915 theory of repression.

THE DEFENCE OF REPRESSION

In the same text that Freud describes masculinity as ego-syntonic in a way that femininity is not, he also elaborates on the difference between repression and defence. But many of the differences he has in mind are foreshadowed in the Metapsychological paper on 'Repression' (1915d). The first thing to note is that

> repression is not a defensive mechanism which is present from the very beginning, and that it cannot arise until a sharp cleavage has occurred between conscious and unconscious mental activity – that *the essence of repression lies simply in turning something away, and keeping it at a distance, from the conscious*. This view of repression would be made more complete by assuming that, before the mental organization reaches this stage, the task of fending off the impulses from the drives is dealt with by the other vicissitudes which drives may undergo – e.g. reversal into the opposite or turning round upon the subject's own self.
>
> (1915d, *GW*: 249–50, *SE*: 147)

In short here we have a view of repression that suggests that it is a later defence mechanism, and one that keeps things at a distance. Elsewhere Freud will suggest that repression has a specific relation to the libido's genital organization, 'and that the ego resorts to other methods of defence when it has to secure itself against the libido on other levels of organization'.[37] The passage quoted at length above also states that the cleavage between conscious and unconscious mental activity is something that has to occur. It is not a given thing but a manufactured one. I argued in the last section that the repression of hallucination is equivalent to primal repression, and the condition of the repressed unconscious coming into being. But it is only one condition. The unconscious also needs repression proper, which I want to tie to secondary inertia.

37 In chapter 5, Klein's appeal to this quotation (Klein 1952a: 87, n. 1) will be significant.

To clarify this, more needs to be said about both phases of repression in Freud's terms. Primal repression is established with 'the psychical (ideational) representative of the drive being denied entrance into the conscious' (1915d, *GW*: 250, *SE*: 148). In this formulation, Freud appears to contradict his previously insistent refusal to distinguish between a somatic drive and its ideational representative. That is to say, given that before his Metapsychological papers Freud had maintained that a drive lay on the frontier of the somatic and the mental, and that it could not be reduced to one or the other, the shift to the idea that a drive has a psychical or ideational representative needs to be noted.

Both phases of repression have a psychical or ideational content. However any difference between the psychical or ideational bearings of the two forms of repression is not elaborated by Freud, nor is it his reason for introducing the distinction between them. In fact, he introduces the distinction between them because his theory of repression requires that the repressed idea is not only pushed away from consciousness. It is also pulled towards, and attracted by, something that has already been repressed.

> The mechanism of repression cannot be understood unless account is taken of . . . two concurrent processes. They may be compared with the manner in which tourists are conducted to the top of the Great Pyramid of Giza by being pushed from one direction and pulled from the other.
>
> (1905b, *Studien*: 83, *SE*: 175–6, n. 2, 1915 edn)[38]

Freud, as ever, stresses the quantitative factor in repression. But in doing so, elsewhere in the paper 'Repression' he seems, unwittingly, to complicate his argument on repression's mechanism. He notes again that 'repression demands a persistent expenditure of force' (an idea critical to my concept of constructed inertia). The repressed idea is not disposed of once and for all; its repression is an ongoing psychical, energetic demand. It is this because 'the repressed exercises a continuous pressure in the direction of the conscious' (1915d, *GW*: 253, *SE*: 151). In other words, the repressed idea strives to become present to consciousness. This means in effect that two energetic processes are at work. On the one hand, a repressed nucleus is attracting further repressions towards it. On the other, that repressed nucleus, and/or the repressions it attracts, is striving for liberation. How the same factor, the repressed, can both

---

38 Both in his use of the term 'fixation', and in his Giza exemplification, Freud evokes his earlier work on hysteria. The Giza example is given to supplement a claim that the mechanism of hysterical amnesia 'is only explicable by the fact that the subject is already in possession of a store of memory-traces which have been withdrawn from conscious disposal, and which are now, by an associative link, attracting to themselves the material which the forces of repression are engaged in repelling from consciousness' (1905b, *Studien*: 83–4, *SE*: 175, 1915 edn).

strive to become conscious, and to keep ideas related to it, and itself, unconscious is not addressed. But Freud needs both arguments. He has to explain why it is that the repressed returns. He also has to explain why adult experiences and desires that could be dealt with by reasoned judgements are in fact dealt with by the economically inefficient process of repression.

To explain the economic inefficiency, Freud adduces primal repression. With primal repression, and it is this that seems to make primal repression different from repression proper, a fixation [*Fixierung*] is established. The consequence of fixation is that the psychical representative remains unaltered and the drive 'remains attached to it' (1915d, *GW*: 250, *SE*: 148). This definition suggests that another difference between the two forms of repression is that in primal repression, the nature of the idea that is repressed remains fixed (which is consistent with my argument on the repressed still point of hallucination), while in repression proper any subsequent idea with a relation to the primally repressed idea will suffer the same repressed fate. So that if the primally repressed idea consisted of an hallucinatory devouring of the breast or the mother, any subsequent idea concerning, say, an oral demand, or, say, a union with the mother, would be drawn towards the first repression. It follows that the ideas that are primally repressed are primitive ones.

The next question is: What is the relation between the primitive nature of the ideas, the mechanism of primal repression, and the other forms of defence that Freud suggests come before 'repression proper'? On the first question: primitive ideas are visual (thinking in pictures comes before thinking in words). Primal repression, accordingly, should be directed towards visual images, or other forms of hallucination. On the second question: Freud has given three indications as to what these other prior forms of defence involve: (i) reversal into the opposite; (ii) turning round upon the subject's own self (p. 54, n. 26, n. 27); and (iii) projection (see chapter 2, pp. 49–53). The first two forms of defence will be of interest in discussing the drives (chapter 4). The third, projection, is of interest now. Actually, projection could come before primal repression, let alone repression proper, in so far as an hallucination is a projected image, and 'turning around upon the subject's own self' takes on a whole new dimension in view of the part played by attention in forming the subject's initial image, and identity maintenance. But we will leave that to one side. The thing now is that Freud contradicts the idea that projection is a primitive defence mechanism in elaborating on the three stages of repression in the Schreber analysis, to which we will now give more attention.

The first stage consists in *fixation*. Freud defines this in a way that makes it equivalent to subsequent definitions of primal repression, in that he says it is 'the precursor and necessary condition of every "repression"'. In fixation, one drive or drive-component

> fails to accompany the rest along the anticipated normal path of development, and, in consequence of this inhibition in its development, it is left behind at a more infantile stage.
>
> (1911b, *GW*: 304, *SE*: 67)

For the second stage of repression described in the Schreber case, Freud uses the expression 'repression proper'. It 'emanates from the more highly developed systems of the ego. ... It gives an impression of being an essentially active process, while fixation appears in fact to be *a passive lagging behind*' (1911b, *GW*: 304, *SE*: 67, emphasis added). Now one might expect, given the association between femininity, passivity, and the girl's lingering in the Oedipus complex, that Freud would tie primal repression to femininity, just as he made projection an early defence mechanism in the girl's case. But this is emphatically not the case. Freud writes that repression proper is 'the phase to which most attention has hitherto been given' (1911b, *GW*: 304, *SE*: 67), which certainly suggests that 'repression proper' is the type of repression found in hysteria, the feminine neurosis. In addition, and this is where he contradicts his assumption that projection is an early defence mechanism, projection is tied to repression proper in the analysis of Schreber. Schreber's homosexual cathexes were unacceptable to him, and he withdrew them from the external world. In this context, Freud writes that

> repression proper consists in a detachment of the libido from people – and things – that were previously loved. It happens silently; we receive no intelligence of it, but can only infer it from subsequent events. What forces itself so noisily upon our attention is the work of recovery, which undoes the work of repression and brings back the libido again on to the people it had abandoned. In paranoia this process is carried out by the method of projection.
>
> (1911b, *GW*: 308, *SE*: 71)

This is the third stage of the three phases of repression: the return of the repressed, and in it projection is tied to a late stage of psychical development. Yet, as I have indicated, Freud subsequently wrote that the defence mechanism of projection 'is favoured by the early age of the [girl] child's psychical development' (1933a, *GW*: 128, *SE*: 120).[39] If Freud is right that projection in Schreber's case is a late defence mechanism, and also right that projection is an early defence mechanism in girls, then two

---

39 Freud evidently thought that the mechanism of projection warranted more attention, and promised to return to it. Strachey notes that he did not in fact return to it, and, as mentioned in an earlier note, infers that projection may have been the topic of one of the missing Metapsychological papers (1911b: 66, edit. n. 1).

forms of projection are at work. As femininity 'lags', like primal repression, and yet, as femininity presupposes repression proper, there must be a means by which a secondary 'lag' comes into being in femininity. This lag should operate like primal repression, and yet presuppose higher levels of organization of the ego. This buttresses my belief that there is a secondary as well as a primary inertia. Yet in some way that remains to be determined, the two 'lags' are tied to projection as an early defence mechanism, and projection as a subsequent one.

This problem turns our attention to Freud's enumeration of the vicissitudes of the defence mechanism of repression as such, rather than of the defence mechanisms that come before it. Most of the Metapsychological paper on 'Repression' is devoted to the vicissitudes of repression. In discussing them, Freud introduces an argument which various commentators have seized on as prefiguring the part played by chains of linguistic association in psychoanalysis. He argues that if the derivatives of what was primarily repressed had been sufficiently removed from it

> whether owing to the adoption of distortions or by reason of the number of intermediate links inserted, they have free access to the conscious. It is as though the resistance of the conscious against them was a function of their distance from what was originally repressed.
> (1915d, *GW*: 252, *SE*: 149)

The significance of free association in psychoanalysis is that by following the chain of ideas or representations, unravelling the associations between, or puns within, words, one arrives at the repressed idea (p. 105). The closer this chain leads to the repressed idea, the greater the resistance to it. Evidently the linguistic chain is a distancing mechanism, a spatial phenomenon, as Derrida (1980) has argued. This spatial factor must be noted, because otherwise, while this vicissitude of repression fits neatly with the emphasis on language, the chain of signification of itself will not help us situate projection, or the earlier defence mechanisms.

For Freud is clear that repression involves other vicissitudes. Not only can the idea be repressed and sent on its way along the path of signification; the energy of the drive linked to the idea can also follow its own path. In stating this, Freud distinguishes between the idea or representation [*Vorstellung*] and 'some other element representing the drive'. For this other element, Freud uses the term 'quota of affect'. Now this distinction between quantitative excitation and affect, although otherwise they seem to be in the same class, will be very helpful. It will help explain how primary and secondary inertia come into being. It will do this because we will postulate that the fixed point of an hallucination and its repression are the means by which quantitative excitation and affect are split in the first instance, and that the consequences of this split spill over into femininity. They spill over after the advent of language, which we will treat as an attempt at recapturing the motion of the original excitation, while arguing that this attempt can be successful only to the extent that it disposes of the affects that result from the primary split. In hysteria (the prototype of the secondary lag of femininity) these affects are retained with a visual image that imprisons the word (pp. 131–2 below).

This is not to say that Freud is clear about the distinction between affects and excitation. He is confused. Yet his confusion indicates that he sensed a problem. His discussion of this quota of affect is confusing because, on the one hand, he suggests that the 'quota of affect' is a different form of representation of the drive, which 'corresponds to the drive in so far as the latter has become detached from the idea and finds expression, proportionate to its quantity, in processes which are sensed as affects' (1915d, GW: 255, SE: 152). In this, he separates the affective quantitative factor from the ideational representative. On the other, he refers to the 'quantitative factor of the representative of the drive [Triebsrepräsentanz]' (1915d, GW: 255, SE: 153). It is unclear whether this means that the representative is both ideational and affective, or whether he has a strictly affective representative in mind. We will give him the benefit of the doubt, believe him to be consistent, and assume the latter.

In other words, two things can represent the drive. One is a linguistic idea. The other is an affect. Moreover, for the drive to be expressed as an affect, it has to be detached from the symbolic idea. It is important to note that the affect is still a representative of the drive, rather than a direct expression of it. It is also important to reiterate that Freud does not express the distinction between the 'quota of affect', as a psychical representative of the drive, and the drive itself, clearly. For instance, he speaks of following the vicissitudes of the idea on the one hand, and the 'energy of the drive attached to it [an ihr haftenden Triebenergie]' on the other (1915d, GW: 255, SE: 152). As I said, it is helpful for our purposes that Freud thought the energy of the drive need be represented in an affect, and that the affect and the energy of the drive need not be one and the same thing, and that the drive has to be detached from the idea before the drive can be expressed as affect. But Freud is not making these distinctions to support the idea that, ultimately, quantitative excitation is split into language and affect by fixed points (or images), nor even making them because he recalls his own idea that a 'common substance' lay at the origin of language and bodily symbol alike. He was making them because, to explain his case material on obsessional neuroses especially, he needs affects to be representatives of the drives. He needs the affect contingent on the drive to be capable of transformation into another affect. He needs affects, like ideas, to be capable of displacement. He also needs the affect to be able to follow a path of displacement which bears no necessary relation to the path of the idea.

Let us note three things before moving on.

1 While the quota of affect represents the energy of the drive, Freud at no point suggests that a particular affect corresponds to a particular drive. He indicates that particular drives are involved, to the extent that he writes of an objectionable idea as something 'cathected with a definite quota of psychical energy (libido or interest) coming from a drive'. The libido is composed of component drives. On the other hand, as the component drives are already ideational, in that they embody oral, anal, or phallic ideas, the 'drive' in question has to be different from the component drives as such; it seems to be 'idea-free'. As I noted in the Introduction, the drives are meant to be like the 'quantity', or Q, Freud referred to in the *Project*, when he invoked a source of energetic pressure whose nature was entirely unspecified. The difference between Q and the drive is that Q comes from without as well as within, while drives are endogenous in origin.

2 Freud also points out (again) that the suppression of the affect is especially characteristic of obsessional neurosis, which I have noted is the masculine neurosis *par excellence*, and in which the vicissitudes of the linguistic idea are most evident in the 'chain of signification'. This, incidentally, resonates with how it is that Elisabeth von R.'s masculine identification is expressed only in words (p. 104).

3 The third thing is that Freud's wish to separate the vicissitudes of the affect, the idea, and the drive, is not only prompted by the need for clinical explanation. It is also prompted by the belief that repression is caused by the desire to avoid unpleasure. It is anxiety 'especially' that leads him to follow the vicissitudes of the quota of affect. For anxiety and other 'feelings of unpleasure' indicate that a repression has failed. Freud stresses that 'the vicissitude of the quota of affect belonging to the representative is far more important than the vicissitude of the idea' (1915d, *GW*: 256, *SE*: 153). Failure is not evident in the fate of the linguistic idea; the idea is either repressed or it is not. Of itself, it does not lead to the unpleasant feelings or anxiety. Accordingly, it is the existence of anxiety and unpleasant feelings that led Freud to suppose that the psychical energy of drives could be transformed into affects, which fits with the picture presented in the preceding section. It does so in more than one way. For while Freud presents this transformation of energy into affects in general terms, the only exemplifications he gives of it refer to unpleasant feelings. It is not just a transformation into any old affect that matters; *it is its transformation into unpleasant feelings, 'anxiety especially'*.

Anxiety, in every instance discussed thus far, accompanies a tie to the past. It accompanies the frozen affects of hysteria and the stalling of the neurotic ego. I related these ties to the past to the fixing of attention, and suggested that fixed attention was a form of repression. From this perspective, anxiety not only accompanies but seems to be the transformation from moving attention to the present to fixed attention to the past. Transformation is also crucial in Freud's paper on repression: anxiety, he argues, is an affect produced by the transformation of unexpressed libido. In other words, he believed that the repression of libido produced anxiety. The view that libido was transformed into anxiety was how Freud solved the problem of the fate of the energy attached to the drive. It was transformed from one affect representing the libidinal image into another, represented by anxiety. He gives the specific example of an anxiety hysteria in which an animal substituted for the father, and fear of the father resulted in an animal phobia. The love for the father, the 'quantitative portion' of the drive's representative, had been transformed into anxiety. So far, so good. Both arguments focus on transformation.

But Freud subsequently argued that anxiety was not transformed libido, but a signal from the ego. He suggested that the ego was able to stop the libidinal, excitatory process from occurring in the id at all, and notes that 'If this is so, the problem of "transformation of affect" under repression disappears' (1926a, *GW*: 119, *SE*: 91). Yet, as Freud goes on to note, this means according a considerable power to the ego. He suggests that it derives this power (which is, let us not forget, an economic power) from its 'intimate connections with the perceptual system – connections which, as we know, constitute its essence and provide the basis of its differentiation from the id' (1926a, *GW*: 119, *SE*: 92). But this leaves him with the further problem of where the ego gets the energy it uses in signalling unpleasure. Freud cannot really answer this question. He suggests that an answer may come from the idea that the ego's response to 'an unwelcome *internal* process will be modelled upon the defence adopted against an *external* stimulus' (1926a, *GW*: 119, *SE*: 92, Strachey's emphases) and that repression based on anxiety is equivalent to flight from a threat also based on fear or anxiety. But this does not solve his economic problem. In the end, he writes that 'Anxiety is not newly created in repression; it is reproduced as an affective state in accordance with an already existing mnemic image' (1926a, *GW*: 120, *SE*: 93). What he means by this is that affective states are not due to transformations, but are memories. He even suggests that these affective states are similar, if not identical, to hysterical attacks, and in some sense that an affect is an hysterical symptom. This is perfect for our argument and it also clarifies the secondary inertia of femininity. The idea that an affect *is* an hysterical symptom, and one that restricts by anxiety, is consistent with my analysis, and moreover reveals that affects or feelings are not generic entities, but symptomatic of disorder. They are produced, or constructed. The stuff out of which they are constructed is, by Freud's account, a drive out of which language also comes.

Before returning to this linguistic conundrum, I want to note how my

argument will solve the economic quantitative problems that continue to
plague Freud throughout the discussion of anxiety. These problems are as
follows. (i) If anxiety is a signal from the ego (modelled on its response
to external stimuli) this means the ego has considerable economic power.
(ii) Anxiety can exhaust the ego, which, once more, means that anxiety
represents an economic demand. If it is the revival of a mnemic trace, it
is none the less an economically demanding one. Nor (iii) can Freud
dispense altogether with his earlier argument that anxiety is transformed
libido, because he is committed to a quantitative view in which

> it cannot be denied that the libido belonging to the id-processes is
> subject to disturbance at the instigation of repression. It might still be
> true, therefore, that in repression anxiety is produced from the libidinal
> cathexes of the drive's impulses. But how can we reconcile this con-
> clusion with our other conclusion that the anxiety felt in phobias is an
> ego anxiety and arises in the ego, and that it does not proceed out of
> repression but, on the contrary, sets repression in motion?
>
> (1926a, *GW*: 138–9, *SE*: 110)

Freud writes that 'It will not be easy to reduce the two sources of anxiety
to a single one' (ibid.), and shortly thereafter gives up the attempt. But if
we take account of the idea that anxiety is the concomitant of the ego
turning attention back to its old pathways in order to preserve itself in
circumstances which jeopardize its identity, if we take account of how
fixed attention is the same as repression, and if we take account of the
idea that attention can also be directed towards the other from without,
in a way that fixes it, thereby producing anxiety, these two sources of
anxiety can be explained. They are even more explicable when the anxiety
produced by another's fixing or freezing attention is also libidinal in origin.
Which it is, if the imposition of this fixed attention embodies the other's
libidinal economic drives.

Whether or not this attention will fix depends, naturally, on the nature
of the libidinal drive. I have suggested that the other's attention works at
two levels and in two ways; it either colludes in fixation in an interlock,[40]
or it facilitates (p. 114). I have suggested that masculinity must be endowed
with an extra dimension of moving attention, and raised the question as
to how it is that this dimension is absent in femininity and pathology (p.
118).

The obvious if provisional answer for the relative absence of this moving
attention in femininity is this: the libidinal masculine drive, the attention
or gaze from the masculine other felt in femininity, must work in the
same way as the inward-turning of attention in producing a fixed point.

40 At the primary level, this interlock would bear on the fact that the Kleinian infant, in
   an hallucinatory split, divides its object into a good (facilitating?) and bad (repressing,
   restricting, or fixing?) breast.

In the case of neurosis, other factors also increase this inward-turning, and the consequent fixation on past pathways. These other factors consist of anything that imperils the supply of attention the ego diverts to itself as a rule. But if we restrict ourselves for now to femininity, the point is that the masculine drive and gaze may also produce anxiety, although this would normally be as subliminal or even unconscious as the deathly factor in the masculine drive itself. Yet as I hinted earlier (p. 90), there is no more than an economic difference between the fixation produced by an actual gaze of this order, and the fixation produced by daydreams. And it seems the fixation is as necessary for maintaining a feminine identity as it is for establishing the ego in the first place. In this connection, it is striking how the need to daydream about an object, and almost any object will do, increases when a woman is not in a sexual relationship. On the other hand, there is something about the nature of the attention directed towards a masculine being from a feminine one which is in some way ego-syntonic, meaning it coheres with his self-image in a way that facilitates active strivings. It is the nature of the attention received in femininity that parallels the repression of hallucination by the ego before the Oedipus complex. In both cases attention produces a 'fix', and it produces anxiety.

It remains to tie this analysis back to the repression of active strivings in femininity. We will begin with the fact that apart from the two sources of anxiety, two forms of projection have also been identified: one an early, and one a subsequent defence mechanism. Can these two forms of projection be tied to the two sources of anxiety? More precisely, can the recognition of these two forms, these two sources, help us with understanding the greater tendency to repression in women? We have seen that the only explanation Freud leaves us with is that women have to repress phallic activity, and that his explanation is not tied to the primitive defence mechanisms that characterize the undifferentiated pre-Oedipal and Oedipal phases in girls.

Freud's psychical economy has been criticized because, at times, it appears that 'the force repressed and the repressing force might have the very same source' (de Sousa 1982: 150). We have resolved this contradiction (at the primary level) by breaking down the 'self-contained' assumptions that give rise to it; there is even less of a contradiction (at the secondary level) if what one party experiences as a drive, the other experiences as a projection; that is to say, if 'his' drive is 'her' repression. Before proceeding, I should reiterate, and not at all for the last time, that 'his' and 'her' refer to the masculine and feminine positions in phantasy rather than the actual positions of either men or women. Or, as Freud would have it, 'his' and 'her' positions are, respectively, the positions of subject and object, to the extent that the masculine position is that of the subject, the feminine that of the object. Again, the important thing here is not the sex of the being in question, but thinking of the psyche as other than a self-contained entity, affected by the drives and libidinal attention of the other. From this perspective, not only the two sources of anxiety, but the two forms of projection, and Freud's account of the greater repression in women, pose fewer problems.

However the discussion here will rely on the assumption that phallic activity is a specific instance of externally directed activity, or active strivings in general, together with moving attention to the present. The identification of phallic activity and externally directed activity in general is borne out by Freud's last words on femininity, and the idea that femininity is not ego-syntonic. This suggests that it is not only phallic activity, but externally directed activity in general, that is repressed, for both externally directed activity as such, and its regulation, is the province of the ego.

Before attempting to specify the difference between the two levels of projection, it is worth noting that the idea that externally directed activity is repressed in femininity introduces spatial terms; it presupposes that the direction of this activity has changed. It has been turned back against the self. The stress on spatiality is relevant to connecting the two forms of anxiety to projection, as I indicated earlier in an allusion to the Derridean linguistic chain. Spatiality, of course, is also implicit in the idea that the attention or gaze or even the desire of the other all presuppose externality, an outer world and other people.

Taking account of the idea that the repression of phallic activity is the repression of externally directed activity, and the discussion of the two levels of anxiety, the relation between the two levels of projection, and the repression of active strivings in femininity can be specified this way. When the ego is formed, and the ego-fix and interlock with the other is felt as restrictive or negative, the anxiety it produces is projected on to another as hostility. This projection frees up the ego. It is an active, and initially hallucinatory, projection. But having projected the hostility one feels externally, one imagines that the other will retaliate, and makes them hostility's source rather than its recipient. This produces more anxiety.[41]

It would make sense if the second level of anxiety was also projected again; that is to say, if it were projected out as hostility. It would also be consistent if it led to further fear of retaliation. Yet the fear of retaliation is only one among three psychical responses to the projection of hostility. That is to say, this projection can lead to paranoia, and more fear of retaliation (hence paranoia as a later as well as an earlier defence

41 This explanation is entirely consistent with Freud's observation that the girl's aggressive impulses towards her mother only come to light after being changed into anxiety ideas (p. 53). There is also a sense in which this logic accounts for the 'fear of retaliation', so basic to Kleinian theory: if a phantasmatic retaliation is similar in structure to the more negative effects of the attention that fixes identity in the first place, the 'fear of retaliation' is also a form of longing for attention that will secure identity. From the ego's perspective, if its sense of coherence is at stake, negative attention is better than none at all, even if it leads to death.

mechanism), but it can also be a successful projection, meaning the hostility is disposed of in a way that means it does not return, or the hostility can return in the form of a further fixation. When it returns, we have a further parallel with the formation of the ego and of femininity, provided that hostility is tied to active strivings.

For what I am saying here is that when active strivings are turned back against the self in femininity, they carry hostility in their train. In phantasy or reality, 'hostility', or whatever hostility is composed of, is directed back against the self. But for this explanation to really work, two conditions need to be fulfilled. Not only does externally directed activity have to be tied to hostility.[42] Reality and/or phantasy has to have a pivotal role,[43] and be capable of turning 'active strivings' (and the attention and affects embodied in them) backwards. Several grounds for fulfilling these conditions have been established in this chapter.

Both from the standpoint that ideas are physical, and from the analysis of Freud and Breuer's case material, I have argued that when the feminine being turns her phantasy inwards, this phantasy carries motor activity in its train. From the standpoint that active strivings are the province of the ego, and attention implicated in them, I have suggested that when the woman represses her active strivings, she fixes herself as an object in phantasy. The *Studies* especially suggested that fixation was tied to a split in attention and affective visualization. This visualization is paramount in

42 Concerning this, Laplanche and Pontalis have argued that primitive defence mechanisms have their 'privileged site' in phantasy: 'turning against oneself, switching to the opposite position, projection, denegation; these defences are even indissolubly linked with the primary function of fantasy – the staging of desire – if it is true that desire itself is constituted as a prohibition, that the conflict is a primordial conflict' (Laplanche and Pontalis [1964] 1968, cited Borch-Jacobsen 1989: 25). Borch-Jacobsen notes that this passage implies that 'desire is linked to repression in a much more complex, radical way than Freud first imagined'.

43 The idea that phantasy itself is the means whereby this translation is effected would also account for how it is that phantasy is not 'the object of desire' as such; 'it is a scene' in which 'the subject is not seeking after the object or its sign, it figures itself caught up in the sequence of images. It does not represent the desired object to itself, but it is represented as participating in the scene without any possibility, *in the forms that are closest to the original phantasy*, of a place being assigned to it' (Laplanche and Pontalis [1964] 1968, cited Borch-Jacobsen 1989: 25, emphasis added). The original phantasy, for Laplanche and Pontalis, is a primal phantasy. The primal scene is the main exemplar of a primal phantasy; it is the phantasy appropriate to the question 'Where do I come from?'. In addition, the closer a phantasy approximates to its original form, the more likely it is to be visual: a visual representation of an event or a sequence of events, rather than a verbal narrative. Now much has been made of how, by Laplanche and Pontalis's account, the subject has no certain position. As noted above (p. 99) there is an argument that in fact *two* positions (subject and object) are the ones at stake. A related conclusion has been reached by Borch-Jacobsen who argues that phantasy leads towards the 'wishing subject's' position (1989: 25). If phantasy is the tie between his subjective drive or desire and her 'objective' repression, the fact that both his phantasy and hers lean towards the subject's wish begins to be comprehensible. It will be more so after we consider the second point that this argument needs to establish, about how activity needs to be tied to hostility.

the private theatre of daydreams, in the cinema-photographer who presents a feminine being with an image of herself; literally, she becomes an object before her own eyes. This constitutes a form of identity, but at a price. The price, which I initially estimated on the basis of Breuer's account of daydreaming (although the same process of course works unconsciously in the maintenance of identity), is that a woman splits her capacity for attention, and diverts some of this attention, together with the quantity embodied in it, back against herself. Presupposing that daydreams constitute a self-image, she can, if she is anxious enough, be frozen within the frame of her image. For she is frozen by fright or anxiety, according to Breuer; these are the affects that produce her symptom, when she is in a daydreaming or hypnoid state. For Freud, she is fixed by repression which (at the unconscious level it works on) is synonymous with paralysing affects. For both Freud and Breuer, the chances were high that the hysterical symptom would reflect a contiguous set of associations: that is to say, an hysteric's symptom would reflect a kind of (frozen?) snapshot in time, in which various extraneous visual associations present at the moment of the symptom's formation combine with the relevant affective associations. It is because of Freud's assumptions in this respect, as well as Anna O.'s 'private theatre' and Jung's cinema-operator, that I have used the term 'frame'.

Throughout this chapter (and this book), I have drawn conclusions about the structure of femininity on the basis that hysteria is an index to that structure. I have also read obsessional neurosis as an index to the structure of masculinity, as did Freud. While obsessional neurosis is the masculine neurosis, it fails in that it is not ego-syntonic. Its failure, as with so much else in Freud's work, tells us as much about normality as it does about pathology. Freud implied that obsessional neurosis is not ego-syntonic because the obsessive is indecisive, 'doubting his own love and therefore every lesser thing', divided between love and hate, which gives us another tie between activity and hostility. The obsessive cannot dispose of his latent hostility or hatred, and this underpins his inability to act decisively, and ineffectual displacement of affect on to ideas which conceal his hatred.

Hysteria almost works, but it is excessive femininity; the freeze-frame it establishes is too fixed. Which means that normal femininity requires a frame with more flexibility or freedom to move. Similarly, while obsessional neuroses almost work, the split between affect and linguistic representation (a split in an original form of excitation, or 'common substance'), and the indecision prompted by hostility, is disabling. Let us suppose then that normal masculinity effects a split between affect and representation which is productive, and which productively disposes of hostility; let us suppose too that normal femininity is a freeze frame which permits a little warm movement. What would this mean? Given that neurosis, like normality, requires some relation to the external world, we can venture that normal masculinity is able to dispose of its otherwise disabling feelings by projecting them on to the other, or the outer world. Of course this projection too is unconscious, just as its affects are unconsciously rather than consciously felt. And at one level, we are saying no more than Freud and Lacan did when they said that the man split woman into two types, directing aggression towards one, affection towards another, in what I called a narcissistic short-cut to securing identity. Except that I am also saying that normal femininity physically accepts some of this projection, but not too much. While femininity 'feels' more than the man who (by his projection?) is able to float away from the flesh and off down the linguistic current, normal femininity is none the less protected from that projection in some way that enables it to direct some of its attention, together with its activity, to the outside world. At the same time, femininity divides its own attention, to the extent that some of it is employed in maintaining its own image: this is narcissism, but a necessary narcissism.

In line with the chain of reasoning established thus far, we can suppose that successful masculinity has in some way split affect and representation, and disposed of its hostility, without negative consequences for itself, and secured the attention from outside that maintains its identity, without having to divert its own stream of attention to the same end. The question, of course, was, From whence does it secure this extra attention? There is a strong case being built now for the idea that the surplus of attention in masculinity is extracted from the feminine other, and that femininity, when it is pushed to its pathological limit, is carrying the disordered feelings of the masculine other. This means that she provides him with an anchor in the flesh, while he floats down the linguistic current, but the flesh is not his own. This anchor provides the man with a boundary or borderline for his identity. Thus, while the first step in the construction of his identity was the construction of a temporal still point, the second step is the spatial projection of the consequences of the first repression on to the feminine other. For I am presuming that the consequences of the first repression was that it split affect from excitation. There will be more discussion of this presumption, but, in part, it has already been established: the notion of a split between forms of excitation is entirely consistent with Freud's assumption that hallucination gratified a wish, while leading to unproductive 'excitations' divorced from that wish. Like an hallucination, the masculine projection of unwanted affects is active. But because it has a real point of reference that is other than itself, it has a fixed place in space and time. At the same time as it endows him with moving attention, this other reference point gives him a literal sense of perspective, and enables him to think without unproductive feeling, to be decisive because his hostility does not disable him.

On the other hand, the feminine being is unable to act or attend (that is to say, think) not only because she is turning her attentive energy back on herself, but also because some of her attention is going to another in the secondary inertia constituted by the intermesh of masculine projection and feminine repression. After all, those hysterics were sick-nursing. Yet we can suppose too that normal femininity has secured a boundary that protects its identity, and secures it against the projections of successful masculinity, in a way that frees some of its attention and activity for externally directed ends. We might suppose too that the security provided by this boundary bears on *why* it is that femininity gives moving attention to the other.

The corollary of what I have supposed so far is that the more successful the masculinity (where a masculine and feminine subject are in a dyadic relationship), and the less successful the femininity, the more likely the woman is to be hysterical. And equally certainly, the converse holds; the more successful the femininity, the more likely the masculine being is to be obsessive, if not depressed, with the depressive indecision that also characterizes obsessional neurosis. The ideal feminist type, the good man, is left with unattractive options here. If he does not project his hostility outwards, he must dispose of it through sublimation, which could lead to genius in a fortuitous case, or just creative reparation (the long path rather than the short-cut to identity (p. 77)); or he can turn hostility back against himself in depression. Or he can do both.[44]

As I indicated at the outset, the block on knowledge, the key to forget-fulness in terms of censorship, is tied to the conviction that subjects are physically self-contained, and the notion that the energetic emotions or phantasies of one subject do not have a physical impact on another. The suggestion that these forces do have an effect, and the proposition that the energies, emotions, and phantasies of the one affect the other, can now be made more concrete. The fact that the affect is displaced in obsessional neurosis, and the notion that the affect is detached from an original energy and displaced in obsessional neurosis has provided one key, the division of attention in hysteria has provided another. In successful masculinity (this is the most contentious conclusion, and will require the next chapter for more plausibility) the displaced affect, a variation on the theme of the original unspecified energy, is not turned inwards in the miserable convolutions of obsessiveness. It is projected on to the other in a confused disorder, felt by the other as 'feelings', which marshals itself into a new and artificial order of rigidity for her. In doing so, it produces an object, where an object is defined as passive. For in this projection, the other becomes relatively fixed or still, and this is exemplified in

44 On the notion that hostility can be sublimated, see Freud's correspondence with Marie Bonaparte concerning the relation between the death drive and the force of sublimation. (See the Editor's Note to Freud 1915c.)

hysterical paralysis. However it is critical to remember that the feminine being is perfectly capable of effecting this paralysis and relative stillness of her own accord. The masculine gaze only overlays and interlocks with an existing psychical, phantasmatic structure, as do the social realities which enforce a retreat to the world of phantasy.

The obsessional neurotic, the archetype of masculinity, is unsuccessful, in that he does not project his disorder outwards. I am venturing that when he does so, the result is ego-syntonic masculinity. In short, when the masculine being, or would-be masculine being, does not project his disorder outwards, he is neurotic, for the projection is turned back against himself, producing anxiety and forgetfulness. On the other hand, no matter how un-neurotic he is, meaning how successfully he projects, he has to forget one thing: he has to forget anything that would tell him that he maintains his sanity by projecting his disorder on to another.

By means we have yet to establish in detail, the other, by virtue of this projection, becomes an object, a still point of reference for the subject. But of course if she is at the mercy, as it were, of the subject's disordered projected energy, she would be psychotic. To be sane, even hysterically sane, she has to have an internal boundary that protects her from this projection.[45] We have supposed here that whatever that boundary is, it is tied to visualization, and that its nature casts light on the similarity, as well as the difference, between femininity and psychosis. Moreover, as anxiety holds a visual mnemic image in place and as anxiety produces repression, it would seem that the visual image is the border or boundary between what is repressed and the anxiety that represses it. There will be more on the precise nature of this boundary, and how it comes into being, in chapter 5; there, we will discuss the superego's part in bringing the boundary into being, and how an identity maintained by feminine means is protected. First, we need to fill out the speculation that the subject projects his disordered energetic affects outwards to maintain a sane masculinity, producing the secondary inertia of femininity, and constituting himself as a subject in the process. If this is right, his own capacity for visualization, in successful masculinity, has to be directed towards another, and it has to be tied to hostility. This notion takes us directly to Freud's theory of the drives.

---

45 It is over this point especially that this argument diverges from Irigaray's, who has also criticized an 'economy of metaphor' and the separation of language and body on different grounds (cf. Irigaray 1985a: 346). The problem with this often brilliant criticism is that it contradicts Irigaray's insistence on the need for a system of symbolic representation for women, a contradiction which could be avoided if the focus was on projection, and the precise dynamics by which the power to represent and metaphorize is acquired.

Chapter 4

The involution of the drives

INTRODUCTION

It is in the context of a brief article on disturbances of vision that Freud (1910f) introduces the first dualistic theory of the drives, arguing that there is a fundamental antagonism between the sexual drive and the self-preservative drive. This dualism was later to be displaced on to one between Eros and Thanatos, Life and Death. It was an essential metapsychological displacement. Freud had argued himself into a situation where he could not consistently maintain grounds for a distinction between the ego drives and the sexual drives. In shifting the emphasis to the struggle between life and death he was right, yet he was also wrong. For the form, function, and force of the ego cut two ways. One way is, or appears to be, on the side of life. The other sides with death. Revealing the ego's two faces depends on a more detailed identification of the level of fixation involved in the production of secondary, not only primary, inertia. It also depends on clarifying why the ego is ego-syntonic in masculinity, and why it is not in femininity. Its masculine syntony makes it lifelike. The absence of syntony in femininity makes it similar in structure to the deathly or inert ego, and understanding this will help unravel the feminine tie to the past further still.

The last chapter noted that it was in relation to the death drive that Freud reformulated his views on anxiety; and established some grounds for the idea that some hypothesis about how attentive energy works not only within but between beings is necessary if one is to make sense of the fixity that characterizes the anxious ego and femininity alike. In this chapter I will establish further grounds for a parallel between the formation of the ego and femininity, concentrating on the passivity and inertia common to both. I will also establish a parallel between the formation of the lively ego and masculinity; both are active.

Yet throughout, it is vital to remember that these parallels are only that. The essential difference between the formation of femininity and the inert or deathly ego is that the former overlays the latter, which is ontologically prior; there is an homology in their structures, but femininity only over-lays the ego; they are not the same thing.

It would be helpful here if an already foreshadowed terminological distinction could be made explicit (p. 115). I have referred to the *formation* of the ego, and the difference between the ego before the Oedipus com-plex, and masculine and feminine identity. Before the Oedipus complex, only one side of identity is created in the fixed point or hallucinatory interlock. The terms 'masculinity' and 'femininity' presuppose fully formed identities that have passed beyond the intermediate mirror stage and are spatially cemented in place. Masculinity and femininity are thus equivalent to masculine and feminine identity. It would be useful if we could reserve the term 'ego' for the psychical self-centred entity that exists before the Oedipus complex, and the term 'identity' for the subject-centred psychical entity that is created by it. But it is difficult to maintain such a distinction because Freud uses the ego to refer to part of the psyche before and after the Oedipus complex. As far as possible however I will try to use 'ident-ity', or its synonyms masculinity and femininity, in the context of the post-Oedipal psyche, and the term 'ego' in the context of the pre-Oedipal one. When Freud's quotations or reference points make this impossible, I will try to indicate which level of the 'ego' I mean.

That said: this chapter will establish more grounds for the parallel, and the difference, between femininity and the inert ego by concentrating on how successful masculinity (and the visual gaze it projects) bears on the nature of fixation in femininity. This concentrated exercise will, of necess-ity, elucidate the difference between the lively ego and masculinity as well. In doing so, it draws out the difference between activity and passivity, and the masculine and feminine identities that emerge with the Oedipus complex. This chapter will do these things through an investigation of Freud's first theory of the drives, which also, ultimately, introduces the 'innate' factor necessary for making the argument on how energetic con-nections between beings lead to their freedom or fixation.

The first theory of the drives is frequently misunderstood as a develop-mental theory of sexuality, and developmental readings of it have been extensively criticized in 'structuralist' interpretations of Freud. But the rejection of the developmental reading sometimes extends to the theory of the drives as such. Wollheim has observed that it is the tie to the body that gives Freud's theory its particular explanatory force (Wollheim [1975] 1976), but this tie has been neglected in recent criticism. Mitchell, for instance, justifies her summary treatment of Freud's theory of the drives by an appeal to Lacan. 'The inadequacy of Freud's "theory of instincts" is precisely an indication of Freud's contempt for its significance' (Mitchell (1974: 27). Lacan writes:

In any event one has only to go back to the works of Freud to gauge to what secondary and hypothetical place he relegates the theory of drives. The theory cannot in his eyes stand for a single instant against the least important particular fact of a history, he insists, and the *genital narcissism* which he invokes when he sums up the case of the Wolfman shows us well enough the disdain in which he holds the constituted order of the libidinal stages.[1]

While Freud's theory of the drives is definitely confused, an examination of that confusion will help the reformulation of the economic riddle of femininity begun in the last chapters, and take us further towards unravelling the confusion over physicality and the psyche. The next three sections of this chapter elaborate on the theory of the *Triebe* as it was first outlined in the *Three Essays on the Theory of Sexuality*. The first section (pp. 137–43) also refers to lecture XXI of Freud's *Introductory Lectures*, which follows the *Three Essays* closely, but which has the advantage that it is one of the rare occasions when Freud mentions the analogy theory, his first theory of femininity. It provides an opportunity for elaborating on the contradiction between the analogy theory and the theory of the libido (p. 28 above).

Moreover the libido theory yields a more productive contradiction: it is this that helps reformulate the questions arising from Freud's second theory of femininity. The second and third sections (pp. 143–7 and 147–58) draw this contradiction out through a discussion of (i) the quantitative matter of the drives, and of (ii) activity and passivity, and by showing (iii) how the drives that make the libido complex fall into two distinct classes. Once the distinction between them is recognized, the relation between the formation of the ego on the one hand, and femininity and masculinity on the other, is clarified. The *Three Essays* have additional interest because their discussion of the transformations of puberty returns us to the question of phantasy in the development of femininity: in discussing this question, the fourth section (pp. 158–70) confronts issues similar to those raised in the second chapter, concerning the quantitative relation between repression, identity, and creative labour, and in the last chapter's discussion of the division of attention. The fifth section (pp. 170–7) returns to the hypothesis whose preliminaries were outlined in the Introduction.

THE ANALOGY THEORY AND THE LIBIDO

In lecture XXI of the *Introductory Lectures* (1916–17 [1915–17]), Freud writes of the Oedipus complex that 'Things happen in just the same way with little girls, with the necessary changes; an affectionate attachment to her father, a need to get rid of her mother' (ibid., *GW*: 345,

---

1 Lacan (1953b: 54–5) quoted Mitchell (1974: 27). Mitchell's reference is to A. Wilden's translation.

SE: 333). Lecture XXI is an account of 'The Development of the Libido'. As such, it canvasses more than the specifics of the Oedipus complex. It dwells especially on the theory of the drives; it refers to object-choice, repression, and latency. Albeit briefly, it exemplifies the manner in which Freud consistently attempts to weave his different theoretical strands into an integrated whole.[2]

Like the *Three Essays*, lecture XXI begins with a discussion of perversion. The existence of perversion is the anchor for two of Freud's canons: that sexual life begins in infancy and that the sexual drive (libido) is constructed rather than natural: 'the sexual drive itself may be no simple thing, but put together from components which have come apart again in the perversions' (1905b, *Studien*: 71, *SE*: 162, first and subsequent edns). Through emphasizing construction, Freud is able to show, more or less in passing, that the difference between normal and aberrant sexuality is one of degree, rather than one of kind. In its time, that idea provided a relieving counterpoint to the dominant belief in the constitutional degeneracy of perverts. Freud writes, 'It has become the fashion to regard any symptom which is not obviously due to trauma or infection as a sign of degeneracy' (1905b, *Studien*: 50, *SE*: 138, first and subsequent edns). That aside: in this case, the polemical thrust of Freud's lecture is otherwise.

Freud wants to convince his audience that some of the bodily experiences of infants and small children are sexual. To do so, he points to the correlation between aspects of normal sexuality that would be perverse if isolated from a heterosexual genital aim, and certain chronological infantile experiences and activities. The experiences give rise to the 'component drives' (*Partialtriebe*): these are the constituents of the libido; or, to say the same thing, the libido is constructed out of the component drives. Freud numbered them as the oral drive, the anal-sadistic drive, the scopophilic drive, the drive for cruelty, the drive for mastery, the drive for knowledge, and the phallic drive. These libidinal constituents are defined in relation to an organic reference point (thus the mouth for the oral drive, and the penis or clitoris for the phallic drive) and in relation to the aim of the drive (thus the drive for mastery). Sometimes the aim and the organic reference point are evident enough. At other times the correlations are not so clear.

The organic reference points for the drives can constitute the erotogenic zones significant in normal sexuality's forepleasure (thus the labial zone is connected to kissing) or as ends in themselves in the perversions;

2 The *Introductory Lectures* were written after the major Metapsychological papers, after or during the major revisions to the *Three Essays* Freud made in 1915, after the secessions of Adler and Jung, but well before the metapsychological turning-points of 1920 and 1923. Delivered in the first years of the war, as the last of Freud's lectures at the University of Vienna, they mark a midway point in his thought. Because of this, and because lecture XXI like its counterparts is an attempt at synthesis, it shows how unswervingly the inconsistency between the analogy theory and the theory of the drives persists.

thus the scopophilic drive dominates the sexuality of the voyeur and the exhibitionist, in that orgasm is contingent on the fulfilment of certain visual requirements. As Freud was the first to point out, the line between normal and perverse sexuality can accordingly be very fine: the pleasure in sexually flavoured looking is perverse where it is an end in itself; merely forepleasure when it is not.

When the norm is established, and the norm here means of-the-norm, on-the-average, and the drives have a heterosexual genital aim, they constitute what Freud (in 1915) terms a genital form of organization. However, this form of organization is building on other pre-genital organizations of the component drives. In the lecture I have taken as a focal point, Freud says that the anal and sadistic drives – the latter he ties to a drive for mastery [*Bemächtigungstrieb*] – constitute a loose pre-genital organization. Elsewhere, he writes that the 'first (pregenital) organization to be discerned is the oral one' (1923a, *Studien*: 13, *SE*: 245). Evidently these pre-genital organizations cross-reference to the oral and anal phases which, together with the phallic phase, constitute one of the best-known theories of psychoanalysis: the theory that the libido develops in relation to those parts of the body which have prime significance for the infant and child at different points in time: the oral phase when it is being breast-fed, the anal phase when it is being toilet-trained, the phallic phase as it becomes aware of genital (clitoridal or penile) excitation, and as its drives come to focus on an object. In these cases, the erotogenic zones acquire significance when a satisfaction that was originally associated with a vital function (taking nourishment, defecation) becomes detached from that function: it is detached when the pleasure associated with the vital function is repeated in wishful 'auto-erotic' phantasy. In a not identical but related vein, Freud argues that the pleasurable feelings produced by the internal and accidental external stimulation of the erotogenic zones of the *glans penis* and the clitoris lead to a need for its repetition (1905b, *Studien*: 94–5, *SE*: 187–8, first and subsequent edns). We will return to the derivation of these drives shortly; there is another aspect of the phallic phase which requires more immediate elaboration.

Despite his recognition of the significance of the phallic drive at the time of the *Three Essays*, it is not until the implications of the second topography that the phallic phase is credited with any organizational significance. Before that, Freud believes that puberty is the occasion when a genital aim takes precedence. This is why the analogy theory could be maintained until then. Even so, it persists in spite of other internal contradictions whose full significance will emerge only after more discussion of how the libido is constructed, and of the nature of its components.

In this discussion, it is important to take account of the common-sense objection that sexuality cannot only be a matter of the construction of the sexual drive out of various components. Freud believed that sexuality had a diphasic onset. It was evident in early childhood, generally repressed in a latency period, and returned at puberty, accompanied by changes in primary and secondary sexual characteristics. Freud did not ignore the hormonal factor in the sexual drive; in fact his *Three Essays* on sexuality postulated something akin to sexual hormones well before they were discovered (1905b, *Studien*: 120, n. 1, *SE*: 216, n. 1). Freud's argument rather is that these substances trigger a drive that has been constructed out of various components. The 'stream' of the libido, to borrow a favourite metaphor of Freud's, takes its character from the pathways along which it flows, but these pathways, together with the aims and objects of the sexual drive, what stimulates it and what does not, are constructed in early childhood. When the libido is reactivated, so are the pathways from which it cannot be distinguished.

The diphasic onset of sexuality may be particularly significant in women. At the risk of straying a little beyond the limitations of this book, but in view of the fact that Freud's theory of femininity is also a theory of how curiosity and knowledge are inhibited in women, the idea that puberty is a time when girls are more likely to turn from abstract thought should be mentioned.[3] For this idea may suggest that when the construction of femininity is repressed after or during the girl's positive Oedipus complex, that repression, and the consequent latency period, is also the *repression*, or redirection, of what inhibits abstract thought.[4] This possibility is even more interesting when we recall the tie between anxiety and repression, and the inability to sustain creative attention under the impact of anxiety.

Puberty will be discussed again. We can note now that the neglect of the chemical factor in sexuality in recent attempts at using Freud to explain the construction of femininity is because discussions of sexual identity which focus on biology tend to be reductive, and developments in psychoanalysis which emphasize its biological connections are extremely reductive.[5]

3 Walkerdine (Walkerdine *et al.* 1984) discusses the evidence on girls' flight from mathematics at puberty in one of the rare psychoanalytically informed accounts of said flight.
4 This suggestion is also pertinent to Freud's refusal to concede to Jung over the latter's wish to generalize the concept of libido, so that it would mean psychical energy in general. Jung regarded 'sexual libido' as only one form of psychical energy, and thought that there was no necessary tie between the former and the energy deployed in thought and phantasy. Jung (1944–78, vol. 6: 61–3) argues against the idea of reducing creative phantasy and the principle of imagination to sexuality and instinctual repression. The force of this argument, that 'it is short-sighted to treat fantasy ... as a thing of little worth' when it is the condition of any 'creative work', is that it counters an historically specific (by Jung's account) emphasis on rationality. Its limitation is precisely that it cannot account for how phantasy and daydreams, in the case of femininity, obstruct the thinking process.
5 The most notorious being Wilhelm Reich (1970). At the other end of this reductive reasoning, one finds H. Hartmann's attempts at locating ego structure in the brain. See the discussion in Guntrip (1971: 40–1). Probably the most systematic attempt at arguing that Freud's relation to biology is fundamental rather than incidental to his psychology is Sulloway (1979).

Furthermore, arguments from or for biology have endured, despite intensive criticism, while Freud's psychophysics has been discredited.[6]

Biological arguments run counter to the notion that the libido is constructed, rather than natural. For many commentators this is the founding discovery of the psychoanalytic theory of sexuality. This is absolutely true, although the redeeming emphasis on construction has closed the door on any possibility of a non-reductionist, physical explanation. But at this point the significant issue is construction.

As I indicated, in its time, the emphasis on construction meant that the perversions were no longer subject to the weak explanation of degeneracy: rather they were to be explained by fixation in a particular phase, and the domination of a specific component drive. Subsequently, the idea of construction, as I also noted in the Introduction, has become the motif for the rejection of essentialism. Freud's own most trenchant arguments for construction are cast in the discussion of the perversions, amongst which he includes homosexuality. They focus on the distinction between the innate and the acquired. He rejects the distinction as inadequate on two grounds: the same things can happen to different people without producing the same result; on the other hand the effects of external circumstances are plain in some case histories. In other words, external events do affect psychosexual disposition (so they cannot be discounted) but they are insufficient to explain a final outcome. Given that different people react differently to the same external events (they might not become homosexual) but given that the events none the less have an effect (they might) we have to enquire into the meaning of innateness. The alternative is to accept 'the crude explanation that everyone is born with his sexual drive attached to a particular object' (1905b, *Studien*: 52, *SE*: 140–1, first and subsequent edns). Yet having recognized the need to do so, Freud never enquires into the meaning of innateness, or what the innate factor involves. His emphasis and his argument are on how the libido is constructed.

In showing how the libido is constructed, Freud stressed that the heterosexual genital norm is not the only form around which the component drives come to be finally organized. They can also be organized around a perverse aim, which means that some variation of a 'pre-genital stage' is an outcome rather than a precursor. When it is an outcome, it is not an unorganized one.

Perverse sexuality is as a rule excellently centred: all its actions are

6 Of course the fact that Freud himself shifted from a physical or, in his terms, mechanistic explanatory focus to a more biological one is a contributory factor here, although he continued to equivocate between physical and biological explanation. For instance, in discussing the stimulus prompted by the drives, as late as 1915, he writes: 'We do not know whether this process is invariably of a chemical nature or whether it may also correspond to the release of other, e.g. mechanical, forces' (1915c, *GW*: 215–16, *SE*: 123).

directed towards an aim.... In that respect there is no distinction between perverse and normal sexuality other than the fact that their dominating component drives and consequently their sexual aims are different. In both of them, one might say, a well-organized tyranny has been established, but in each of the two a different family has seized the reins of power.

(1916–17, *GW*: 334, *SE*: 322–3)

We have here an argument that the centring, the aiming of sexuality, has nothing to do with innate properties of the genitalia.[7] But this anti-natural argument is also contradicted by Freud.

In the polemics of lecture XXI, Freud supports his argument for the existence of infantile sexuality by an appeal to nature. Just as it is 'biologically more correct' to say the seed of a dicotyledonous plant is already sexed, even though its sexuality is not revealed until its flowering, so we may 'call the pleasure in the activities of an infant-in-arms a sexual one' (1916–17, *GW*: 336, *SE*: 325). This remarkable reversal of the constructive logic of his previous argument may stem from nothing more than a tendency to gild the lily, if not the dicotyledon. But it goes against the grain of his argument that the libido is constructed, and seems a banal and contradictory supplement to the linking of libido, perversion, and childhood experience.[8]

When Freud turns to object-choice in lecture XXI, he does so on the basis of the theory of the libido. He notes that while some drives retain their aim, as with the drive for mastery, others,

more definitely linked to particular erotogenic zones of the body, have [an aim or an object] to begin with only, so long as they are still attached to the non-sexual functions, and give it up when they become separated from them. Thus the first object of the oral component of the sexual drive is the mother's breast, which satisfies the infant's need for nourishment. The erotic component, which is satisfied simultaneously during the [nutritive] sucking, makes itself independent with the act of *sensual* sucking [*lutschen*]; it gives up the outside object and replaces it with an area of the subject's own body.

(1916–17, *GW*: 340–1, *SE*: 329)

Similar things happen with the other erotogenic drives. After this, writes

7 This idea and its implications for sexuality are pursued in Freud's posthumously published work on the splitting of the ego ([1938] 1940d). It is worth adding that it reopens the question as to what is the principle by which 'centring' is effected. As noted above (p. 113, n. 31), it is the ego that Freud credits with the capacity for synthesis, and synthesis and centring have the idea of coherence in common. Yet it is plain that synthetic psychical entities (cathected by attention?) need not take the form of the 'normal' ego.

8 This appeal to nature is the more surprising in view of Freud's removal of other teleological appeals to 'nature's purpose' from the *Three Essays* in 1915, the year the introductory lectures commenced (1905b, *Studien*: 94, *SE*: 188).

Freud, development has two aims. One is the replacement of the subject's own body with another outside object. The other is the unification of the various objects of the component drives, accomplished through their replacement by a single object. Now after a brief caveat on the complexity of the process involved in finding an object, Freud goes on to write that

it may be specially pointed out that when, in the years of childhood before puberty, the process has in some respects reached a conclusion, the object that has been found turns out to be almost identical with the first object of the oral pleasure-drive [*oralen Lusttriebe*] . . . Though it is not actually the mother's breast, at least it is the mother. We call the mother the first *love*-object.

(1916–17, *GW*: 341, *SE*: 329)

The oral demand for the mother's breast is significant in the choice of mother as love-object. To this choice, 'everything . . . under the name of the "Oedipus complex" ' becomes attached. Freud then elaborates on the Oedipus complex, having established a clear line of causal connection from the construction of the libido to the choice of object. Or so it seems. It is after describing the course of the boy's complex that Freud introduces the claim that 'Things happen in just the same way with little girls, with the necessary changes . . .'. It should now be evident that in this unproblematic assertion of the primacy of the girl's attachment to her father, Freud is undermining the connection he has just established between libido formation and object-choice. He establishes that connection only five pages before asserting the primacy of the girl's paternal attachment. Yet within the small space of those five pages, it was forgotten.

THE QUANTITATIVE FACTOR

When Freud does recognize that his analogy theory of femininity is incompatible with his second topography, and that the girl, 'being already castrated', lacks a strong motive for establishing a superego, he none the less continues to insist that women are more subject to repression. As I have established, this presents him with a further contradiction, to the extent that the superego becomes the agency affecting repression (p. 56 above). The greater tendency to repression in women was based on a quantitative argument, and we have seen that Freud's emphasis on the quantitative factor derived from the study of psychoneuroses, especially hysteria.

We are continuing to seek an alternative explanation for this quantitative factor of more repression in femininity, concentrating here on how it is overlaid by a projected image from the masculine other. An investigation of the quantitative factor in *Three Essays* will eventually contribute to this explanation, but the path to it is not direct. While Freud notes in *Three*

Essays that women have a greater tendency to repression, his investigation of the quantitative factor in the *Essays* has its point of departure in the perversions. The quantitative factor in the perversions is my concern in this section.

In an argument similar to that adumbrated in the *Studies on Hysteria*, Freud argues that symptoms are built on the transformation of libidinal drives, which, for psychical or external reasons, have no outlet. But

> it is by no means at the cost of the so-called normal sexual drive that these symptoms originate . . . they also give expression (by conversion) to drives which would be described as *perverse* in the widest sense of the word if they could be expressed directly in phantasy and action without being diverted from consciousness. These symptoms are formed in part at the cost of *abnormal* sexuality; *neuroses are, so to say, the negative of the perversions.*
>
> (1905b, *Studien*: 74, *SE*: 165, first and subsequent edns;
> original emphases)

Where the perversions and the component drives which underlie them are not repressed, the subject, perversely, is *healthier*.[9] When the perverse impulses are repressed, and a psychoneurosis results, its analytic investigation will reveal any or all of the component drives existing in their independent, that is to say, their perverse forms. These include unconscious libidinal fixations on persons of the same sex, the substitution of mouth or anus for the role of the genitals, and sadism and masochism. While normal sexuality is produced when some of the component drives are repressed and others are subordinated 'under the primacy of the genital zones in the service of the reproductive function' (1906a, *GW*: 156, *SE*: 277), neuroses are due to an excessive repression of the libidinal components (ibid.). This formula, in which health is a matter of less rather than more repression, normality the result of a compromise, and neuroses the result of excessive repression is echoed in Freud's formulation of the second theory of femininity, where 'normality' is enough repression of masculine sexuality, neuroses is too much, and the third alternative is a 'masculinity complex'. It should be added that Freud, in a discussion of the question of hereditary factors in the psychoneuroses and perversions, says that it is not uncommon to find both in the same family. A male in the family will be more likely to be a 'positive pervert', meaning he will act on his perversion, 'while the females, true to the tendency of their sex to repression, are negative perverts, that is, hysterics' (1905b, *Studien*: 139, *SE*: 236, first and subsequent edns). The more perverse the man in the family, the more hysterical the woman (cf. p. 52 above).

9 In fact, Freud's generally economic definitions of health are tied to normality at one point, but the norm in this case is based on 'ideal harmony . . . of the three main ways of employing the libido in the economy of the psyche' (1931a, *GW*: 511–12, *SE*: 219).

When it comes to accounting for why some people become perverse and others develop symptoms, the direction of Freud's reasoning is similar to that discussed in the Introduction. He focuses not on the real event as the cause of hysteria, nor on the phantasy of seduction, but on the relative force of repression in either case. However in this instance he does not only write that the individual outcome is determined by whether individuals react to events by repression, and how extensively they repress if they do so.

> The fact is we must put sexual repression as an internal factor alongside such external factors as limitation of freedom, inaccessibility of a normal sexual object, the dangers of the normal sexual act, etcetera, which bring about perversions in persons who might perhaps otherwise have remained normal.
>
> In this respect, different cases of neurosis may behave differently: in one case the preponderating factor may be *the innate strength of the tendency to perversion*, in another it may be the collateral increase of that tendency owing to the libido being forced away from a normal sexual aim and sexual object . . . neurosis will always produce its greatest effect when constitution and experience work together in the same direction. Where the constitution is a marked one it will perhaps not require the support of actual experiences; while a great shock in real life will bring about a neurosis even in an average constitution.
>
> (1905b, *Studien*: 78–9, *SE*: 170–1, first and subsequent edns, emphasis added)

But if we ask of what does the innate tendency to perversion consist, the only answers we find are (i) that if the genital zone is weak, 'the strongest of the other components of sexuality will continue its activity as a perversion' (1905b, *Studien*: 140, *SE*: 237, first and subsequent edns) and (ii) that in homosexuality, the bisexual disposition which Freud assumes exists in all human beings is somehow involved ('though we do not know in what that disposition consists') (1905b, *Studien*: 55, *SE*: 144, first and subsequent edns).

That much said: as homosexuality is the context for much of the discussion of perversion, and the argument that psychoneurotics have a greater tendency to perversion, but that they have repressed that tendency, this 'bisexual disposition' deserves some attention. When Freud writes that the constituents of this disposition are uncertain, he does so when reviewing a literature on hermaphroditism, and other biological factors bearing on bisexuality. He finds the literature inadequate, but he is clear that 'bisexuality' means some combination of masculinity and femininity. The difficulty is with defining masculinity and femininity. As we shall see, the various additions to the *Three Essays* indicate that Freud's difficulty actually consists of establishing the relation between masculinity and femininity, and activity and passivity respectively.

This discussion introduces another aspect of the drives theory that needs to be noted here. Whether repressed or expressed, each of the perversions has a passive and an active form. More exactly, homosexuality seems to be an expression of activity and passivity, to the extent that these are replayed, however imprecisely, in masculinity and femininity, while the component drives and their respective perversions have an active and a passive form (1905b, *Studien*: 67, *SE*: 157). Whenever we find the one we find the other; a sadist is always a masochist, a voyeur an unconscious exhibitionist. While all the component drives are characterized by active and passive forms, when Freud exemplifies, he habitually refers to the pairs of scopophilia and exhibitionism, cruelty and suffering, or sadism and masochism. He also says that this last pair has more to do with masculinity and femininity 'which are combined in bisexuality' than with the element of aggressiveness (1905b, *Studien*: 69, *SE*: 160, first and subsequent edns). In a clause added to this remark in 1915, Freud makes masculinity and femininity equivalent to activity and passivity, although in 1924, the year he relinquished the analogy theory, he modifies the claim. The contrast between masculinity and femininity 'often has to be replaced in psychoanalysis by that between activity and passivity' (ibid.).

In addition, Freud refers especially, both in the *Three Essays* and subsequently, to the contrast between activity and passivity as governing the anal-sadistic, pre-genital organization of the libido. In this organization, the

> contrast between 'masculine' and 'feminine' plays no part. . . . Its place is taken by the contrast between 'active' and 'passive', which may be described as a precursor of the sexual polarity and which later is soldered to that polarity. What appears to us as masculine in the activities of this phase, when we look at it from the point of view of the genital phase, turns out to be an expression of a drive for mastery.
>
> (1916–17, *GW*: 339, *SE*: 327)

So here we have a confusing situation, where what appears to be masculine in the anal-sadistic stage is really an expression of a drive for mastery, while sadism and masochism have more to do with masculinity and femininity than they do with aggressiveness. Moreover activity and passivity dominate the anal-sadistic stage; each of the component drives has an active and a passive form (most evident in the scopophilic drive, and sadism and masochism); activity and passivity are closely tied to, but not identical with, masculinity and femininity; masculinity and femininity are combined in bisexuality, and the strength of bisexuality is somehow involved in whether a person becomes homosexual.

As activity and passivity are here by implication tied to the tendency

to fall ill, and as they are elsewhere tied, although not reduced, to masculinity and femininity, the foregoing becomes particularly significant. As I
noted above (p. 81), during the years of secession,[10] when Adler and Jung
left the psychoanalytic movement, one of the disputes concerned whether
repression and bisexuality went hand in hand; that is to say, the idea that
what is repressed is always one's feminine self if one is male, and vice
versa, and that this repression underlies the disposition to neurosis. Freud
rejected this idea (see especially 1919b). Although, as we have seen, something similar returns when he argues that we have reached 'bedrock' in
an analysis when a woman will not relinquish her wish for a penis, and
a man cannot conquer his fear of being in the feminine position (1937).
His argument, as we have also seen, is that health is a matter of more or
less repression, but whether repression is a failure depends on how much
needs to be repressed. Yet this is determined, in part, by external events,
and in part by an 'innate' tendency to perversion which, on examination,
reimplicates masculinity and femininity via the uncertain pathways of
activity and passivity, and the strength of the component drives, all of
which have active and passive aims.

My concern now is with finding an alternative explanation for the
implication that activity and passivity are implicated in an innate and/or
externally induced disposition to perversion or pathology, which, first,
takes account of the innate factor without discounting externality; second,
does not lose the primacy accorded the quantitative force of repression in
inducing pathology; third, recognizes that the active and passive trends
are connected to masculinity and femininity; but, fourth, does not reduce
what is repressed to the denial of masculinity in the female case and vice
versa in the male. It is only this explanation that would absolve Freud of
casuistry in dealing with his opponents, but this is not the only reason
for seeking it. Some such explanation seems to take account of Freud's
observations, and to reconcile his internal contradictions while recognizing
the force of the conclusions underlying them. My argument here will
hinge on the notion that much of what Freud ascribes to bisexuality
should be ascribed to the ego and its vicissitudes. It will also hinge on
clarifying much of what he ascribes to the ego as innate. As I mentioned
in the Introduction, this can be done in the light of the contrast between
uterine and post-uterine states. These points will be clarified after the
confusion in the theory of the drives has been examined.

THE UNCLEAR ORIGINS OF THE DRIVES

That the theory of the drives is confused has been noted. For de Sousa,

> Freud's characterization of the aims of all instincts – including the

10 See the discussion in Gay (1988: 225ff).

libidinal – is unacceptably vague . . . there are no criteria for distinguishing one instinct from another. Conflict does not provide a sufficient
criterion of difference, for two component instincts of the libidinal
group can have opposite effects. . . . Nor does Freud himself invariably
assume that conflict provides distinctness. For though he seems to have
assumed that the conflict leading to the transference neuroses
'compelled' him to posit two independent groups [the sexual and ego
drives] (1914c: 77) he was also willing to consider, at about the same
time, the possibility that in repression 'it is precisely the cathexis
which is withdrawn from the idea that is used for anti-cathexis'
(1915e: 181).

> (de Sousa 1982: 150)

This comment is fairly typical, although it is concisely put. That is to say,
many commentators have focused on the confusion evident in Freud's
assumption of an antithesis between hunger and love, or the sexual drive
and the 'self-preservative' ego drive, because, as Freud's essay on narcissism was to reveal, the origin of the ego drives and the self-preservative
drives cannot be separated. Yet this indistinguishability is already foreshadowed by the account of the derivation of the drives in the *Three
Essays*. Through a discussion of the latter, I shall come to a similar
conclusion to that reached by Freud's commentators, and Freud himself.
But I shall come to this conclusion by a different route, one that facilitates
an alternative account of the derivation of the ego.

De Sousa notes that Freud was not unaware of the vagueness of *die
Triebe*. 'Drives are mythical entities, magnificent in their indefiniteness'
(1933a, *GW*: 101, *SE*: 95), writes Freud, making a virtue of necessity,
something to which he is usually not prone. More honestly, the theory
of the drives 'is the most important but at the same time the least complete
portion of psychoanalytic theory' (1905b, *Studien*: 77, n. 1, *SE*: 168, n.
2, 1924 edn). In defining a drive Freud echoes the language of the *Project*.
A drive seems to be the same as an excitation without quality in that it
is to be understood as

the psychical representative of an endo-somatic continuously flowing
source of stimulation . . . without quality, and, so far as mental life is
concerned [the drive] is only to be regarded as a measure of the demand
made upon the mind for work.[11] What distinguishes the drives from
one another and endows them with specific qualities is their relation
to their somatic sources and to their aims.

> (1905b, *Studien*: 76–7, *SE*: 168, 1915 edn)

This resonates with the preceding chapter's argument on the idea that
affects are psychical representatives of the drives. Yet in this case it is the

11 A demand for work is the classical definition of energy. Cf. More's *Energia*.

drives that are representatives of 'an endo-somatic continuously flowing source of stimulation'. Affects are not drives; drives must be a different sort of representative. Moreover in the *Project* excitation was not only endogenous. It was also exogenous.[12] How these inconsistencies are to be resolved is not clear, except that we have already raised the possibility that affects too are not, or not only, endogenous, in so far as they can be deposited in the one by the other (p. 125ff). And to complicate things further, Freud stresses it is their relation to their aims, as well as their somatic sources, that makes drives distinctive. It is not clear if an affect has an aim, although an affect can be produced by turning a drive back against oneself (hostility, which involves drives, can be turned back against itself, producing affects, such as anxiety or melancholia). And it is possible that an affect can also result from another's drive.

Part of the difficulty with the concept of the drive is that Freud regards it as 'lying on the frontier between the mental and the physical [*Trieb ist so einer der Begriffe der Abgrenzung des Seelischen vom Körperlichen*]' (1905b, *Studien*: 76, *SE*: 168), although (p. 120 above) this definition is not one he maintains consistently. It is possible that this inconsistency could be resolved eventually if drives are treated as representatives of quantity once it has become tied down and to some extent bound in primary inertia, while affects and representational ideas would be attempts at recapturing the energetic connections between beings that existed hitherto. But the inconsistency I intend to concentrate on now concerns the derivation of the drives. While they are meant to develop in relation to their somatic sources, this derivation does not hold for all the drives.

Let us recall that Freud lists seven component drives: the oral drive, the anal-sadistic drive, the phallic drive, the drive for mastery, the drive for cruelty, the scopophilic drive, and the drive for knowledge. We noted that the oral drive is initially attached to the vital function of taking nourishment and then becomes detached from it when the subject seeks to repeat the pleasurable accoutrements of the experience by itself. It becomes independent of its object, the breast or mother, but may well retain that object in its phantasy. The anal drive, as I have also mentioned, originates from the stimulation of the anal mucous membrane, so this drive too is tied to a vital function (eliminating faeces). The phallic drive is more problematic.

It was noted that the phallic drive is meant to derive from stimulation of the penis or clitoris in the course of the infant's being cared for, and that everyday events such as washing stimulate pleasurable responses in an area that Freud describes as particularly sensitive. These pleasurable responses lead to a desire for the repetition of the pleasure involved, which

12 See the Editor's Note to Freud (1915c: 114) on how Freud maintained a distinction between exogenous and endogenous excitations, drives belonging in the latter category.

in turn introduces masturbation. In this connection, Freud makes the observation that 'The preference for the hand which is shown by boys is already evidence of the important contribution which the drive for mastery is destined to make to masculine sexual activity' (1905b, *Studien*: 95, *SE*: 188, first and subsequent edns). Freud adds a significant note to this idea in 1920. It concerns how it is that guilt attaches to memories of masturbation.

> The most general and most important factor concerned must no doubt be that masturbation represents the executive agency of the whole of infantile sexuality [*die Exekutive der ganzen infantilen Sexualität darstellt*] and is, therefore, able to take over the sense of guilt attaching to it.
>
> (1905b, *Studien*: 95, n. 3, *SE*: 189, n. 1, 1920 edn)

The guilt which pertains to the masculine Oedipus complex especially is here identified with the notion of executive capacity and related to the drive for mastery. Subsequently, Freud will make the superego that source of guilt. He will do this after he ties the superego's formation and the coming together of (some, not necessarily all) the component drives to a phallic aim via the threat of castration. But this identification is a subsequent one. I am raising it now because the term 'executive' will feature again.

Returning to the main thread, the derivation of the drives, but bearing the reference to the drive for mastery in mind, let us reconsider the anal drive. The anal drive is peculiar, in that it is tied to the drive for mastery from the outset; this peculiarity is evident already in the fact that this drive is referred to as the anal-sadistic drive. Freud notes that stimulation by faecal elimination is a passive experience; the sadism enters with the effects of the drive to mastery (1905b, *Studien*: 85–6, *SE*: 198–9, 1915 and subsequent edns).

Yet from where did this drive for mastery emerge? In fact, it would seem that in reality only three of the component drives have organic sources: the oral, the 'passive-anal', and the phallic drives. But that this is so emerges slowly. Freud points to it when he writes that

> it must, however, be admitted that infantile sexual life, in spite of the preponderating dominance of erotogenic zones, exhibits components which from the very first involve other people as sexual objects. Such are the drives of scopophilia, exhibitionism and cruelty, *which appear in a sense independently of erotogenic zones*; these drives do not enter into intimate relations with genital life until later, but are already to be observed in childhood as independent impulses, distinct in the first instance from erotogenic sexual activity.
>
> (1905b, *Studien*: 97–8, *SE*: 191–2; emphasis added)

So here we have three drives – or really, as scopophilia and exhibitionism are two sides of the same drive, two drives – which 'in a sense' have nothing to do with organic reference points. Elsewhere however Freud does assign these drives their organic reference points. But as he does so, he makes them 'more remote' from the body. The context is an observation that hysterical symptoms are the ones most closely tied to the oral and anal erotogenic zones as genital substitutes, while in obsessional neurosis and paranoia, they are still as significant, but 'less recognizable'. It is particularly striking that hysterical (feminine) symptoms are more evidently tied to the actual organic drives, while in the (masculine) obsessional neuroses and paranoia, they are not. But Freud does not easily relinquish the claims on the body of the more remote drives.

> In obsessional neurosis what is more striking is the significance of those impulses which create new sexual aims and seem independent of erotogenic zones. Nevertheless, in scopophilia and exhibitionism the eye corresponds to an erotogenic zone; while in the case of those components of the sexual drive which involve pain and cruelty the same role is assumed by the skin.
>
> (1905b, *Studien*: 77–8, *SE*: 169, first and subsequent edns)

The first sentence quoted is clearly a statement about organic reference points, but a 'correspondence' does not solve the derivation problem. I shall return to the drives for scopophilia, exhibitionism, and cruelty, which we will term the 'less organic' component drives, shortly. More immediately, let us concentrate on the drive for mastery. While the oral drive, to take the most clear-cut example, derives from the memory of pleasurable oral sucking, the drive for mastery only *expresses* itself through an organic reference point. Moreover it seems to have a predetermined quantitative strength. Earlier, I noted that the boy's putative preference for the hand is *evidence* of the drive for mastery's contribution to masculine sexual activity. Elsewhere, when Freud refers to the organism in discussing the drive to mastery, as he does in one of the many interpolations into the *Three Essays* made in 1915, he says that 'activity is put into operation by the drive for mastery through the agency of the somatic musculature [*Die Aktivität wird durch den Bemächtigungstrieb von seiten der Körpermuskulatur hergestellt*]' (1905b, *Studien*: 104, *SE*: 198, 1915 and subsequent edns).

On the one hand, the drive puts activity into operation. On the other, it does so through the musculature. But either way, the drive for mastery is the moving force. This is one significant deviation between this drive and others of the *Triebe*, and it needs to be noted because there is a tendency in writing on Freud to assume that all the drives have similar genealogies in principle.[13] This is not so.

13 Even Laplanche and Pontalis (1983) give this impression in a book otherwise marked by much exactitude.

The drive for mastery does not derive in part from sucking at the breast or the stimulation of 'the erotogenic mucous membrane of the anus'. It is just there. It is not a source of the libido in the same way that orality and anality are; rather, it combines with these sources to produce a variety of effects ranging from 'activity' to the perversion of sadism, in which sexuality and cruelty are combined. For Freud, 'the fundamental psychological analysis of this drive has as we know not yet been satisfactorily achieved' (1905b, *Studien*: 99, *SE*: 193, 1915 edn). How we know this is unclear, except in that in earlier editions of the *Three Essays*, Freud, in attempting to explain the cruelty or sadism that he attributed to the drive for mastery, said that it arose 'from sources which are in fact independent of sexuality but may become united with it at an early stage owing to an anastomosis near their points of origin' (1905b, Studien: 99, n. 1, *SE*: 193, n. 1). As we shall see in a moment, these sources may also have a 'cannibalistic' connection.

There are two other features of the *Bemächtigungstrieb*. (i) Freud does not always refer to it as a drive: on an occasion where he presents us with a formula very similar to that mentioned above, to the effect that cruelty and aggressiveness *derive* from mastery trends, he refers, not to a drive, but to the 'apparatus for obtaining mastery [*Bemächtigungsapparat*]' (1905b, *Studien*: 68, *SE*: 159, 1915 edn).

By way almost of an aside at this point, I note that the drive for mastery appears to be pivotal in the relation between activity and passivity, and masculinity and femininity. The full context for the quotation just given is a discussion of sadism and masochism and the 'aggressive element of the sexual drive'. Freud wonders if the latter does not have a cannibalistic origin, which would make it, and 'the apparatus for obtaining mastery', independent of the sexual drives (1905b, *Studien*: 68, *SE*: 159, first edn). He adds that sadism and masochism are perversions which have a 'special position . . . since the contrast between activity and passivity which lies behind them is among the universal characteristics of sexual life' (1905b, *Studien*: 68, *SE*: 159, 1915 edn). Yet as we have seen, in the 1924 edition of the *Three Essays* Freud expressly connects sadism and masochism with masculinity and femininity (this is the 'contrast which often has to be replaced in psychoanalysis by that between activity and passivity') (1905b, *Studien*: 69, *SE*: 160, 1924 edn). This is why I suggested that the drive for mastery might be pivotal in the relation between activity and passivity, and masculinity and femininity; there seems to be something in the drive that connects it with the latter pair from the outset, and yet it is also tied to the former. But I shall defer further discussion of this pivotal possibility now (while recalling that phantasy has also been assigned a pivotal role, p. 130 above), in favour of the second point about the drive.

(ii) The *Bemächtigungstrieb* even more than the other *Triebe*, conjures up the idea of force, and it is important to remember this precisely because this drive is 'less organic', which might mean it is more physical. Force, the idea of force directed towards something, connotes the vocabulary of pressure and quantity found in the *Project* and which we encounter again in the Metapsychological papers. And in most of the contexts in which Freud refers to the drive for mastery, it connotes a force directed externally. While there are partial exceptions to this connotation of externality, in that they involve the drive being directed inwards, these are none the less consistent with the idea of physical force. One is the concept of masochism, the vicissitudes of which involve a turning of sadism, with its mastery component, back against the self. The other exception is partial because there is a shift in terminology, although the concept is similar. Freud also refers to 'the child's efforts to gain control [*Herr werden*] over his own limbs' (1915c, *GW*: 223, *SE*: 130) which suggests that something akin to domination by force can also be directed inwards towards the self.[14] Needless to say, this echoes the idea of attention turned inwards, carrying motor activity in its train.

These points about the drive for mastery have been stressed here because, aside from the fact that that drive has a special part to play in the contrast between activity and passivity (and hence of masculinity and femininity), the drive for mastery will be critical in understanding how some of the other component drives come to be directed externally, and moreover it will help account for the derivation of the drives mentioned above. That is to say, if the drives for scopophilia, exhibitionism, and cruelty only have a 'correspondence', at best, with organic reference points, do they have a common derivation in something else? I have hinted that they are related to the vicissitudes of attention, and noted their prominence in (masculine) obsessional neuroses, but first we have to consider the prime candidate for this common origin by Freud's account. It is that these drives involve other people, objects external to the subject. In support of this, one can note that visual impressions (by nature external) are meant to be the most common pathway [*der Weg*] of libidinal arousal (1905b, *Studien*: 66, *SE*: 156, first edn), and also that seeing is 'an activity that ultimately derives from touching' (ibid.).

But if we now consider the component drives *in toto* again, it seems, although Freud does not comment on this, that even more of the drives have no organic derivation. Moreover all of these 'less organic' component drives, excluding scopophilia, are tied to the drive for mastery. This is obscured, in part, because the drive for mastery itself is not mentioned in Freud's reference to the 'exceptional' component drives – scopophilia, exhibitionism, and cruelty. It is also less than plain because the drive for

14 In fact the context for this quotation – the reversal of drives into their opposite – does suggest this. When Freud (1915c) writes that a preliminary stage in which the subject takes itself as its own object is absent in sadism (unlike scopophilia), he adds that the child's efforts to master its limbs might provide the missing first stage (pp. 155–6 below).

cruelty itself has a somewhat *ad hoc* introduction, and its relation to the drive for mastery is simply mentioned in passing. And it is complicated because yet another drive without an organic reference point, the drive for knowledge, is also excluded from Freud's initial recapitulation of the renegade 'less organic' component drives: but knowledge, too, has a relation to the drive for mastery. In addition, if the drive for knowledge is taken into account a connection between the scopophilic drive and the drive for mastery emerges. Let us take these points in order.

1 We begin with the *ad hoc* introduction of the 'drive for cruelty'. Initially, this drive was referred to in this chapter without comment, and it appears in the *Three Essays* some thirty pages before Freud accounts for its derivation. When it first appears, it is described as

> essential to the understanding of the fact that symptoms involve suffering . . . it is also through the medium of this connection between libido and cruelty that the transformation of love into hate takes place, the transformation of affectionate into hostile impulses, which is characteristic of a great number of cases of neurosis, and indeed, it would seem, of paranoia in general.
> (1905b, *Studien*: 75, *SE*: 166–7, first edn)[15]

A subsequent reference to the 'impulse of cruelty' (1905b, *Studien*: 99, *SE*: 193, first and subsequent edns) says that it 'arises from the drive for mastery' (ibid., 1915 edn). And as I have already indicated, the cruelty which the drive for mastery underlies, in turn underlies the sadism of the anal-sadistic stage.

2 We turn now to the drive for knowledge, also exempted from the admission that half of the *Partialtriebe* do not derive from organic reference points. Freud considers it subsequently. He stresses that it is intimately connected with sexual life, since it is possibly aroused by sexual questions in early childhood. At the same time,

> This drive cannot be counted among the elementary drive components nor can it be classed as exclusively belonging to sexuality. Its activity corresponds on the one hand to a sublimated manner of obtaining mastery, while on the other hand it makes use of the energy of scopophilia.
> (1905b, *Studien*: 100, *SE*: 194, 1915 and subsequent edns)[16]

3 The last sentence quoted indicates that scopophilia is also connected to the *Bemächtigungstrieb* via the drive for knowledge. This is not to say that scopophilia derives from the drive for mastery directly, by Freud's

15 Projection on to an object external to the subject is the defence mechanism favoured in paranoia, which reinforces the possibility that a common origin of the 'less organic' *Partialtriebe* is the explicit presupposition of an object external to the subject.

16 And where, we ask in passing, did scopophilia as a less organic drive, get its energy?

account, but the connection is significant. Whenever Freud discusses the active and passive forms of the *Partialtriebe*, his main exemplars are scopophilia and cruelty.

Thus far, I have suggested that a common feature of all the inorganic component drives, excluding scopophilia, is the drive for mastery. I have also noted that Freud accounts for 'scopophilia, exhibitionism, and cruelty' on the basis that they involve other people.

In sum, I want to suggest now that the significance of scopophilia is that it is a means for formalizing the distinction between the subject and other people (as well as the fact that sight stimulates sexual desire), and that this formal distinction is the condition of the drive for mastery taking an external other as its object. While this does not account for the drive for mastery's origin as such, it means that what the more abstract *Partialtriebe* have in common is that they are means for mastery of the visually distinct other, and indeed that this distinctive visualization of the other is a means for mastery in itself.[17] This is the other side of, the active subjective side of, the visualization that holds the hysteric or feminine being in her place. What is required now is that we show: (i) how it is that the more abstract *Partialtriebe* are one and the same as the energetic attention and capacity for activity that are turned back against the self in femininity and hysteria; (ii) how this turning-back differs from the backward pressure that brings the ego into being. In other words what is required now is that we show that attention and activity in reverse are the same as the passive forms of the *Partialtriebe*. These passive forms involve subjects 'taking their own body' as their object, and the fact that the subject's body becomes the object through the medium of a real or imagined other. The point is that this reversal operates at two levels.

The idea that the reversal operates at two levels is directly supported by Freud's discussion of the four stages of the drives in 'Instincts and their Vicissitudes' (1915c). In this discussion Freud once more focuses on scopophilia and sadism. He notes that in scopophilia, there are four stages. The first is passive; it involves a sexual organ being looked at by oneself. Its other, active side is oneself looking at a sexual organ. The third and fourth stages of scopophilia once more introduce the relation to other people. They consist of active scopophilia ('oneself looking at an extraneous object') and 'an object which is oneself or part of oneself being looked at by an extraneous person (exhibitionism)' (1915c, *GW*: 222, *SE*: 130). A similar turnabout holds in sadism, although Freud originally argued that the first stage paralleling passive scopophilia was absent in sadism, and that the vicissitudes of the sadistic drive accordingly had only

---

17 The connections my interpretations point to between a systematic reading of Freud's theory of the drives, and Foucault's and Heidegger's theories, will not be explored in this study, but they are pursued in my forthcoming *History After Lacan* (Routledge 1993, forthcoming).

three stages: an active sadistic first stage, a passive masochistic second stage, and an active sadistic third stage, which once more involved another person who took the place of the subject's own self. It is of note that in this discussion, while Freud habitually uses the word 'object' for the thing or person that the drive is directed towards, he in this instance uses the word 'subject' for the active sadistic party, and 'object' for the passive masochistic one (1915c, GW: 220, SE: 127).

Three things are of further interest in Freud's discussion of the four stages. The first is that he ties the first stage of scopophilia to narcissism; he also ties the second stage of passive scopophilia, in which another subject takes the place of the subject's ego, to narcissism; and he ties masochism as a secondary formation based on primary narcissism to sadism. In both 'passive scopophilia and masochism, the narcissistic *subject* is, through identification, replaced by another, extraneous ego' (1915c, GW: 224, SE: 132). Coming to the second point: if the above argument on the tie between sadism and scopophilia is right, it would make sense if the first stage of scopophilia, which, we have argued, is produced by the imprint of another's attention, was also tied to a first passive stage of sadism: masochism, in other words. Subsequently, Freud did conclude that there was a first stage in the vicissitudes of sadism, which he termed primary masochism. He concluded this in a discussion of inertia, which echoes the argument of the *Project* (1920a), in which he introduces the death drive (1920a). By the argument of the last chapter, the death drive is in one sense superfluous: the original trend to inertia will account for it provided we take account of the moving force of the other's attention as a source of life. At the same time, it is the imprint of the other's attention, and its interlock with the repressed hallucination, that constitutes primary inertia which is felt as a restricting force, and it is the projection of this imprint which accounts for one form of repression, and the turning of hostility and motor activity inwards. What matters now, which brings me to the third point, is that the two stages of inertia described in the last chapter in terms of the vicissitudes of attention and repression, are in Freud's account of the vicissitudes of the drives, also described as a process in which one set of active and passive attitudes is then overlaid by another. Freud expressly refers to the first experience of the active and passive vicissitudes of the drives as 'an underlying situation [*Grundsituation*]' (1915c, GW: 226, SE: 133). He also makes it plain that it is then overlaid by a second situation in which the same process is repeated through the medium of an external other. All we are adding here is that the first stage also involves an external other's attention, and it is by this addition that we can account for the quantitative force of the urge to project in the first and second stages. Except that, as we shall see, the externality of the external other in the first stage is not recognized by the nascent subject;

no spatial distinction exists, no judgement (the distinction between an inside and an outside) is present.

Yet precisely how it is that the energetic attention and motor activity which Freud allocated to the ego operate at two levels requires more elucidation. One comes before masculinity; the other, by this account, *is* masculinity. By showing this we shall establish the difference between activity and passivity on the one hand, and masculinity and femininity on the other. We will also perforce return to the quantitative factor and the question of innateness.

The tie between the less organic *Partialtriebe* and the ego's capacities for attention and motor activity is implicit in an earlier reference to sensory attention (p. 97, n. 16). Of the five senses implicated in sensory attention (smell, touch, hearing, taste, and sight), sight and touch (in so far as 'seeing is derived from touching') also feature in the less organic drives, more evident in obsessional neuroses and paranoia. Taste and smell[18] feature in the more organic drives, more evident in hysteria. There is no mention of hearing in this context, although it is worth mentioning that the superego is formed out of voice residues. The matter of sensory perception was first raised in the context of 'consciousness', and an argument that one could talk of activity and passivity in that context only if it was allowed that direction was embodied in attention (p. 96 above). The recollection of direction takes us to an explicit connection between (egoic) attention and (sexual) drives. Freud makes it in an observation concerning 'pathways of mutual influence'. He notes that:

> if sexual satisfaction arises during taking of nourishment, then the same factor also enables us to understand why there should be disorders of nutrition if the erotogenic functions of the common zone are disturbed. Or again, if we know that concentration of attention may give rise to sexual excitation, it seems plausible to assume that by making use of the same path [*auf demselben Wege*], but in a contrary direction, the condition of sexual excitation may influence the possibility of directing the attention.
>
> (1905b, *Studien*: 110–11, *SE*: 205–6)

Given that 'attention' is a prime function of the ego, its connection to the sexual drive confirms that the ego drives and the sexual drives have the same source. But in addition, given that the sexual drives are structured, and that two of the component drives in the drive for mastery are also means for sensory perception, it would seem that these means for perception are also structured by a drive for mastery, unless we are to suppose two independent sources of sight.

Thus the tie between attention and the drives has already been drawn,

18 I am assuming that 'smell' is related to anality and the 'disgust' Freud mentioned in draft K as one of the motive forces of repression.

at least in part. And its very drawing appears to be an argument against any effective distinction between the ego drives and the sexual drives. But it also points to an argument for it, if we take account of the two levels of attention and fixation. This argument, and an argument for the idea that the secondary inertia of femininity is the (overlaid) passive experience of the *Partialtriebe*, will emerge through a reflection on Freud's discussion of the fate of the sexes at puberty.

INVOLUTION: FEMININITY AND THE 1911 THEORY OF THE EGO

When the component drives combine, when the other erotogenic zones are dominated by the genital zone, a new sexual aim appears. The sexual aim of males is accompanied by intensification of libido at puberty. But in girls, puberty is marked 'by a fresh wave of repression, in which it is precisely clitoridal sexuality that is affected' (1905b, *Studien*: 124, *SE*: 220, first and subsequent edns). Accordingly, as Freud showed at length in the three papers on femininity, it is masculine and therefore active sexuality that is repressed.

> Since the new sexual aim assigns very different functions to the two sexes, their sexual development now diverges greatly. That of males is the more straightforward and understandable, while *that of females actually enters upon a kind of involution [Rückbildung]*.
> (1905b, GW: 108, SE: 207, first and subsequent edns, emphasis added)

This is a remarkable statement, no less so for being completely unexplicated. What precisely is a kind of involution?

Freud uses the term *Rückbildung* rarely.[19] This is almost the first time he introduces it; he uses it next in the fourth of the *Five Lectures* he

19 While the *SE* includes 'involution' in the index, the index omits the *Three Essays* reference to involution in the sexual life of women. *SE* is not accurate in respect of this term. We next meet *Rückbildung* in the case study of Little Hans, where the term is used in passing, and connotes psychosis; in fact 'involution', more than 'regression', carries that connotation. Freud uses *Rückbildung* especially between 1909 and 1911. With one exception, it does not figure in his late work at all. But for my argument, that exception is significant. It occurs when he is writing of the division of the mind into id, ego, and superego, in 1932. 'It is highly probable that the development of these divisions [id, ego, superego] is subject to great variations in different individuals; it is possible that in the course of actual functioning they may change and go through a temporary phase of involution. Particularly in the case of what is phylogenetically the last and most delicate of these divisions – the differentiation between the ego and the superego, something of the sort seems to be true' (1933a, GW: 89, SE: 79). Apart from the usages discussed in the text, and in this note, Freud's only other reference to 'involution' seems to be a reference to the menopause (1910b). The term 'ego-syntonic', used in connection with femininity in Freud (1937), is also not listed in the *SE* index in connection with femininity.

presented in Massachusetts in 1909, during his visit to the United States
with Sandor Ferenczi and C. G. Jung.[20] There he writes that

> the highly complicated development of the sexual function . . . does not
> occur smoothly in every individual; and, if not, it leaves behind it either
> abnormalities or a predisposition to fall ill later along the path of
> involution [*Rückbildung*] (i.e. regression).

(1910a, *GW*: 48, *SE*: 45)

The context of this quotation, where involution is made synonymous
with 'regression', is a discussion of the component drives, perversion and
neurosis. To the extent that regression has sexual connotations, all that
may be meant by *Rückbildung* is a regression to pre-genital erotic stages.
The plausibility of this view is borne out by Freud's subsequent endorsement of Andreas-Salomé's view that the vagina, as the neighbour of the
cloaca, 'is only taken from it on lease' (Andreas-Salomé 1916: 259). But
this was a subsequent endorsement: Andreas-Salomé's paper was published
eleven years after the *Three Essays*.[21] The notion that the vagina is taken
on lease from the anus plays no part in the *Three Essays*, where Freud
sees the vagina as deriving its sexual excitability from the clitoris (1905b,
Studien: 125, *SE*: 221, first and subsequent edns). Moreover while involution has the connotation of regression to earlier erotic stages in the
instance just quoted (and it is important to remember this, given that we
are arguing that 'backward-turning' operates at two levels), it has broader
connotations in another reference to the process in the last lecture of the
Massachusetts series. These connotations in no sense exclude the erotic
ones, but they tie them to the circumstances in which the subject retreats
into phantasy. Freud writes that when the satisfaction of 'an erotic need
in reality is frustrated' either because of external obstacles or an internal
lack of adaptation, this can lead to a 'flight from reality'. This

> takes place along the path of involution [*Rückbildung*], of regression,
> of a return to earlier phases of sexual life, phases from which at one
> time satisfaction was not withheld.

(1910a, *GW*: 53, *SE*: 49)

The flight from reality does not only involve a return to earlier points

20 This was the time when Freud and Jung were 'on their most intimate terms [although]
   signs of strain and tension between them could be detected' (Roazen 1967: 255). Given
   that the term 'introversion', which echoes 'involution', almost disappears from Freud's
   vocabulary, although Freud thought 'introversion' a good term, it is possible that maintaining a distinction between his work and Jung's affected Freud's preferences in his
   conceptual vocabulary. But there was a real conceptual disagreement with Jung over the
   specificity of introversion as a process (below, pp. 166ff).
21 Freud adds a footnote to the *Three Essays* concerning Andreas-Salomé (1916) in 1920
   (1905b, *Studien*: 93, n. 2, *SE*: 187, n. 1, 1920 and subsequent edns). The reference to
   involution in the sexual life of women occurs in the first edition, and is neither removed
   from nor qualified in subsequent editions.

of gratification. It also leads to a life of phantasy. All human beings, not simply neurotic ones, make up for reality 'by the production of wish-fulfilments'. But they differ in terms of what they do with them.

> The energetic and successful man is one who succeeds by his efforts in turning his wishful phantasies into reality. Where this fails, as a result of the resistances of the external world and of the subject's own weakness, he begins to turn away from reality and withdraws into his more satisfying world of phantasy, the content of which is transformed into symptoms should he fall ill.
>
> (1910a, *GW*: 53, *SE*: 50)

Contained in this passage is a very interesting evocation of the pleasure and reality principles, which Freud was to discuss the following year in a major metapsychological contribution on the 'Two Principles of Mental Functioning' (1911a, *GW*: 238, *SE*: 226). The passage evokes these principles by contrasting wishful phantasy with acting; instead of phantasy as an end in itself, one acts to make those phantasies real. I will try to draw this contrast out, before returning to involution and its significance for femininity.

As mentioned in the Introduction, in essence, the distinction between pleasure and reality had figured in the *Project*, where it was elaborated in relation to the role of the ego, and in the metapsychological chapter of *The Interpretation of Dreams*, where it was discussed in terms of the primary and secondary processes. I shall briefly recapitulate: initially the psychical apparatus is dominated by the pleasure principle, which expresses itself in 'hallucinatory wish-fulfilment': the subject hallucinates its wishes as fulfilled, and takes the hallucination for a real perception. The pleasure principle and the inability to distinguish between a wish and its fulfilment continue to hold sway in the primary process. However while the wish-fulfilment procedure has literally immediate results, it is ultimately productive of more unpleasure (p. 25 above). It is unpleasurable because the desired satisfaction is not obtained, and because the motor-discharge that accompanies hallucination is itself unpleasurable when it is excessive.

The reality principle is instituted as the means for distinguishing between hallucinatory wish-fulfilment and actual perception. It entails recognizing that 'what was presented in the mind was no longer what was agreeable but what was real, even if it happened to be disagreeable' (1911a, *GW*: 232, *SE*: 219). With this recognition, the reality principle substitutes for the pleasure principle. At the same time, this substitution

> implies no deposing of the pleasure principle but only a safeguarding of it. A momentary pleasure, uncertain in its results, is given up, but only in order to gain upon the new path an assured pleasure at a later time.
>
> (1911a, *GW*: 235–6, *SE*: 223)

This 'new path', it is implied here, is that pursued by the 'energetic and successful man'. In pursuing it, he converts the motor discharge that accompanied the primary process into motor activity, by which means he strives to bring about an alteration of reality (as Freud expressed it in the 'Two Principles'). The conversion of motor discharge into action necessitates a major innovation in the psychical apparatus, the experimental activity of thinking that informs the secondary process. Thinking makes it 'possible for the mental apparatus to tolerate an increased tension of stimulus while the process of discharge was postponed' (1911a, *GW*: 233, *SE*: 221). Let us pause right here.

Thinking, it seems, might begin when the reality principle substitutes judgement for repression, in so far as it involves deciding whether a given idea was false or true. But it also represents 'a major innovation' in the psyche which hinges on the idea of postponement. Given our concern with how it is that mental and motor activity come to be divorced, this suggests that the divorce is connected with the capacity to wait. But if my argument about the two levels of projection and the two stages of inertia is right, this capacity to wait also operates at two levels. These two levels are collapsed in the term 'thinking'. Thinking initially takes place in pictures, and we can include perceptions here.[22] Thinking subsequently takes place in words.

Freud is supposing that all the 'increased tension of stimulus' goes into thinking. I have supposed that it *may* do so, in which case it will be thinking of a fairly high and concentrated order. But as a rule, the increased tension of stimulus will be projected out. It will be projected on to another who carries it in order that the subject may think. In the first instance it is projected in an hallucinatory way and embodies hostility. In the second, the projection is tied to the recognition of spatio-temporal reality, and to language. More slowly . . .

If an hallucinated wish-fulfilment failed to bring satisfaction, it was false, but the recognition of this falsity depends on a distinction between hallucinations and perceptions (a form of 'thinking') and waiting. The recognition entails splitting 'thinking' and acting, indicating that the waiting involved is instrumental in the splitting of mental and physical

---

22 In the 'Two Principles' there is a different slant on the mechanism of 'repression'. Freud writes that 'a system living according to the pleasure principle must have devices to enable it to withdraw from the stimuli of reality. Such devices are merely the correlative of "repression", which treats internal unpleasurable stimuli as if they were external – that is to say, pushes them into the external world' (1911a, *GW*: 232, n., *SE*: 220, n.). Surely this is nothing less than the mechanism of projection. In this connection, it is worth adding that Freud in the same paper writes that thinking, before it became connected with verbal residues, and thus became available to consciousness, was probably 'directed to the relations between impressions of objects [*sich den Relationen der Objekteindrücke zuwendete*]' (ibid., *GW*: 233–4, *SE*: 221) which is suggestive of space. A concept of the internal and the external is predicated on space, and some concept of space, as we have seen, would seem to be the condition of projection.

processes. It was for this reason, in part, that I suggested that the fixing of an hallucination was critical to this splitting. But at the same time as it is 'thinking', the subject-to-be is also projecting hostility (cf. Bion 1970). When it thinks in language, when and as the second border for its identity is established, the subject is still projecting hostility. It is inextricably bound to the drive for mastery. But it is doing so in a way that maintains a sane identity; it is able to perceive the spatio-temporal reality that the fixed point of the other helps it secure, and its pleasure is the pleasure of phantasy, rather than hallucination.

Yet for Freud there is no straightforward coupure between hallucinatory pleasure and the pleasure of phantasy. Both are counterposed to the reality principle. He argues that sources of pleasure *simpliciter* are tenaciously clung to, even where they are formally renounced.

> With the introduction of the reality principle one species of thought-activity was split off; it was kept free from reality-testing and remained subordinated to the pleasure principle alone. This activity is phantasy-ing, which begins already in children's play, and later, continued as daydreaming, abandons dependence on real objects.
>
> (1911a, *GW*: 234, *SE*: 222)

In other words, some 'thoughts' remain tied to 'phantasy', and by this tied to the past, in that they are not oriented to the future through the medium of postponement. But as we have seen, there are two ties to the past. One is the tie of hallucination, the primary inertia which attracts subsequent repressions towards it. The other is the secondary inertia of the phantasies that are subsequently repressed, and the projected drives which are the other side of those phantasies. These levels are elided by Freud, although it is significant that the above quotation, which emerged from a discussion of hallucination, ends with a reference to daydreams.

This reference to daydreaming has to evoke the evidence from the *Studies on Hysteria*. The *Studies* provided a further opportunity to reflect on the interplay between psychical and material reality, and its relation to health. While habitually this interplay has been approached in terms of the cultural symbolic representation of women, and its relation to psychical phantasy, the fact was that Freud's and his co-author Breuer's patients did not have outlets for concentrated labour in reality. The marriageable daughter of middle-class Vienna lacked opportunity to labour thought-fully. To say the same thing differently, they lacked the opportunity for motor activity commensurate with whatever thoughts they might have had, which meant, in technical terms, that they lacked the opportunity for a spatial extension commensurate with thought. In the dark of a restricted and closed space, the thoughts could grow into daydreams that had less and less to do with reality or practicality. This restriction also bears on why phantasies tied them to the past: these phantasies could not be 'tested' in the present. To point this out is not to reduce psychical to material reality, but to note that the conscious daydreams that accompany the lack of quantitative release (which thoughtful labour can provide) replicate a similar unconscious process. In other words, the material reality, the lack of a creative outlet, overlays and reinforces a psychical structure, in which attention is turned inwards. The overlay of inward-turning attention can lie in the image projected by the other, an 'other' which extends to the entire social and symbolic world which accords woman her place, and literally fixes her within it. By contrast, a different kind of image, one which facilitates movement, at the same time as it enables a self-image to cohere, an image which is consistent with the fact of an active ego, is present in masculinity, as we have already suggested (pp. 118ff).

None the less, the connection between sexual regression and phantasy, suggestively implied in the concept of involution, has to be explicated more fully. So has the question of narcissism. In the 'Two Principles', Freud makes it plain why the sexual drives and the turn to phantasy are closely connected. He argues that the existence of auto-erotic activity means that the sexual drives are less affected than the ego drives by the demands of reality. For while the ego drives, as the guardians of self-preservation, have to take account of what can and cannot be done, the sexual drives, to the extent that they are auto-erotic, have a life of their own. Accordingly, they remain longer under the dominance of the pleasure principle.

> The continuance of auto-erotism is what makes it possible to retain for so long the easier momentary and imaginary satisfaction in relation to the sexual object in place of real satisfaction, which calls for effort and postponement.
>
> (1911, *GW*: 235, *SE*: 223)

This situation is compounded by the effects of the latency period, which interrupts the process of finding an object before it has encountered the earnest resistance of reality. In short, because the sexual drives are more subject to the pleasure principle, Freud argues that they are genetically connected with the phantasies and daydreams that also obey it. What he does not say is that there is a difference between phantasies and daydreams on the one hand, and hallucinations on the other: the former acknowledge space and time; hallucinations, in a sense, obliterate them. The distinction between phantasies and hallucinations is also blurred by Freud's commentators, even the best.

In a remarkable critique of Freud's theory of auto-eroticism Laplanche has argued that the auto-erotic pleasures of infancy can only come into being via the mediation of phantasy. In this critique, where he builds on his earlier work with Pontalis (p. 151, n. 13) (Laplanche and Pontalis [1964]), Laplanche argues that the infant has to hallucinate *or* phantasize the breast as its desired object before it can repeat the pleasure associated with it auto-erotically, because the auto-erotic pleasure, by Freud's account, requires the desired object to be absent, in order to come into being. This phantasy functions as the 'first seducer'. It is the concomitant and condition of desire, of the longing for what one cannot have, and phantasy as the first seducer is also the first 'invader' of the psyche. On this basis Laplanche ties auto-eroticism to Freud's theory of narcissism, presenting this as an argument for the inseparability of the ego drives and sexual drives (Laplanche ([1970] 1976: 79). More on this, and the elision of phantasy and hallucination, in a moment.

Narcissism is especially significant as the concept constitutes a bridging concept between the 1911 theory of the ego and the later theory of the superego. In fact Freud first mentioned narcissism as the necessary stage between auto-eroticism and object-love towards the end of 1909.[23] He first refers to it in print in a footnote added to the *Three Essays* in December 1909 and elaborates on it in the Leonardo (1910b) and Schreber (1911b) 'case histories'. In short, the concept is contemporaneous with the theory of the ego we have just discussed. In addition, it is in Freud's paper on narcissism (1914c) that he introduces the concept of the ego-ideal, the 'prototype' of the superego. But the question of the prototype of the superego is as complicated as the question of narcissism itself, when narcissism is viewed from the perspective adopted in this discussion. The key to the complication is precisely the elision of phantasy and halluci-nation. Laplanche, like many others, makes these psychical acts equivalent. Yet hallucination is immediate in a way that conscious phantasy is not. Conscious phantasy is aware that what it imagines is not present in the here and now. Hallucination is truly delusory. The fact that this distinction is not made causes problems in Freud's theory of narcissism.

His paper on narcissism begins with a discussion of looking at one's own body. Narcissists treat their own bodies in the same manner that an external sexual object is treated. The narcissist 'looks at [the body], that is to say, strokes it and fondles it' (1914c, *GW*: 138, *SE*: 73). Here again, looking is derived from, in fact it is made identical with, touching. At its extreme, this is narcissism as a perversion, but Freud also sees a more general use for the term. He notes that narcissism as an attitude is a 'libidinal complement to the egoism of the self-preservative drive' (ibid., *GW*: 138–9, *SE*: 73–4). So a little narcissism is a good thing. But a lot of narcissism accompanies psychosis, and leads to the inaccessibility of the narcissist to psychoanalytic influence. If too much libido is turned back on the subject's ego, the result is psychosis. But Freud makes it plain that the inward-turning of the libido is not of itself the source of psychosis, and his very insistence on this point confirms the necessity for a distinction

23 But even as he does so, he overlooks the problem that auto-eroticism has solved for him: why the sexual drives were tied to the past.

between phantasy and hallucination in his argument on narcissism (and the pleasure principle), although he never makes this distinction explicit.

Freud argued *contra* Jung that there is a neurotic inward-turning of the libido which is other than psychotic. In this inward-turning, the libido is attached to phantasies about people and things. It is the presence of these phantasmatic attachments that means the subject still has a relation to others, even though the subject's libido is inward-turned, which means that psychosis is due not only to the inward direction of the libido, but to the absence of phantasmatic objects. In turn this absence should imply that the sense of space and time is not present, or is in some way disordered in psychosis.

Let us now place this argument in the context of Freud's distinction between two types of narcissism, primary and secondary narcissism. In the first, the narcissist looks at the body 'in the same manner' as an external object, and in this process complements the egoism of the self-preservative drive. But as Borch-Jacobsen (1989) has noted in his thorough critique of Freud, the discussion in which this idea is embedded is deeply confused: the fact that the ego sees itself in narcissism helps constitute the ego, or body image, but what is it that does the 'seeing' before the 'ego' comes into being? Freud's theory of narcissism presupposes that initially there is something that is able to see, and therefore presupposes a pre-existing subjective property directed towards an end, although there is no account of how it could come to be directed towards that end (Borch-Jacobsen 1989: 119). Borch-Jacobsen also establishes that the theory of narcissism presupposes that the ego begins before not only any specular relation, but any relation at all (ibid: 117). In fact the essence of Borch-Jacobsen's critique overall is that Freud consistently presupposes what he is in fact obliged to explain: the formation of the subject. Borch-Jacobsen carries this critique through to its logical conclusion, arguing that it is a 'womb-mother' out of which the ego comes, and that it is this womb-mother the subject has to dispose of, in order to constitute its myth of itself. It has to believe that it is the breast, and indeed, as Borch-Jacobsen records, Freud, in a throwaway note in the last year of his life, said exactly this: the first form of identification involves no differentiation; one *is* the breast (1941b [1938], *GW*: 150, *SE*: 299). Now what I want to do is agree entirely. But what I then want to do, and will do below, is to ask, What happens if we take this womb-mother as origin entirely seriously? What if we make her the depository which the subject draws on in order to constitute itself? Will this give us grounds for reconciling the conflicting insights which will otherwise dissolve Freud's theory into a 'myth' of the subject's origins, despite its phenomenal explanatory force?

From the standpoint adopted in the last chapter, 'seeing' is a directed activity that helps constitute the ego through the eye of the other. But, and this is critical, it is clear that in the case of primary narcissism, the impact of the other's attention is not perceived as something that emanates from an external source. No external other is recognized as such. The flood of libido that comes back on the self, as the imprint of the other's attention, and as the return of the energy that resists that imprint (pp. 114–15), is thought of as one's own, regardless of its actual energetic origin. The grandiosity that can result from a flooding of libido on to the self, the megalomania to which narcissism can lead, is explained if the subject takes the other's capacities to be its own. And in infancy, the other, or mother, is an all-powerful being. A further note: I said that the nascent subject does not differentiate between the energetic imprint of the other's attention, and the return of the energy that resists that imprint. But while no differentiation is made, the return of the energy that resists the imprint of course presupposes resistance. In this resistance lies the beginning of activity, and the formation of the active ego. In other words, this formation means that the ego begins to do to the other what it imagines the other is doing to it. It projects out what it experiences as restrictive, as the imposition of inertia, but this projection is not only its first active act; it also, by this argument, depends on a 'borrowing' of the capacities of the other, in so far as it is the attention received from the other that enables it to move, at the same time as this attention makes its fledgling self-image cohere. Yet, I repeat, this active ego, like the passive ego formed through the imprint of the other, does not recognize or know of that other, in either its passive experience of it, or the exercise of the active capacities it borrows.

The first experience of activity and passivity does not differentiate self and other. But such differentiation is present in secondary narcissism: in this state, attention is refracted back on the self through the medium of an imagined other, which means of course that an other has to be recognized. With this in mind, let us consider Freud's discussion of 'introversion', a term that resonates with 'involution'. As I noted, in the disagreement with Jung, Freud insisted that 'introversion' had to involve phantasy objects, meaning phantasies about others. He argued that where the libido is turned inwards but still has its phantasies of external others, even if it has no relation with them, the state can properly be termed 'introversion'.[24]

The state of introversion means that the subject 'has renounced the initiation of motor activities for the attainment of his aims in connection with [imaginary] objects' (1914c: 74). For my purposes, what matters here is first that the subject recognizes difference (the existence of the other) but that this recognition entails passivity. It is a different form of passivity

24 Because Freud criticizes Jung for indiscriminate use of the term 'introversion'(1914c: 74, 1912a), and because that word today has Jungian connotations, I have preferred the term 'involution' to describe the state where the libido is turned inwards but still attached to phantasy objects.

than the experience of infancy; in this 'secondary' passivity, motor activities are renounced. This accords with the argument of the last chapter on how inward-turning attention carries motor activity in its train; the renunciation is not a mere putting to one side of motor activities, but a redirection of those activities, or rather capacity for activity towards the subject's self. In conversion hysteria, of course, parts of this 'somatic musculature' lose their sovereignty, and in this connection we can note Freud's observation that in hysteria, something like the process of erection occurs in inappropriate parts of the body (1905b, *Studien*: 77, *SE*: 169, first and subsequent edns). As if, I suggest, it was directed inwards, towards the wrong end.

So if we now hark back to the mysterious 'kind of involution' encountered by the sexual life of women at puberty, what can be said about the possible implications of that statement? If it refers to sexual regression of the kind that takes place when an erotic need encounters an obstacle in reality, it also refers to the retreat from reality expressed in the predilection for phantasy. It implicates the retreat to phantasy for three reasons. The first of these reasons is associative. When Freud describes the flight from reality involved in the turn to stages where erotic gratification was more easily obtained, he also describes that flight in terms of the contrast between acting on reality, and retreating to phantasy for consolation. The second reason is that sexual drives and phantasy are tied under the pleasure principle. The second tie is strengthened if we consider that the stages where erotic gratification was more easily obtained are suggestive of 'auto-erotic activity', and it is auto-erotic activity especially that escapes the reality principle. Yet, as we have stressed, there is a clear spatio-temporal difference between primary auto-erotic activity and involution or introversion.

If 'involution' in the sexual development of women has the meaning Freud gives involution in other contexts, then it involves sexual regression and the retreat from reality to phantasy. In this, it involves both the ego drives, as the relation to reality is their business, and the sexual drives, as regression is theirs. However as the nature of any sexual regression on women's part is unspecified in the *Three Essays*, the 'kind of involution' Freud refers to does not sit readily with this picture of what involution involves. More to the point: 'involution', like primary narcissism and auto-eroticism, indicates that the ego drives and sexual drives have a common origin, but a common origin that can act for or against the self-preservative drive, and that operates at two distinct spatio-temporal levels.

It was under the rubric of the self-preservative drive that Freud collapsed his initial distinction between the ego drives and the sexual drives, opposing both to the death drive. But involution is not 'self-preservative' except in one very special sense. It preserves one's image (in phantasy) but at the price of limiting one's capacity for logical thought, and motor activity directed towards reality. While the self-preservation of an image could of course have a deathly price, as it did for Narcissus, the crucial difference between primary narcissism and hallucination, and secondary narcissism and involution, means that the notion that the ego drives and the sexual drives are on the same side is not straightforward. Involution and secondary narcissism are self-preservative precisely because they preserve identity. They also presuppose recognition of an external other; the phantasies about that other, because of this, serve in the construction of an identity distant from the over-inflation to which it may be subject in psychosis. In other words phantasies, by virtue of their spatio-temporal difference from hallucination, preserve identity, an identity which psychosis can destroy or distort when the ego is flooded by an unmediated flow of libido, a flood which can carry an image, projection, or archetype ('I am Napoleon') which swamps the subject's constructed identity in its train. At the same time, involution, because it restricts thought and motor activity, results in a secondary inertia or 'psychical rigidity' which parallels the deathly restrictions of primary narcissism. We have now explained how that secondary inertia comes into being.

This involution contrasts with the 'energetic and successful' behaviour that marks fully fledged masculinity, although masculinity too needs to preserve its spatial distinction from the other. It does this, I have argued, by projection of its visual and other drives on to another, depositing its disordered affects in that other, and clearing its head in the process. It is able to plan, wait, and act, and to act with a realistic grasp of what phantasies can be actualized through their deferral, for it is practised in this art. Of course it was through the initial correlation between deferral, as a characteristic of the masculine Oedipus complex, and as a characteristic of the ego, that we began. This correlation took us to the conclusion that the ego drives and the sexual drives have a joint origin, but it did so in a way which reveals that it is in masculinity, and masculinity alone, that the ego functions syntonically. In part its syntony rests on the fact that before and after the Oedipus complex, it projects hostility.

The genealogy of the joint origin of the ego drives, or the ego's capacities, given here can account for how it is that the ego drives and the sexual drives are experienced actively, in a way that means they are on the same side, opposed to death on the face of it. But this genealogy can also account for how it is that the ego's capacities and sexual drives are initially experienced passively (an experience that correlates with the inertia of the death drive), and then reversed into activity. One can also account for how it is that this initial experience is then overlaid by a subsequent passive identification in femininity, which preserves some of the inert effects of its predecessor while preserving identity. And one can account for how it is that the primary experience of activity is cemented by, and made ego-syntonic with, masculinity. To make this even clearer, I will sum up the argument thus far, before returning to the hypothesis outlined in the Introduction.

The idea that Freud's descriptions of the drive for mastery are descriptions 'in other words' of the same psychical processes he elsewhere assigns to the ego takes us to a more productive conclusion regarding the joint origin of the ego drives and sexual drives, and ultimately to the metapsychological impasse of femininity in this way. First, these 'other words' entail a description of the active and passive forms of the drives, and introduce the question of the relation to other people. But it is plain that these active and passive forms operate at two levels, and 'other people' only feature *as distinct entities* on the second level, through the medium of phantasies about those others, and the spatial distance these phantasies effect (pp. 115ff).

While this argument relies on a discussion of the ego's capacities as Freud defines them in 1911, there are indications of a tie between the drive for mastery and the ego in the *Three Essays* themselves. Critically they lie in Freud's use of the term 'executive agency'. In fact as much of this argument hinges on forces and capacities which are either discerned in the drives or in the ego, I have borrowed from the notion of executive agency, and termed them executive or subjective capacities.

In addition to Freud's reference to executive agency, we have the fact that he refers at one point not to a 'drive', but to an apparatus for obtaining mastery. In this reference, by introducing a connection between an aggressive element in the sexual drive and 'cannibalistic desires' he also ties the apparatus for obtaining mastery to the 'older of the great instinctual needs [i.e. hunger rather than love]' (1905b, *Studien*: 68, *SE*: 159, first and subsequent edns). Freud's eventual recognition that hunger and love provided 'an insufficient basis for conflict' is accordingly presaged in this theory well before 'the dark moment' of 1914. It is presaged in a way that ties it to cannibalism, or the incorporation of the breast, which the infant believes to be its own. The drive for mastery, in its cannibalistic connection, marks a struggle over who does, and who does not, possess the capacities associated with the breast, the mother, or any relevant other. It is not entirely an imaginary or phantasmatic struggle, for the musculature is the means by which, in part, the drive for mastery will be exercised, and its exercise begins with the first scream.[25] None the less, it remains a struggle, a protracted moment of confusion, over and about the executive capacities the infant believes to be its own. Which returns us to our hypothesis, which has four parts. I will try to indicate how much of it has been established, sum up more of this argument in the process, and indicate what remains to be done.

25 Cf. Freud's observation in the *Project*: the 'scream', he notes, characterizes the object for the infant. The infant does not distinguish between the object and itself, in terms of who or what is the source of pain and aggression.

HYPOTHESIZING

The first part of the hypothesis is this: in infancy, the subjective capacities were experienced passively, at the hands of 'another person'. The ostensible 'identification' with this other is in fact an imprint from that other. That imprint is basic to the process whereby the subject-to-be is able to identify with others. It is basic in that the imprint helps structure the nascent subject's means for perception or attention. The nascent subject is looked at, handled, fed, and listened to, and these sensory factors all enter into the imprint it receives together with the living attention that imprint embodies. But that imprint interlocks with the repression of its primal hallucination, and one result is a series of phantasmatic permutations, in which the subject-to-be does not know who causes what and what belongs to whom. The other result is that this interlock constitutes the first fixed point out of which a subject-centred identity will be constructed. This construction also introduces primary inertia and the death drive. In the next chapter, I will try to establish that this construction and the imprint from the other it entails constitute the original superego which Melanie Klein and Lacan believed in, and makes sense of more of Freud's inconsistencies. For instance, Freud at one point attributes the capacities for testing reality to the ego-ideal (1921a); it is only in 1923 that he gives them to the ego. All we are adding is that at times they remain, or rather, are given back to the 'ego-ideal'. Of further interest is the remarkable fact that it is precisely the capacities which are most evidently those of the other that constitute the 'less organic' *Partialtriebe*. While the 'more organic' orality remains rooted in the body of the hysteric, the capacities to see, to know, which feature in obsessional neuroses, and by implication, masculinity, are precisely the capacities which the infant depends on in the other, and which it struggles to claim through the pivotal drive for mastery. The less organic capacity which I have omitted to mention in this context is the drive to cause pain: it is a drive that emphasizes the projective process in acquiring those capacities; the drive for mastery is pivotal because it is the drive to claim from the mother or other the very mastery that other possesses in actuality, and it does this, in part, by projecting on to the other the subjugation it feels with the other's imprint. It only comes to know of this other through this spatial projection and the activity and hostility involved in it; it does not recognize the distinctness of the other in the first instance.

The second part of the hypothesis bears on why it is that initially, the infant does not, and cannot, distinguish psychically between the mother and itself ('I am the breast'). Its inability to make this distinction originates not only in a hostile and loving interlock, but in a reality. The infant is one with the mother's unconscious in the intra-uterine state, and this connection continues after birth, in terms of the sensory ties, the confusion over what belongs where in imprinting, and living attention. This literal, non-metaphorical, reading of the 'original identification with the mother' assumed in so much psychoanalytic writing, *might* bear on the innate quantitative factor which Freud assumed was one of the governors of the strength of activity and the drive for mastery (pp. 145ff). It could be explained not only by the force of the imprint received from the other(s), and the consequent resistance to that imprint, but also by differences in the energetic tie to the mother. The argument for the first line of this explanation was laid out in chapter 3, and it is probably enough to explain the innate factor in terms of that argument alone. However there is another aspect to innateness which deserves more attention, as it is relevant to the question of inertia.

To point to the idea that the infant's belief that the mother's capacities are its own has some basis in fact, in that it was part of the mother before birth, is to point to something else: namely, to a different experience of time. If we suppose that the infant's experience of the mother as part of itself is predicated on the infant being part of a closed system in which there is no or less delay between the registration of a need and the response to it, if, in other words, foetus is connected to mother as hand is to brain, then the experience of need after birth is inevitably connected with the experience of delay. Moreover, if foetus is connected to mother as hand is to brain, the nature of this connection has to be one in which communication functions through physical codes which are also intelligent.

Recognizing that such communication takes place, more accurately, labelling this intra-uterine interaction 'communication', may point to the source of the 'common substance' Freud presupposed lay at the origin of language and physical symptom alike.[26] More generally, recognizing that such communication takes place means recognizing the physicality of ideas as a concept. This concept makes it possible to think in terms of the experience of physical codes of communication *in utero* living on as a fleshly memory. It is this fleshly memory, I suspect, that actually lies at the base of 'the origin of language'. If language is always in the first instance 'a call', as Lacan has it, it can only be a call if, by definition, a concept of an answer is always already present. To the obvious objection to this, namely: that the expectation of an answer is established through the response to screaming, etc., one can reply that screaming too is

26 To engage with the question of the origins of language with any earnestness would require far more detailed discussion than can be provided here. While I am aware that this argument goes against Derrida's critique of Rousseau (Derrida [1967] 1974, discussed brilliantly in Spivak 1974), my difference from Rousseau's romanticism should be apparent. My reference to uterine communication as foundational is not much more than a suggestion at this point, but it is a suggestion that would account for how some words are more tied to expressiveness than others are without the need to invoke an epochal 'prelapsarian' state (W. Benjamin 1979: 107ff). We have all lapsed, at the moment we are severed from a more rapid, logical expressive code.

predicated on the expectation of a response. What I am stating, in other words, is that the experience of call and answer exists *in utero* in bodily codes. And, anticipating a more extended argument, it is worth adding that discussing, let alone deciphering, these codes might also cast Chomsky's theories of universal grammar in a different light, one which took account of the most cogent criticism levelled against his theory of generative grammar and language: namely, its neglect of communication.[27] This would make Chomskyian linguistics literally generative, rather than genetic.

But the present concern is with how it is that the pre-natal communication between mother and child is connected with time and delay. Needless to add, the experience of delay has to be a retroactive one. For what I am saying is that a notion of delay, and with it a notion of time, can come into being only by virtue of a comparison with a prior state in which delay was not experienced as such. Retroaction of course is critical in Freud's understanding of castration. He argued that the fear of phallic castration built on previous experiences (birth, weaning) but that these were only experienced as castrating after the fact.

The above notions, especially the notion of a retroactive experience of delay, place the hallucinations which provide instant gratification in a different light. They are an attempt to recapture a lost immediacy, in which the 'delay' between a need and its fulfilment was not experienced. Yet these hallucinations, as we have seen, also constitute the tie to the past; they are intrinsic to the fixed point of primary inertia. I have established (pp. 114ff) that hallucinations do contribute to a constructed psychical inertia, different (although Freud did not realize it) from the inertia of thermodynamics, an inertia which causes the subject unpleasure, and from which it seeks to escape. Yet the subject-to-be needs this inertia; it establishes the first boundary for identity. *As it does so, the foreclosure of the knowledge that there are energetic connections between beings begins.* This foreclosure is foreshadowed by the mental (pictorial) image of the hallucination, which is a condition of a subject-centred perspective. This inaugurates delay, while the hallucination itself is born of delay. However as the intra-uterine world is not the haven that some accounts assume it to be, and as the nature of the experience within it, as well as the contrast between this and subsequent post-natal experience, will vary, the 'innate factor' Freud presupposed may have more to it. But none of this should be read, although unfortunately I cannot stop its being read, as a prescription for parents to meet infantile needs under the speed of the four-minute mile. Were they to do so, in fact, they would only be likely to perpetuate

---

27 Recently I had a conversation with Gillian Beer about the language of biochemistry. Gillian Beer had observed that certain biochemists were referring to biochemical codes as 'sentences'; their explicit problem was that they did not understand the 'punctuation' of these sentences. But as punctuation is tied to time and space, the original language of the flesh may know nothing about it, or as little as the poets and the Hebrew Talmud.

the omnipotent confusion which needs to recognize the other as a spatially distinct entity in order to be moderately sane.[28]

The third part of this hypothesis is that in the femininity constructed by the Oedipus complex, the infant's passive experience of subjective capacities is reinforced and overlaid in the constitution of a second interlock: the secondary inertia femininity carries. This overlays the first passive experience of executive capacities, and it means that femininity consists of a state where these capacities are not 'ego-syntonic'; they are directed inwards rather than externally, as they are in masculinity. In femininity, these capacities stand opposed to the ego; they are not reclaimed. None the less this opposition, because it entails recognition of spatiality and externality, does confer a distinct identity in a way that the first passive experience does not. In the next chapter, I will try to establish how this works through discussing the phantasy of the father, and its role in protecting a spatially distinct feminine identity. In masculinity, subjective capacities become ego-syntonic because the ego and 'original superego', meaning the interlock with the imprinting of the other's subjective capacities, come together. In the same process, the sexual drives that focused on the mother are either desexualized, and available, potentially, for sublimation, or directed away from the mother. But this is nothing more than the reacquisition and redirection, away from the ego, of subjective capacities that once 'belonged' to the mother, and were then experienced as turned inwards. I have inferred that the ego, before the Oedipus complex, is formed in the acquisition of these capacities, meaning the reversal of the passive identification with the 'less organic drives' into their opposites. I have also assumed that the extent to which the ego will become 'active', or syntonic with sexual identity, depends on its receiving a supply of moving or living attention which enables its self-image to cohere, while freeing it to act. As chapter 3 established, the anxiety of repression is immobilizing at two levels: in primal repression, and in femininity. And, as we have seen in this chapter, the inertia or rigidity of femininity differs from the inertia of the death drive as such, although it is also similiar. It is similar because it restricts activity, and turns attentions inwards. It differs in that the nature of the attention received in femininity confers spatial distinctness, coherence or identity.

None the less, 'femininity' (like hysteria) is at metapsychological odds with the 'reality principle' and the secondary process means by which the ego knows reality, and is willing to wait and plan in order to change it. For the capacities with which it could act are reversed, turned back from the activity by which the ego acquired them, into a feminine (passive)

---

28 Incidentally, the notion that intrauterine experience is more rapid and more lively is a particular point of temporal differentiation between this argument and that of Rank [1924], Ferenczi [1924], and especially Norman O. Brown (1959), who imagines the womb to be slow and sluggish, representing the ultimate pull of the death drive.

overlay on an original imprinting. As I said, this secures identity, of a sort. The extent to which the feminine being is more likely to depend on an identity secured by this means will depend on the nature of the imprint she receives from the masculine other, and on the opportunities available for acting on reality. The imprint she receives from the other is part of and reinforced by a social symbolic order which accords her a certain place. The effects of this cannot be underestimated. At the same time, the fact that the 'image' (meaning imprint) received from the other is a physical idea, a physical energetic affair, means that reversing or changing the impact of this image, as Freud put it in almost the same context, 'demands a considerable expenditure of psychic energy'. It also demands the opportunities to expend this energy: to act on reality, in other words. The fact that this action may entail sacrificing a secure identity will explain why a woman will remain attached to phantasies, and a disabling image, even when the opportunities for acting on reality increase.

The fourth part of the hypothesis is that femininity and masculinity replay the hypothetical original connection between beings, but do so in a parody of that original connection, in which entropy and the secondary inertia of femininity are reinforced. This parody works at a slower pace than the original connection we have hypothesized exists *in utero*; the energetic connections between beings are distanced by space and time. This parody is also slower and more complex than the sensory ties of the first stage of imprinting. I am proposing that it is slower precisely because language and the distinct recognition of spatiality are involved in it, and because it depends on making knowledge of energetic connection entirely unconscious[29] for the masculine subject especially.

It is plain how the unconscious construction of spatio-temporal bearings is concealed at the first level of fixation: hallucinations are *repressed*. The repression of the hallucination defers as well. Language also defers, removing the subject one degree further away from the flesh. This removal seals the subject off from any residual consciousness of energetic connections between beings, as it constructs the spatial boundary that secures identity (cf. Kristeva 1986).

This point can be appreciated only in terms of the crucial differences between the two levels of deferral. The repression of an hallucination is initially the repression *of* an image. At the second level, it seems that an image is not only repressed; it is also an image that *represses*. Now if it

---

29 Towards the end of his life, Freud made a brief jotting. '*August 22* – Space may be the projection of the extension of the physical apparatus. No other derivation is probable. Instead of Kant's *a priori* determinants of our physical apparatus. Psyche is extended; knows nothing about it' (1941b: 300). This is a radical statement of what I have hinted at, which is that the sense of space, like the sense of time, is constructed. Except that I have added that it is constructed in the projections and introjections that mark the intermesh of masculine and feminine identities, in which these identities find a point of reference outside themselves.

works in a manner similar to hallucinations, that 'picture' is in some way responsible for the illusion that mental and physical processes are distinct. In the first deferral this illusion is born of the difference between real perceptions and lagging hallucinations: to a large extent, the difference itself is pictorial, although it can also be auditory.[30] But in the second deferral, language as well as images are involved, and it is an affect-laden image that is not only repressed; it is also repressing.

To make this plainer, I need to stress that femininity, like hysteria, retains the intelligent physicality of the hypothetical original connection: I suggested earlier (p. 93) that if thought and action are understood as one system, rather than as distinct modes of expression, the idea that attention turned inwards would have effects on the motor apparatus (as it does in hysterical paralysis or symbols) would become more explicable. But while physicality is retained, it obviously works at a slower pace, so slow it can paralyse. This we attributed to its 'inward-turning', while stressing that the only way psychophysical energy could 'turn' in any direction at all depended on the establishment of a fixed point: the initial, subject-centred, reference point of primary constructed inertia.

At the second level, hysteria (which remains the best exemplar for current purposes) has a relation to energy and language that goes beyond Freud's postulate of a common substance at base of affective responses and the words used to describe them ('the stab in the heart', p. 104 above). Notoriously, an hysterical paralysis of a hand covers the area we designate 'hand', and which we visually perceive as a hand. So the common substance would appear to have been 'split' or reordered into symbolic or representational categories before it returns as the form psychophysical energy takes when it is inwardly directed attention.

At the same time, it is not language itself that does the repressing. Freud emphasized the pictorial nature of the memory underlying the hysterical symptom, the picture that fades when it is put into words. I suggested above (p. 131) that it is the image, together with the affect that is retained with it and perhaps by it, that interferes with linguistic expression. From this perspective, rather than thinking of the hysterical symptom only as a failed attempt at linguistic expression, one can think of it as the product of a visual image that contains the attempt at symbolization in words, and that it is the image that misdirects the memory's release away from words, and on to the body. Evidently this is not an argument against the releasing power of language; it is an argument that a particular type of visual image prevents language flowing in the same direction as motor activity oriented outwards. Yet the very idea that words can release, and can flow in the

30 Auditory and olfactory hallucinations require more treatment than I have given them. I hope to discuss the role auditory hallucinations and sound play in establishing the psychical time-space barrier in a subsequent study on inertia. But at this point this study is, so to speak, only projected.

same direction as activity, points to how the parody of the original connection comes about. It is words that play out this parody; they try to remake connections from a subject-centred position. Yet they lag, caught at an imaginary crossroads. For words to release in hysteria, they have to release affect. They have to release both a repressed hallucinatory image and a repressing one.

But, as pathology is always the index for the workings of normality, this means that *as a rule*, repressed and repressing images are released by language. Yet if the repressed primal repression of hallucination, the foundation of the unconscious, primal phantasy and identity, were all released *as a rule*, the result would be that there could be no identity. The ego, as agent of perception, would be overwhelmed by the id, the embodiment of excitations and the drives. It would become psychotic.[31] So *as a rule*, something keeps appropriate repression in place. On the first level of inertia, this repression results from an interlock, in which another 'more experienced person' generally facilitates syntony.

On the second level, things are not so simple. A repressing image has to be projected out in order for words to flow. I have argued (p. 132) that *as a rule*, this constricting image with its unwanted affects is projected out in activity, but if the subject wants to secure an identity at the same time as it projects this constriction outwards, it can do so, most easily, if its unwanted affects are carried by an external other. For this to be done, that other must also carry the repressing image. We have seen the results of a double repression in hysteria, and assumed that a similar double load is carried in femininity. This means that in femininity, as a rule, the repressing image is not released by language. In masculinity, it is. But for words to work from a subject-centred position, they cannot express the truth that their working depends on another's carrying a repressing image and unwanted affects. Accordingly, the notion that the feminine other

31 It is, of course, well known that a psychotic is likely to feel invaded by others' feelings, or 'the rays of God', or CIA probes. These can be read as attempts at describing the energetic connections between beings (cf. Deleuze in Deleuze and Guattari [1972]). But what is missing here is the idea that there is a connection that is other than distorted. It is because psychosis is a compromise in this sense that the argument of Deleuze and Guattari [1972] has to founder. It mistakes this compromise, the remains of the battle encapsulated in psychosis, as the alternative to Oedipus in itself. The notion that order-as-harmony rather than order-as-rule is an alternative to the regimented laws of Oedipus is ruled out accordingly. Deleuze and Guattari work on the assumption that any form of order is a bad thing, and thus have to take the psychotic path as the only alternative. Just as Kristeva [1974b] assumes that her semiotic embodies the laws of condensation and displacement that mark the primary process, so does Deleuze assume that disorder is endemic in the 'schizoflow'. What these arguments miss is that the disorder may be laid upon something that is not of itself disordered, and that psychosis presents itself as such because it has to struggle through the subject-centred boundaries that would otherwise contain it. Psychosis, like the 'primary process', is a mixture of the censorship and what is 'beneath it'. There is no reason for assuming that psychosis is the only way connections can be experienced, even if it is the only way they can be expressed from other than a subject-centred position.

may be carrying the masculine subject's unwanted affects cannot be conscious. The masculine subject's sense of self-containment, and with it, his repressed psychical reality, depends on any experience of energetic connections between beings remaining unconscious.

They remained unconscious for Freud, who failed to perceive the homology between the formation of the ego and masculinity, and the fact that both need to project hostility. The failure to distinguish between these two formations left the spatial second border of the construction of psychical reality and the unconscious unrevealed. For it is with the projective repression of an image that masculinity garners its sense of perspective: hallucinations are cut down to size. By this argument, femininity marks the border not only between the neuroses and psychoses, but between 'inner' and 'outer' reality. Or, to make both points at once, it marks the border between 'psychical reality' and the unknown reality of a world unbound by time and space. One only functions well in the known world by action based on planned deferral and 'knowledge of reality', rather than being tied to the past.

The tie to the past of the one facilitates the other's attempt to catch up with the future, except that the longed-for future of the unconscious is a time when there was no time, a time when delay was not known to be such. Deferral never catches up with the rapid motion and thought it once knew as one. Deferral cannot catch up without sacrificing the identities it maintains. It is part of the cementing in place of the masculine and feminine positions, in that it brings the drives of the external other into play 'at a distance', and thereby strengthens the cement. The feminine party carries some of the unwanted affects of the masculine one. In doing so she provides him with an emotional anchor that helps him to function ego-syntonically. By carrying his disordered emotions or affects, which she does as her subjective capacities are turned back against herself, she enables him to follow the line of language (to reason) in a straightforward way.

From this perspective, overcoming femininity is not just a matter of the woman's reversing the direction of word and deed. It is a matter of reconnecting words to affects in a way that preserves her identity while it facilitates acting on reality. The reason this reconnection is difficult to make is precisely because the inward-turned image she has of herself preserves her identity, and (related) the psychical dynamics involved are not purely intrapsychic; they involve energetic connections with others. The 'desire of the other' is not only felt in relation to parental others. It is also felt at a second level, the level of the overlay, in which a masculine drive imprints its own message on the feminine other. Yet if the masculine drive consisted of nothing more than the drives analysed in this chapter, it could not preserve feminine identity in the way we have supposed that it must. It remains to see how this is done.

Chapter 5

The original superego

INTRODUCTION

A leading contradiction outlined in chapter 2, between the idea that women are more repressed and yet have weaker superegos, is resolved if repression is not contingent on the Oedipal formation of the superego. Another related contradiction, between the idea that women's fixations and repressions take place in the pre-Oedipus phase, and the notion that repression is tied to the superego, is also resolved if the superego is not contingent on the Oedipus complex. While Freud noted, after the second topography was established, that 'There is a danger of over-estimating the part played in repression by the super-ego' (1926a, *GW*: 121, *SE*: 94), he did not develop an account in which another agency is given the responsibility for repression.

Freud credited the ego with this capacity before 1923; and could perhaps appeal to it for an explanation of feminine repression, as indeed, he did. In hysteria, the ego, dealing with the sense of guilt the superego would impose on it, represses it. 'We know that as a rule the ego carries out repressions in the service and at the behest of the super-ego, but this is a case in which it has turned the same weapon against its harsh taskmaster' (1923b, *GW*: 281, *SE*: 52). But how or why the ego would repress the feminine Oedipus complex is not something he addressed. The only substantial repression Freud accounts for is that of her masculine sexuality, her negative Oedipus complex, which he attributes to *Penisneid*. He does not attribute it to the superego; penis-envy rules this out, as penis-envy is also meant to account for why girls have less motivation to establish a superego. But if we reconsider the seven characteristics of femininity (passivity, masochism, narcissism or vanity, a weaker sense of justice, less social sense, an inhibition in knowledge, and envy or jealousy), all but passivity have a relation to the superego. Of these characteristics, the weaker sense of justice, less social sense, one aspect of knowledge-inhibition and envy can be accounted for by Freud's model: they are byproducts of the feminine failure to establish a strong superego, and to sublimate. But passivity, knowledge-inhibition in another respect, narcissism, and especially masochism, cannot. Passivity and one aspect of knowledge-inhibition are accounted for, in part, by upbringing, social disincentives, and intimidation. But masochism directly implicates the superego, while narcissism is founded in relation to the superego's precursor, the ego-ideal.

In this chapter, I will approach the argument advanced in chapter 3, on the division of attention and the two stages of repression, and the argument in the last chapter on the vicissitudes of the drives, from the angle of the superego. A dissection of Freud's conflicting theories on the superego confirms the conclusions of these chapters. It does so because Freud's internal inconsistencies on the superego become consistent from the viewpoint that there is an initial imprinting at the hands of the other, an image full of drives, which interlocks with the nascent subject's hallucinations. I have hypothesized that this constitutes an original superego. This superego embodies the capacities the subject has to acquire for itself, as it is not born with its reality-testing ego (that is a developmental myth). The subject will acquire these capacities with more success when ego and superego are syntonic in masculinity, and less success when the subject needs the 'superego's' attributes to remain inward-turned in maintaining its identity.

The next section (pp. 179–90) discusses Freud's theory of the superego. A detailed reading of *The Ego and the Id*, and a comparison of this second topography with the first topography, shows that Freud presupposed, in fact, that a form of superego existed before the Oedipus complex. In this respect, and in the particular place he accorded repression amongst the defences, his theory is close to Klein's postulate of an original superego. Klein's theory is discussed in the third section (pp. 190–4). It leads to a brief reflection on love and hate (pp. 194–6), which in turn leads to the final section on masochism (pp. 196–215). This, the fount of the riddle of femininity, will return us to the spatial question of distance, the father and the death drive.

FREUD AND THE SUPEREGO

Freud's account of the superego emerged relatively late. It is known well enough that he first used the term *das Über-Ich* in *The Ego and the Id* (1923), although the superego concept is supposedly prefigured by the 'critical agency' put forward in the Metapsychological papers of 1914; and the correlate concept of an ego-ideal. In 'On Narcissism', Freud had hypothesized that the ego-ideal is established when infantile narcissism gives way to adult devotion to an ego-ideal. This concept was developed in 'Mourning and Melancholia' (1917) and in *Group Psychology and the Analysis of the Ego* (1921).

In all, Freud attributed the existence of conscience, the mechanism of paranoia, pathological mourning states, and the dream censorship to the critical agency. The first two attributes are retained in the superego concept. Significantly, the dream censorship is not. The fact that the dream censorship is dropped from the list is related to the fact that reality testing was attributed to the ego-ideal in *Group Psychology*; to the ego in *The Ego and the Id*. As I noted, this shift, and other inconsistencies, can be resolved by the notion that the original superego embodies the reality-testing capacities in the first instance, and that the 'ego' may or may not acquire them, and having acquired them, the subject may none the less give them away again. The first argument that supports this emerges through analysing the nature of the dream censorship. In the first topography, this censorship is inextricably intertwined with the agency that tests reality, an agency Freud terms 'the critical agency'. A second argument (there will be others culled from masochism) that supports the idea of an original superego comes from Freud's own theory of 'the origin of the ego-ideal' in *The Ego and the Id*. I will take these arguments in turn.

The critical agency

The critical agency acts as a censor that stands between the primary and secondary processes. An analysis of these processes, and the difference between them, was, as we saw in the Introduction, the essence of the first topography, and the censorship it holds in common with the second topography. It was an analysis cast in the context of dream interpretation. All dreams express a primary-process wish, but the wish is disguised:

> dreams are given their shape in individual human beings through the operation of two psychical forces [*zwei psychiche Mächte*] (or we may describe them as currents or systems): and that one of these forces constructs the wish which is expressed by the dream, while the other exercises a censorship upon this dream-wish, and, by use of that censorship, forcibly brings about [*erzwingt*] a distortion in the expression of the wish. It remains to enquire as to the nature of the power enjoyed by this second agency [*zwei Instanz*] which enables it to exercise its censorship.
>
> (1900, *GW*: 149, *SE*: 144)

By chapter 7 of *The Interpretation*, which is well known as the main theoretical section of that book, this second agency will have transformed itself into the secondary process on the one hand, and the critical agency on the other. On the path to this transformation, Freud refers both to 'two psychical agencies and a censorship between them [*zwei psychischer Instanzen und die zwischen ihnen bestehende Zensur*]' (1900, *GW*: 241,

SE: 235) and to the 'inhibition [of the suppressed wish] by the second system [*das zweite System*]' (1900, *GW*: 242, *SE*: 236). At yet another point, he will refer to 'the suppressed and suppressing agencies' (1900, *GW*: 483, *SE*: 479). He also refers to 'two psychical systems [and] the censorship upon the passage from one of them to the other [*beide psychischen Systeme, die Übergangszensur zwischen ihnen*]' (1900, *GW*: 613, *SE*: 607).

When Freud finally turns to an explicit discussion of the primary and secondary processes (he takes his time throughout *The Interpretation* to get to this point), he introduces the second system as one which seeks both to alter the external world in order to achieve satisfaction, and in doing so, to inhibit, as well as selectively release, quantities of excitation and related trains of thought: '*the second system [das zweite System] can only cathect an idea [Vorstellung] if it is in a position to inhibit [zu hemmen] any development of unpleasure that may proceed from it*' (1900, *GW*: 607, *SE*: 601), and this leads Freud to introduce the expression 'secondary process'; it results from the inhibition – or, if we take another 'non-psychological' meaning of *hemmen*, delay – imposed by the second system (1900, *GW*: 607, *SE*: 601). This bears back on our argument that hallucination (itself a still point in time, despite its apparent immediacy) will lead to unpleasure through the motor excitations it generates but cannot release, at the same time as checking out whether an hallucination is real or imagined will lead to further delay, and the need to wait (p. 111): the ego's calculative capacity.

Shortly after discussing inhibition, Freud again refers to the 'censorship between two systems' (1900, *GW*: 616, *SE*: 611).[1] This should leave the second system and the secondary process separate from, if closely connected to, the censorship; it should leave the correlation between the second system which seeks to alter external reality by voluntary movement, and the ego a straightforward one.[2] But Freud has, at an earlier point in chapter 7, also referred to a 'critical agency' which censors ideas. It is not identified with the second system as such, in that like the censor at certain points, it is given an intermediate position. The critical agency 'stands in a closer relation to consciousness than the agency criticized: it stands like a screen between the latter and consciousness' (1900, *GW*: 545, *SE*: 540). On the other hand, Freud 'found reasons' for identifying the critical agency with

1 This time, he refers to it in terms of a telescope analogy. He compares 'the censorship between two systems to the refraction which takes place when a ray of light passes into a new medium'.
2 It is a remarkable fact that while the ego features in the *Project*, and in Freud's work after *The Interpretation*, its role in *The Interpretation* itself is peripheral. It is mentioned only once in the theoretical chapter, when Freud notes that he cannot discuss the relations between the ego and the repressed, and the conscious and unconscious, respectively, without taking account of the psychoneuroses, and for that reason he will leave the matter to one side (1900, *GW*: 563, *SE*: 558).

'the agency which directs our waking life and determines our voluntary, conscious actions' (1900, *GW*: 545, *SE*: 540).[3]

In brief, as with the relocation of reality-testing from the ego-ideal of *Group Psychology*, to the ego of the *The Ego and the Id*, one of the functions Freud attributes to the reality principle ('directing our waking life, determining voluntary conscious actions') is identified with the precursor of the superego, the critical agency. It is identified with it in a strikingly confused discussion of second systems [*das zweite System*], secondary processes [*Sekundärvorgang*], secondary agencies and censorship [*zwei psychische Instanzen, Zensur*], which both does and does not warrant the alliance between the secondary process and the ego, as distinct from the superego. This confusion is due less to an *ad hoc* style of reasoning, than an accurate reflection of a situation[4] where voluntary alterations of reality, which implement a deferred gratification, are 'ego-syntonic' with the superego's censoriousness in the masculine case (or in the case of health), and where, on the other hand, the censorious superego stands opposed to the 'ego' in the case of pathology.

In the context of the argument that the ego's capacities are acquired from the original superego, Freud's confusing discussion is also significant because it shows that conscious thought is suspended *with* motility, and that censorship is inseparable from the processes involved in conscious, as well as unconscious, thought overall. This has already been indicated, but there is a particular illustration of it which Freud mentions in the context of 'criticism' which I want to note. In discussing the path of consciousness and its application to a train of ideas, Freud writes that 'If, as we follow this path, we come upon an idea which will not bear criticism, we break off: we drop the cathexis of attention' (1900, *GW*: 598, *SE*: 593). In other words, if it is essential to us to maintain an idea, if that idea cannot be criticized, we cease to attend to the line of reasoning that would lead us to criticize it. In ceasing to attend, we withdraw energy from that idea; (it is worth recalling here that attention and the sexual drive are connected (p. 157)).

If one examines other activities of the critical agency, its relation to conscious secondary-process thinking, and its parallels with the ego become even plainer. The critical agency not only censors dreams, it also interpolates and makes additions in and to them. Through these efforts, the dream loses its appearance of absurdity and disconnectedness, and may, on the face of it, become faultlessly logical and reasonable. But the

3 In this connection, Freud comments that this critical agency or system should thus be located at the motor end of the psychical apparatus (1900, *GW*: 545–6, *SE*: 540), and it is the suspension of motor activity in dreams that explains for Freud why the censorship is also, if not entirely suspended, at least disempowered. This means that the identification of the critical agency with voluntary activity is not incidental to his argument.

4 Wollheim (1973: 109) puts the matter finely in another context: 'the ambiguity lies in the situation itself, not in [Freud's] conception of it'.

meaning of these apparently rational dreams is, Freud thinks, as far removed as possible from their true significance (1900, *GW*: 495, *SE*: 491). The rational façade is only another means of disguise, although it is more elegant than the undisguised censorship that simply blocks out large slabs of the dream or its recollection.

Shortly I shall discuss a similarity between this censorship process and the activity of the critical agency in waking life. First, there are two other points which Freud associates with the critical agency to be noted. One concerns the agency's behaviour in its construction of façades. 'It exerts its influence principally by its preferences and selections from psychical material in the dream-thoughts that have already been formed' (1900, *GW*: 495, *SE*: 491). He says further, and this takes us to the second point, that the critical apparatus is spared the labour of constructing a façade when a façade already exists and is available for use in the material of the dream-thoughts. Such ready-made façades are nothing less than phantasies, analogous, says Freud, to the daydreams of waking life. These phantasies and dreams are also wishes, but they have been chosen and constructed by consciousness. They are constructed by the same censorship. In other words, *not only are these phantasies admissible to that agency, they are its products* (1900, *GW*: 493, *SE*: 489). Given that daydreams are, for Freud, representations at a further remove of the family romances of the Oedipus complex, this suggests that the latter have a closer tie to the secondary process than they do to the primary process with which they are usually affiliated, and they can have this tie only if they function in the service of repression. For one form of (projective) repression, we have argued, daydreams do in fact pave the way (pp. 117ff above).

In the course of this discussion Freud also recalls the finding that 'phantasies or day-dreams are the immediate forerunners of hysterical symptoms, or at least of a whole number of them' (1900, *GW*: 495, *SE*: 491). Hysterical symptoms, he writes at this point, are not attached to actual memories, but to phantasies erected on the basis of those memories (ibid.). These phantasies may be consciously present as daydreams or they may be excluded from consciousness. It needs to be stressed that the key connection between the secondary revision in dreams, including the overlay of a rational sequence, and the construction of daydreams is precisely the fact that both are processes of construction. The critical agency seeks to mould the material; to make up a story that pleases it. In sum, the critical agency which acts as the censoring apparatus in dreams also constructs seemingly rational revisions, phantasies, and daydreams. Through 'secondary revision' dreams are given an appearance of logic and connectedness they do not possess. This appearance is invariably the consequence of the demand for intelligibility made of ideas or events, regardless of whether they actually possess it. In this connection, Freud refers to Havelock Ellis with approval. Ellis writes:

> Sleeping consciousness we may even imagine as saying to itself in effect: 'Here comes our master, Waking Consciousness, who attaches such mighty importance to reason and logic and so forth. Quick! gather things up, put them in order – any order will do – before he enters to take possession.'[5]

Our master, waking consciousness, is not only a censor but a desperately reasonable being, whose ability to reason while covering things up is intertwined with other reality-testing attributes; motility, voluntary action, and so forth. In hysteria, and its modified form, femininity, these capacities stand opposed to the self, reverting back to the original unity that characterized them. In masculinity, this original unity is concealed as the subject presents the capacities for acting, planning, and thinking as its own from the outset, hiding the source from which they were appropriated. Similarly, by the time of the second topography, Freud's original secondary-process union of ego and superego capacities comes asunder. But other arguments for that union emerge, in spite of themselves, in the later theory of the superego.

The superego

In acounting for the origin of the ego-ideal in *The Ego and the Id*, Freud explains:

> behind it [the 'ego-ideal'] there lies hidden an individual's first and most important identification, his identification with the father in his own personal history [*persönliche Vorzeit*]. This is apparently not in the first instance the consequence or outcome of an object-cathexis; it is a direct and immediate identification and takes place earlier than any object-cathexis.
>
> (1923b, *GW*: 259, *SE*: 31)

Freud adds that it might be safer to say that this identification is with the parents, as a child does not value its father more in early life (1923b, *GW*: 259, *SE*: 31 n.). It is a fortuitous addition. For a little, it forestalls the otherwise contradictory implications of a comment he makes, to the effect that object-cathexis and identification are indistinguishable in the 'primitive oral phase'. Actually he needs to distinguish this indistinguishable primary identification from the distinct identification with the father, as I will make plain. However the main issue at this stage is that a 'primary identification' with the parents lies behind the ego-ideal. It is only after this that the (boy) child enters the familiar passage of the Oedipus complex. Yet not only the superego, but the position of the Oedipus complex itself is prefigured before that complex comes into being. Freud makes it clear

5 Havelock Ellis (1911: 10). Ellis shared Freud's interest in dreams too.

that the child's love and desire for its mother predate what he terms the Oedipus complex. This point is under-appreciated. So I quote at length:

> At a very early age the little boy develops an object-cathexis for his mother, which originally related to the mother's breast and is the prototype of an object-choice on the anaclitic model; the boy deals with his father by identifying himself with him. For a time these two relationships proceed side by side, until the boy's sexual wishes in regard to his mother become more intense and his father is perceived as an obstacle to them; *from this the Oedipus complex originates.* His identification with his father then takes on a hostile colouring [*feindse-lige Tönung*] and *changes* into a wish to get rid of his father in order to take his place with his mother.
>
> (1923b, *GW*: 260, *SE*: 31–2, emphases added)

By these remarks Freud divorces the earliest object-cathexis and identification. But there is a more striking contradiction contained here, a reversal of the earlier reversal: the pre-Oedipal identification with the father disappears from view; Freud writes simply that the superego 'owes its existence' to the repression of the hostility to the father and of desire for the mother (1923b, *GW*: 262–3, *SE*: 34). Eventually in *The Ego and the Id*, these different 'origins' of the superego will be drawn together (1923b, *GW*: 277, *SE*: 48). The superego that owes its existence to the resolution of the Oedipus complex is also based on the boy child's identification with his father. As Freud points out, this is unexpected by the logic of his argument on introjection: the identification that *results* from the Oedipus complex introduces the father rather than the abandoned (mother) object into the ego (1923b, *GW*: 260, *SE*: 32). However he notes that in some cases identification with the mother can take place. Moreover the positive and negative forms of the Oedipus complex are usually present in some combination. At one level the boy does identify with his mother and 'displays an affectionate attitude to his father' (1923b, *GW*: 261, *SE*: 33); the word 'affectionate' is Freud's preferred term for the Oedipal attitude of girls, rather than boys. A complementary reversal holds for and is more common in girls, who can bring their 'masculinity into prominence' identifying with the lost (father) object. In sum, the Oedipus complex results in a 'precipitate in the ego, consisting of these two identifications in some way united with each other' (1923b, *GW*: 262, *SE*: 34). This precipitate 'confronts the other contents of the ego as an ego ideal or superego'.

It seems we are dealing, once more, with a two-stage process, in which remarkably similar things occur. Before and during the Oedipus complex, the child desires its mother. Before, during, and after the Oedipus complex it identifies with its father. That identification enters into the formation of the superego. Of what then does the Oedipus complex consist? How, if at all, does the pre-Oedipal identification with the father differ from that which succeeds it?[6] For that matter, what is the status of 'identification' here?

By Freud's account, what delimits the Oedipus complex is not an attachment to the mother and identification with the father. It is rather the hostility to the father, resulting in the ambivalence 'inherent in the identification from the beginning' (1923b, *GW*: 260, *SE*: 32) becoming manifest. As sexual wishes towards the mother exist prior to the Oedipus complex, as ambivalence is present if latent, it seems the changes bringing on the Oedipus complex are quantitative. Wishes intensify. Freud's logic here is consistent with the idea that the ego is governed by the pleasure principle. It appears that too much intensity leads to unpleasure. With this intensity, hostility to the obstacle preventing its release comes to the surface.

The question then becomes, does the quantitative change result in a qualitative change in the father-identification forming the superego? The earlier identification with the father did not take the form of an internal prohibition on desiring the mother. The second identification does. Indeed it is the prohibitive nature of the superego that gives it its distinctive post-Oedipal character. Superficially, this distinctive character appears to be forged by two means: in addition to identification, there is also an energetic change. In fact these processes are so intertwined that they cannot really be separated. Freud indicates this in two contrasting (although not entirely contradictory) statements. In the first, he discusses the energetic alteration wrought by repression. In this context he again stresses that the superego is a new psychical entity born of the Oedipus complex's resolution.

> The super-ego is ... *not simply a residue* of the earliest object-choice of the id; it also represents an energetic reaction-formation against those choices. Its relation to the ego is not exhausted by the precept: 'You *ought to be* like this (like your father)'. It also comprises the prohibition: 'You *may not be* like this (like your father) – that is, you may not do all that he does; some things are his prerogative'. This double aspect of the ego ideal derives from the fact that the ego ideal had the task of repressing the Oedipus complex; indeed, it is to that revolutionary event that it *owes its existence*.
>
> (1923b, *GW*: 262–3, *SE*: 34 first and last emphases added, other
> emphases in the original)

In the following statement, where Freud also writes of the superego's

---

6 In a detailed reading of the relevant paragraph in *The Ego and the Id*, Kristeva also notes that there is an identification with the father prior to the Oedipus complex. Her enquiry does not focus on the contradictory aspects of Freud's account, but on the origin of the pre-Oedipal identification. She explains it in terms of the infant identifying with the father as the object of the mother's desire.

prohibitive character, he shifts the emphasis away from the newness of the psychical entity forged by the Oedipus complex.

> The super-ego owes its special position in the ego, or in relation to the ego, to a factor which must be considered from two sides: on the one hand it was the first identification and one which took place while the ego was still feeble, and on the other it is the heir to the Oedipus complex and has thus introduced the most momentous objects into the ego. . . . [It] preserves throughout life the character given to it by its derivation from the father complex – namely, the capacity to stand apart from the ego and to master it. . . . As the child was once under a compulsion to obey its parents, so the ego submits to the categorical imperative of its super-ego.
>
> (1923b, *GW*: 277, *SE*: 48)

This statement makes explicit the notion that superego formation begins before the Oedipus complex (and adds that the 'father complex' is the source of mastery over the ego). I suggest that the only way the second quotation can be reconciled with the previous one is to say that the repression of the Oedipus complex alters the nature of the first father identification; or, in Freud's express terms, of the superego formed while the ego was still feeble. This has to be Freud's intention, and the meaning underlying the idea that the ego-ideal has a 'double aspect'. Yet while the meaning of Freud's text is clear, for over fifty years he has been heard as saying that the superego is inaugurated by the resolution of the Oedipus complex and therefore cannot predate it.[7] But if the significance of the resolution of the Oedipus complex for the superego is that it changes its nature, the issue remains as to how the change manifests itself. As I said, the prohibitive nature of the post-Oedipal superego gives it its distinctive character. Yet Freud's discussion of the change focuses more on energetic than on characterological alterations: what distinguishes the Oedipus complex proper from the sexual feelings that precede it is the greater intensity of the desire for the mother and hostility to the father, while the prohibitive nature of the post-Oedipal superego distinguishes it from its precursor. It would be interesting to know the nature of the connection between the intensity of the feelings and the advent of their repression. The threat of castration features here, although it is little emphasized in *The Ego and the Id*. When it is, the context is the origin of the 'fear of conscience' (1923b, *GW*: 287, *SE*: 57).

Before turning to the qualitative change, which is very relevant to femininity, there is a related point to be made about the quantitative one, and the threat of castration (see p. 223 below). We can resolve the question

---

7 This is why Klein's theory is said to be riddled with metapsychological contradictions. She makes the superego independent of the Oedipus complex. But by this account, the contradictions could be explained.

of why the boy appears not to identify with his mother in spatio-temporal terms. In fact, he does identify with her subjective, executive capacities, whose imprint, and the living attention that underpins it, he initially received from her. But in the momentous resolution of the Oedipus complex, he redirects these capacities to the outer social sphere, following his father's path. His 'identification' with his mother is, accordingly, the appropriation, or gift, of her energetic (quantitative) subjective capacities. His identification with his father is a matter of the spatial *redirection* of those capacities, a redirection that goes hand in hand with a temporal deferral. 'You may not be like your father ... not yet, at any rate.'

In part, my thinking that there is a qualitative change in the father 'identification' also rests on its double and deferred nature after the Oedipus complex. Then it embodies precept *and* prohibition. However in *The Ego and the Id*, there is no explicit discussion of the qualities of the 'first' superego, or, in Freud's more frequently used terms, of the qualities of the father identification before the Oedipus complex. Nor is there any discussion of characteristics that are changed by internalizing the parental prohibition. One can infer, strongly infer that there is a character change. One cannot point to it in this text. Yet the basis for the inference becomes stronger still if one here recalls the characteristics women lack because they have no strong superego: a lack consequent on the fact that their Oedipus complex does not have a dramatic resolution. Women lack moral sense in general, and have less sense of the great exigencies of life. These lacks, and their associated virtues (justice and inexorability), correlate with the positive aspects of the superego. What women do not lack are the symptoms of melancholia, or other symptoms of the punitive superego. It is because the hysteric's symptoms involve suffering that Freud, in 1926, cannot absolve the superego of any part in hysterical repression, although he would otherwise like to do so.

With this in mind, it is worth noting that the characteristics Freud ascribes to the superego as a whole break down into two classes. In the first class are characteristics which, while their universal desirability may be disputed, are none the less ethically positive. They include the 'religious sense of humility', the 'tensions between the demands of conscience' and actual performance, resulting in a sense of guilt (1923b, *GW*: 263, *SE*: 35), 'morality and a social sense – the chief elements in the higher side of man' (1923b, *GW*: 265, *SE*: 37). In the second class are characteristics with no positive value, ethical or otherwise. These are evident in the descriptions of the superego in melancholia and obsessional neurosis. In such illnesses the superego 'often rages against the ego in a cruel fashion' (1923b, *GW*: 280, *SE*: 51); and (in melancholia) 'with merciless violence, as if it had taken possession of the whole of the sadism of the person concerned' (1923b, *GW*: 283, *SE*: 53). In these circumstances, 'What is now holding sway in the superego is, as it were, a pure culture of the death instinct' (1923b, *GW*: 283, *SE*: 53).

Remembering here that hysteria is the archetype of femininity, we can note that this passage is striking for two reasons. It is both a tacit acknowledgement of a consistency requirement, namely, that repression in the feminine case behaves in some respects independently of the superego, and at the same time, it echoes the language of a passage cited in the preceding chapter, in which 'the fact that symptoms involve *suffering*' (1905b, *Studien*: 75, *SE*: 166, first and subsequent edns; emphasis added) was attributed to the 'passive forms of the drive for cruelty'. In turn, this drive (or impulse) was, as I have shown, attributed to the drive for mastery and 'a period of sexual life at which the genitals have not yet taken over their later role' (1905b, *Studien*: 99, *SE*: 193, 1915 and subsequent edns).

This suggests that the negative aspects of the superego predate its Oedipal formation. It also suggests, if it does not confirm, that executive capacities turned inwards, or an early form of superego, also predate the Oedipus complex. If both these suggestions are read together, they give birth to another: the early form of superego, or the involuted executive capacities, is aggressive and destructive towards the self, in a way that the later superego need not be, if hostility is 'integrated' or directed away from the self, as it is in masculinity.

One might object that Freud addressed the presence of destructiveness turned inwards by postulating the death drive as a primary force which initially took the subject as its object, and that this is sufficient to account for involuted aggression, and that a concept of a pre-Oedipal superego is unnecessary. On the other hand, the death drive is an extremely problematic and controversial concept; many of the revisions of psychoanalytic metapsychology have aimed at its elimination, and those who have retained it have had difficulty accounting for it. But this argument does account for it: it does so (i) in terms of the tie between delay and inertia; (ii) in terms of the resistance to the restrictions of the hallucinatory interlock with the other's imprint as a source of hostility; (iii) in terms of the idea that the initial imprint of the other is unmediated, so that the aggression against the self is aggressive precisely in that no 'self' or distinct identity is likely to survive or come into being in its presence. Moreover this argument accounts for a puzzling and oft-commented feature of the death drive. The death drive is meant to be a peaceful longing for Nirvana, meaning a state of perfect rest, and yet it is meant to be ragingly sadistic, against the self or the other. This apparent contradiction is resolved if the longing for Nirvana is the longing for a state in which there was no delay between the perception of a need and its fulfilment, while raging sadism is the response to a feeling of imprisonment that results from the hallucinatory response to that delay, which, as we have seen, the subject-to-be confuses with the imprint of the other. More to the present point, if the drives for cruelty and mastery that mark the death drive are connected through a hallucinatory interlock to subjective capacities first experienced at the hands of the other, this explains why the death drive is first experienced as something that is directed against the self, and only subsequently projected outwards. And if these capacities *are* the original superego, there is no difficulty accounting for the superego's sadism, and its connection with the passive, masochistic form of drives that are unmistakably sexual.

But how does Freud himself explain the cruel characteristics of the superego? Before addressing this directly, I want to note a connection Freud makes between manifest hostility and identification when discussing 'social feelings'. This connection does not really fit with the flow of the argument at this point, but there is no other obvious place to put it. Also, it bears on the question of 'identification', and the two-stage 'identification' with the father needs more attention. When Freud attributes social feelings to the superego, he says they 'rest on identifications with other people, on the basis of having the same ego-ideal' (1923b, GW: 265, SE: 37). Social feelings are the one feature of the superego which Freud does not attribute to the internal role of the father. They are built upon jealous rivalries with brothers and sisters. 'Since the hostility cannot be satisfied, an identification with the former rival develops' (1923b, GW: 266, SE: 37). In addition, Freud points out that in 'mild cases of homosexuality . . . the identification is a substitute for an affectionate object-choice which has taken the place of an aggressive, hostile attitude' (1923b, GW: 266, SE: 37). Let us note here that as the subject cannot develop a sublimated homosexual identification, which presupposes an identification with a subject of the same sex, his social feelings will be confined to that sex. His aggressive, hostile attitude to 'sister' siblings cannot take this path, a fact which returns us to the notion of aggression projected on to the female other. When these projections were discussed in chapter 2, Klein's theory was introduced. I shall now return to her work, mainly for the support it gives to the notion of an original superego.

FREUD AND KLEIN

We can begin by noting that there is a critical difference between Freud and Klein, when it comes to discussing the origin of the superego's cruel characteristics. Freud hinges much of his explanation for melancholia on repression having overreached itself; that is, on the 'later' superego being too strong. Klein situates melancholia, or manic-depressive psychoses, as a product of the ego's dealings with the 'early' superego, which she distinguishes from a later superego.

The 'depressive position' is the aspect of Klein's theory of the change from early to later superego which has been discussed most. This is the

condition of reparation, and creative labour discussed above (p. 79), in
that the depressive position is the result and accompaniment of recognizing
that good and bad coexist in the same object, and in the subject. Yet there
is another aspect of Klein's theory of psychic change which has received
less attention. It is her particular use of the concept of repression. This
builds on a line of reasoning which is present in Freud, while establishing
grounds for completing it. While Klein and Freud differ on the later
superego, they are in striking agreement over the nature of the impact of
repression. Klein clarifies Freud's sometimes conflicting comments on the
later superego by writing of repression as marking a boundary between
forms of psychical, personality organization which are predominantly psychotic, and forms which are neurotic. Her assumptions about this boundary resonate with my argument, and this and other resonances should be
obvious enough.

The emphasis in comparative controversial discussions of Klein and
Freud has been on the areas of apparent disagreement. Klein's critics
have concentrated on her earlier dating of the superego. Kleinians have
concentrated on the explanatory power of the depressive position concept
which is tied to this early dating. In fact Klein's understanding of
repression is thoroughly informed by the depressive position, and once the
focus of discussion is shifted to her agreement with Freud on repression it
is clear that the issue is not *when* the superego is formed. It is *what* form
of superego predominates when.

Taking these points more slowly: in 1926 ('Psychological Principles'),
Klein proposed two major revisions to Freud's concept of the superego
and its relation to the Oedipus complex. First, she proposed that the
superego is formed at the beginning of the Oedipus complex, rather than
in the course of its resolution. Second, she shifted the Oedipus complex
itself back in time, arguing it began with the end of breast-feeding. Klein
proposed that the superego 'exists very much earlier than Freud supposed'
because of her unexpected finding that guilt exists in very small children
(p. 49 above). Klein's logic is plain: if guilt arises from and with the
superego's formation, and if guilt exists earlier than Freud supposed, then
the superego must be formed earlier too. There is no problem with this
logic, provided one accepts the premiss. Of course an alternative explanation is that guilt is constituted independently of the superego, but this
is not an explanation that Klein appeared to entertain at any point. Even
after she placed the superego in the first three months of life (more on the
implications of this for the Oedipus complex in a moment), she still links
its existence to guilt (Klein 1935 and 1957). There is another alternative,
which I favour: it is that guilt is very like shame, and that very early guilt
(in infancy) is in fact shame. Shame is scarcely mentioned in the four
volumes of Klein's collected writings. When it is, the context is shameless-
ness accompanying exhibitionism. There are no apparent grounds for

thinking Klein made a sharp distinction between the emotions of shame and guilt. Moreover shame is an emotion with an established relation to scopophilia. Scopophilia is one of the drives which is tied, in this argument, to the executive capacities first experienced passively (the original superego).

In terms of the two classes of superego attributes, the characteristics of Klein's early superego belong in the second. Her superego is 'terrifying', 'deforming', and can be 'crippling', especially in terms of the intellectual inhibition it effects. Indeed this early superego is so persecutory in nature that it is the source of greatest anxiety to the psyche (Klein 1929). But as I have indicated, Klein distinguishes the early superego from what she describes as its 'developed' form. Edna O'Shaughnessy in the excellent notes to Klein's collected *Writings* comments that the early superego is marked by anxiety or fear, the later form by guilt.[8] This particular distinction is affirmed in Klein's first major work, *The Psychoanalysis of Children* (1932). Despite making this distinction, despite the radical relocation of the superego back in time, Klein none the less in her earlier work adheres to Freud's belief that the superego is tied to the Oedipus complex. She thinks the Oedipus complex begins at 3 to 6 months, and that the Oedipal introjects that form the superego are introjected at the start of the Oedipus complex, not the end, but she still thinks the introjects are precisely Oedipal. Or at least this is her formal position in 1932. Shortly thereafter, she will abandon any tie between Oedipus complex and superego; and indeed, as O'Shaughnessy notes, there is an indication of what is to come in *The Psychoanalysis of Children*; the context is a discussion of the organism's means for mastering the destructive impulses Freud attributes to the death drive. Klein argues that in addition to thrusting the death drive out towards its objects (Freud 1924b, *GW*: 376–7, *SE*: 163–4) the ego can mobilize one part of the destructive impulses 'as a defence against the other part'.

> In this way the id will undergo a split which is, I think, the first step in the formation of instinctual inhibitions and of the superego and which may be the same thing as primal repression. We may suppose that a split of this sort is rendered possible by the fact that, as soon as the process of incorporation has begun, the incorporated object becomes the vehicle of defence against the destructive impulses within the organism.
>
> (Klein 1932: 127)

In 1935, Klein accounts for the superego without referring to the Oedipus complex. In 'A Contribution to the Psychogenesis of Manic-Depressive States' she argues only for the shift from one form of superego to another. Subsequently, Klein will correlate repression with the super-

8 Klein 1985, vol. 1: edit. n. 430–1.

ego's later form, and in this context describe the superego in classical terms, as the moral arbiter born of genital strife. In this context, it is worth quoting again a remark Freud made, which Klein cites with approval. It refers to

> the possibility that repression is a process which has a special relation to the genital organisation of the libido and that the ego resorts to other methods of defence when it has to secure itself against the libido on other levels of organisation.
>
> (quoted in Klein 1952a: 87, n. 1)

This footnote is important. It resurrects an idea mentioned in preceding chapters, viz. that repression is a later defence than that of splitting, the defence associated with the earlier superego. Moreover repression is of 'vital significance ... for normal development' (1957: 231) precisely because it marks a shift from a psychotic to a neurotic psychical organiz-ation. While splitting is a psychotic defence mechanism, repression becomes 'the main defence against emotional disturbances' for neurotics (1957: 223). This idea resonates with the idea that the Oedipal neuroses of childhood are the resolution of earlier psychotic anxieties, and with my idea that repression proper is established only with masculine and feminine identities, and the spatial distinctions they consolidate. But where for Freud the Oedipus complex terminated with a shock, for Klein, its resol-ution and the emergence of the later superego are 'gradual' (1952a: 87); it comes about through a growing psychical integration, which 'allows' the ego to substitute the defence of repression for that of splitting.

In earlier chapters, the possibility that the man secures his identity via a narcissistic short-cut, in which he projects his aggression on to the other woman, or the father, was discussed. When the man projects this aggression on to the other woman, this projection also involves a splitting. He splits women into two types: the mother, or good woman, for whom he retains his affection, and the whore, towards whom he directs his sexually imbued aggression (pp. 80ff).

The direction of this argument has now reached a point where we can specify further how an external splitting in the masculine case reinforces the involution of subjective capacities in the feminine. It has reached this point for two reasons: (i) I have noted that the hostility the man directs towards members of the same sex can be sublimated in a social bond, and suggested that the hostility directed towards the other sex cannot; (ii) at the same time, the idea that the man continues to split and project, and yet establishes a strong superego, indicates that he purchases not only his identity, but his ego-syntonic superego and masculinity through a form of repression which is actually a projection on to the other. This projective repression comes after or with the formation of the later superego; that is to say, with the Oedipus complex. One might also surmise that this projection is necessary to the impersonal nature of his superego, and hence his sense of justice, in that it disposes of unwanted affects. This is not to suggest that this is the only means by which he represses his Oedipus complex, but that it is a supplementary means, and the extent to which it is developed will depend on the extent to which he has achieved a 'gradual' integration through labour of what he has hitherto split. This projective repression reinforces the involution of the drives in the feminine case to the extent that it interlocks with them. This is so especially at puberty, when the second stage of the diphasic onset of sexuality asserts itself. But it is vital to stress that reinforcement means only that. The notion that femininity is constructed in terms of an overlay of an original passive experience of executive capacities is an internal psychical notion, internal in that attention is turned inwards. The notion that the construction is reinforced is a social one, which is not to say that the social force involved is immaterial, i.e. lacking a physical energetic dimension. But leaving this aside for now, the immediate question concerns how it is that the girl achieves some measure of psychical integration, without the option of projecting hostility for a second time.

While Freud perceived repression as a result of shock (the threat of castration), Klein perceives it as gradual. Her theory makes the problem of bringing love and hate together that much harder. Partly for this reason, it might be useful to reflect a little on love and hate. Love and hate, for Klein, are the forces that encapsulate the life and death drives, and the forces that inform the notion of 'good' and 'bad' objects. A little speculation about love and hate thus seems an appropriate note on which to leave her theory. It will also provide us with a bridge to the discussion of masochism, which necessarily entails some discussion of the death drive.

LOVE AND HATE

Hatred helps one take one's distance (cf. Benjamin 1988). Whatever else it involves, it involves a refusal of empathy, or in psychoanalytic terms, identification. Yet in the Oedipus complex, the boy both hates his father and identifies with him. The refusal of empathy may protect him, in that it stops that identification going too far. We could say the same of the girl in relation to her mother. The difference is that the boy has not always hated his father, in the hatred born of ambivalent strong love. He originally hated (as he loved) his mother. Freud has told us that he deals with this hatred of the mother by redirecting it towards the father, and that his hostility helps him smash the Oedipus complex. Moreover he does not only redirect his hatred to his father; he redirects it to the other woman, and we have inferred that this helps him cement his social bond with his own sex.

What does redirecting an emotion from one person to another mean?

The answer that comes to mind is that it relieves a pressure. I am only speculating here, but will follow this line of thought for a minute, because it puts the argument on the response to 'imprisonment by the other' (p. 115) in more available terms. The idea that pressure is relieved in turn suggests that hatred, before it is redirected, binds one to the other. That is to say, when one hates, one is bound to what one hates, but there is relief from bondage when hate is redirected. When one is bound, the parameters for action or being are in some way limited. By contrast, when one loves it should follow that one is not bound to what one loves, but this is nonsense. One is bound; the difference is, one does not bind or limit. In terms of the analysis of living and fixed attention (pp. 114ff) one might say that when one loves one directs living or facilitating attention towards the other (or oneself), when one hates one's attention fixes the other, and one is fixed in turn. Attention does not liberate; it limits. Conceivably, if limitation results in the containment of something that seeks release, the result would be pressure. So the notion that the redirection of hate relieved pressure makes a little sense if the redirection provides an outlet for what was otherwise contained. But what is this thing that is otherwise contained? Before attempting to answer that, the continuation of this train of speculation should be justified. The only justification for continuing is that two of the terms used echo Freud, and evoke concepts that may turn out to be pertinent. The first evocative term is 'release', which evokes the pleasure principle: the build-up of tension or pressure leads to unpleasure, release to pleasure; in seeking release the organism seeks pleasure. The second evocative term is 'pressure': aside from its pleasure-principle connotations, pressure resonates with repression; conceptually, one of the terms used by Freud for repression was after-pressure. Now all this suggests that the pressure of the build-up from something seeking release (or discharge, as Freud has it) and repression are in some way related. Which of course they are. Repression creates pressure, and whatever it is that is repressed behaves in the same way as whatever it is that seeks discharge. Here my line of reasoning reconnects with Freud.

> Let us call what becomes conscious as pleasure and unpleasure a quanti-
> tative and qualitative 'something' in the course of mental events. . . .
> Clinical experience . . . shows us that this 'something' behaves like a
> repressed impulse.

> (1923b, *GW*: 249, *SE*: 22)

The repressed impulse is the thing that can lead to a symptom, and ultimately to a pathology. It is the repression, rather than the sublimation of the Oedipus complex, that can make it pathological. Sublimation involves redirection. The difference here is that what is redirected is not the libido, but hatred. In the girl's case, this hatred is not redirected. It remains tied to her mother. If the earlier hypothesis is correct, the hatred in which she is trapped is overlaid by more hostility which is also turned against the girl, involuted, rather than directed outwards. Hatred and aggression turned in against the self characterize two pathologies: masochism and melancholia (or depression). As masochism prompted Freud's real riddle of femininity, i.e. how is it that the psychical state of femininity also occurs in men, we will concentrate on it.[9]

MASOCHISM

Freud distinguished three types of psychical masochism: a primary erotogenic masochism, feminine masochism, and moral masochism. He also discussed masochism as a real-life perversion. Primary *erotogenic* masochism is meant to underlie both feminine and moral masochism. It is 'pure death drive' turned in against the self. That should be stressed. First, because this argument accounts for the origins of a primary erotogenic masochism (which Freud does not, other than by the death drive, which he wants to counterpose to the sexual or life drive). It accounts for it because the involuted form of executive capacities is also the fount of the sexual drives; the difference between the life and erotic drives on the one hand, and the death drive on the other, is not a qualitative difference, but one of direction. Second (related), if primary erotogenic masochism underlies feminine and moral masochism, this means that, by definition, the death drive features in feminine masochism. I am stressing this because the role of the death drive in feminine masochism receives less attention from Freud than its more obvious manifestations in moral masochism, as we shall see.

Feminine masochism is the overtly sexual form of masochism in phantasy, and it parallels masochism in sexual reality. It is evident in phantasies of being bound, whipped, gagged, and so on, phantasies which, it is clear from Freud's account, are conscious (1924b, GW: 374, SE: 162). But these conscious or manifest phantasies have a deeper unconscious phantasy underlying them. When analysed, these phantasies reveal a wish to be beaten by the father. This, says Freud, 'stands very close to the other wish, to have a passive (feminine) sexual relation to him, and is only a regressive distortion of it' (1924b, GW: 382, SE: 169). The condition of this wish is castration. In general, masochistic phantasies 'signify' that the subject is being placed in a 'characteristically female situation'. The characteristic female situation consists of castration, copulation, childbirth (1924b, GW: 374, SE: 162). There is also in feminine masochism a factor of guilt, and desire for punishment. Freud says this guilt is connected with infantile masturbation (1924b), although he had earlier developed an

---

9 Although much of what follows is also relevant to melancholia.

explanation of it in terms of the reaction to the wish to see a rival punished, or denied love (1919b). In brief then, three ingredients constitute feminine masochism: (i) primary erotogenic masochism, consisting of the death drive turned inwards; (ii) female situation phantasies occasioned by an attachment to an object – namely, the father; and (iii) guilt.

There are two further points to be noted about feminine masochism. The feminine masochistic phantasy is the paradigm for the re-creation of a situation where the subject is or appears to be at the mercy of its phantasmatic environment. The other specific feature of feminine masochism is that in it, unlike the moral masochism to which we are about to turn, the superego plays no large part. However given that the parental introject is basic to the superego, and the factor of guilt, it should be noted that the relation between parent and child is embodied in the structure of feminine masochism. Freud says that the feminine masochist wants to be treated like a small helpless naughty child. This desire and the desire to be in the 'characteristically female situation' are – Freud's word – *stratified*. He says the explanation for this stratification is simple, although he never says precisely why. However it seems that the helpless naughty child originates in the pre-Oedipal anal-sadistic phase, while the desire for the castrated female situation is of course Oedipal. Which means an Oedipal structure parallels a pre-Oedipal one. Indeed it overlays it neatly enough to mean one can talk of stratification. Freud's otherwise unexplicated notion of stratification fits well with our hypothesis that femininity overlays an earlier pre-Oedipal relation in which the subject's executive capacities are experienced as opposed, turned in against the self.

Moral masochism is focused on the relation to the superego. Freud defines it as masochism on the grounds that it involves a libidinal relationship between the superego and the ego. In this relation, the superego has become 'murderous', in that it is governed by the death drive, while the ego is the masochistic victim. There are three striking things in Freud's account here. The first is that the superego has been detached from a personal phantasmatic attachment to either parent (it is worth noting that, ideally, this detachment also occurs in the resolution of the masculine Oedipus complex). The second thing is that Freud presents the significance of the inward-turning of the death drive in terms of the opposite situation: the external direction of aggression is the 'way out' of moral masochism. The third point to be made is that the moral masochist obtains satisfaction from real-life disasters or failures. Freud believes that these disasters are unconsciously contrived.

So far, the emphasis, following Freud, has been on the superego's role in masochism. The ego's role has not been considered. It appears only as a passive victim, albeit a libidinally satisfied one. But the ego's part in the proceedings deserves close attention. I shall give it this attention by assessing not only feminine masochism and moral masochism, but masochism as a perversion, in terms of the 'adult' ego's capacities. As discussed in preceding chapters, these capacities include the ability to judge, and to make estimates of reality in order to realize pleasure, which in turn involves the capacity for deferred gratification (planning), together with motility (the muscular apparatus) directed towards the fulfilment of those plans. And of course, 'the ego' (in our terms, the active ego) belongs to the reality principle and reality-testing, rather than to the pleasure principle, and the escape from reality in phantasy.

In feminine masochism as a conscious phantasy, one has conscious control of the phantasy, but does not participate in any event other than masturbation. In feminine masochism when it is acted out, that is to say, when it is a perversion, one has joint custody, and to this extent conscious control, of the phantasy and the events. In moral masochism, one has unconsciously ceded control to 'fate' or 'destiny'. One is unconscious of any underlying phantasy (indeed, it has disappeared, although the libidinal relation it involves has been transferred to destiny) and one has no conscious control of the events.

In the first case, where the subject is conscious of the phantasy, the capacity for constructing a phantasy belongs to the ego in that some degree of coherence in the form of planning a narrative or imagining a scene is available (cf. p. 100). But the narrative or scene is governed by the pleasure principle; it escapes or retreats from reality.

In the second case, perversion, the capacity for acting on reality in order to actualize a phantasy is evidently present. The pleasure deferred is gained by constructing a real-life sadomasochistic encounter. Nor, in perversion, is there any impairment of the ego's other capacities. In this connection, it will be remembered that for Freud the neuroses are the negative of the perversions. They are this precisely because the acting out of what is only phantasized in the neurotic case (and it can be phantasized consciously and/or unconsciously) does not entail the introversion or involution of libido that carries the denial of reality and neurotic ineffectiveness in its train (the passive or inert ego). Nor does it involve the considerable expenditure of energy involved in the repression of what is inadmissible to consciousness. The acting-out of the phantasy liberates the subject from the introverted or involuted libido which Freud so often, if so elliptically, holds responsible for neurotic enervation.

In moral masochism, neither thought, nor judgement, nor the capacities for affecting reality through motility directed towards a given end are available to consciousness. The moral masochist's real-life failure has to be contrived. The means for testing reality, judging it, making estimates of it, have to be at the disposal of the death drive. That is to say, they have to be at the disposal of the superego. Yet, as we have seen, these capacities are all assigned by Freud to the ego.

I now return to the interpretation of Freud which explains this inconsistency; this situation wherein the capacities of the (pre- and post-Oedipal) ego for testing and acting on reality are borrowed by the superego and used against the subject, rather than on its behalf. That moral masochism embodies a situation where the ego's capacities are appropriated by the superego is not an aberrancy, but an illustration of the more general psychical process that founds femininity and neurotic pathology and marks its characteristics: the superego returns to its original position; it stands opposed to the ego, *and* it once more embodies the executive capacities which it was the subject's task to acquire for the ego.

It is evident that moral masochism is a secondary construction. In fact both the turning of the death drive back against the self, the sadistic superego of moral masochism, and the stratification of the infantile and female situations in feminine masochism, are secondary constructions. But the examination of the secondary constructions in Freud's writing on masochism reveals a difference between them and thereby introduces another factor to be taken into account. This is the significance of phantasy, and its relation to the division between the conscious and the unconscious.

In moral masochism, the attachment to a libidinal object in phantasy has been lost. As I noted, it has lost its 'personal' (as Freud terms it) parent/child form.[10] One of the first things Freud notes about moral masochism is that by its nature, it is fundamentally distanced from the personal father. There is no longer even the phantasmatic remnant of the feminine relation to him. And with its departure, the symptoms of masochism are exacerbated. On the other hand, there is a way in which the symptoms accompanying feminine masochism (for instance, impotence) are not as severe as the dramatic, sometimes suicidal disasters of moral masochism and its murderous superego. So what, then, is the role of the death drive in feminine masochism? It matters here that I have already drawn a distinction between primary inertia (the unmediated death drive) and the secondary inertia of femininity, in which the subject's identity is protected, at the same time as its activity is restricted. It matters too that femininity and pathology, I have argued throughout, are closely connected. For Freud the death drive is active in any neurosis, and the degree of its force depends on its state of fusion with Eros. Given that the introversion of neurosis, like femininity, retains a phantasy object, this is significant precisely because it means that the death drive is still active, even though the neurotic subject has an identity, is not psychotic. It strengthens the similarities between the secondary inertia of femininity and neurotic pathology in general. And given the relation between anxiety and the death drive, and the argument on the special role of anxiety in femininity (p. 108), it can be added here that in the *New Introductory Lectures* Freud

10 This personal parent/child relation is described at more length in Freud 1927c.

identifies anxiety as the hallmark of neuroses, and the thing of which neurotics most frequently complain.

But how, exactly, do feminine masochism and its phantasy object somehow protect the subject from the dire effects of the death drive evident in moral masochism? We can infer that because the father is a loved person, and one who is supposed to love the child in its phantasy, Eros somehow screens out the worst effects of the death drive. The role of the personal father in femininity also fits with the structure of femininity as pathology, to the extent that the attachment to the father as an object in phantasy is precisely why no strong superego (a condition of sublimation) is established. On the other hand, as we have seen, a strong superego may be a necessary, but it is in no way a sufficient, condition of sublimation. The superego has not only to be detached from the personal phantasy object; it has also to be directed the right way. If it is detached from its phantasy object and inverted, moral masochism is one result.

Here it is important to recall that the detachment of libido from a phantasy object is what characterizes the ideal resolution of the masculine Oedipus complex. On the other hand the girl's sexuality 'lingers in phantasy' (Freud 1912d). So before discussing the role of the death drive in feminine masochism in more detail, we should digress from masochism for the moment to recall what the ideal masculine Oedipal resolution involves. It involves the detachment through sublimation, as distinct from the repression, of the attachment to the mother in phantasy. However as Freud notes, the process of sublimation involves some defusion of Eros and Thanatos; he otherwise presupposes that Eros and Thanatos are in some degree fused in the sexual drives. This presupposition was already present in Freud's theory before he conceptualized the death drive: he argued that some element of aggressiveness or sadism is always present in masculine sexuality (pp. 146–52 above). Masculine sexuality is to some degree aggressively directed towards the object it seeks to possess in a process we have termed projective repression. But when the sexual drive is sublimated, that is to say, when it is redirected away from the libidinal object to a 'higher aim', the possibility arises that the death drive will then become defused or detached from the libido. Indeed the fact of sublimation raises the question, In sublimation, what happens to the death drive, where does it go? One tentative answer is that the death drive is also redirected, and that it is this redirection that makes sublimation into something different from the sexual drive; in sublimation the death drive is directed towards a different end from the one it is directed towards in the case of normal sexuality.

That is to say, in sublimation one external aim, viz. the sexual object, is replaced by another, viz. the higher pursuit. Can a shift in the direction of the death drive explain this shift in aim? Recalling that by Klein's account, anxiety derives from the death drive working within, and recalling too that it is present in the pre-Oedipal ego, hysteria, and obsessional neurosis, an observation of Freud's on the mystery of anxiety becomes very relevant to this question.

> Why does the affect of anxiety alone seem to enjoy the advantage over all other affects of evoking reactions which are distinguished from the rest in being abnormal and which, through their inexpediency, run counter to the movement of life [*dem Strom des Lebens*]?
>
> (1926a, *GW*: 180, *SE*: 148)

Strom, incidentally, has a liquid and electric connotation that it lost in its translation as 'movement', although movement will do. When sublimation is directed towards the higher aim of cultural or creative pursuits, it is psychical energy directed externally in an ongoing process. As we noted, sublimation has another form: it can be redirected towards the social tie with members of the same sex (sublimated homosexuality) and Freud suggests that this sublimated homosexuality is the means by which residual libidinal energy is available for social and other cultural or creative pursuits, or the means by which it is directed towards those pursuits in its entirety. But for now, I will continue to concentrate on the process of sublimation. Even if this process has an ultimate aim, this seems rather different from energy directed externally towards the object of sexual desire, in so far as the latter represents a fixed point. Is there a relation between the fixity of anxiety (running 'counter to the movement of life') and the direction of the sexual drive? Part of that question, the part depending on the idea that sublimation has an aim which is ongoing, an aim whose fulfilment rests in movement rather than the possession of a fixed object, phantasmatic or real, should be held in mind for a moment. The other part, concerning the relation between fixity, phantasy, and sexuality, can be addressed now.

In one regard, I have already established a connection between sexuality, anxiety, fixity, and phantasy, but I have done so in relation to the first stage of inertia, femininity and the masculine short-cut (pp. 132–5). Here, we have been discussing the *ideal* resolution of the masculine Oedipus complex. Three things need noting: (i) ideal types do not exist in psychology, and because any subject has some neurotic or psychotic propensities, extensive sublimation is a rarity; Freud argued (especially in Freud 1910b) that sublimation of the order found in genius was accompanied by the absence of any apparent sexuality at all; (ii) for the same reason, that is, because any subject has some neurotic or psychotic propensities, some part of the death drive will be present in everyone; (iii) as we saw in preceding chapters, there is no sexuality without phantasy. This leads to the question. What is the relation between phantasy, the death drive, and the sexual drive? We need to pay more attention to the fate of the death drive where an attachment to a libidinal object persists in phantasy. This is the common case, and it returns us to feminine masochism.

The heart of neurotic enervation is the repressed attachment to a phantasy (masochism as a perversion is the 'negative' of a neurosis in that the perversion does not entail neurotic enervation; it is literally acted out). On the other hand, without the attachment to a phantasy, things, in the case of moral masochism, become much worse. From this perspective, the phantasy that characterizes feminine masochism as distinct from moral masochism appears to have a positive value. Or rather one might say, with more accuracy, the phantasy has a positive and a negative effect. Its negative effect, as we have just seen, is that it entails repression, hence enervation. Its positive effect seems to be, I repeat, that it shields the subject from the worst effects of the death drive.

It is also worth reiterating that what emerges from Freud's account is that the phantasmatic attachment in feminine masochism is to the father. This is so whether a boy's, a man's, a girl's, or a woman's phantasy is involved. For either sex, the basis of the phantasy that figures in feminine masochism is a phantasy of castration. The fact that castration figures as a phantasy for both sexes, rather than the reality it is meant to be for the girl, is a great equalizer. It dispenses with Freud's argument from phylogeny, which he offered when attempting to account for why femininity occurred in women. But it does not solve the economic problem of femininity. Or does it?

If the phantasy of the father shields the subject from the worst effects of the death drive, then it stands as a 'protective shield' (so to speak) in the event that the subject is unable to dispose of the death drive by directing it externally (in perversion, hostility to the father, the sadistic component in sexuality, or general aggressiveness). The 'protective shield' [Reizschutz], in Freud's original meaning of that term, was introduced in Beyond the Pleasure Principle (1920a). He argued that the protective shield functioned to protect the organism from external excitations, whose intensity was intolerable. He specifically notes that this protective shield, however necessary, is divested of the characteristics of living matter. Its job is to shield the organism from too much energy without, while admitting enough perceptual information for the subject to survive. Note, too, that he locates the perception-consciousness system, the receptive sensory organs, underneath the protective shield (1920a, GW: 27, SE: 28).[11] Freud assumes that the protective shield exists from the earliest period of psychical life.[12] He also does not suggest, in fact he expressly denies, that the shield protects the subject against internal stimuli. At the same time, Freud

---

11 Compare the discussion in Freud 1925a.
12 While the protective shield is described in spatial terms in Beyond the Pleasure Principle, it is also described in temporal terms as something which assures the subject of the relief of excitations from time to time (1925a, GW: 8, SE: 231).

also refers to the protective shield in the context of anxiety (1926a) and suggests that anxiety is modelled on the 'flight' signal when it warns against a dangerous internal idea. This has already been discussed from another angle (cf. p. 126 above). It was a discussion that raised the puzzle of how the ego could raise the economic resources it needed to make anxiety, 'an hysterical affect', into a force with such repressive power. But what if the protective shield is equivalent to the phantasy not only of, but to a drive-ridden imprint *from* the father, that works in a manner similar to yet different from the projected masculine drive (as I am about to argue it is)? This would make the protective shield external in one sense.

Beyond the Pleasure Principle is well known as the work which comes closest to Freud's *Project*, where he also posits the existence of some protective apparatus against external stimuli. What I want to suggest now is that although the protective shield is assigned to earliest psychical life, the phantasy of the father discernible in feminine masochism, a phantasy that may interlock with and be reinforced by a projected imprint from the father, has a similar function amidst the later defences. To suggest this, I need to assign the first protective shield, Freud's protective shield, to the period of the ego's formation in order to keep the parallel between the first passive identification, and a secondary feminine overlay. This can be done by making the primary hallucination which interlocks with the imprint from the primary other, into an equivalent of the first protective shield. While this is a foundation for identity, it is also a still image, and its stillness makes it inimical. That is to say, it is felt as something opposed to the movement of life. If life is movement, it is by virtue of its stillness that the *repressed* primary hallucination (and its later figuration in the hallucinatory ego-ideal) becomes divested of the properties of living matter, and in this respect parallels Freud's description of the protective shield. The protective shield, in this sense, becomes the shield that separates the subject from the flow of information and feeling that connects being to being (after all, 'perception' is part of the flow of information; and Freud has located it *beneath* his protective shield. Which again suggests that a 'common substance' once carried information in streams or currents that were neither physical nor mental but both; it is later overlaid by a form of perception which is structured through the directed attention that helps bring identities into being). Moreover, given that I have argued that the primary repressed hallucination is connected to delay and the subsequent sense of time, I have to note that there is direct support for these inferences in Freud.

In discussing the protective shield, Freud interpolates a brief reference to 'a subject which would merit the most exhaustive treatment'. He continues:

As a result of certain psycho-analytic discoveries, we are today in a position to embark on a discussion of the Kantian theorem that time and space are 'necessary forms of thought'. We have learnt that unconscious processes are in themselves 'timeless'. This means in the first place that they are not ordered temporally, that time does not change them in any way and that the idea of time [*Zeitvorstellung*] cannot be applied to them. These are negative characteristics which can only be clearly understood if a comparison is made with *conscious* mental thought processes. On the other hand, our abstract idea of time seems to be wholly derived from the method of working of the system Pcpt.-Cs. [perception-consciousness system] and to correspond to a perception on its own part of that method of working. This mode of functioning may perhaps constitute another way of providing a shield against stimuli. I know that these remarks sound very obscure, but I must limit myself to these hints.

(1920a, GW: 27–8, SE: 28)

Not only this, but Freud suggests in 'The Mystic Writing-Pad' (1925a) that the concept of time has an origin which is connected to the 'protective shield'. It is connected to the protective shield in this way. First, Freud notes that 'It is as though the unconscious sends out feelers, through the medium of the system Pcpt.-Cs., towards the external world and hastily withdraws them as soon as they have sampled the excitations [*Erregungen*] *coming from it*' (1925a: 231; emphasis added). He also says that the feelers by which the unconscious samples these external excitations are sent out in rapid periodic impulses. It is a condition of perception that these periodic impulses are cathected by the perception-consciousness system, but they are only cathected from time to time, and it is the discontinuity in when and how they are cathected that Freud suspects 'lies at the bottom of the origin of the sense of time'.

   These self-confessed obscure allusions seem to draw a distinction between the rapid periodic impulses and the abstract 'idea of time' (*Zeitvorstellung*, which also implies the way that time presents itself) in the perception-consciousness system. Of what does the distinction consist? The rapid periodic impulses are unconscious, unless they are the focus of perception, but the word 'periodic' has temporal connotations. On the other hand, periodicity does not connote linear or causal time, and it is precisely that that fits with our abstract idea of time. And Freud, while he argues that it is 'the unconscious' that sends out feelers in 'The Mystic Writing-Pad', writes later the same year (that forgetful year, 1925) that it is the *ego* that sends the feelers out. He does so to make the point that 'perception is not a purely passive process' (1925b: 238). The idea that it is the ego that sends out the feelers is compatible with the idea that it is the unconscious that does the sending because of this: Freud has also argued that one is only conscious of the information these feelers glean if they are cathected by perception. They are sending periodically, but they are attended to only occasionally, and when they are, the perception is active. As the last sentence suggests, the idea that feelers are cathected by perception is equivalent to saying that they are the beneficiaries of actively directed attention. And indeed, Freud said exactly this in the *Project* (1950b: 337).[13] In addition, the idea that we can have an actively perceiving ego that is simultaneously unconscious of excitations from without, unless it chooses to attend to them, is consistent with my claim that it is impossible that psychopsychical energy is subjectively self-contained: 'feelers' go out; excitations come in.

But I am straying too far from the notion of father as protective shield. There are two difficulties with this argument so far. The first is that if the phantasy of and imprint from the father shields the subject from the worst effects of the death drive, this makes the death drive external. The second difficulty with this argument is that it effectively makes the first protective shield, Freud's protective shield, into the partial equivalent of an hallucination. In turn this means that the ego, as the agent of perception, has to be different from the ego's product, hallucination, as a protective shield, and I have been arguing for two chapters that the means for testing reality are acquired from capacities that are first identified with the primary other. But this second difficulty is only superficial, and anyway, it has been substantially resolved by the above interpolation on Freud, time, and the protective shield: it was the confusing interlock between its hallucinated phantasies and the undifferentiated capacities of the other that laid the first keystone of the identity-arch; these structure perception through directing attention in certain channels.

The first difficulty is less of an obstacle than an idea that has been present all along. Masculine sexuality, to the extent it embodies sadism, projects this on to the other. If this projection is at some level felt by the other (as projective repression), then the death drive, at this level, would be experienced as external. Yet we have just been arguing that the phantasy of and, more importantly, the imprint from the father functions to shield the feminine subject from the worst effects of the death drive. Is there then a difference between what is projected out in masculine sexuality, and what is projected out by the father? I have stressed repeatedly that the unconscious drives *from*, as well as of, the other can affect the shape of the subject's psyche, and there is no reason why drives from the father should be exempt.

Yet given the history of psychoanalysis, any talk of fathers entertaining

13 The context is a discussion of how the sense organs that are capable of being closed are closed in sleep. What I have argued about the equivalence of active, directed perception and attention (and the idea that attention is direction) is confirmed in this discussion. This reference to sleep is discussed in a detailed analysis of the *Project* above (specifically, p. 97 and p. 97, n. 16).

phantasies about or directing drives towards daughters is dodgy. Indeed illustrations of the 'desire of the other' conspicuously neglect the desire of the father in relation to the daughter. It is allowed: (i) the son desires his mother (and father); (ii) the daughter desires her father (and mother); (iii) the mother sees the son as the realization of her desire, the phallus she never had. But the fourth term, which would bear on the nature of the father's desire in relation to his daughter, is never specified. The father's desire in relation to his daughter is of course the most problematic of all the terms, for it is the rejection of the actuality of the father's sexual desire for his daughter that founds psychoanalysis. But without treading on to the disputed territory of the real event, we can still enquire into the effects of the father's 'desire' regarding the daughter.

The idea that there is an imprint from the father that differs in some respect from that which is projected on to the other in masculine sexuality is essential to this argument. It explains the difference between 'masculinity' as something that embodies the death drive, and 'masculinity' as something that protects the subject from the death drive. The former is what we discussed in the last chapter; it is what Freud termed the sensual current, unmediated by affection. The latter is the affectionate current. I am postulating that the affectionate current is (or should be) embodied in the imprint from the father. This means that the imprint from the father embodies Eros, but it does so in a way that forbids sexuality. As Freud has it concerning the boy's feelings for the mother: the affectionate current in Eros is permitted; the sensual forbidden. The imprint from the father, I am suggesting, forbids anything that crosses the boundaries between subjects, as sensuality strives to do. It forbids it in that it is a restriction on the father himself, and a restriction the father imposes on other men. In this way it protects feminine identity. Needless to say, just as the desire of the mother for a phallus (the boy-man who will be what she is not) can carry over to the phantasy of the woman-in-love, the imprint from the father can carry over to the imprint from the man, which points to why heterosexuality can be felt as an imperative necessity, especially when identity is in jeopardy because of other circumstances. But the significant point now is that as what the subject most fears from the death drive is the loss of its identity, I have indicated how the imprint from the father can confer and maintain that identity. I have also indicated why the daughter will cling to the feminine Oedipus complex, rather than risk the identity-loss at stake in being the object of a masculine drive that does not have elements of the protective affectionate current within it. For there is no reason why the affectionate (or protective) aspects of Eros should necessarily be combined with the sensual ones in masculine desire; indeed, much if not most of Freud's writing on masculine sexuality is premissed on the difficulty of effecting this combination.

All the foregoing reintroduces the matter of identity-formation. The child's phantasy of the father fuses a protective love (a form of Eros) and the death drive. Moral masochism left us with a situation where Eros departs from this fusion, and the departure echoes the defusion that can occur in sublimation, excepting that in the case of moral masochism, the death drive returns, defused from the erotic admixture that protected the subject from the death drive's worst effects. Why, then, does Eros depart? Is it because Eros by its nature is always directed away from the self, towards another? This is an unsatisfactory answer, for Eros in the case of narcissism is also directed towards the self. But is this quite right? In the narcissistic neuroses (the old name for the psychoses) when the ego is aggrandized by the return of the libido on to itself, when there is no attachment to an object in phantasy, we have seen that the ego is 'flooded with libido'. Under these circumstances the subject becomes psychotic, and no matter how well it thinks of itself, it is destroyed in that it loses its identity. So this return of Eros is worse than useless. Indeed, given that it destroys identity, can we still call it Eros? Or is this libido turned inwards without a mediating phantasy object rather the death drive itself, thinly disguised by the residues of self-admiration? In which case, the difference between Eros and the death drive is one of direction, except that it has to be something more, as one can direct the death drive towards another, as well as oneself. One can also direct living attention, or love, towards another, as well as the self, which, incidentally, points to whence the residues of admiration arose: namely, the other's living attention, everyday non-psychotic narcissism, and, as we shall show, the protective paternal imprint. In everyday narcissism, the libido is directed inwards via a mediating phantasy object. In the phantasy the child has about the father, the libido is externally directed (towards the attachment of the father in phantasy) and the child phantasizes that it is the sole loved object of the father (of which more in a moment): the beneficiary of masculine love without its sadistic component. But in turning its libido inwards, there is no guarantee that, in fact I do not see how, an entirely fictitious phantasy could secure identity. Or, in other words, how a phantasy of one's own construction could really protect the subject from the effects of the death drive. In this connection, it is no accident that Freud saw the fictions of psychoses as an attempt at recovery. For this reason, I am inclined to think that an interlock between the phantasy of and imprint from the father is essential to preserving identity, but that it will do so only because the phantasy from the father carries living attention in its train. In other words, the father's imprint may well confirm feminine narcissism, and a feminine identity that is restricted in its sphere of activity, but if living attention is not part of what it projects out, I do not see how identity could be preserved, for this requires an injection of life, particularly when it is inward-turned. Needless to say, the impact of the mother's living attention and the nature of her imprint will effect the extent of this need, and it may be she who supplies the father with the living attention his imprint should convey. And the father's personal role in securing identity is also played by the social constellation in which the child lives. As *Group Psychology* makes plain, the social constellation will often take over the personal father's role in later life. Thus the effects of an 'absent father' are, ultimately, the effects of an absent social constellation. This absence would only make for psychosis in the event of effective social isolation.

It should now be clear that the preservation of feminine identity is effected in two ways. First, because an other is presupposed in the phantasmatic attachment to the personal father (or his social substitutes), and this presupposition involves the recognition of externality or difference. Second, in the same movement by which this other is presupposed, the other also has a material affect on the subject that further distances her (or him) from the death drive. Even as the imprint from the father overlays an inward-turning, it also lays a prohibition on sexual fusion, and it embodies living attention in the image it gives.

To say some of this more harshly, the 'protective shield' formed through the interlock of the phantasy of and imprint from the father still directs the death drive inwards, but it does so in a more benign manner. It directs it backwards precisely because it *fixes* identity, at the same time as it confers identity. This is consistent with the secondary inertia of femininity; identity survives, but it is less active or effective. But the fact that it survives at all is because the imprint from the father is, or should be, preservative. I reiterate that its preservative function is also a function of the recognition of the father as an external and distinct other. This is where contemporary stress on sexual difference is particularly pertinent. The union which I have hypothesized exists with the mother would mean one is not fundamentally differentiated from the experience of the mother as oneself in other respects. But the imprint from the father is *different*, and even while it does not originate from the subject, it stakes out a territory that marks the subject as other.[14]

This is why the superego is identified with, even retroactively identified

14 In support of this argument, an aspect of Freud's discussion of the case of Schreber might be usefully considered. This remarkable analysis of a psychotic's memoirs has one conclusion which is intellectually unsatisfactory, in that the order of explanation Freud offers is not on a par with the rest of the analysis. This conclusion concerns why it is that paranoia should precede megalomania, when Freud's logic otherwise leads him to the opposite inference (see p. 54, n. 6 above). But by this argument, the reason paranoia precedes megalomania is that paranoia would be a last-ditch struggle with the phantasy of the father that otherwise maintains the subject's separate identity from the mother. It seeks to return to the situation in which it experienced itself as an omnipotent being, when it took the mother's capacities to be its own, and the phantasy of the father stands in its way. This explanation would also accord with why it is that in paranoia, the subject 'makes external', projects outwards, the paternal identification that marked it as separate and gave it an identity.

with, the paternal figure. The sense of an imprint from another was there all along; but this imprint was initially indistinguishable. After the father is recognized, the distinctness this recognition confers is projected back on to the imprint from the mother: the two are confused, hence Freud's difficulties with differentiating between the 'identification' with the parents, and that with the father, and for that matter, specifying the change wrought by the Oedipus complex between the father identification that precedes and postdates it. Once the concept of an 'imprint' is substituted for that of 'identification' in the formation of the subject (who can only identify with another once it has acquired the means to do so (p. 170 above)), these difficulties disappear. Not only is the father's different imprint, by virtue of its difference, projected back. In the boy's case, the first identification with the father is the imprint from him; after receiving this imprint, he is then able to identify with the father. This means he identifies with the being who projects out into the larger spatial sphere, and this is why the mother identification appears to (but does not really) disappear with, and why the father identification changes its character at, the Oedipus complex (p. 187). The problem in the girl's case is that there is no directional distinction between the imprint she receives from the father in a narcissistic interlock, and her original passivity in relation to her mother. We might suppose it is the precariousness this similarity engenders for identity that leads the girl to turn from the mother, and cling to the father in phantasy, for it is this that establishes her otherness. We can suppose further that the risk to identity embodied in the union with the mother also contributes to this turning.

But the force of the death drive that accompanies this union should also be as threatening to the boy, and the only explanation for how he avoids this threat is that he projects the death drive outwards; in so doing, he makes the subjective or executive capacities his own. However as Freud's discussion of masochism reveals, the boy too has a 'first stage' in which the phantasy of the father situates him in a 'feminine position'.[15] This feminine position also shields and preserves his identity, when it interlocks with the others' imprints. But the difference between the boy and the girl, and explanation of the advent of masculinity in the former, is that the boy, ideally, subsequently abolishes the personal attachment to the father in phantasy, while the girl does not. He projects his hostility not only on to his father, but, as we have seen, on to a woman unlike his mother (the divergence of the sensual and affectionate streams). The girl might try to project this hostility on to her father, but something gets in her way and prevents her from doing so. Or rather, some things. The first thing is the masculine imprint that resituates her in a position where her capacities stand opposed to her, of which the father must also to some extent

15 Cf. the discussion of Klein on the subject of the femininity phase (chapter 2).

partake. The second thing is that while the masculine being can project his hostility outwards, the girl cannot, and thus the short-cut available to the boy in securing identity is not available to her.

The girl is only able to secure identity by creative labour, which brings us to her third obstacle. The means by which she could accomplish this creative labour have been economically and culturally circumscribed. Each of these obstacles requires more specific attention, but first the bearing of the above on femininity in men needs to be explicitly stated. Simply put, it is that if the boy cannot dispose of the death drive by projecting it on to the other or through sublimation (or both), he will seek to deal with the death drive by feminine means, by seeking protection from the phantasy of and imprint from the father that places him in a feminine position, while it preserves his identity. This places him in a castrated position, but it also indicates why he might welcome castration. It will be recalled that the qualitative change between the original superego and its successor came about as love and hostility intensified (p. 185 above). Now on the one hand, this can and usually does lead him to identify with his father, and cut off his sensual desire for his mother. The problem as to why he identifies with his father, when it is his mother he has had to forgo, is less of a problem if what this identification is really about is this: the intensifying hostility results from an increasing pressure within the arena in which he is confined in relation to his mother; this has no sexual outlet, and what is more, sex is also a threat, in the sense that sex represents not only a release through but a fusion with the mother, but it is an outlet the boy is seeking. He finds this outlet through directing his hostility to others outside ('sister siblings', women of a certain type) and depositing in them the unwanted hostility and affects that constrain him, through a visual affective projection that displaces his temporally constructed inertia on to another. The fact that these others are 'outside' involves a spatial reorientation. He identifies with his mother in a highly specific sense, in acquiring the subjective capacities he first experienced at her hands. His 'identification', in fact, is a redirection of those capacities towards the outer sphere. He identifies with his father by becoming an imprinter, rather than an imprintee. *In the outer social sphere, subjective capacities, originally maternal, are masculine.* On the other hand, if the boy is unable to effect this spatial reorientation, either because of the strength of his love for his mother, or because he fears the father will not share it, or (related) feels the imprints of the parental others, especially the father, as imprints that forbid it, or because of any of the reasons that prevent the girl from effecting the same spatial shift, then the increasing intensity of both love and hate remains a threat to identity. The nature of the living attention and weighty imprints he receives is especially pertinent here, as much of this argument has established, and I will draw out the full implications of this in a moment. Enough at this point that if a boy's hostility has no outlet, he will try to maintain his identity by feminine means. But if he turns his libido back and maintains his self-image narcissistically, this backward-turning is destructive, unless it is conditionally mediated and reinforced by the father's (or social others') living attention. These points will be clearer after a brief discussion of the obstacles mentioned above that stand in the girl's way; in certain cases, they may also stand in the boy's.

Turning first to why the father should get in the way of the girl's projecting her hostility away from the mother, we should note, first, that Freud writes that the father even encourages this hostility!

> The affections of the little girl are fixed on her father, who has probably done all he could to win her love, and in this way has sown the seeds of an attitude of hatred and rivalry towards her mother.
>
> (1919b, GW: 206, SE: 186)

This probably does not affect boys, but the vicissitudes of hostility do. Let us consider in more detail what projecting his hostility outwards means for the boy, before considering what the fact that she cannot project it out means for the girl. In redirecting the death drive, which it does by projecting it away from the self, masculinity, in the same movement, separates the death drive from subjective capacities, which it thereby incorporates as its own; they now belong to it. Masculinity is able to accomplish this because by projecting the death drive outwards, it turns subjective capacities outwards as well. Yet how does it come to experience these subjective capacities as its own? These capacities have to be cemented indissolubly with its identity, or, to say the same thing, its identity has to embody these capacities.

This reintroduces, once more, the problem of identity-formation. Is the process whereby identity is formed also the process whereby subjective capacities are acquired? The answer to this is yes and no. Yes, in that the preconditions for identity are laid down in the first still point of hallucination. No, in that there is nothing in the first imprinting that tells the subject-to-be where it finishes and the other begins. By Lacan's theory, identity begins to be established in relation to a mirror phase, in which the Gestalt, the image of the whole self, is counterposed to the infant's experience of itself as a disconnected bundle of parts. At the same time, by Borch-Jacobsen's critique, the identification with one's mirror-image presupposes the very thing it is meant to explain: the formation of the ego.[16] He argues that something has to exist before, because 'something'

16 At the beginning of his book, I thought Borch-Jacobsen had arrived at the same thesis outlined in this one. In his introduction, he puts forward the hypothesis that the unconscious is the 'umbilical cord' connecting the one with the other with whom it identifies. I am not sure if he meant 'umbilical cord' metaphorically, as he does not detail the physical attachment to the mother as the point of origin for the unconscious (but cf. p. 165). But his argument is consistent with this implication, although he cannot be held responsible for it (my implication I mean, not his argument).

makes a visual identification with itself in the mirror. Yet, as I suggested in the hypothesis elaborated in the last chapter, and this means taking the Lacanian concept of the 'desire of the other' literally, this 'something' *is* the attention, capacities, and, in a sense, the unconscious of the other: it is the complex of drives, psychical energy, and images which form the other's unconscious. From these in the first instance the infant is not shielded. It is one with its mother in the way that it was one before birth. In other words, the 'something' with which the infant is able to make its visual identification is the unconscious connection with the mother, which supplies it with the mother's subjective capacities, perception borrowed and structured through directed attention. It is this that also enables it to perceive its mirror-image, the mediating identification by which it begins to perceive itself as separate. Yet, as I have shown, because it interlocks with hallucination, including the hallucinatory mirror-image, this directed attention, this imprint from the other, is also felt as an imprisonment, however life-enhancing it might be. It is castrating, in the sense that its stillness cuts it off from a connection with the movement of life. In the masculine case, this movement is rejoined when the infantile phantasy of oneself as helpless, held still, a disconnected, disordered bundle of parts, is projected on to the other in order that the subject assumes the position of 'superego', and makes the superego syntonic with the ego by reversing a passive experience into an active one. In this reversal, the visual anatomical difference is significant not only because of the difference it marks, but because the capacity for visualizing the other is part of the force of projective repression, the economic drives, which in their interlock with the inward-turning phantasy that maintains identity by feminine means, can literally hold the other still.

In reversing the passive experience of the primary inertia that is the first plank of its separate identity, the masculine subject projects its primary castration on to the other (cf. Ragland-Sullivan 1986). Because this option of reversal is not open to the feminine being, the personal connection, the personal father matters because the connection with him means that ident-ity is not at the mercy of the subjective capacities, intertwined with the stream of attention and the movement of life, which would otherwise swamp separateness (a situation that moral masochism replays, as we have seen).[17] Of course, if there is no personal father present, both the benefits of his attention, and the negative effects of his masculine drive, will be less. To say the same thing differently, the literally imaginary effects of the father will not be the same, although his place can of course be taken by others. Yet if these others are more distant, then the process of identity-formation has to be effected. As I have already indicated, the social

---

17 The role of the personal father in femininity fits with the structure of femininity in another respect, to the extent that the attachment to the father as an object in phantasy is precisely why no strong superego (a condition of sublimation) is established.

constellation can and also does play the father's role. But in childhood especially, this, and the symbolic role of language in effecting separation, will play a different part than they do when combined with a personal imprint from the other. The absence or lesser impact of this personal imprint could be liberating, if the imprint from the father is more constraining than facilitating. It could be bad, if separation and identity are less certain without the intervention of that personal imprint. Or both could be true. One is more able to act and think, without imprints from the other intervening, and influencing or determining the sphere of activity. One is less sure of who one is as one does so.

Freud's insistence on the retroactive significance of phallic castration (p. 172) could be read as an insistence that phallic castration, and the masculine and feminine positions it cements in place, is the point at which identity finds its final spatio-temporal bearings. In other words, it is only after the subject has taken up a sexed position that the various events that constructed its sense of time and space fall into place behind it, so to speak. And this of course means that there must be something in the formation of masculinity and femininity which means, as we have already inferred, that the spatial distinctness necessary for sanity is secured by this formation. For masculinity, this security depends on femininity's carrying the initial inertia that brought the ego into being *at a distance*. For femininity, it depends on a distance from the death drive that is guaranteed only by a living attention that protects her from the aggression turned towards or back against herself. This protection may be preferable to its alternatives.

I mentioned a third obstacle that stood in the way of the feminine being's securing identity, namely, that the alternative means by which she achieves identity, that is to say, creative labour, have been circumscribed economically and culturally. This circumscription has been so extensively documented and demonstrated by the women's movement, which is a testament to its existence, that it requires no elaboration – except for one forceful aspect of it that I will elaborate on in the conclusion: it is about how the curtailment of the economic and cultural opportunities available to women is reinforced by a physical social force which benefits masculine identity. In concluding this chapter, I shall elaborate on its critical but still underdeveloped idea: the difference between masculine sexuality and the imprint from the father.

The law of the father precisely dictates that he does not direct his sexual drive towards his daughter;[18] in terms of the typology Freud constructed

18 It is when he does so that we get another type of default on the law of the father, which may be related to the default (on the subject's part) which produces psychosis. For by the above argument on identity, it is the active sadistic component in sexuality that is most destructive of identity. In this context it should be added that the idea that the protective shield functions as a barrier against trauma (Freud 1920a) could be discussed in terms of the relation between trauma and primal repression, focusing especially on incest as a piercing of the protective shield.

for masculine sexuality, the daughter should be the beneficiary of the affectionate rather than the sexual current. I suggested that this is the critical difference between the imprint from the father and masculine sexuality. However because the imprint from the father, as a projected, specific expression of the 'desire of the other', is not discussed in the clinical literature, we are still a little in the dark as to how the difference would manifest itself. Moreover the phantasy of the father, as Freud describes it in the subjective experience of feminine masochism, is of course associated with the other side of sadistic masculine sexuality; the phantasy embodies sadism at the hands of the other. Yet, if we turn to Freud's elaboration of feminine masochism in 'A Child Is Being Beaten' (1919b) (based on the analysis of four female and two male patients) we find that the phantasy of a sadistic father is the missing stage, the 'silent phantasy' that psychoanalysis has had to infer. In the girls' phantasy that a child is being beaten, 'The child being beaten is never the one producing the phantasy, but is invariably another child' (1919b, GW: 204, SE: 184). The phantasy that presents itself to consciousness is of *another child* being beaten.

Freud reasons that the beating phantasies have three phases. As they present themselves to consciousness, they are an 'end-product', and their first phase in girls 'must belong to a very early period of childhood' (1919b, GW: 204, SE: 184).[19] This phase in girls is represented by the idea that a child is being beaten by an indeterminate adult, who, on examination, appears to be the girl's father. He is beating a child whom she hates, presumably a sibling. The existence of siblings means that

> many children who believed themselves securely enthroned in the unshakable affection of their parents have by a single blow been cast down from all the heavens of their imaginary omnipotence.
>
> (1919b, GW: 206, SE: 187)

The second phase of the phantasy is expressed by the words ' "*I am being beaten by my father.*" It is of an unmistakably masochistic character' (1919, GW: 206, SE: 187). But this second phase

> in a certain sense . . . has never had a real existence. It is never remembered, it has never succeeded in becoming conscious. It is a construction of analysis, but it is no less a necessity on that account.
>
> (1919b, GW: 204, SE: 185)

It is a necessity because of the third phase, similar in structure and personnel to the first, in which a teacher or other representative of 'the class of fathers' is beating a (usually male) child, who, again, is not the girl herself. Because this third phase is unambiguously sexual and sadistic,

19 Freud makes a distinction between the phases of the beating phantasy in girls and boys.

Freud infers that a second phase, also sexual in character, preceded it. But the masochistic pleasure experienced in the inferred phantasy of being beaten by the father has been completely repressed.

For my purposes, the change in direction exemplified by the shift from the subject to another child could also exemplify the notion that the imprint from the father protects the child from the death drive, at the same time as this change in direction marks the difference between the imprint of the father, and the overlay of a masculine sexual imprint with a sadistic component. As noted, Freud interprets the first phase as the child's egoistic response to the existence of other children. It is also dependent upon the 'erotic side', as it involves jealousy. Both the erotic and the egoistic are gratified by the thought: ' "My father does not love this other child, *he loves only me.*" ' (1919b, *GW*: 206, *SE*: 187). But the erotic and the egoistic can also figure conjointly in another way in our interpretation. The erotic figures in that the inferred, silent, second phase of the phantasy represents a tacit acknowledgement of sadism in masculine sexuality, of which the father also partakes in his male capacity. In fact many of the contributions to the 'Great Debate' on sexuality focus on the girl's fear of being damaged by the father's 'too big' genitals. In this context, it should be recalled that one of Horney's early contributions to the debate suggested a different origin to the seduction phantasy, which is that the daughter is connected with her mother's unconscious in a manner which means she does not differentiate between her mother's experience and her own (pp. 41–2 above). However the idea that the father is beating *another* child deflects or redirects the sexual aspect of the desire of the father together with the death drive that underpins it. But of course, this interpretation of the beating phantasy relies on the most controversial part of my four-part hypothesis, which is that initially the child and mother are a psychical as well as a physical unity, in which the mother's capacities are taken by the child as its own. This interpretation also rests on how the different pathways and directions from that original unity are elaborated; all depends on the directions, and the still points and phantasies that bring these different directions into being, moments of inertia that left the riddle of femininity intact for so long.

Chapter 6

Conclusion: the riddle again

The riddle with which we began was a riddle about how it is that men, too, turned their aggressiveness back against themselves. This energetic or economic riddle was recast in the context of Freud's two metapsychologies, and the question as to whether the spatial reference points of the first illuminated the tripartite structure of the second. I did not dispute that 'femininity', as Freud described it, existed. It does, and inhibits both sexes. It bears all the marks of pathology, yet it is also the means by which a biological female becomes a woman, and it is, or apparently has been, more likely to afflict the female sex *tout court*. So, rephrasing the riddle, we might ask: Why does femininity appear to afflict more women than men, yet why does it affect men at all? For that matter, why does it affect some women more than others, and why does its impact on both sexes vary and fluctuate?

Femininity was something Freud tried to explain by two theories: the first, an analogy theory developed in the context of his work with hysterics, his discovery of the Oedipus complex, and the psychical reality of phantasy. This theory he discarded in favour of a theory that women too first desired the mother, and only made the transition to heterosexuality with difficulty. He described this transition as a psychically exhausting task, and it was from this description that the pathological aspects of femininity emerged. The task left the woman rigid, inhibited, less conscious or capable of thoughtful curiosity, masochistic, envious, and less willing to deal inexorably with social justice and the exigencies of life. Freud's theory of how a woman effected the transition from mother to father hinged on castration and penis-envy, although he was the first to suggest that penis-envy was carrying an explanatory burden beyond its strength. In fact all the reasons he gave himself for the daughter's turning to the feminine path were never quite good enough. Penis-envy was insufficient, although the effects of castration cannot be overestimated, he said, as do we, as did many participants in the first and second debates over his theory, who also raised questions about the interplay of social and psychical reality, and the more contemporary concern with how it is that identity is formed.

Identity especially has figured in the explanation of the riddle offered here, and it has done so in two ways. The first is our argument about how identity is constructed, and how it is that a subject-centred position comes into existence. The construction of this subject-centred identity depends on severing, and making any knowledge of the energetic connections between beings, unconscious. The same process also constructs 'the unconscious' and psychical reality. Identity has also featured in a thoroughly Freudian context. That context is Freud's assumption that femininity is always and only *defined in relation to masculinity*. Once this is taken utterly seriously, the riddle is less of a conundrum. For one can understand the 'relation to masculinity' not only in terms of the idea that there is only one libido, and it is masculine, or in terms of a visual difference that shocks the man and makes the woman envious. One can also understand that relation in terms of its *benefits* to masculinity. Once the emphasis is placed on 'who benefits?', it is possible to understand why femininity is different from passivity, why it is more likely to occur in women, why its pathological aspects present themselves as normal, while understanding why it also occurs in men. Because those who benefit are those who are placed in a position where they are able to project what would otherwise distort their judgement and inhibit them on to the other.

This means that what they project is at least consistent with, if not responsible for, any being following the feminine path. If this is so, the masculine projected imprint or image should be consistent with narcissism, masochism, a weaker sense of justice, less social sense, less capacity for sublimation, and greater repression or rigidity. To be consistent with these things, of what would that projection need to consist?

To be consistent with more repression, the masculine projected image has to hold something back; to be consistent with rigidity, it has to be willing to keep something fixed; to be consistent with masochism, it has to have a sadistic component; to be consistent with narcissism, it has to be willing to admire. If it is consistent with these things, the relation of the masculine projection to a lesser capacity of sublimation and a limited social sense is relatively easy to specify. In being willing to keep something fixed and hold something back, the projected image is consistent with less capacity for sublimation, in that sublimation requires giving something out in active movement. Note here Freud's observation that 'It is possible that sublimation arises out of some special process which would be held back by repression' (1919b: 182). Sublimation also requires a capacity for curiosity and knowledge-seeking which the masculine imprint, if it is consistent with the feminine path, has to be willing to censor. The social sense requires an awareness of others, an awareness which is inconsistent with narcissism, and we have to suppose that the drives projected out in masculinity are at least willing to maintain this ignorance.

The weaker sense of justice is the most problematic of the characteristics of femininity in terms of the foregoing argument. For while the relation of the other characteristics of femininity to the masculine overlay seems straightforward, in that the overlay models the involuted or inward-turned executive capacities that shape psychical femininity, a weaker sense of justice seems to have nothing to do with any capacity capable of being turned inwards or outwards (unlike the drive for mastery in sadism/masochism, or the related scopophilic drive in voyeurism/narcissism). But this seeming lack of any relation to inward or outward directions is misleading.

Justice, or the 'impartial insistence on right and wrong', presupposes judgement, as the capacity to distinguish between right and wrong. Judgement in fact is the capacity to make appropriate distinctions overall. Judgement in the first case is, for Freud, an orally derived faculty connected to the desire to keep something in, or spit something out. Hence judgement is critical in founding projection as a defence mechanism, and the difference between the internal and the external ('what is bad is outside; what is good is within').[1] Moreover judgement is tied to the ability to distinguish between hallucination and perception. It is tied to the repression of an hallucination that founds the unconscious and primary inertia, a repression that brings a still point, and with it, a sense of direction into being. Judgement is also tied to the spatial mechanism of projection, and thus it is at the very foundation of whether anything is turned in or out.

Given the connection between justice and judgement, between keeping something in or spitting something out, the stronger masculine sense of justice should be critical in the process whereby masculinity comes to project its disordered affects into the feminine other, in order to maintain its impartiality and dispassionate chain of reasoning. The feminine sense of justice, on the other hand, will be over-emotional and confused. The difficulty here is that justice is meant to have an ethical dimension which considerations of externality and internality do not encompass on the face of it. Yet, bearing the ethical dimension of justice in mind, it is worth recalling Freud's note that justice is the reaction formation to envy, which raised the unanswered question of how this reaction-formation came into being in the masculine case, and of the origin of the envy that reaction-

1   In addition, the priority of the internal/external division in relation to the justice question is recognized by Freud in another context. He remarks that conscience is imposed from without, and that its external origin is manifest in the regressions of paranoia (1914c: 96). The ego-ideal is projected back externally to its place of origin. From these standpoints, the difference, the weakness in the feminine sense of justice, is one of lodgement. In femininity, it is tacked on, still partly an external construction. In the masculine case it is securely lodged inside.

formation supposed (p. 62). The envy is bypassed by Freud. By Klein's account, it is built into the megalomania of infancy, which denies that the subjective capacities on which it depends did not belong to it in the first place. Which means that justice, as a reaction-formation to envy, may be nothing more than part of, and perhaps the condition of, the masculine reclamation of these capacities, a reclamation which depends on a projection of disordered affects (including envy) on to the other.

Yet those who benefit from femininity do not only benefit because femininity is a convenient depository. They also benefit in that they secure a certain attention, an identity, from the deposed. With reference to the ego's two tasks, preserving identity and acting on the world, this means being placed in a position where those two tasks are not in conflict. In everyday language, it means being loved for what one does, rather than in spite of it. In terms of this analysis, it means being on the receiving end of a stream of living attention that helps maintain identity at the same time as it facilitates activity or an active ego; it also means having a space to act. Finally, it means clearing this space either through sublimation or dumping disorder in another. In other words, it means 'giving' and receiving the right images, but images, by this argument, have a literal physical force of their own. This is why, although its effects cannot be overestimated, the emphasis on the part played by cultural symbolic tradition in maintaining masculine power is not enough. For if men neither direct the emotions they would rather do without towards another, nor benefit from the libidinal economy of living attention, they are more likely to be placed in the feminine position; and less likely to accede to their own symbolic. If the fact of the ubiquity of a masculine symbolic tradition was a sufficient explanation for the empowerment of men, there would be no riddle of femininity. You might say, echoing Freud's metaphor on repression, that you are not only pulled into the symbolic; you have to be energetically pushed, and you have to have an anchor in it in order to stay there, an anchor provided by the one who carries the affects that otherwise interfere with the ability to act and think in a direct line of logic.

Otherwise you fall back on maintaining identity by feminine means, for femininity also secures identity, but by a different route, and at a higher price. The feminine route is an inverted one. Attention is turned inwards via phantasy, in order to maintain one's own image. The price is that when attention is received from another, it overlays and fixes that image in place. It is immobilizing, because in a feminine state, one is the depository for the other's unwanted affects and inertia. Femininity, too, works on a push-me-pull-you fulcrum. As if there has to be something that attracts a type of immobilizing attention from the other, a phantasy that is already lodged within. More exactly, by this argument, it is phantasy that makes the woman complicit in her inertia. For in addition to the unconscious phantasy that is always deployed in maintaining one's self-image, another overlay of phantasy was assigned a pivotal role in the feminine object's turning her activity back against herself, just as the drive for mastery was assigned a pivotal role in the transformation of activity and passivity into masculinity and femininity. This suggested that if one is on the receiving end of a projection of the drive for mastery, this of itself, leads to phantasy as conscious daydreams. In turn, this would mean that phantasy is part of the pivot by which primary constructed inertia, and the initial experience of passivity, becomes the secondary inertia, the entropic rigidity of femininity.

A problem lies though in charting a precise relation between a specific projection of the drive for mastery, and the daydreams of a feminine object. The intuitive appeal provided by the experience of withdrawing attention (without the conscious knowledge of the daydream-object), or having it withdrawn, and the immediate interest this withdrawal generates, is not enough. The feminine being is perfectly capable of daydreaming in the absence of any sexual relation at all, and by previous argument may even be more likely to do so. Daydreaming or conscious phantasy seems to work in a way that parallels the attention provided by an actual other, and there are distinct indications as to why this might be so. I have suggested that the social reality which imposes a feminine identity will facilitate a similar psychical structure, and that a psychical identity maintained by feminine means seems to attract a like-minded external image towards it. So that if the split attention of daydreaming helps maintain identity, then the attention of a real other will maintain it in a similar manner, but at a similar price. It will maintain it on the condition that a surplus of living or moving attention is extracted in return for the image basic to the origin of the masculine subject. And, as should now be plain, this surplus need not be extracted from women alone. The man who relies on identity by feminine means also seems to attract a castrating image from without. Alternatively, if he receives that negative image from without, and is placed in the position that fits it and attracts it, he is more likely to find his psychical identity by the feminine path.

Not that maintaining identity by feminine means is without its own benefits. It relieves one of the obligation to act, and, depending on the extent to which it is socio-economically sanctioned, may provide one with the luxuries of idleness, relief from responsibility, and other secondary gains. That these benefits can be literally sickening, that they are inevitably accompanied by self-hatred because their is no direct outlet for aggression, whose only escape route lies in the indirect side-swipes and backbiting of the powerless, is clear enough. While the 'epoch of hysteria' is an epidemiological fiction, it coincided with the socio-economic endorsement of femininity taken to an extreme as an expected and respectable form of identity for women of a certain class. On the other hand, if the feminine path to identity is not socially sanctioned, it will either veer towards neurotic pathology or incapacity (the feminine Wolfman); or it will result in an immiseration of any identity at all. For instance, the situation of the immigrant worker who is castrated by the image he receives, and because of this, is more likely to fall back on the feminine psychical path, does not make for a secure identity. He may try to compensate by directing more aggression towards the woman near him (if there is one). But he will not have the reassurance of feminine narcissism, let alone the love of paternal protection, nor is he likely to be securely masculine, socially inexorable, or 'just'.

Now obviously the account I am rendering here relies on the interplay of psychical and material reality. Obviously, if one is placed in a position where one receives an image of oneself as powerful, where one is given the opportunity to act and is loved for doing so, obviously, if one is male, white, privileged, and without compunction, the chances are far higher that one will accede to the masculine position. The point is that there is nothing inevitable here. For not only the chances of acceding to the masculine position, but the concept of that position as such, depend on the interplay of psychical and material reality. I have laid out an argument on how masculine and feminine identities are constructed, but by this argument, masculine identity especially depends on the manufacture of the illusion of self-containment. In a culture where that illusion is not a psychical necessity, where psychophysical connections with others are acknowledged, it should follow that both the spatio-temporal co-ordinates of that culture, and the identities constructed within it, will be different (cf. Strathern 1988). It may also follow that that culture will not be subject-centred. There is a whole other research agenda at issue here.[2] Within the subject-centred culture in which my analysis of Freud's theory is cast, focusing on the interplay of psychical and material reality has the advantage that it brings together various and otherwise conflicting psychoanalytic insights generated by that culture. Its emphasis on psychical reality is consistent with aspects of Lacanian and Kleinian theory; its spatio-temporal emphasis, and its attention to material reality, evoke the language of object-relations. But the thing that makes these insights cohere is my intersubjective reading of Freud's theory of the 'drives': a theory spurned by Lacanians and object-relations theorists alike. In turn, the fact that my account of Freud's economic dimension is intersubjective means, once more, that within the material reality of this culture, there is nothing preordained about who accedes to the masculine position. Nor is it ever

2 Felman's reading of Lacan argues that the Oedipus complex is itself a representation of how an individual situates itself as a distinct being, and that there might be other forms of representing this distinctness, which would also be fated to be repressed (Felman 1987: *passim*). Her (and Lacan's) attention to repression means that the implications for cross-cultural variation here avoid the Malinowski trap.

the case that one human being is purely masculine or feminine all of the time.

But to the extent that penis-envy remains a factor in the girl's turning from mother to father, and to the extent that the boy fears castration, we are left with biological factors in the riddle of femininity. We might have explained femininity in men, but is this explanation consistent with the girl's turning from mother to father, and the boy's fear of castration at the father's hands? To consider this, I need to retrace some of the steps that led to this conclusion.

I have argued that masculinity is forged at the Oedipus complex through the acquisition, and cementing in place, of capacities which originally belonged to, and were experienced passively at the hands of, the mother, and the reversal of this passive experience into its opposite. I have also argued that this is a two-stage process: the first stage consists of an interlock between the immediate, atemporal hallucination and the imprint of the other; the second of interlocks between the child's Oedipal drives and phantasies, and, once more, the imprints from the parental others. These imprints mark the difference between activity and masculinity, and passivity and femininity, when they coalesce in the 'identification' with the father. They protect feminine identity while restricting it, and secure masculine identity while liberating it. These imprints perform a similar function to the distancing role of language, but they are not reducible to that role.

The second stage of the two-stage process is replayed in adult masculinity and femininity. But femininity is so similar in structure and direction to the first interlock that it is hard to tell the difference between it and infantilism. In masculinity the reversal of a passive experience into its opposite is fixed in place, but the price of this fixed security may be that the passive position is forcefully projected on to the other (unless the masculine being achieves full 'sublimation', meaning he establishes his identity through his creative labour). This introduced a whole other side to the visual dimension in castration, perceived, as it were, from the feminine standpoint. It was the sight of the absent penis that was meant to shock the man into giving up his desire for his mother. From the other side, it is the visual gaze of a real or imagined other that affectively freezes the woman in place and ties her to the past. We saw that it was the backward-turning of attention against herself, a turning that carried a visual image and disordered affects in its train, that brought the feminine object into being. This placed us in a position to understand the role of the masculine subject in confirming and overlaying this image: the projection of his drives, the capacity for visual projection that is inextricably intertwined with the ego's capacities for testing, acting on, and changing reality, help bring the masculine subject into being.

Freud ascribed the masculine subject's origin to the fear of castration, and this, too, is true. The key is in the term 'castration' itself. In Freud's writing (and generally, the psychoanalytic corpus as a whole) castration is traditionally associated with blindness, with lacking the power to see. Or, in our terms, the ability to project a visual image and the disorder affects it carries in its train on to the other. And literally castration means to be cut off. In the light of the analysis of attention, a two-stage imprinting process, and a connection with some original 'common substance', being castrated is being cut off from that substance, and being cut off from it by a visual energetic projection that places one outside the movement of life. Of course the notion that this projection can castrate the other presupposes that psychical energetic connections work not only within but between beings, but at a different level, and in a different manner, from the original connection that I have hypothesized exists. For the subject, the advantage of this projection is that it disposes of the affects and anxiety that otherwise inhibit his ability to follow a train of thought, and/or a linguistic chain of association; the disadvantage is that this ability depends on maintaining critical blind spots.

I have indicated how, by this same process, the masculine drive represses the feminine other's ability to symbolize.[3] For Freud, in repression, the energy of the drive is split into an affect, which is one psychical representative of the drive, and a word or chain of words. I suggested above that she (meaning, as ever, the feminine being of either sex) contains the affect, while he says or writes the word. How? The repressed affect of anxiety is what interferes with the logical process. He is able to think logically, provided the anxiety that would otherwise prevent his doing so is contained by her. But what, then, is logical thought? Whatever else it is, it is the ability to make consistent connections. It is when something gets in the way of these connections that such thought cannot be sustained. If, as I have suggested, some part of the structure of language is based on an original form of intra-uterine communication, then the question had to arise as to why language works in ways that either facilitate or hinder connections. Presumably facilitating connections are basic to the language of the flesh, which has to be logical, in the sense that one thing connects with another in a way that facilitates growth. This suggests that logical thought, the connections made through words, is a kind of mimesis of a hypothetical original form of communication which was both mental and physical. And if, as I have argued, the word can be turned in certain directions, a turning hinged on its connection with a visual image, affects, and motor activity, then this direction will affect the ease with which connections are made. This must be so, given that the image can lock a word inside in hysteria (femininity). In masculinity, the outward forceful

3 This argument echoes that of Le Doeuff (1980) on philosophy's need for an unknowing (feminine) other, although Le Doeuff's argument is couched in metaphorical rather than (psycho)physical terms.

projection of image and affects should allow those words to flow more freely, but at the price of a divorce from affective feeling. While this divorce cannot be understood unless the spatial underpinnings of language are taken into account, the physical, spatial projection of an image and affect help secure the grounding or anchor any subject needs to follow a chain of words. Moreover it is a divorce that suggests that affects, or emotions, are the confused residue of the original logic of the flesh, left over and muddled up once they have been subtracted from that original logic through speech, after the subject has been cut off from that fleshly logic, or castrated.

What all this implies is that his fear of castration is a literal projection. It returns, as do all projections, as the belief that the other is doing to the subject what the subject is doing to it. And yet there is a truth in his fear, for his own original castration resulted from the confusing interlock of the hallucination and imprint from the mother that established his bearings. It established the first fixed point that enabled him to view the world from a subject-centred perspective, and yet it is fixity he fears. He fears something similar from the father, which suggests that an imprint from the father can also place him, if it fixes him, in the feminine position. This psychical similarity between his experience of these imprints means that the fact that the maternal imprint facilitated movement, as it carried living energy in its train, is the fact that he forgets, as he represses knowledge of the source from whence he came.

As the source from whence he came is a woman (it need not be the being who mothers him, but it is indubitably a woman, at least at the time of writing) there is a sense in which this account allows for no amicable divorce between biological sex and constructed sexual identity. My argument on the retroactive sense of time and delay depends on the fact of a uterine connection, as do the associated speculations on language and the logic of the flesh. This uterine connection lays the basis for a primary constructed inertia, and the imperative to hallucinate and project, and these in turn undoubtedly strengthen the imperative to repress the fact of a maternal origin. Yet there is, on the face of it, nothing about the post-natal maternal or paternal roles that is tied to biological sex, any more than femininity or masculinity. In other words, while I have consistently spoken of the mother in the post-natal connection, this at one level has to be a matter of convention. Mothering can be and occasionally is done by men, which suggests that the living attention in the initial imprinting need not only come from women. Paradoxically, the only argument for the idea that living attention does only come from women, and thus that the attention men give is always borrowed from another woman (from the mother onwards), is an argument demanded by the idea that the symbolic order of language and differentiation is necessarily identified with the father and the man. For if we assume that the identification of living attention with the mother is conventional, we are still left with the problem of situating this account in relation to the familiar, biological factors of the Oedipus complex, and the question of whether the social arguments are good enough to account for the role of the father as castrator.

Certainly these social arguments work well enough on the lateral level: that is to say, they work well in terms of the relation between adults. We have seen that castration is effected whenever a subject is on the receiving end of an immobilizing and negative projection, and that while the subject can immobilize itself in the interests of constructing a pathetic identity, the force of the other's projection is often an overlaying force. We have also seen that by denying while benefiting from the energetic attention it receives, any one subject can castrate another. It can be done by male to male, female to female, female to male, as well as, if most commonly, by male to female. It can be done provided that the subject colludes in it, in so far as collusion implies the existence of an internal psychical structure that attracts or is reinforced by an external projection, although it may be that force of social circumstance means that the subject appears to have no choice but to collude. None the less we, some of us, persist in colluding by turning to the narcissistic path of gratifying daydreams, even when the opportunities for action are there. For relinquishing that path means relinquishing the most familiar means for maintaining identity, and jeopardizing a familiar identity is no easy matter.

Yet it is the very idea of the *familiarity* of identity, the fact that its origins are familial, that puts the father, as symbolic castrator, in his place, and shows how this argument applies to the linear level of the Oedipus complex. It shows how the dialectics of fixity and living attention work between the generations on a push-me-pull-you model of their own. It also indicates why it is that much harder for women to relinquish a feminine identity. These things are more evident in the light of other aspects of the economics of a two-stage imprinting process, and an analysis of how the active and passive forms of the drives also operate at two levels.

There is nothing about the two directions of the drives (the subjective capacities of the active and passive ego) that identifies them with men or women before the Oedipus complex. As Freud noted, 'our women analysts' have provided ample clinical evidence of the existence of sadistic and aggressive impulses in pre-Oedipal girls, which are just as strong as those in boys. He also noted that the curiosity and intelligence of pre-Oedipal girls are comparable, at the least, to those of boys. But while both the externally directed and involuted forms of these drives and capacities exist in both sexes prior to the Oedipus complex, after it, these different directions are cemented to men and women as a rule; activity and passivity become masculinity and femininity. As I noted earlier, the social circumstances that are instrumental here are clear and much discussed.They consist of the paternal symbolic cultural tradition and the socio-economic material opportunities for effective action. But what my argument is suggesting is that something more is needed for the cement to stick, and bring the conventional Oedipus complex into being, and this something I am calling social force. By this, I mean the economic or psychophysical force shaping sexual identity at any given historical moment. The available socio-economic material opportunities are evidently critical in relation to social force as much as social circumstance, if not more so. Understanding their effects on, and the concept of, the physical force of masculinity and femininity in general, takes us back to the two-stage imprinting process, and then back to the father.

The first level of imprinting is something experienced by all subjects. Still the idea that an imprint is received from the other in infancy, and that it may look like an innate factor when it is not only that, cannot be overstressed. For what it means is that all the projections of rage, hostility, and disordered affects on to the other in the second level will depend on the economics of this first psychical level. Consequently the strength of what is projected in masculinity, and the entropy of femininity, will also depend on the force and nature of, and the resistance to, the first imprinting.

In other words, I have assumed that there are two levels of 'imprinting'. The second level helps constitute masculinity and femininity, but the economic force of masculinity and femininity does not originate in masculinity and femininity as such. It originates in the psychophysical level underlying them. In part, this is significant precisely because it brings the social dimension into play in another respect: 'the desire of the other', whether the attention given to the infant is mobilizing as well as inevitably restricting, will also depend on the social force in the environment of its significant others. The hostility they have to contain, the aggression they have to project, the nature of the imprint they give, are all variables dependent on the way in which their own capacity for acting on the world is enhanced or diminished. Moreover the nature of the imprint they give is variable in two ways. It is not only a matter of whether that imprint, in turn, is attentively enhancing or diminishing; it is also a matter of the interlock between the desires the child directs towards the parents, and the unconscious desires or expectations directed towards a child on the basis of its sex. This returns us to the 'symbolic' image and desire of the other in the conventional sense, in so far as these project a conventional image on to the child because of its sex. The desire of the other, in short, embodies an image and attention that can enhance or diminish one's capacities (thus the complaint from Freud's women's patients that their mothers did not give them enough 'milk').

What needs to be reiterated is that the 'image' also has physical effects. Hence my loose usage of the term 'image' and the way I have made it interchangeable with the 'imprint', and at times, the drives from, and desire of, the other. But at the risk of wandering from the paternal line which is our next concern, something more has to be said about this vocabulary of imprints, drives, desires, and so forth. As I have accused Freud of striking confusion in his discussion of primary and secondary processes, first and second instances, etc., I can at least acknowledge that my own discussion of primary and secondary inertia, two-stage processes, and overlays is also the result of groping towards concepts which are, as yet, unclear. That said: it is time that the old vocabulary of the economic level and the drives, 'magnificent in their indefiniteness', was reviewed.

I will try to indicate briefly where the concepts I have introduced clarify the situation, as much as they may complicate it. I have introduced the term 'imprint', made it synonymous with 'image' in an affect-laden or energetic sense of that word, and synonymous to an extent with desire. The term 'imprint' is useful in that it embodies the notion that the one has a physical effect on the other; this effect shapes and defines, and how it does so will depend on whether it embodies living or fixed attention. 'Desire', depending on its context, can refer either to an imprint, or to a phantasy. An unconscious phantasy is in the first instance a repressed hallucination; subsequent conscious and unconscious phantasies are the longing for an imprint. An imprint needs a drive, and has to interlock with a phantasy in the other, to have an effect. A drive is directed psychophysical energy. It is directed along the interlinked pathways of structured attention and constructed libido. An affect, which has not really been separated conceptually from feeling or emotion, is formed in two ways. It is both the residue of the excitations split from the hallucinatory image after the latter is repressed, and also the unconscious registration of an interlocked imprint. A feeling or emotion is its conscious registration. Both language and affects, by Freud's account, emerge either from the drives, and/or from some 'common substance'. By my argument, they emerge from both. The common substance is the logical communication of the flesh, experienced *in utero*, which language will attempt to mime. But the grounds for this mimesis are only established by space and time, in the two stages of constructed inertia which seal the subject off from any conscious knowledge of imprinting, and make it unconscious of its identity boundaries. In part, these two stages are tacitly recognized in Freud's concept of 'excitations', which is not the same as 'drives'. Excitations are exogenous and endogenous. They are the post-natal form of energetic connections between beings and the environment. Excitations are psychophysical stimuli that flow within and without. The drives are endogenous only. The first boundary, the first 'protective shield' that is erected against excitations, depends on the repression of an hallucinatory image, which can be accomplished only with the aid of another's imprint and living attention. This hallucination depends on temporal delay. Its

repression inaugurates further delay. Its repression divorces 'mental' regis-
trations from physical ones: it divorces unconscious phantasies (or
repressed hallucinations) from excitations, and these left-over excitations
become endogenous drives and affects. They become endogenous because
the hallucination's repression establishes a still point from which the
psychophysical energy of the drives can flow in different directions. This
is the fixed point necessary for subject-centred direction. Whether energy
goes in or out, and whatever form it takes, it does so, henceforth, from
a subject-centred point. Drives will seek to follow the same projected path
as hallucination, but they can only do so, sanely, if the other accepts them
as an imprint. This imprint in turn is felt by the other as an affect. The
extent to which this drive is accepted as affect will facilitate reasoning in
words and motor activity directed towards a conscious goal. The extent
to which this drive is not disposed of, or turned back in against the self,
will interfere with such activity or reasoning, and, as noted, be felt as
affect. The projected drive, when it is accepted as an imprint, establishes
a second spatial boundary for the one who projects it. At the same time,
the spatial boundary for the one on to whom it is projected depends on
a protective imprint which differs from the imprint of a drive without
affection. The former is the second protective shield of the father. This
attempt at specifying the vocabulary of the economic level needs far more
work. But as this limited specification has ended with a return to the
paternal imprint, it is time to go back to the main theme in this conclusion.

Which means going back to the father. The desires and imprints the
child receives do not only come from the mother, or the one who mothers,
but from the one who takes the father's place. I argued above that precisely
because the child is originally undifferentiated from the mother (or primary
other), it should follow that the child needs an image or imprint from
another to mark out a separate identity; and this other, conventionally, is
the father. As always, any reference to an actual father's effects has to be
immediately qualified. He might be there, or he might not. So for that
matter might the actual post-natal mother, but we will keep to the father.
His problematic presence means that his role in distinguishing child from
mother has to be rethought in alternative terms.

It might be thought that these terms have already been provided. In
discussing how the entry of the father breaks up the imaginary dyad of
mother and child, Lacan distinguished between the imaginary and the
symbolic father. The imaginary father gives an 'image'; the symbolic father
is identified with language, as a distancing mechanism that separates one
from the other. It enables the distinction between the phantasized or
hallucinatory other to be made because the other – according to whether
it is real or imagined – does or does not respond to the linguistic call.
Lacan's main point is simply that language will do the father's job: it
establishes distance from, and the distinctness of, the other.

But this symbolic distance does not silence the question of the effects of the images and sensory connections into which the child is born. Indeed, taking account of these connections makes the 'imaginary dyad' more concrete and more comprehensible. If the dyad remains unbroken, the child is prone to psychosis, to omnipotent illusions. The reason for this is plainer if one allows that the dyad relies on sensory connections (smell especially, but also touch, taste, and the hearing and the sight that can be misled by hallucination). Therefore the dyad relies on connections which give no clear markers as to where the other ends and the child begins. The senses are structured as, and through, attention. Given that they are structured, the child's omnipotent confusion has an experiential basis; the child is literally closer to, without the means for differentiating itself from, the other it conceives of as all-powerful. That the mother is the habitual purveyor of the first imprint, and the living attention that accompanies it, is, as I stressed, probably a matter of convention. That the identification of the father with the symbolic function of language is equally a matter of convention has been argued for *ad nauseam* in my own and others' writing. I have added something new here in terms of understanding the man's ability to follow a direct chain of reasoning that mimes the original logic of the flesh through splitting language from affects, and depositing those affects in the other in a final appropriation of the original logic. As this appropriation distances the masculine party from that fleshly logic, it makes him more committed to a belief in the arbitrary nature of signification, a belief that denies any origin at all.

None the less it is the material distance he has, and the cultural tradition he embodies, that identify the man with this function, and these conditions of his identification can be changed. The only reason they could not be changed is if the father is the only means by which distinct identities come into being, which means men alone have the ability to effect separation and distance in a manner analogous to language. But this in turn would mean that men are not bound by boundaryless connections between beings, while women in some way are. And the connections between beings, by my analysis, are coterminous with the supply of living attention on which those connections depend. So this means that if one wants to insist on a necessary identification between the father, the man, and the differentiating function of language, one can only do so by insisting that he is exempt, *by virtue of his biological sex*, from the living attention that connects being to being. Which in turn means acknowledging the female source of what keeps him going, while recognizing his separating, identity-protecting function. If it has to be a man who severs connections, it has to be a woman who lends herself to their persistence. The point is one cannot have it both ways. If one insists that conferring identity is a masculine prerogative, one has also to acknowledge that this prerogative can only be exercised on the basis of a living energetic attention that he borrows from the woman. Moreover there is nothing here that means the woman cannot symbolize herself, provided her distinct identity is guaranteed.[4]

The ever-rising flight away from the flesh into the world of metaphor that marks the linguistic turn, and the related neglect of a maternal origin for language, makes me wonder if there is something in the idea that biological women have a natural surplus of living attention, a surplus that men can draw on in the way that infants do (cf. Bion 1970 and 1967, Segal 1984).[5] In other words, it may be that the neglect of the implications of maternal origins covers up the possibility that the source of living energetic attention really does come from women alone. If this is so, it means that the nature of what is symbolically represented, the truths admitted to and by a culture, would have to recognize the vital psychical roles of both sexes: the woman as the origin of energetic connection; the man as the protector of identity. It would mean language has to be used to trace a path that mimed the original logic of the flesh more accurately than it has done hitherto, and in this sense tell the truth of the literal matter.[6] However if this is a truth, it is a truth that can be established only by another science; if biological women are the source of attention, this means that the origin of attention is, as Freud thought it was in the *Project*, a question for biology. As I cannot answer that question, and as I am disinclined to give an affirmative answer until I know if it rests on residual radical feminist prejudice or fact, I return to the assumption that the cultural symbolic tradition and the 'right material circumstances' are masculine by convention, and that the means for changing this are social.

By this analysis, the relevant social changes could not be wrought unless those attempting them can dispose of the unwanted affects that are the conditions of masculine symbolic power. This means they need the energy and identity to carry these changes through, and the material opportunities, at every level, to do so. 'Levels' here are the domain of social force. 'Levels' mean (i) the physical, attentive, energetic level, which, as I have indicated, is affected by the socio-economic level; (ii) the material factors

4 See Cornell (1991) for an excellent discussion of the question of signification and the mother; also Sprengnether (1990).
5 Hanna Segal and Wilfred Bion are major post-Kleinian analysts. Segal makes Bion, who is almost as obscure as Lacan, that much clearer. Bion has given more attention to attention in theory than any other analyst, Kleinian or non-Kleinian (1970). Moreover his argument resonates with mine in that the mother is presented as a 'container', who literally contains projective identifications. But Bion's argument ends with mothers; it does not extend to women (or men). At the same time, and in a very different field, there is an almost tacit recognition that the attention of the other is a condition of sustained creativity. Kraakman notes how at the point where the possibility that a woman might be a genius was first seriously discussed, both George Sand and Madame de Staël were accused of writing their books on their lovers' backs and sucking 'the marrow of their bones' (1990: 12).
6 See the discussion of Joseph Goux and the mother/matter connection in Jardine (1985).

in the environment of those who have to contain or try to dispose of aggression and inertia.

At these levels, conventions have their massive power, and it is in terms of these imaginary, yet ever so physically imaginary, levels that the traditional Oedipus complex can be understood, together with its assumptions about actual boys and girls, and biological mothers and fathers.[7] In the western context, and only in the increasingly problematic context, that the conventional family is the norm, these imaginary effects can be illuminated by two observations of Freud's. The first is that a man's and a woman's love are a phase apart. A woman begins by relating to her husband as she did to her father; she ends by relating to him as she did to her mother. The second is that a woman does not give her husband the mother-love he aspires to; she gives it to her son. She sees in her son the phallus she never had. In the concrete terms of this analysis, what does this mean? It means, regarding the second observation, that a particular type of living attention is no longer given to the man, but to the son (Freud 1933a, GW: 143–4, SE: 133). This attention, this desire of the other, was given to and imprinted on the boy or the man on the basis that he would be what she could never become: an actor on the world. In terms of the first observation, it means she might have hoped that her husband would give her something she once longed for, or received from the father. But it seems the hope was misplaced. As I argued above, the 'something' that she wanted in the first instance was an identity that distinguished her from the mother, and this would also hold for the boy. There is no doubt that the father gives her identity. The feminine Oedipus complex is a haven of refuge because the image the girl receives from the father does at the least protect her from the annihilating aggression that will destroy identity when that aggression has nowhere to go, which the son's evidently does. Yet the woman who begins by relating to her husband as she did to her father, and ends by relating to him as she did to her mother, is evidently disappointed. We might suppose that she feels constrained by her relation to her husband (in which he becomes the target for aggression that has nowhere else to go) in a recapitulation of a similar imaginary constraint at her mother's hands. Yet in the beginning of this marital relation, she is hoping for something else. She is not holding out for mere identity. She is hoping the man will confer an identity that facilitates action at the same time as it marks her out as distinct. As she begins by relating to the man as she did to her father, it seems she identifies the father as the potential, if not actual, source of this facilitating identity. Of course the father is a source of living attention, in so far as he loves her, and directs an unadulterated current of affection towards

7 By the same token, whether actual parents are present or not will also affect the relations of fixity or moving attention involved.

her. The issue is whether this living attention has its limits, and what they are.

Clearly, the daughter hopes that the father will give all, in that she hopes for a penis from him, 'as a gift'. In terms of my analysis, it is now more than plain why this longing is a longing for a faciliating identity without limits. The penis is the perfect emblem of the ability to project a visual image on to the other, and the phallic means to deposit affects in the other, to secure the attention that maintains identity while acting in the line of external direction. Feminine penis-envy is the envy of the being who is able to receive that attention at the same time as he directs his aggression outwards, who gains a living attention that enables his self-image to cohere, while he projects his visual image and the associated aggressive drives on to the other. However while this is the content of penis-envy, the strength of penis-envy is another matter. As the feminine party's penis-envy is also the projected underside of the masculine sense of justice, penis-envy's strength will depend on the force of what she (or he) has imprinted upon her (or him), in terms of what restricts her, and what enables her to resist it.

In lieu of a penis, she settles for a baby, which means settling for the means to exercise the mother's executive capacities by the established route convention has permitted. Is this how it is that the identity she receives from the father both does and does not give her what she really wants, while laying the grounds for future optimism? That is to say, the baby-option gives her a facilitating phallic identity, but it is conditional; she can only reclaim the executive capacities she originally identified with the mother on the condition that they are exercised within a confined (spatial) sphere. Yet the father may not of himself be the source of this condition; it may be inbuilt to the imprint he gives the daughter, or it may be that the limits on the facilitating identity he gives her are circumscribed by social convention. What is clear is that the son does receive an image from the father which as a rule enables him to exercise those executive capacities in the larger sphere. Except of course that the father might withhold this image; hence, again, the boy's fear of castration at the father's hands.

To begin to talk in terms of the father's withholding this image is to reintroduce the energetic reading of attention. For this reading will explain why sons, too, can be castrated, or placed in the feminine position. This energetic reading is also the basis on which one can estimate whether what the daughter hoped for from the father was something she received. I have argued that feminine identity overlays and confirms the partly self-imposed restrictions of the first imprinting, restrictions for which the girl continues to blame her mother, without acknowledging the living attention she received from her, even if she feels there was not enough of it. But is it the father who colludes in the inward-turning phantasy that sustains femininity, or the man?

The answer to this question is possibly, and probably, both. The ambiguity depends both on the conventional nature of the image given, and on the economy of the relations of attention between father, mother, daughter, and son. Conventionally, if, for the boy, the father's imprint permits him to go forth, it is conditional on his giving up his desire for his mother. At the same time, this very condition enables the man-to-be to dispose of some measure of the aggression in his sexually informed executive capacities by splitting the affectionate and sensual currents. A similar split is essential to the father's preserving the daughter's identity, and this means the father's imprint is different from that of the man. As we saw above, this makes the question complicated: does the (ideal) father's splitting facilitate the daughter's going forth, or does it have nothing to do with it? The thing is that both mother and father not only embody the conventions that have governed them. They can also default on them. I have alluded to this much in mentioning that if he gives the daughter a facilitating identity, the father may or may not be responsible for the baby-option.

The desire of the other can work in many ways, to many ends. The oddities, the inconsistencies in children's behaviour in relation to their socialization, can be explained by the unconscious desires of their others. These inconsistencies cannot be readily explained otherwise. At the same time they show that the others' desires can work for good or ill. The feminist who finds her way out of a fundamentalist household, the ethical man whose political and emotional commitments conflict with his rearing, may be expressing the repressed unconscious desires of those who raised them, as much as the subsequent social contradictions they encounter. Thus the mother may give her daughter a conventional image, or see the daughter as her phallus. She may even give to the daughter what she should conventionally give to the son. In this case, the son is less likely to get the push he needs into the symbolic, and will fall back on neurosis, and finding his identity by more feminine means. Except that we have to allow for the fact that the father is pushing too. He, like the mother, is likely to be pushing the boy in a direction that is ego-syntonic, but he may not. Whether the father pushes the girl in this direction is also open to change (as we saw in chapter 3, 'her father saw in Fraülein Elisabeth an intellectual companion'). It is also a question of how the phantasies of the daughter and the imprint of the father interlock (the daughter's masculine identification may or may not receive a paternal endorsement). But it is, in the final analysis, a question of libidinal economy. Whatever the father's conscious belief, whatever his unconscious desire, the limits on how far the separate identity he gives facilitates or fixes are set by his own economic force, and what it depends on. I suggest that this force, or the lack of it, will also affect his conventionality. If the father is ill, or if his energy is diminished in other ways, his need for a womanly woman will increase accordingly. But the main point is that the attention the father gives out will be affected in such circumstances. As Freud pointed out in the context of narcissism, illness may mean that one withdraws libido back from its objects: the world counts for nothing in the event of a serious toothache.

To enhance rather than diminish the daughter's potential the father has to have a certain economic force. This will determine how far the imprint from the father differs from the masculine sexual drive (meaning, as always, that form of masculine drive that lacks the affectionate current). This difference is the second pivot on which the daughter's psychical fate depends (the first being the interlock between her repressed hallucinatory image and her mother's imprint). In other words, the imprint from the father is pivotal, as is the love of any adult man, in the extent to which it embodies living attention, and the extent to which it demands it. To say the same thing differently, it is pivotal to the extent that it immobilizes, and to the extent that it facilitates. The imprint of the masculine sexual drive, unlike the affectionate paternal imprint, is meant to immobilize, hold back and hold still, to make the other an anchor by depositing unwanted affects in her, and thereby secure a surplus of living attention. If the father is looking to the daughter for this surplus, he will to some degree transgress the identity barrier he is meant to establish.

From this standpoint, and given the idea that 'phantasy is the first invader', there is, after all, something in the seduction theory that gave birth to Freud's mistakes about femininity. There is even more to it if one accepts that psychical reality is constituted by a repressed fixed point and the secondary inertia, the feminine fixity which overlays it. In fixing the feminine, the father, like the man, may make the daughter the second still point, the second border that makes femininity literally borderline. However, *contra* the seduction theory, whether the father gives rather than receives is an open question, and the idea that he gives is reinforced by this: the girl, like the boy, functions ego-syntonically until puberty. Usually it is only after her own drives are reactivated, and interlock with the projections of masculine others, that involution comes into being. That much said: when the father's imprint on the daughter embodies a masculine sexual drive, and transgresses its protective function, it pierces the protective shield it is meant to establish. It can do so in reality, and be literally more traumatic because of that. Or it can do so in phantasy. In either case, the daughter's masochism and anxiety will be reinforced, and she will be more repressed. But even if the father brackets out these components of the masculine sexual drive, he can still look to the daughter for the admiration that is complicit with his narcissism. This is to his psychical advantage in terms of the ego's two tasks: directing attention and activity towards reality, and maintaining its self-image or identity. The father would benefit if one or both of these tasks were accomplished, a burden shared, through his desire in relation to the daughter. It should be the daughter's image that is maintained in relation to her father's admiration; for while his willingness to admire is complicit with her narcissism, it also relieves her of the need to divert some of her attention inwards. But the converse can hold, and if the father's supply of living attention is short, he can always extract a surplus of admiration from his daughter. He is more likely to look to his daughter for feminine admiration if his wife is no longer directing her living attention towards him, or if he receives no admiration or recognition in his life-contexts.

Not that this form of recognition is a guarantee that a man will cease to seek as much living attention as he can lay hands on, as it were. In fact, the economics of energetic attention might explain why it is that men of a certain type look, as they age, to younger women. It would explain it if energetic attention is tied to that adaptive energy that diminishes with age, and we have every reason to suppose that this is so. The pathways the ego lays down as it establishes itself make it less able to adapt, and more prone to the anxiety that runs counter to the movement of life. Anxiety arises precisely because the ego feels itself to be imperilled when its familiar pathways are jeopardized, for these are also its nascent or established sense of self. As time passes, as experiences multiply, ever more fixed pathways for dealing with 'life's exigencies' are established. Identity, accordingly, becomes stronger but less plastic. Indeed it would seem that as the very establishment and maintenance of the ego is itself entropic in one respect (while it helps one stay alive in another), the identity the ego underpins is the key to the entropy or rigidity that Freud associated with ageing, although he could not account for the process involved. This does not mean that having an identity is something that can be dispensed with (unless one follows the path of the mystics). Nor does it mean that identity necessarily cuts one off from the movement of life: the more open an identity is to inspiration, from art that retains enough of life to transmit it, from life in nature, or living prose, the less likely an identity is to lose its capacity to adapt. The thirst for these forms of living beauty in those who age well differentiates them from the other type, which grasps life in beings whose youth means their energy is the greater, as their identities are undefined, and the light of their vitality undimmed. Nor is it only men who grasp in this way. It is an interesting fact of latter-day feminism that established and older women are looking to younger apprentices, and taking on the phallic role in relation to them. On the one hand, the fact that these women can take on this role suggests that the ability to separate and confer distinctness is tied to stronger, firmer identities, which are, by definition, opposed to connection, and which can be acquired through age rather than sex. On the other hand, whether the identity these established women confer is a facilitating one cannot be guaranteed. One can only be on guard against one's own capacity for exploitation, as much as the other's capacity for envy.

But I digress. The point was that the father is more likely to look to his daughter for admiration, as men, conventionally, look to women for this form of attention. But there is no reason why the father could not make a similar demand of his son, or, for that matter, direct an unconscious sexually sadistic drive towards a son. In those cases, the son, too, will fall back on a feminine identity, in that the father's projected imprint will reinforce his own feminine desire. This completes my argument as to why the libidinal economy of either or both parents is at bottom of the mystery of femininity in men. It remained a mystery as long as the imprint from the other was neglected. It had had to be neglected because the imposition involved sailed so close to the seduction theory whose overthrow established psychical reality and psychoanalysis. At the same time, psychical reality itself depends on a constructed inertia, which is the foundation of subjects' imaginary yet material illusion that they are physically self-contained, the source of their own capacity to act, and impermeable to the drives, imprints, or 'desires' of the other. The unthematized question of permeability in turn depends on the neglect of the physical connections between beings, connections that enable the imprints of the one to affect the other.

But does this abolish the traditional Oedipus complex? Not at all. It merely says that there is an additional side to the story, a heavy side. Marx termed it the dead weight of previous generations. That weight may be lighter if a parent is absent, heavier if those who take the figurative place of parents lack love. I have talked throughout in terms of conventions. Within the limits of those same conventions, sons continue to desire mothers, as do daughters, sons and daughters wish to take the feminine place in relation to their fathers, and the Oedipus complex persists accordingly. The thing is that the drives and desires of boys and girls are informed by the spatio-temporal inertia of the first and second imprinting, and the weight of the images projected through them. Whether a boy or girl takes an ego-syntonic masculine path to sexual identity, or an involuted feminine one, depends on their own impulses. But it also depends on the imprint of the other, the direction it points in, and the exchange of energetic attention that underpins that direction. The economic riddle of femininity only resolves itself when all the forces in a familiar constellation declare themselves, as the Oedipus complex is not just the point at which sexual identity is conferred and confirmed; it is the point at which the generations interlock.

In the context of the interlock between the generations, we can also cast a fresh glance at the arguments against psychoanalysis, which see psychoanalysis as an imposition in itself. Freud imposed his own story on Dora, and as Borch-Jacobsen (1989), Butler (1990), Derrida (1980),

Foucault (1981), Deleuze (Deleuze and Guattari [1972]) and others have argued, psychoanalysis performs a cover-up job through imposing a myth that conceals the subject's origins.[8] I suspect that there is real resentment, as well as analytic acumen, in arguments such as these: it is a resentment directed at the neglect of the unconscious impositions of previous generations, an imposition psychoanalysis replays when it makes the child the sole source of its drives and phantasies. When no one else is held accountable. Yet psychoanalysis is also the means for bringing the past to account, especially when its neglected economic dimension is explored.

Anyone who enters that dimension must do so reluctantly, if the space they inhabit sustains a force-field in which a mother, father, or significant other depends on them for living attention in maintaining their self-image. To withdraw this attentive energy and use it in creative pursuits can be a kind of death for the other, which could contribute to, for example, the guilt the son feels at surpassing his father, the guilt which prevented Freud from journeying to Rome. Yet how much worse would this guilt be in the daughter's case, when she lacks the legitimating social image, the sublimated social bond, that authorizes her to surpass the father or protective man, that makes the act literally unthinkable. The father himself, like the mother, will probably authorize the son. How much harder for the woman to turn back the image she receives from the father, if this image protected her identity. But what makes it harder still is that while this protection secured her identity, it also prepares the ground where, in later life, she can be fixed in a still place by a masculine drive.

While a boy, and a man, can be fixed in the same way, the fixing of the woman is the means by which both the masculine social bond and the man's individual identity is secured. Where social force and social circumstance collude to sustain this bond, the woman we know is likely to be feminine. The masculine social bond lessens the hostility between men, by directing aggression towards women of a certain kind. This helps the man's individual (ego-syntonic) identity, because by fixing the woman in place, he transfers the fixity he fears, but needs outside, away from the initial hallucination and imprint that both constituted and threatened him. In another context, it would be worth exploring how the fixity produced by this transfer into the outside world has affected the living environment overall. It would also be worth exploring whether any alteration affected by this transfer has contributed to the woman's refusing, or beginning to refuse, the projection that fixed her in place. After all, by this account, the energetic force of what is projected, and the urge to project it in the first place, do not lie in any inherent masculinity or femininity. It is rather that the formation of masculinity and femininity is an arena in which an underlying war between inertia, anxiety, and projected hostility is played

8 In fact not all psychoanalysis does this, not at all. For a good exchange on the question, see Segal (1990).

out. The forces determining that underlying war accordingly are the forces that determine the strength of 'masculinity' and 'femininity' at any given historical moment.

These forces also determine what kind of masculinity and femininity prevail. When Freud remarked that a man resented the consideration a woman extracted from him through sex, he could not have given a clearer indication of the fact that the masculine drive does not willingly or necessarily entail the protective function. It does so, when it combines the paternal affectionate current with the sensual one, but the paternal function was sustained by conventions that are changing. It was sustained by notions of lifelong commitment, which meant the older model could not be traded in for a younger one, and by fathers who were present rather than absent. A good man (who we can define as one who kept his side of a bad bargain) had major social incentives and ethical reinforcements for the 'affectionate current'; it was harder, or at least more expensive, to seek a surplus of living attention from other women, and more admirable when he gave of this attention himself. Of course such beings still exist, and today what they give abets a woman's acting on the world. What they gave hitherto may have kept a woman in her place, but it did so with more affection and security. In the west, both the increasing divorce rate since the 1950s, and the fact that the family without a father is becoming more of the norm in what MacCannell has termed 'the regime of the brother' (MacCannell 1991a), are the underexplored underside of the rise of feminism. They may have compelled women at the same time as they released women to find an alternative social contract. However the issue here is that masculinity without affection, femininity without facilitation, will lead to forms of masculinity that embody more aggression and less love, and an inert, commodified version of womanhood. Unless, and it is a big unless, the underlying forces of inertia, anxiety, and hostility find other fields in which to play themselves out. The immobilizing projection that mars and marks femininity could as well be projected on to another race or class.

But within the compass of this book, it is enough to conclude that the characteristics of femininity, as Freud defined them, will be more evident when the strength of the subject's need to project an immobilizing image and disordered affects on to the other is greater. I have supposed that this need will be greater whenever the relevant imprint embodies less life and more anxiety. I have also supposed that this need and what it results in will vary. It will vary cross-culturally and has varied historically. Currently, more accurately, since the Second World War, identity crises and narcissistic disorders figure more prominently on the therapeutic agenda. Yet these identity crises also encapsulate the disabling characteristics of femininity. The dependence on another for an image, the inability to act, the new West Coast obsession with 'being energized', the difficulty in maintaining a logical chain of thought (perversely, a subject of celebration in contemporary postmodern theory), the unwillingness to ask too many questions, even, possibly, a weaker sense of justice, all these show that femininity remains a problem in both sexes. Not because it is a riddle, but because it is an affliction that requires all the weight of their energetic capacity and ability to think to shift it off the shoulders of those who carry it. Our politics did not begin with our feelings (which reflect paralysing restrictions as much as sympathetic bonds) but with our perceptions and ability to sustain a train of thought without forgetful anxious interruptions. The sympathetic bonds, the capacity for 'relating' which has received so much favourable publicity in recent feminist theory is a two-edged sword. On the one hand, this capacity probably encapsulates the original connection between beings which I have signalled needs more investigation. On the other, these connecting 'feelings' also slow us down; they tie us to the past.

This tie to the past is broken by outwardly directed aggression, which provides temporary relief from inertia, or creative labour which redirects the attention that maintains identity, provided that another identity is secured. From this perspective, the 'French feminist' emphasis on symbolizing and representing women is only half the story, a necessary but not a sufficient condition for change. But it is a difficult story to tell in full, because of the anxiety and forgetfulness which repress it.

The story can be told only when this anxiety is overcome and this forgetfulness surpassed. It becomes coherent only when words follow an uncensored chain. It is forcefully expressed only when the inertia that is the condition of a masculine logic maintaining its ellipses is projected back, and when the being who carries it thinks, and acts on a reality that provides her with a space for activity, and the opportunity to bring dank phantasies out into the measurable light of day. The woman who does this has reclaimed her subjective capacities. If she reclaims them in rage, which she may well do, she can sustain them only by creating an anchor for her own disorder, or through creative sublimation, or both. If she sustains them through sublimation, she will not have the illusion that she is the all-powerful mother, although she may be subject to that ultimately destructive illusion (megalomania is rife amongst feminist theorists) in the rite of passage from a spatially distinct identity that slowed her down, to an identity based on new forms of shared recognition of what a woman can become. Which means recognition based on reciprocal relations of attention, and acknowledging the separate reality of the other. Nor does this recognition necessarily come from women. It can come from a man, or men, and its effects will depend on the libidinal economy of the relations of attention involved. The point is that in order to act upon the world, any being needs an identity, and living attention from within if not from without. When the libidinal economy is balanced in favour of acting, at the same time as identity is guaranteed, then any living being can deploy the subjective capacities first identified with a mother. A woman, or any feminine being, can reclaim her heritage, and sever her tie to the past. All that stands in the way of her doing so is an identity by which she is protected, but which none the less slows her down. It slows her down because of the death drive it contains. Yet the power of the death drive is only time, whose power in turn is naught but the delay between the conception of an idea, and its execution.

Bibliography: Freud

Titles abbreviated in the text are as follows:

GW Sigmund Freud, *Gesammelte Werke, chronologisch geordnet*, ed. Anna Freud, Edward Bibring, Willi Hoffer, Ernst Kris, and Otto Isakower, in collaboration with Marie Bonaparte, 18 vols; vols 1–17, London, Imago, 1940–52; vol. 18, Frankfurt am Main, S. Fischer Verlag, 1968.
Letters Sigmund Freud, *The Complete Letters of Sigmund Freud to Wilhelm Fliess, 1887–1904*, ed. and trans. Jeffrey Moussaieff Masson, Cambridge, Mass., Harvard University Press, 1985.
Origins Sigmund Freud, *The Origins of Psycho-Analysis: Letters to Wilhelm Fliess, Drafts and Notes, 1887–1902*, edited by Marie Bonaparte, Anna Freud, and Ernst Kris, translated by Eric Mosbacher and James Strachey, introduction by Ernst Kris, London, Imago, 1954.
SE Sigmund Freud, *The Standard Edition of the Complete Psychological Works of Sigmund Freud*, ed. and trans. James Strachey, in collaboration with Anna Freud, assisted by Alix Strachey and Alan Tyson, London, Hogarth Press and the Institute of Psychoanalysis, 1953–74, 24 vols.
Studien Sigmund Freud, *Studienausgabe*, Frankfurt am Main, S. Fischer Verlag, 1969–75, 10 vols.

(1887) Review of Weir-Mitchell's *Die Behandlung gewisser Formen von Neurasthenie und Hysterie*, *SE*, vol. 1, p. 36.
(1888 [1888–9]) 'Preface to the Translation of Bernheim's *Suggestion*', *SE*, vol. 1, pp. 75–85.
(1893a) (with Joseph Breuer) 'Über den psychischen Mechanismus hysterischer Phänomene: Vorläufige Mitteilung', *GW*, vol. 1; 'On the Psychical Mechanism of Hysterical Phenomena: a Lecture', *SE*, vol. 3, pp. 27–39.
(1893b) 'Quelques considerations pour une étude comparative des paralysies motrices organiques et hystériques' [in French], *GW*, vol. 1, pp. 39–55; 'Some Points for a Comparative Study of Organic and Hysterical Motor Phenomena', *SE*, vol. 1, pp. 160–72.
(1894) 'Die Abwehr-Neuropsychosen', *GW*, vol. 1, pp. 59–74; 'The Neuro-Psychoses of Defence', *SE*, vol. 3, pp. 45–61.
(1895a [1894]) 'Obsessions et phobies (leur mécanisme psychique et leur étiologie)' [in French], *GW*, vol. 1, pp. 345–53; 'Obsessions and Phobias: their Psychical Mechanism and their Aetiology', *SE*, vol. 3, pp. 74–82.
(1895b) (with Joseph Breuer) *Studien über Hysterie*, *GW*, vol. 1; *Studies on Hysteria*, *SE*, vol. 2.

(1895c) 'Zur Kritik der "Angstneurose" ', *GW*, vol. 1, pp. 357–76; 'A Reply to Criticisms of my Paper on Anxiety Neurosis', *SE*, vol. 3, pp. 123–39.

(1896a) 'L'hérédité et l'étiologie des névroses' [in French], *GW*, vol. 1, pp. 407–22; 'Heredity and the Aetiology of the Neuroses', *SE*, vol. 3, pp. 143–56.

(1896b) 'Weitere Bemerkungen über die Abwehr-Neuropsychosen', *GW*, vol. 1, pp. 379–403; 'Further Remarks on the Neuro-Psychoses of Defence', *SE*, vol. 3, pp. 162–85.

(1896c) 'Zur Ätiologie der Hysterie', *GW*, vol. 1, pp. 425–59; 'The Aetiology of Hysteria', *SE*, vol. 3, pp. 191–221.

(1898a) 'Die Sexualität in der Ätiologie der Neurosen', *GW*, vol. 1, pp. 491–516; 'Sexuality in the Aetiology of the Neuroses', *SE*, vol. 3, pp. 263–85.

(1898b) 'Zum psychischen Mechanismus der Vergesslichkeit', *GW*, vol. 1, pp. 519–27; 'The Psychical Mechanism of Forgetfulness', *SE*, vol. 3, pp. 289–97.

(1900) *Die Traumdeutung*, *GW*, vols 2–3; *The Interpretation of Dreams*, *SE*, vols 4–5.

(1901a) *Über den Traum*, *GW*, vols 2–3; *On Dreams*, *SE*, vol. 5.

(1901b) *Zur Psychopathologie des Alltagslebens*, *GW*, vol. 4; *The Psychopathology of Everyday Life*, *SE*, vol. 6.

(1905a [1901]) 'Bruchstück einer Hysterie-Analyse', *GW*, vol. 5, pp. 163–286; 'Fragment of an Analysis of a Case of Hysteria', *SE*, vol. 7, pp. 7–122.

(1905b) *Drei Abhandlungen zur Sexualtheorie*, *GW*, vol. 5; *Studien*, vol. 5; Three Essays on the Theory of Sexuality, *SE*, vol. 7.

(1905c) *Der Witz und seine Beziehung zum Unbewussten*, *GW*, vol. 6, *Jokes and Their Relation to the Unconscious*, *SE*, vol. 8.

(1906a [1905]) 'Meine Ansichten über die Rolle der Sexualität in der Ätiologie der Neurosen', *GW*, vol. 5, pp.149–59; 'My Views on the Part Played by Sexuality in the Aetiology of the Neuroses', *SE*, vol. 7, pp. 271–9.

(1906b) 'Tatbestandsdiagnostik und Psychoanalyse', *GW*, vol. 7, pp. 3–15; 'Psycho-Analysis and the Establishment of the Facts in Legal Proceedings', *SE*, vol. 9, pp. 103–14.

(1907a [1906]) *Der Wahn und die Träume in W. Jensen's 'Gradiva'*, *GW*, vol. 7; *Delusions and Dreams in Jensen's 'Gradiva'*, *SE*, vol. 9.

(1907b) 'Zwangshandlungen und Religionsübung', *GW*, vol. 7, pp. 129–39; 'Obsessive Actions and Religious Practices', *SE*, vol. 9, pp. 117–27.

(1907c) 'Zur sexuellen Aufklärung der Kinder', *GW*, vol. 7, pp. 19–27; 'The Sexual Enlightenment of Children', *SE*, vol. 9, pp. 131–9.

(1908a) 'Hysterische Phantasien und ihre Beziehung zur Bisexualität', *GW*, vol. 7, pp. 191–9; 'Hysterical Phantasies and their Relation to Bisexuality', *SE*, vol. 9, pp. 159–66.

(1908b) 'Charakter und Analerotik', *GW*, vol. 7, pp. 203–9; 'Character and Anal Eroticism', *SE*, vol. 9, pp. 169–75.

(1908c) 'Über infantile Sexualtheorien', *GW*, vol. 7, pp. 171–88; 'On the Sexual Theories of Children', *SE*, vol. 9, pp. 209–26.

(1908d [1907]) 'Der Dichter und das Phantasieren', *GW*, vol. 7, pp. 213–23; 'Creative Writers and Day-Dreaming', *SE*, vol. 9, pp. 143–53.

(1909a [1908]) 'Allgemeines über den hysterischen Anfall', *GW*, vol. 7, pp. 235–40; 'Some General Remarks on Hysterical Attacks', *SE*, vol. 9, pp. 229–34.

(1909b [1908]) 'Der Familienroman der Neurotiker', *GW*, vol. 7, pp. 227–31; 'Family Romances', *SE*, vol. 9, pp. 237–41.

(1909c) 'Analyse der Phobie eines fünfjährigen Knaben', *GW*, vol. 7, pp. 243–377; 'Analysis of a Phobia in a Five-Year-Old Boy', *SE*, vol. 10, pp. 5–149.

(1909d) 'Bemerkungen über einen Fall von Zwangsneurose', *GW*, vol. 7, pp. 381–463; 'Notes upon a Case of Obsessional Neurosis', *SE*, vol. 10, pp. 155–249.

(1910a [1909]) *Über Psychoanalyse*, *GW*, vol. 8; *Five Lectures on Psycho-Analysis*, *SE*, vol. 11.

(1910b) *Eine Kindheitserinnerung des Leonardo da Vinci*, *GW*, vol. 8, *Leonardo da Vinci and a Memory of his Childhood*, *SE*, vol. 11.

(1910c) 'Die zukünftigen Chancen der psychoanalytischen Therapie', *GW*, vol. 8, pp. 104–15; 'The Future Prospects of Psycho-Analytic Therapy', *SE*, vol. 11, pp. 141–51.

(1910d) ' "Über den Gegensinn der Urworte" ', *GW*, vol. 8, pp. 214–21; ' "The Antithetical Meaning of Primal Words" ', *SE*, vol. 11, pp. 155–61.

(1910e) 'Über einen besonderen Typus der Objektwahl beim Manne', *GW*, vol. 8, pp. 66–77; 'A Special Type of Choice of Object made by Men (Contributions to the Psychology of Love, I)', *SE*, vol. 11, pp. 165–75.

(1910f) 'Die psychogene Sehstörung in psychoanalytischer Auffassung', *GW*, vol. 8, pp. 94–102; 'The Psycho-Analytic View of Psychogenic Disturbance of Vision', *SE*, vol. 11, pp. 211–18.

(1911a) 'Formulierungen über die zwei Prinzipien des psychischen Geschehens', *GW*, vol. 8, pp. 230–8; 'Formulations on the Two Principles of Mental Functioning', *SE*, vol. 12, pp. 218–26.

(1911b) 'Psychoanalytische Bemerkungen über einen autobiographisch beschriebenen Fall von Paranoia (Dementia Paranoides)', *GW*, vol. 8, pp. 240–316; 'Psycho-Analytic Notes on an Autobiographical Account of a Case of Paranoia (Dementia Paranoides)', *SE*, vol. 12, pp. 9–82.

(1911c) 'Die Bedeutung der Vokalfolge', *GW*, vol. 8, p. 348; 'The Significance of Sequences of Vowels', *SE*, vol. 12, p. 341.

(1911d) ' "Gross ist die Diana der Epheser" ', *GW*, vol. 8, p. 360; ' "Great is Diana of the Ephesians" ', *SE*, vol. 12, pp. 342–4.

(1911e) 'Die Handhabung der Traumdeutung in der Psychoanalyse', *GW*, vol. 8, pp. 350–7; 'The Handling of Dream-Interpretation in Psycho-Analysis' (Papers on Technique), *SE*, vol. 12, pp. 91–6.

(1912a) 'Zur Dynamik der Übertragung', *GW*, vol. 8, pp. 364–74; 'The Dynamics of Transference' (Papers on Technique), *SE*, vol. 12, pp. 99–108.

(1912b) 'Ratschläge für den Arzt bei der psychoanalytischen Behandlung', *GW*, vol. 8, pp. 376–87; 'Recommendations to Physicians Practising Psycho-Analysis' (Papers on Technique), *SE*, vol. 12, pp. 111–20.

(1912c) 'Über neurotische Erkrankungstypen', *GW*, vol. 8, pp. 322–30; 'Types of Onset of Neurosis' (Papers on Technique), *SE*, vol. 12, pp. 231–8.

(1912d) 'Über die allgemeinste Erniedrigung des Liebeslebens', *GW*, vol. 8, pp. 78–91; 'On the Universal Tendency to Debasement in the Sphere of Love (Contributions to the Psychology of Love, II)', *SE*, vol. 11, pp. 179–90.

(1912e) 'Zur Onanie-Diskussion', *GW*, vol. 8, pp. 332–45; 'Contributions to a Discussion on Masturbation', *SE*, vol. 12, pp. 243–54.

(1912f) 'A Note on the Unconscious in Psycho-Analysis' [in English], *SE*, vol. 12, pp. 260–6.

(1913a) 'Zwei Kinderlügen', *GW*, vol. 8, pp. 422–7; 'Two Lies told by Children', *SE*, vol. 12, pp. 305–9.

(1913b) 'Die Disposition zur Zwangsneurose', *GW*, vol. 8, pp. 442–52; 'The Disposition of Obsessional Neurosis', *SE*, vol. 12, pp. 317–26.

(1913c [1912–13]) *Totem und Tabu*, *GW*, vol. 9; *Totem and Taboo*, *SE*, vol. 13.

(1913d) 'Weitere Ratschläge zur Technik der Psychoanalyse: I. Zur Einleitung der Behandlung', *GW*, vol. 8, pp. 454–78; 'On Beginning the Treatment (Further

Recommendations on the Technique of Psycho-Analysis, I)', *SE*, vol. 12, pp. 123–44.

(1913e) 'Das Interesse an der Psychoanalyse', *GW*, vol. 8, pp. 390–420; 'The Claims of Psycho-Analysis to Scientific Interest', *SE*, vol. 13, pp. 165–75.

(1913f) 'On Psycho-Analysis' [in English], Aust. Med. Congr. (Transactions of the Ninth Session, held in Sydney, September 1911) 2, part 8, 839; *SE*, vol. 12, pp. 207–11.

(1914a) 'Weitere Ratschläge zur Technik der Psychoanalyse: II. Erinnern, Wieder-holen und Durcharbeiten', *GW*, vol. 10, pp. 126–36; 'Remembering, Repeating and Working-Through (Further Recommendations on the Technique of Psycho-Analysis, II)', *SE*, vol. 12, pp. 147–57.

(1914b) 'Zur Geschichte der psychoanalytischen Bewegung', *GW*, vol. 10, pp. 44–113; 'On the History of the Psycho-Analytic Movement', *SE*, vol. 14, pp. 7–66.

(1914c) 'Zur Einführung des Narzissmus', *GW*, vol. 10, pp. 138–70; 'On Narciss-ism: An Introduction', *SE*, vol. 14, pp. 73–102.

(1915a) 'Mitteilung eines der psychoanalytischen Theorie widersprechenden Falles von Paranoia', *GW*, vol. 10, pp. 234–46; 'A Case of Paranoia Running Counter to the Psycho-Analytic Theory of the Disease', *SE*, vol. 14, pp. 263–72.

(1915b [1914]) 'Weitere Ratschläge zur Technik der Psychoanalyse: III. Bemerkun-gen über die Übertragungsliebe', *GW*, vol. 10, pp. 306–21; 'Observations of Transference-Love (Further Recommendations on the Technique of Psycho-Analysis, III)', *SE*, vol. 12, pp. 159–71.

(1915c) 'Triebe und Triebschicksale', *GW*, vol. 10, pp. 210–32; 'Instincts and their Vicissitudes', *SE*, vol. 14, pp. 117–40.

(1915d) 'Die Verdrängung', *GW*, vol. 10, pp. 248–61; 'Repression', *SE*, vol. 14, pp. 146–58.

(1915e) 'Das Unbewusste', *GW*, vol. 10, pp. 264–303; 'The Unconscious', *SE*, vol. 14, pp. 166–204.

(1915f) 'Zeitgemässes über Krieg und Tod', *GW*, vol. 10, pp. 324–55; 'Thoughts for the Times on War and Death', *SE*, vol. 14, pp. 275–300.

(1916a) 'Mythologische Parallele zu einer plastischen Zwangsvorstellung', *GW*, vol. 10, p. 398; 'A Mythological Parallel to a Visual Obsession', *SE*, vol. 14, pp. 337–8.

(1916b) 'Einige Charaktertypen aus der psychoanalytischen Arbeit', *GW*, vol. 10, pp. 364–91; 'Some Character-types met with in Psycho-Analytic Work', *SE*, vol. 14, pp. 311–33.

(1916–17 [1915–17]) *Vorlesungen zur Einführung in die Psychoanalyse*, *GW*, vol. 11; *Introductory Lectures on Psycho-Analysis*, *SE*, vols 15–16.

(1917a [1915]) 'Metapsychologische Ergänzung zur Traumlehre', *GW*, vol. 10, pp. 412–26; 'A Metapsychological Supplement to the Theory of Dreams', *SE*, vol. 14, pp. 222–35.

(1917b [1915]) 'Trauer und Melancholie', *GW*, vol. 10, pp. 428–46; 'Mourning and Melancholia', *SE*, vol. 14, pp. 243–58.

(1917c) 'Über Triebumsetzungen insbesondere der Analerotik', *GW*, vol. 10, pp. 402–10; 'On Transformations of Instinct as Exemplified in Anal Eroticism', *SE*, vol. 17, pp. 127–33.

(1917d) 'Eine Schwierigkeit der Psychoanalyse', *GW*, vol. 12, pp. 3–12 'A Diffi-culty in the Path of Psycho-Analysis', *SE*, vol. 17, pp. 137–44.

(1918a [1914]) 'Aus der Geschichte einer infantilen Neurose', *GW*, vol. 12, pp. 29–157; 'From the History of an Infantile Neurosis', *SE*, vol. 17, pp. 7–122.

(1918b [1917]) 'Das Tabu der Virginität', *GW*, vol. 12, pp. 161–80; 'The Taboo of Virginity (Contributions to the Psychology of Love, III)', *SE*, vol. 11, pp. 193–208.

(1919a [1918]) 'On the Teaching of Psycho-Analysis in Universities', *SE*, vol. 17, pp. 171–3.

(1919b) ' "Ein Kind wird geschlagen" Beitrag zur Kenntnis der Entstehung sexueller Perversionen', *GW*, vol. 12, pp. 197–226; ' "A Child Is Being Beaten": a Contribution to the Study of the Origin of Sexual Perversions', *SE*, vol. 17, pp. 179–204.

(1919c) 'Das Unheimliche', *GW*, vol. 12, pp. 229–68; 'The "Uncanny" ', *SE*, vol. 17, pp. 219–52.

(1920a) *Jenseits des Lustprinzips*, *GW*, vol. 13; *Beyond the Pleasure Principle*, *SE*, vol. 18.

(1920b) 'Über die Psychogenese eines Falles von weiblicher Homosexualitat', *GW*, vol. 12, pp. 271–302; 'The Psychogenesis of a Case of Homosexuality in a Woman', *SE*, vol. 18, pp. 147–72.

(1921a) *Massenpsychologie und Ich-Analyse*, *GW*, vol. 13; *Group Psychology and the Analysis of the Ego*, *SE*, vol. 18.

(1921b) 'Introduction to J. Varendonck's *The Psychology of Day-Dreams*' [in English], *SE*, vol. 18, pp. 271–2.

(1922a) 'Traum und Telepathie', *GW*, vol. 13, pp. 165–91; 'Dreams and Telepathy', *SE*, vol. 18, pp. 197–220.

(1922b) 'Über einige neurotische Mechanismen bei Eifersucht, Paranoia und Homosexualitat', *GW*, vol. 13, pp. 195–207; 'Some Neurotic Mechanisms in Jealousy, Paranoia and Homosexuality', *SE*, vol. 18, pp. 223–32.

(1923a [1922]) ' "Psychoanalyse" und "Libido Theorie" ', *GW*, vol. 13, pp. 211–33; 'Two Encyclopedia Articles', *SE*, vol. 18, pp. 235–59.

(1923b) *Das Ich und das Es*, *GW*, vol. 13; *The Ego and the Id*, *SE*, vol. 19.

(1923c) 'Eine Teufelsneurose im siebzehnten Jahrhundert', *GW*, vol. 13, 'A Seventeenth-Century Demonological Neurosis', *SE*, vol. 19.

(1923d) 'Die infantile Genitalorganisation (Eine Einschaltung in die Sexualtheorie)', *GW*, vol. 13, pp. 291–8; 'The Infantile Genital Organization: an Interpolation into the Theory of Sexuality', *SE*, vol. 19, pp. 141–5.

(1924a [1923]) 'Neurose und Psychose', *GW*, vol. 13, pp. 387–91; 'Neurosis and Psychosis', *SE*, vol. 19, pp. 149–53.

(1924b) 'Das ökonomische Problem des Masochismus', *GW*, vol. 13, pp. 371–83; 'The Economic Problem of Masochism', *SE*, vol. 19, pp. 159–70.

(1924c) 'Der Untergang des Ödipuskomplexes', *GW*, vol. 13, pp. 395–402; 'The Dissolution of the Oedipus Complex', *SE*, vol. 19, pp. 173–9.

(1924d) 'Die Realitätsverlust bei Neurose und Psychose', *GW*, vol. 13, pp. 363–8; 'The Loss of Reality in Neurosis and Psychosis', *SE*, vol. 19, pp. 183–7.

(1924e [1923]) 'Kurzer Abriss der Psychanalyse', *GW*, vol. 13, pp. 403–27; 'A Short Account of Psycho-Analysis', *SE*, vol. 19, pp. 191–209.

(1925a [1924]) 'Notiz über den "Wunderblock" ', *GW*, vol. 14, pp. 3–8; 'A Note upon the "Mystic Writing-Pad" ', *SE*, vol. 19, pp. 227–32.

(1925b) 'Die Verneinung', *GW*, vol. 14, pp. 11–15; 'Negation', *SE*, vol. 19, pp. 235–9.

(1925c) 'Einige psychische Folgen des anatomischen Geschlechtsunterschieds', *GW*, vol. 14, pp. 19–30; 'Some Psychical Consequences of the Anatomical Distinction between the Sexes', *SE*, vol. 19, pp. 248–58.

(1925d [1924]) *Selbstdarstellung*, *GW*, vol. 14; *An Autobiographical Study*, *SE*, vol. 20.

(1926a [1925]) *Hemmung, Symptom und Angst*, GW, vol. 14; *Inhibitions Symptoms and Anxiety*, SE, vol. 20.

(1926b) *Die Frage der Laienanalyse*, GW, vol. 14; *The Question of Lay Analysis*, SE, vol. 20.

(1927a) 'Die Zukunft einer Illusion', GW, vol. 14, pp. 325–80; 'The Future of an Illusion', SE, vol. 21, pp. 5–56.

(1927b) 'Fetischismus', GW, vol. 14, pp. 311–17; 'Fetishism', SE, vol. 21, pp. 152–7.

(1927c) 'Der Humor', GW, vol. 14, pp. 383–9; 'Humour', SE, vol. 21, pp. 161–6.

(1928 [1927]) 'Dostojewski und die Vatertötung', GW, vol. 14, pp. 399–418; 'Dostoevsky and Parricide', SE, vol. 21, pp. 177–94.

(1930a [1929]) *Das Unbehagen in der Kultur*, GW, vol. 14; *Civilizations and its Discontents*, SE, vol. 21.

(1930b) 'Ansprache im Frankfurter Goethe-Haus', GW, vol. 14, pp. 545–50; 'The Goethe Prize', SE, vol. 21, pp. 207–12.

(1931a) 'Über libidinose Typen', GW, vol. 14, pp. 509–13; 'Libidinal Types', SE, vol. 21, pp. 217–20.

(1931b) 'Über die weibliche Sexualität', GW, vol. 14, pp. 517–37; 'Female Sexuality', SE, vol. 21, pp. 225–43.

(1932 [1931]) 'Zur Gewinnung des Feuers', GW, vol. 16, pp. 3–9; 'The Acquisition and Control of Fire', SE, vol. 22, pp. 187–93.

(1933a [1932]) *Neue Folge der Vorlesungen zur Einführung in die Psychoanalyse*, GW, vol. 15; *New Introductory Lectures on Psycho-Analysis* (Lectures XXIX–XXXV), SE, vol. 22.

(1933b [1932]) 'Warum Krieg?', GW, vol. 16, pp. 13–27; 'Why War?' (Einstein and Freud Correspondence), SE, vol. 22, pp. 199–215.

(1936) 'Eine Erinnerungsstörung auf der Akropolis', GW, vol. 16, pp. 250–7; 'A Disturbance of Memory on the Acropolis', SE, vol. 22, pp. 239–48.

(1937) 'Die endliche und die unendliche Analyse', GW, vol. 16, pp. 59–99; 'Analysis Terminable and Interminable', SE, vol. 23, pp. 216–53.

(1939 [1934–8]) *Der Mann Moses und die monotheistische Religion*, GW, vol. 16; *Moses and Monotheism*, SE, vol. 23.

(1940a [1938]) *Abriss der Psychoanalyse*, GW, vol. 17; *An Outline of Psycho-Analysis*, SE, vol. 23.

(1940b [1938]) 'Some Elementary Lessons in Psycho-Analysis' [title in English, German text], GW, vol. 17, pp. 141–7; SE, vol. 23, pp. 281–6.

(1940c [1922]) 'Das Medusenhaupt', GW, vol. 17, p. 47; 'Medusa's Head', SE, vol. 18, pp. 273–4.

(1940d [1938]) 'Die Ichspaltung im Abwehrvorgang', GW, vol. 17, pp. 59–62; 'Splitting of the Ego in the Process of Defence', SE, vol. 23, pp. 275–8.

(1940–1a [1892]) 'Letter to Joseph Breuer', GW, vol. 17, pp. 5–6; SE, vol. 1, pp. 147–8.

(1940–1b [1892]) (with Joseph Breuer) 'Zur Theorie des Hysterischen Anfalls', GW, vol. 17, pp. 9–13; 'On the Theory of Hysterical Attacks', SE, vol. 1, pp. 151–4.

(1941a [1921]) 'Psychoanalyse und Telepathie', GW, vol. 17, pp. 27–44; 'Psycho-Analysis and Telepathy', SE, vol. 18, pp. 177–93.

(1941b [1938]) 'Ergebnisse, Ideen, Probleme', London, Juni 1938', GW, vol. 17, pp. 149–52; 'Findings, Ideas, Problems', SE, vol. 23, pp. 299–300.

(1950a [1892–9]) Extracts from the Fliess Papers, in *Origins* (see abbreviated titles on p. 241); SE, vol. 1.

(1950b [1895]) *Project for a Scientific Psychology*, SE, vol. 1.

(1961) *Lectures of Sigmund Freud*, ed. E. L. Freud, trans. T. and J. Stern, London, Hogarth Press.

(1965) *A Psycho-Analytic Dialogue: The Letters of Sigmund Freud and Karl Abraham 1907–1926*, ed. H. C. Abraham and E. C. Freud, trans. B. Marsh and H. C. Abraham, London, Hogarth Press.

(1972) *Sigmund Freud and Lou Andreas-Salomé: Letters*, ed. E. Pfeiffer, trans. W. and E. Robson-Scott, London, Hogarth Press.

(1974) *The Freud/Jung Letters: The Correspondence between Sigmund Freud and C. G. Jung*, ed. W. McGuire, trans. R. Mannheim and R. F. C. Hull, London, Routledge & Kegan Paul

(1985) *The Complete Letters of Sigmund Freud to Wilhelm Fliess, 1887–1904*, for details see abbreviated titles on p. 241.

Select bibliography

Abraham, K. ([1921] 1922) 'Äusserungsformen des weiblichen Kastrationskomplexes', *IZP* 7: 422–52; 'Manifestations of the Female Castration Complex', *IJPA* 3: 1–29.
Adams, P. (1983) 'Mothering', *m/f* 8: 41–52.
Adams, P. (1988) '(Per)oscillation', *Camera Obscura* 17: 7–30.
Adams, P. and Cowie, E. (eds) (1990) *The Woman in Question*, London and New York, Verso.
Adler, A. (1917) *The Neurotic Constitution*, New York.
Alexander, F. ([1922] 1923) 'The Castration Complex in the Formation of Character', *IJPA* 4: 11–42.
Andreas-Salomé, L. (1916) ' "Anal" und "Sexual" ', *Imago* 4: 249–73.
Anzieu, D. (1959) *L'autoanalyse de Freud*, Paris, PUF.
Assoun, P.-L. (1983) *Freud et la femme*, Paris, Colmann-Levy.
Balint, A. (1939) 'Love for the Mother and Mother-love', in M. Balint (ed.) (1965), *Primary Love and Psycho-Analytic Technique*, New York, Liveright, pp. 91–108.
Balint, M. (1968) *The Basic Fault: Therapeutic Aspects of Regression*, London, Tavistock.
Beauvoir, S. de ([1949] 1972) *The Second Sex*, trans. H. M. Parshley, London, Penguin.
Benhabib, S. and Cornell, D. (eds) (1987) *Feminism as Critique*, Cambridge, Polity Press.
Benjamin, J. (1988) *The Bonds of Love: Psychoanalysis, Feminism and the Problem of Domination*, London, Virago.
Benjamin, W. (1979) *One Way Street and Other Writings*, trans. E. Jephcott and K. Shorter, London, NLB.
Bernheimer, C. and Kahane, C. (1985) *In Dora's Case: Freud–Hysteria–Feminism*, New York, Columbia University Press.
Bion, W. ([1962] 1988) *Learning from Experience*, London, Maresfield Library.
Bion, W. (1967) *Second Thoughts*, London, Maresfield Library.
Bion, W. (1970) *Attention and Interpretation*, London, Maresfield Library.
Bleier, R. (ed.) (1986) *Feminist Approaches to Science*, New York, Pergamon Press.
Bonaparte, M. (1935) 'Passivity, Masochism and Femininity', *IJPA* 16: 325–33.
Bonaparte, M. (1951) *Female Sexuality*, London, Imago.
Boothby, R. (1991) *Death and Desire: Psychoanalytic Theory from Freud to Lacan*, New York and London, Routledge.
Borch-Jacobsen, M. (1989) *The Freudian Subject*, London, Macmillan.
Borch-Jacobsen, M. (1991) *Lacan: The Absolute Master*, trans. D. Brick, Stanford, Calif., Stanford University Press.

Bordo, S. R. (1987) *The Flight to Objectivity*, Albany, NY, University of New York Press.

Bowie, M. (1991) *Lacan*, London, Fontana.

Brennan, T. (1988) 'Controversial Discussions and Feminist Debate', in E. Timms and N. Segal (eds) *Freud in Exile: Psychoanalysis and its Vicissitudes*, New Haven, Conn., Yale University Press, pp. 254–74.

Brennan, T. (1989) 'Introduction', in T. Brennan (ed.) *Between Feminism and Psychoanalysis*, London, Routledge, pp. 1–23.

Brennan, T. (1990) 'History after Lacan', in *Economy and Society* 19 (3) (August): 277–313.

Brennan, T. (1991a) 'An Impasse in Psychoanalysis and Feminism', in S. Gunew (ed.) *Feminist Knowledge: A Reader*, London, Routledge, pp. 114–38.

Brennan, T. (1991b) 'The Age of Paranoia', in *Paragraph* 14: 20–45.

Brierley, M. (1932) 'Problems of Integration in Women', *IJPA* 13: 433–48.

Brierley, M. (1936) 'Specific Determinants in Feminine Development', *IJPA* 17: 163–80.

Brown, N. O. (1959) *Life Against Death: the Psychoanalytical Meaning of History*, London, Routledge & Kegan Paul.

Brunswick, R. M. (1928) 'A Supplement to Freud's "History of an Infantile Neurosis" ', *IJPA* 9: 439–76.

Brunswick, R. M. (1940) 'The Pre-Oedipal Phase of the Libido Development', *PQ* 9: 293–319.

Bunge, M. and Shea, W. (1979) *Rutherford and Physics at the Turn of the Century*, Folkestone, William Dawson & Sons.

Butler, J. (1990) *Gender Trouble: Feminism and the Subversion of Identities*, New York and London, Routledge.

Callois, R. (1935) 'Mimétisme et psychasthénie légendaire', *Minotaure* 7; translated as 'Mimicry and Legendary Psychesthenie' in *October: The First Decade*, ed. Annette Michelson, trans. J. Shepley, Cambridge MA, MIT Press, 1989, pp. 59–74.

Cannon, W. ([1929] 1963) *Bodily Changes in Pain, Hunger, Fear and Rage*, New York, Evanston, Ill., and London, Harper & Row.

Chadwick, M. (1925) 'Über die Wurzel der Wissbegierde', *IZP* 11: 18–27.

Chasseguet-Smirgel, J. ([1964] 1981) *La sexualité féminine, recherches psychanalytiques nouvelles*, Paris, Payot; *Female Sexuality, New Psychoanalytic Views*, trans. anon., London, Virago.

Chasseguet-Smirgel, J. (1984) *Creativity and Perversion*, London, Free Association Books.

Chodorow, N. (1978) *The Reproduction of Mothering: Psychoanalysis and the Sociology of Gender*, Berkeley, Calif., University of California Press.

Chodorow, N. (1989) *Feminism and Psychoanalytic Theory*, London and New Haven, Conn., Yale University Press.

Chomsky, N. (1981) *Lectures on Government and Binding*, Dordrecht, Foris.

Christensen, F. (1981) 'The Problem of Inertia', *Philosophy of Science* 48: 232–47.

Cixous, H. (1981) 'The Laugh of the Medusa', in E. Marks and I. de Courtivron (eds) *New French Feminisms*, Brighton, Sx, Harvester, pp. 245–64.

Cixous, H. and Clément, C. ([1975] 1986) *La jeune née*, Paris, Union Générale d'Editions; *The Newly Born Woman*, trans. C. Porter, Minneapolis, Minn., University of Minnesota Press.

Colletti, L. (1973) *Marxism and Hegel*, London, New Left Books.

Cornell, D. (1991) *Beyond Accommodation*, New York and London, Routledge.

Cowie, E. (1991) 'Fantasia', in P. Adams and E. Cowie (eds) *The Woman in Question*, London and New York, Verso, pp. 149–96.

David-Ménard, M. ([1983] 1989) *Hysteria from Freud to Lacan: Body and Language in Psychoanalysis*, trans. C. Porter, Ithaca, NY, Cornell University Press.

De Beauvoir, S., *see* Beauvoir, S. de.

De Lauretis, T. (1989) 'The essence of the triangle, or taking the risk of essentialism seriously: feminist theory in Italy, the U.S., and Britain', *differences* 1 (2): 3–38.

Deleuze, G. and Guattari, F. ([1972] 1977) *Capitalisme et schizophrénie: L'anti-Oedipe*, Paris, Minuit; *Anti-Oedipus: Capitalism and Schizophrenia*, trans. R. Hurley, S. Seem, and H. R. Lane, London, Athlone Press.

Derrida, J. ([1967] 1974) *De la grammatologie*, Paris, Minuit; *Of Grammatology*, trans. G. C. Spivak, London and Baltimore, Md., Johns Hopkins University Press.

Derrida, J. (1980) *La Carte Postale de Socrate à Freud et au-delà*, Paris, Flammarion.

Derrida, J. (1981) 'Freud and the scene of writing', in *Writing and Difference*, trans. A. Bass, London, Routledge & Kegan Paul, pp. 196–231.

De Sousa, R. (1982) 'Norms and the Normal', in R. Wollheim and J. Hopkins (eds) *Philosophical Essays on Freud*, Cambridge, Cambridge University Press, pp. 139–62.

Deutsch, H. (1925) 'Psychologie des Weibes in den Funktionen der Fortpflanzung', *IZP* 11: 40–53; 'The Psychology of Women in Relation to the Functions of Reproduction', *IJPA* 11: 48–60.

Deutsch, H. (1930) 'Der feminine Masochismus und seine Beziehung zur Frigidität', *IZP* 16: 172–84; 'The Significance of Masochism in the Mental Life of Women', *IJPA* 11: 48–60.

Deutsch, H. (1932) 'On Female Homosexuality', *PQ* 1: 484–510.

Deutsch, H. (1933a) 'Homosexuality in Women', *IJPA* 14: 34–56.

Deutsch, H. (1933b) 'Motherhood and Sexuality', *PQ* 2: 476–88.

Deutsch, H. (1944) *Psychoanalyse der weiblichen Sexualfunktionen*, Vienna, *The Psychology of Women*, vol. 1, New York, Grune & Stratton; (1947) *The Psychology of Women*, vol. II, London, Research Books.

Dinnerstein, D. ([1976] 1987) *The Rocking of the Cradle and the Ruling of the World*, London, Women's Press.

Ellenberger, H. F. (1970) *The Discovery of the Unconscious: The History and Evolution of Dynamic Psychiatry*, London, Allen Lane.

Ellis, H. (1911) *The World of Dreams*, London.

Erikson, E. H. (1953) 'On the Sense of Inner Identity', in *Health and Human Relations: report of a conference held at Hiddesden near Detmold, Germany*, New York, Blakiston.

Fechner, G. T. ([1860] 1966) *[Elemente der Psychophysik]* Elements of Psychophysics, trans. H. E. Adler, New York, Henry Holt, 1966.

Feldstein, R. and Roof, J. (eds) (1985) *Feminism and Psychoanalysis*, Ithaca, NY, Cornell University Press.

Felman, S. (1987) *Jacques Lacan and the Adventure of Insight*, Cambridge, Mass., Harvard University Press.

Fenichel, O. ([1930] 1931a) 'Zur prägenitalen Vorgeschichte des Oedipuskomplexes', *IZP* 16: 239–60; 'The Pregenital Antecedents of the Oedipus Complex', *IJPA* 12: 141–66.

Fenichel, O. (1931b) 'Specific Forms of the Oedipus Complex', *IJPA* 12: 412–30.

Fenichel, O. (1949) 'The Symbolic Equation: Girl = Phallus', *PQ* 8 (3): 303–24.

Ferenczi, S. ([1924] 1938 *Thalassa, a Theory of Genitality*, trans. H. Alden Bunker, New York, Psychoanalytic Quarterly Press.

Ferenczi, S. (1926) 'Psychoanalysis of Sexual Habits', in *Further Contributions to the Theory and Technique of Psychoanalysis*, London, Hogarth Press, pp. 11–31.

Flax, J. (1990) *Thinking Fragments: Psychoanalysis, Feminism and Postmodernism in the Contemporary West in the Recent Decade between 1980 and 1990*, Berkeley, Calif., University of California Press.

Forrester, J. ([1980] 1985) *Language and the Origins of Psychoanalysis*, London, Macmillan.

Forrester, J. (1986) 'The True Story of Anna O.', *Social Research*, 53 (2) (Summer): 327–47.

Forrester, J. (1991) *The Seductions of Psychoanalysis*, Cambridge, Cambridge University Press.

Foucault, M. (1964) Introduction to Ludwig Binswanger, *Le Rêve et l'existence*, Paris, Deschée de Browwer.

Foucault, M. (1981) *The History of Sexuality*, vol. 1, trans. R. Hurley, Harmondsworth, Penguin.

Freud, A. (1923) 'The Relation of Beating-Phantasies to a Day-dream', *IJPA* 4: 89–102.

Freud, A. (1937) *The Ego and the Mechanisms of Defence*, London, Hogarth Press.

Fuss, D. (1989) *Essentially Speaking*, London and New York, Routledge.

Gallop, J. ([1982] 1983) *Feminism and Psychoanalysis: The Daughter's Seduction*, London, Macmillan.

Gallop, J. (1988) *Thinking Through the Body*, Columbia, Columbia University Press.

Gay, P. (1988) *Freud: A Life for Our Time*, London, Dent.

Gilligan, C. (1982) *In a Different Voice*, Cambridge, Mass., Harvard University Press.

Granoff, W. (1976) *La pensée et la féminin*, Paris, Editions de Minuit.

Greenson, R. (1968) 'Dis-identifying from Mother: Its Special Importance for the Boy', *IJPA* 49: 370–4.

Gregory, R. L. (1979) *Eye and Brain: The Psychology of Seeing* (3rd edn), London, Weidenfeld & Nicolson.

Grooten, Angela (1991) 'Coming to your senses', in Alkeline van Lenning and Joke Hermsen (eds), *Sharing the Difference*, London and New York, Routledge, pp. 208–27.

Grosskurth, P. (1986) *Melanie Klein: Her World and Her Work*, London, Hodder & Stoughton.

Grosz, E. (1988) 'Space, Time and Bodies', in *On the Beach* (Sydney), vol. 23.

Grosz, E. (1989) *Sexual Subversions: Three French Feminists*, Sydney, Allen & Unwin.

Grosz, E. (1991) *Jacques Lacan: A Feminist Introduction*, London, Routledge.

Grosz, E. (1992) 'Irigaray and Merleau-Ponty in the Flesh', Cambridge, unpublished lecture.

Guntrip, H. (1971) *Psychoanalytic Theory, Therapy and the Self*, New York, Basic Books.

Hamilton, V. (1982) *Narcissus and Oedipus*, London, Routledge & Kegan Paul.

Hampshire, S. (1974) 'Disposition and Memory' in R. Wollheim (ed.) *Freud: A Collection of Critical Essays*, New York, Anchor, pp. 113–31.

Hampshire, S. (1988) *Spinoza*, Harmondsworth, Penguin.

Harding, S. (1986) *The Science Question in Feminism*, Milton Keynes, Open University Press.

Harding, S. and Hintikka, M. (1983) *Discovering Reality: Feminist Perspectives on Epistemology, Metaphysics, Methodology, and Philosophy of Science*, Dordrecht, London, and Boston, Mass., D. Reidel.

Hartmann, H. (1958) *Ego Psychology and the Problem of Adaptation*, New York, International Universities Press.

Heimann, P. (1950) 'On Counter-Transference', *IJPA* 31: 81–4.

Hodgson, D. (1991) *The Mind Matters: Consciousness and Choice in a Quantum World*, Oxford, Clarendon Press.

Horney, K. ([1923] 1924) 'Zur Genese des weiblichen Kastrationkomplexes', *IZP* 9: 12–26; 'On the Genesis of the Castration Complex in Women', *IJPA* 5: 50–65.

Horney, K. (1926) 'Flucht aus der Weiblichkeit', *IZP* 12: 360–74; 'The Flight from Womanhood', *IJPA* 7: 324–39.

Horney, K. (1932) 'The Dread of Woman', *IJPA* 13: 348–60.

Horney, K. (1933) 'The Denial of the Vagina', *IJPA* 14: 57–70.

Horney, K. ([1939] 1947) *New Ways in Psychoanalysis*, London, Kegan Paul, Trench, Trubner.

Horney, K. (1967) *Feminine Psychology*, London, Routledge & Kegan Paul.

Horvath, T., Friedman, J., and Meares, R. (1969) 'Attention in Hysteria: A Study of Janet's Hypothesis by Means of Habituation and Arousal Measures', *American Journal of Psychiatry* 137 (2): 217–20.

Hunter, R. A. and Macalpine, I. (1955) Introduction to Daniel Paul Schreber, *Memoirs of my Nervous Illness*, London, Dawson.

Irigaray, L. ([1974] 1985a) *Speculum, de l'autre femme*, Paris, Minuit; *Speculum of the Other Woman*, trans. G. C. Gill, Ithaca, NY, Cornell University Press.

Irigaray, L. ([1977] 1985b) *Ce Sexe qui n'en est pas un*, Paris, Minuit; *This Sex which is Not One*, trans. C. Porter, Ithaca, NY, Cornell University Press.

Irigaray, L. (1984) *Ethique de la différence sexuelle*, Paris, Minuit.

Irigaray, L. (1989) 'Is the Subject of Science Sexed?', in N. Tuana (ed.) *Feminism and Science*, Bloomington, Ind., Indiana University Press, pp. 58–68.

Isaacs, S. (1952) 'The Nature and Function of Phantasy', in M. Klein, P. Heimann, S. Isaacs, and J. Riviere, *Developments in Psychoanalysis*, ed. J. Riviere, London, Hogarth Press, pp. 67–121.

James, S. (1990) 'Spinoza the Stoic', Cambridge, unpublished ms.

Janet, P. (1901) *The Mental State of Hystericals*, trans. C. R. Corson, New York, Putnam.

Jardine, A. (1985) *Gynesis: Configurations of Women and Modernity*, Ithaca, NY, Cornell University Press.

Jones, E. (1916) 'The Theory of Symbolism', *British Journal of Psychology* 9 (2): 181–229.

Jones, E. (1922) 'Notes on Dr Abraham's Article on the Female Castration Complex', *IJPA* 3: 327–8.

Jones, E. (1926) 'The Origin and Structure of the Super-Ego', *IJPA* 7: 303–11.

Jones, E. (1927) 'The Early Development of Female Sexuality', *IJPA* 8: 459–72.

Jones, E. (1933) 'The Phallic Phase', *IJPA* 16: 1–33.

Jones, E. (1935) 'Early Female Sexuality', *IJPA* 16: 263–73.

Jones, E. (1951) *Essays in Applied Psycho-Analysis*, vols 1 and 2, London, Hogarth Press.

Jung, C. G. (1944–78) *The Collected Works of C. G. Jung*, ed. H. Read, M.

Fordham and S. Adler, trans. R. F. C. Hull and H. G. Baynes, London, Routledge & Kegan Paul, 19 vols.

Kaplan, M. A. (1984) 'Anna O and Berthe Pappenheim: An Historical Perspective', in M. Rosenbaum and M. Muroff (eds), *Anna O: One Hundred Years of Psychoanalysis*, New York, Collier Mac, pp. 101–17.

Keller, A. (1983) *Infancy of Atomic Physics: Hercules in His Cradle*, Oxford, Oxford University Press.

Keller, E. F. (1985) *Reflections on Gender and Science*, London and New Haven, Conn., Yale University Press.

Klein, M. (1926) 'The Psychological Principles of Early Analysis', in Klein (1985) *The Writings of Melanie Klein*, London, Hogarth Press and the Institute of Psychoanalysis, vol. 1, pp. 128–38.

Klein, M. (1928) 'Frühstadien des Ödipuskonfliktes', *IZP* 14: 65–77; 'Early Stages of the Oedipus Complex', *IJPA* 11: 167–80; references are to Klein (1985) *The Writings of Melanie Klein*, London, Hogarth Press and the Institute of Psychoanalysis, vol. 1, pp. 186–98.

Klein, M. (1929) 'Personification in the Play of Children', in Klein (1985) *The Writings of Melanie Klein*, London, Hogarth Press and the Institute of Psychoanalysis, vol. 1, pp. 199–209.

Klein, M. (1930) 'The Importance of Symbol Formation in the Development of the Ego', in Klein (1985) *The Writings of Melanie Klein*, London, Hogarth Press and the Institute of Psychoanalysis, vol. 1, pp. 219–32.

Klein, M. (1932) *The Psychoanalysis of Children*, in Klein (1985) *The Writings of Melanie Klein*, London, Hogarth Press and the Institute of Psychoanalysis, vol. 2.

Klein, M. (1935) 'A Contribution to the Psychogenesis of Manic-Depressive States', in Klein (1985) *The Writings of Melanie Klein*, London, Hogarth Press and the Institute of Psychoanalysis, vol. 1, pp. 262–89.

Klein, M. (1946) 'Notes on Some Schizoid Mechanisms', in Klein (1985) *The Writings of Melanie Klein*, London, Hogarth Press and the Institute of Psychoanalysis, vol. 3, pp. 1–25.

Klein, M. (1952a) 'Some Theoretical Conclusions Regarding the Emotional Life of the Infant', in Klein (1985) *The Writings of Melanie Klein*, London, Hogarth Press and the Institute of Psychoanalysis, vol. 3, pp. 61–93.

Klein, M. (1952b) 'On Observing the Behaviour of Young Infants', in Klein (1985) *The Writings of Melanie Klein*, London, Hogarth Press and the Institute of Psychoanalysis, vol. 3, pp. 94–121.

Klein, M. (1957) 'Envy and Gratitude', in Klein (1985) *The Writings of Melanie Klein*, London, Hogarth Press and the Institute of Psychoanalysis, vol. 3, pp. 176–235.

Klein, M. (1985) *The Writings of Melanie Klein*, London, Hogarth Press and the Institute of Psychoanalysis, 4 vols.

Kofman, S. ([1980] 1985) *L'énigme de la femme*, Paris, Seuil; *The Enigma of Woman*, trans. C. Porter, Ithaca, NY, Cornell University Press.

Kohut, H. (1978) *The Search for the Self*, New York, International Universities Press.

Kraakman, D. (1990) 'Georges Sand en de travestie van het vrouwelijke', *Lust & Gratie* 27 (Autumn): 11–32.

Kristeva, J. ([1974a] 1981) 'Woman Can Never Be Defined', in E. Marks and I. de Courtivron (eds) *New French Feminisms*, London, Harvester, pp. 137–41.

Kristeva, J. ([1974b] 1984) *La Révolution du langage poétique*, Paris, Seuil; *Revo-*

lution in Poetic Language, trans. M. Waller, New York, Columbia University Press.

Kristeva, J. (1980) 'Motherhood According to Giovanni Bellini', in *Desire and Language: A Semiotic Approach to Literature and Art*, ed. L. S. Roudiez, trans. T. Gora, A. Jardine, and L. S. Roudiez, New York, Columbia University Press, pp. 237–70.

Kristeva, J. ([1980] 1982) *Pouvoirs de l'horreur*, Paris, Seuil; *Powers of Horror*, trans. L. S. Roudiez, New York, Columbia University Press.

Kristeva, J. (1986) 'Freud and Love: Treatment and its Discontents', in *The Kristeva Reader*, ed. T. Moi, Oxford, Blackwell, pp. 240–71.

Kristeva, J. ([1987] 1989) *Soleil Noir: Dépression et mélancolie*, Paris, Gallimard; *Black Sun: Depression and Melancholia*, trans. L. S. Roudiez, New York and Oxford, Columbia University Press.

Kuhn, T. (1966) *The Structure of Scientific Revolutions*, Chicago, Chicago University Press.

Lacan, J. (1948) 'Aggressivity in Psychoanalysis', in Lacan (1977a) *Ecrits: a Selection*, trans. A. Sheridan, London, Tavistock, pp. 8–29.

Lacan, J. ([1949] 1966) 'Le stade du miroir comme formateur de la fonction du Je', *Ecrits*, Paris, Seuil, pp. 93–100; (1977a) *Ecrits: a Selection*, trans. A. Sheridan, London, Tavistock, pp. 1–7.

Lacan, J. (1953a) 'Some Reflections on the Ego', *IJPA* 34: 11–17.

Lacan, J. (1953b) 'Fonction et champ de la parole et du langage en psychanalyse', in Lacan ([1949] 1966) *Ecrits*, Paris, Seuil, pp. 237–322; Lacan (1977a) *Ecrits: a Selection*, trans. A. Sheridan, London, Tavistock, pp. 30–113.

Lacan, J. ([1953–4] 1975) *Les écrits techniques de Freud: Le Séminaire I*, Paris, Seuil; (1988) *The Seminar of Jacques Lacan: Book 1. Freud's Technical Writings*, trans. J. Forrester, Cambridge, Cambridge University Press.

Lacan, J. ([1954–5] 1978) *Le moi dans la théorie de Freud et dans la technique de la psychanalyse: Le Séminaire II*, Paris, Seuil; in Lacan ([1949] 1966) *The Seminar of Jacques Lacan: Book 2. The Ego in Freud's Theory and in the Technique of Psychoanalysis*, trans. S. Tomaselli, Cambridge, Cambridge University Press.

Lacan, J. (1955–6) 'D'une question préliminaire à tout traitement possible de la psychose', in Lacan ([1949] 1966) *Ecrits*, Paris, Seuil, pp. 493–528; and in Lacan (1977a) *Ecrits: a Selection*, trans. A. Sheridan, London, Tavistock, pp. 179–225.

Lacan, J. (1957) 'L'instance de la lettre dans l'inconscient ou la raison depuis Freud', in Lacan ([1949] 1966) *Ecrits*, Paris, Seuil, pp. 493–528; and in Lacan (1977a) *Ecrits: a Selection*, trans. A. Sheridan, London, Tavistock, pp. 146–78.

Lacan, J. (1958) 'La direction de la cure et les principes de son pouvoir', in Lacan ([1949 1966) *Ecrits*, Paris, Seuil, pp. 585–645; and in Lacan (1977a) *Ecrits: a Selection*, trans. A. Sheridan, London, Tavistock, pp. 226–80.

Lacan, J. (1959) 'A la mémoire d'Ernest Jones: sur sa théorie de symbolisme', in Lacan ([1949] 1966) *Ecrits*, Paris, Seuil, pp. 697–717.

Lacan, J. (1960) 'Subversion du sujet et dialectique du désir dans l'inconscient freudien', in Lacan ([1949] 1966) *Ecrits*, Paris, Seuil, pp. 793–827; and in Lacan (1977a) *Ecrits: a Selection*, trans. A. Sheridan, London, Tavistock, pp. 292–325.

Lacan, J. (1963) 'Kant avec Sade', in Lacan ([1949] 1966) *Ecrits*, Paris, Seuil, pp. 765–90.

Lacan, J. ([1964] 1973) *Les quatres concepts fondamentaux de la psychanalyse: Le Séminaire XI*, Paris, Seuil; (1977b) *The Four Fundamental Concepts of Psycho-Analysis*, ed. J. A. Miller, trans. A. Sheridan, London, Hogarth Press.

Lacan, J. ([1972–3] 1975) *Encore: Le Séminaire XX*, Paris, Seuil.

Lacan, J. (1977a) *Ecrits: a Selection*, trans. A. Sheridan, London, Tavistock.

Lacan, J. (1977b) *The Four Fundamental Concepts of Psycho-Analysis*, ed. J.-A. Miller, trans. A. Sheridan, London, Hogarth Press.

Lacan, J. (1990) *Seminar II, The Ego and Psychoanalytic Technique*, trans. J. Forrester and S. Tomaselli, Cambridge, Cambridge University Press.

Lampl-de Groot, J. ([1927] 1928) 'Zur Entwicklungsgechichte des Odipuskomplexes der Frau', *IZP* 13: 269–82; 'The Evolution of the Oedipus Complex in Women', *IJPA* 9: 332–45.

Lampl-de Groot, J. (1933) 'Problems of Femininity in Women', *PQ* 12: 489–518.

Laplanche, J. ([1970] 1976) *Vie et mort en psychanalyse*, Paris, Flammarion; *Life and Death in Psychoanalysis*, trans. J. Mehlman, Baltimore, Md, Johns Hopkins University Press.

Laplanche, J. and Pontalis, J. B. ([1964] 1968) 'Fantasy and the Origins of Sexuality', *IJPA* 49: 1–18.

Laplanche, J. and Pontalis, J. B. (1983) *The Language of Psychoanalysis*, trans. D. Nicholson-Smith, London, Hogarth Press.

Leclaire, S. (1964) 'The Economic Standpoint – Recent Views', *IJPA* 45: 324–31.

Le Doeuff, M. (1980) *L'Imaginaire Philosophique*, Paris, Payot.

Lemoine-Luccione, E. (1976) *Partage des femmes*, Paris, Seuil.

Lewin, B. D. (1933) 'The Body as Phallus', *PQ* 2: 24–47.

MacCannell, J. Flower (1991) *The Regime of the Brother: After the Patriarchy*, London and New York, Routledge.

Malinowski, B. (1922) *Sex and Repression in Savage Society*, London, Routledge & Kegan Paul.

Marcuse, H. ([1955] 1969) *Eros and Civilization: A Philosophical Inquiry into Freud*, London, Sphere Books.

Masson, J. M. ([1984] 1985) *The Assault on Truth: Freud's Suppression of the Seduction Theory*, Harmondsworth, Penguin.

Merleau-Ponty, M. (1962) *The Phenomenology of Perception*, trans. C. Smith, London, Routledge & Kegan Paul.

Merleau-Ponty, M. (1968) *The Visible and the Invisible*, trans. A. Lingis, Evanston, Ill., Northwestern University Press.

Miller, J. B. (ed.) (1972) *Psychoanalysis and Women*, Harmondsworth, Penguin.

Miller, J. B. ([1976] 1983) *Toward a New Psychology of Women*, Harmondsworth, Penguin.

Mitchell, J. (1974) *Psychoanalysis and Feminism*, Harmondsworth, Penguin.

Mitchell, J. (1982) Introduction I, in J. Mitchell and J. Rose (eds) *Feminine Sexuality: Jacques Lacan and the Ecole Freudienne*, trans. J. Rose, London, Macmillan, pp. 1–26.

Mitchell, J. and Rose, J. (eds) (1982) *Feminine Sexuality: Jacques Lacan and the Ecole Freudienne*, trans. J. Rose, London, Macmillan.

Moi, T. (1985) *Sexual/Textual Politics*, London, Methuen.

Moi, T. (ed.) (1986) *The Kristeva Reader: Julia Kristeva*, Oxford, Blackwell.

Moi, T. (1989) 'Patriarchal Thought and the Drive for Knowledge', in T. Brennan (ed.) *Between Feminism and Psychoanalysis*, London and New York, Routledge, pp. 189–205.

Montrelay, M. ([1970] 1978) 'Recherches sur la féminité', *Critique* 26 (Paris): 654–74; 'Inquiry into Femininity', trans. P. Adams, *m/f*: 65–101.

Muller, J. (1932) 'A Contribution to the Problem of Libidinal Development of the Genital Phase in Girls', *IJPA* 13: 361–8.

Müller-Braunschweig, C. (1926) 'Zur Genese des Weiblichen Über-Ich', *IZP* 12: 375–8; 'The Genesis of the Feminine Super-Ego', *IJPA* 7: 359–62.

Nusbaum, M. C. and Rorty, A. O. (1992) (eds) *Essays on Aristotle's* De Anima, Oxford, Oxford University Press.

Ophuijsen, J. H. W. van, *see* van Ophuijsen, J. H. W.

Prigogine, I. (1988) 'Origins of Complexity', in A. Fabian (ed.) *Origins*, Cambridge, Cambridge University Press, pp. 69–88.

Prigogine, I. and Stengers, I. (1979) *La nouvelle alliance: metamorphose de la science*, Paris, Gallimard.

Proust, M. ([1974] 1983) *A la recherche du temps perdu*, Paris, Gallimard, 8 vols; *Remembrance of Things Past*, trans. T. Kilmartin, Harmondsworth, Penguin, 3 vols.

Rado, S. (1932) 'The Paths of Natural Science in the Light of Psychoanalysis', *PQ* 1: 683–700.

Rado, S. (1935) 'Die Kastrationsangst des Weibes', *IZP* 25: 598–605; 'Fear of Castration in Women', *PQ* 2: 425–75.

Ragland-Sullivan, E. (1986) *Jacques Lacan and the Philosophy of Psychoanalysis*, London and Canberra, Croom Helm.

Ragland-Sullivan, E. (1989) 'Seeking the Third Term: Desire, the Phallus and the Materiality of Language', in R. Feldstein and J. Roof (eds) *Feminism and Psychoanalysis*, Ithaca, NY, Cornell University Press, pp. 40–64.

Rank, O. ([1924] 1929) *The Trauma of Birth*, London, Routledge, Kegan Paul, Trench & Trubner.

Reich, W. (1970) *Selected Writings*, New York, Doubleday.

Ricoeur, P. (1970) *Freud and Philosophy: An Essay on Interpretation*, trans. D. Savage, New Haven, Conn., Yale University Press.

Rinsley, D. B. (1968) 'Economic Aspects of Object Relations', *IJPA* 49: 38–48.

Riviere, J. (1929) 'Womanliness as Masquerade', *IJPA* 10: 303–13.

Roazen, P. (1967) *Freud and his Followers*, London, Allen Lane.

Roazen, P. (1985) 'Helene Deutsch's Feminism', *Psychohistory Review* (Winter): 26–32.

Roazen, P. (1992) *Helene Deutsch*, New Jersey, Transaction.

Roche, J. (1986) 'Theories of Matter in the Seventeenth Century', in R. Harre, (ed.) *The Physical Sciences since Antiquity*, London and Sydney, Croom Helm, pp. 41–62.

Rose, J. (1982), *see* Mitchell and Rose (eds) (1982).

Rose, J. (1986) *Sexuality in the Field of Vision*, London, Verso.

Rose, J. (1989) 'Where does the Misery come from?: Psychoanalysis, Feminism and the "Event" ', in R. Feldstein and J. Roof (eds) *Feminism and Psychoanalysis*, Ithaca, NY, Cornell University Press, pp. 25–39.

Rubin, G. (1975) 'The Traffic in Women', in R. Reiter (ed.) *Toward an Anthropology of Women*, New York and London, Monthly Review Press, pp. 157–210.

Sachs, Hans (1929) 'One of the Motive Factors in the Formation of the Super-Ego in Women', *IJPA* 10: 39–50.

Safouan, M. (1974) *Etudes sur l'Oedipe*, Paris, Seuil.

Sagan, E. (1988) *Freud, Women and Morality: The Psychology of Good and Evil*, New York, Basic Books.

Schaffer, S. (1991) *Measuring Victorian Values*, Cambridge, unpublished MS.

Schaffer, S. (1992) 'Where Experiments End', in J. Buchwald (ed.) *Table Top Experiments*, Chicago, Chicago University Press.

Schneiderman, S. (ed.) (1980) *Returning to Freud, Clinical Psychoanalysis in the School of Jacques Lacan*, London, Yale University Press.

Schor, N. (1989) 'The Essentialism Which Is Not One', *Differences* 1 (2).

Segal, H. (1957) 'Notes on Symbol Formation', *IJPA* 38: 391–7.

Segal, H. (1984) *The Work of Hanna Segal*, London, Hogarth Press.
Segal, H. (1990) Hanna Segal interviewed by Jacqueline Rose, *Women: A Cultural Review* 2: 198–214.
Segal, N. (1988) 'Freud and the Question of Women', in N. Segal and E. Timms (eds) *Freud in Exile: Psychoanalysis and its Vicissitudes*, New Haven, Conn., Yale University Press, pp. 241–53.
Segal, N. and Timms, E. (1988) (eds) *Freud in Exile: Psychoanalysis and its Vicissitudes*, New Haven, Conn., Yale University Press.
Sherfey, M. J. (1972) 'On the Nature of Female Sexuality', in J. B. Miller (ed.) *Psychoanalysis and Women*, Harmondsworth, Penguin, pp. 136–53.
Shiach, M. (1991) *Hélène Cixous*, London and New York, Routledge.
Shope, R. (1971) 'Physical and Psychic Energy', *Philosophy of Science* 38: 1–11.
Silverman, K. (1988) 'Masochism and Male Subjectivity', *Camera Obscura* 17: 113–67.
Sontag, S. (1980) *Under the Sign of Saturn*, New York, Farrar Straus Giroux.
Sousa, R. de, *see* de Sousa, R.
Spinoza, B. ([1677] 1989) *Ethics*, ed. G. H. R. Parkinson, trans. A. Boyle and G. H. R. Parkinson, London, Dent; also pub. in 1985 *The Collected Works of Spinoza*, ed. E. Curley, vol. I, New Jersey, Princeton University Press.
Spivak, G. C. (1974) Introduction to J. Derrida (1974) *Of Grammatology*, trans. G. C. Spivak, London and Baltimore, Md., Johns Hopkins University Press, pp. ix–xc.
Sprengnether, M. (1990) *The Spectral Mother: Freud, Feminism, and Psychoanalysis*, Ithaca, NY, Cornell University Press.
Starcke, A. (1921) 'The Castration Complex', *IJPA* 2: 179–201.
Stoller, R. (1964) 'A Contribution to the Study of Gender Identity', *IJPA* 45: 220–6.
Strathern, M. (1988) *The Gender of the Gift*, Berkeley, Calif., and London, University of California Press.
Sulloway, F. J. (1979) *Freud, Biologist of the Mind: Beyond the Psychoanalytic Legend*, London, Burnett.
Thompson, C. (1950) 'Some Effects of the Derogatory Attitude towards Women', *Psychiatry* 13: 349–54.
Tuana, N. (ed.) (1989) *Feminism and Science*, Bloomington, Ind., Indiana University Press.
Van Ophuijsen, J. H. W. ([1916–17] 1924) 'Beiträge zum Männlichkeitskomplex der Frau', *Internationale Zeitschrift für ärztliche Psychoanalyse* 4: 241–51; 'Contributions to the Masculinity Complex in Women', *IJPA* 5: 39–49.
Varendonck, J. (1921) *The Psychology of Daydreams*, London, Allen & Unwin.
Vienna Psychoanalytic Society (1962–75) *Minutes of the Vienna Psychoanalytic Society*, ed. H. Nunberg and E. Federn, trans. M. Nunberg with H. Collins New York, International Universities Press.
Virgil (1934) *Aeneid*, trans. H. Rushton-Fairclough, London, (Loeb) Heinemann, 2 vols.
Walkerdine, V., Urwin, C., Venn, C. *et al.* (1984) *Changing the Subject*, London, Methuen.
Whitford, M. (1986) 'Luce Irigaray: Speaking as a Woman', *Radical Philosophy* 43 (Summer): 1–8.
Whitford, M. (1989) 'Rereading Irigaray', in T. Brennan (ed.) *Between Feminism and Psychoanalyis*, London, Routledge, pp. 106–27.
Whitford, M. (1991) *Luce Irigaray: Philosophy in the Feminine*, London, Routledge.

Wimpfleimer, M. J. and Schafer, R. (1977) 'Psychoanalytic Methodology in Helene Deutsch's *The Psychology of Women*', *PQ* 46 (2): 287–318.

Winnicott, D. W. (1965) *The Maturational Process and the Facilitating Environment*, London, Hogarth.

Winnicott, D. W. (1975) *Through Paediatrics to Psychoanalysis*, New York, Basic Books.

Wollheim, R. (1973) *Freud*, London, Fontana, Modern Masters series.

Wollheim, R. (ed.) (1974a) *Freud: A Collection of Critical Essays*, New York, Anchor.

Wollheim, R. (1974b) 'Identification and Imagination: the Inner Structure of a Psychic Mechanism', in R. Wollheim (ed.) *Freud: A Collection of Critical Essays*, New York, Anchor, pp. 172–95.

Wollheim, R. ([1975] 1976) 'Psychoanalysis and Feminism' [review of Juliet Mitchell's *Psychoanalysis and Feminism*], *New Left Review* 93: 61–9; and 'Reply to Critics' ['Lacan Study Group'], *New Left Review* 97: 109–12.

Wollheim, R. (1982) 'The Bodily Ego', in R. Wollheim and J. Hopkins (eds) *Philosophical Essays on Freud*, Cambridge, Cambridge University Press, pp. 124–38.

Wollheim, R. and Hopkins, J. (eds) (1982) *Philosophical Essays on Freud*, Cambridge, Cambridge University Press.

Young, I. M. (1990) *Throwing Like a Girl and Other Essays in Feminist Philosophy and Social Theory*, Bloomington, Ind, Indiana University Press.

Young-Bruehl, E. (1988) *Anna Freud: A Biography*, London, Macmillan.

Index

Abraham, Karl 39, 40, 46, 47 (n13), 88 (n7)
abreaction 86–8, 89, 94, 106
abstraction, capacity for 98
activity 8, 59–60, 130 (n43), 133; and passivity (compared with masculinity and femininity) 31, 42, 146–7, 152–3, 157, 166–7, 169, 219, 222, 225
Adams, P. 31 (n36), 69
Adler, Alfred 45 (n10), 81, 138 (n2), 147
affect(s) ix–x, 1, 3, 67 (n40), 85–8, 91–5, 102, 105–7, 120, 126, 131–3, 149, 175–7, 201–3, 229–31; displaced and detached 133; overload in femininity 34, 118, 220–2; paralysing 107, 115; quota of 124, 125; strength 1; suppression 125; transformation and words 123–6
affectionate current 206, 234, 238, *see also* splitting
aggression 8, 70, 77, 190, 231; split 193
Alexander, F. 43 (n7)
ambivalence 57
anal-sadistic drive 60, 62, 97 (n16), 139, 146, 149, 150, 154, 197
analogy theory defined 9–10, 19, 25, 27–8 (and n32), 38, 84, 216; and libido 137–43
'Analysis Terminable and Interminable' 63, 82
anatomy, differences 77
Andreas-Salomé, L. 88 (n7), 159
Anna O. 90–6, 113 (n31), 131
anxiety 77, 88, 94, 95, 101, 126, 128, 199, 201, 223, 234, 235, 237; economic problems of 127; and

memory 116; and repression 125ff; and tie to the past 125; in women 108
Aristotle 3
Assoun, P.-L. 2 (n4)
attention 89, 133, 155, 157, 219; actively directed 205; backward turning 222; biological rule of 112–13; compared with consciousness 92–3; consequences of withdrawing 237ff; direction of 96–7 (and n16); disorder of 98, 116 (n35); division of 92ff; energetic 235; equated with repressing force 107; facilitating (also moving and living) 195, 207, 211, 224, 229, 230, 231; fixed 101, 106, 118, 126–7, 195, 227; fixed attention as form of repression 125; and fright 95; from the other 115; frozen 95, 97, 195; gains from surplus 132; nature of 83–4, 128; sexual connection with 157; and structure of sensory perception 96; three forms 95; turned inwards 93, 103, 105, 114, 118, 153, 163, 175
Autobiographical Study, An 10
auto-eroticism 163–4, 167

Balint, A, 67
Balint, M. 67, 68
Beauvoir, S. de 66 (n38)
Beer, G. 172 (n27)
Benjamin, J. 17 (n19), 83, 194
Benjamin, W. 1 (n1), 171 (n26)
Bernheimer, C. and C. Kahane 11 (n16)
Besetzung 67 (and n40)
Beyond the Pleasure Principle 202, 203
biochemistry, language of 172 (n27)

libido 164–5, 166, 198, 207; of love
and hate 195–6; of passivity 42–3; of
phantasy 130, 212, 232; relation to
conscious, unconscious and
daydreams 96–7; of superego 32
disidentification 56 (n28)
Dora case study 11 (n16), 25–6
dreams, censored 182–3; primary-wish
180; secondary revision 183
drive for mastery 142, 149, 151–2,
153–4, 162, 169, 189, 220
drive(s) 44, 227; active/passive 146–58;
and relation to affects 227–8, see also
affects; component 138; Freud's first
theory of 20–1; involution of 43,
135–77 passim; libidinal 127, 128;
listed 149; (in)organic 150–1, 153,
155, 170; origins as unclear 147–58;
and repression 120–9; theory of 73ff,
97 (n16), 135, 136–7, 221; and words
124, see also ego, death drive, sadistic
drive for mastery, cruelty,
scopophilic, oral drives
dual-aspect monism 4
dual personality 113 (n31)
dualism 3–4 (and nn6–7)

economic and economy 21, 75 (and
n54), 76–7, 91, 118–21, 144 (n9),
233–5; use of term 2 (and n3);
generous 76; libidinal 75; psychical
128
ego 15–16, 20–1, 30–1, 35, 52, 55, 67,
116, 126, 157, 176; capacities 198–9;
coherent 113–14; disabled 115; drives
43 (n7), 163, 167, 168, 169; formation
of 21, 71, 108, 116, 117, 129, 136,
166, 177; and id 47 (n15); as innate
147; neurotic 115–18, 125; origin of
148; role of 197–8; self-generating
illusions concerning xi, 70; split 78,
142 (n7); strength of 21; theory of
84, 89; two faces of 135; two tasks of
33–4, 219, 234
Ego and the Id, The 10, 19, 179, 180,
182, 185, 187–8
ego-ideal 32, 43, 61, 77, 164, 170, 179,
182, 184, 186–7, 218 (n1)
ego-psychology 70
ego-syntonic 30–1, 34, 81–2, 119, 128,
129, 134, 135, 168, 173, 182, 193, 234,
236, 237; term defined 30

Elisabeth von R. 90, 91, 101–4, 233;
masculine identification of 106
Ellenberger, H. F. 22 (n25), 84 (n1), 90
(n10)
Ellis, H. 183, 184 (and n5)
emotion(s) x, 2 (n3), 46, 107, 133,
191–4; redirection of 194–5
energy 74–9, 85, 91–2, 95–6, 111–13,
125, 166, 175, 186, 230, 235–7;
definition of 148 (n11); original 133,
177
entropy 63; tie to temporality 64, see
also inertia and rigidity
envy 62; origin of 218–19
equilibrium 76
Erikson, E. 17 (n19)
Eros 199, 200, 206, 207
erotogenic drives 142
essentialism 74
excitation(s) 21, 120, 124, 132, 148, 149,
204, 227; compared with drives 21,
149, 227; flow of (Q) 108, 110
executive agency 150, 169
executive capacities 189, 192, 218
exhaustion 21, 63, 85
exhibitionism 150, 153
Exner, S. 93 (n13)

father, attachment to 56–8, 137;
complex 187; identification with
185–8, 209, 210; law of the 213 (n18);
personal 212 (n17); as protective
shield 173, 205, 228; role of 208;
symbolic 70–1, 228
Fechner, G. T. 84
Felman, S. 221 (n2)
'Female Sexuality' 47–58
'Femininity' 59–65
femininity 6ff, 64, 136, 157, 177, 217;
characteristics of, summarized
178–9; contradictions in theory and
38; dubious benefits of 219, 239;
Freud's two theories of 9–17;
formation of 213, 237–8; inertia and
34, 35–6; in men 15; 'normal' 132,
133; passive overlay 32–3, 173–4; and
pathology of 6–7, 30; and psychosis
134, 177, see also tie to the past; see
also riddle of femininity
Fenichel, O. 47 (n13), 48–9
Ferenczi, S. 44 (n9), 47, 159, 173 (n28)
fixation 121ff
fixed point, as founding direction 97; as